INHALT

Liebe Leserinnen und Leser,

die vorliegende Ausgabe der Interkulturellen Theologie knüpft an das letzte Heft an: Sie versammelt weitere Beiträge, die gegenwärtige »Theologien des Politischen« in verschiedenen Kontexten erkunden.[1] Beide Hefte nehmen damit eine Art Standortbestimmung vor, zwanzig Jahre nach der Jahrtausendwende und rund vierzig Jahre nach der die geopolitische Lage in vieler Hinsicht verändernden Zäsur von 1989/1990. Ausgangspunkt und Motivation für den Themenschwerpunkt war die Frage, wie sich die Situation heute darstellt, sowohl was die politische »Grosswetterlage« (in ihrer jeweiligen lokalen Ausprägung) anbelangt, als auch bezüglich theologischer Konzeptionen des Verhältnisses von »Kirche« und »Politik«. Im Zentrum stand die Beobachtung – oder zunächst ein etwas vages Gespür dafür –, dass es in den letzten Jahren zu markanten Verschiebungen kam: Nach den Demokratisierungsschüben, die die Jahre um 1989 geprägt hatten (als Resultat der »third wave of democracy«) und der mit ihnen verbundenen Hoffnung, dass sich freiheitliche, demokratische Grundwerte an vielen Orten der Welt dauerhaft Geltung verschafft hätten, zeigen sich jüngst Tendenzen hin zu einem »global conservative turn«, der sich zuweilen in rechtspopulistischen Regierungen und Bewegungen verdichtet, wie Jeffrey Haynes in seinem Beitrag in der letzten Ausgabe gezeigt hat. Natürlich ist eine Einteilung in »Epochen« zunächst einmal als heuristisches Gerüst zu verstehen. Während es hilft, gewisse Entwicklungen in einen grösseren Horizont einzuzeichnen, bringt es auch sofort zu Tage, dass die lokalen Gegebenheiten höchst unterschiedlich sind und von Theologie und Kirche andere Schwerpunktsetzungen und Verhältnisbestimmungen zwischen Kirche und Politik verlangen. Das zeigt auch die Lektüre der Beiträge. Dabei wird auf ein grosses Repertoire theologischer Konzepte zurückgegriffen, die helfen, diese Verhältnisbestimmung vorzunehmen: von politischer Theologie Barth'scher Prägung und feministischer Theologie (vgl. bspw. den Beitrag von Meehyung Chung), über kontextuelle und interkulturelle Theologie und mit Bezug auf Dietrich Bonhoeffer (Ruomin Liu), bis hin zu politischer oder öf-

1 Vgl. auch das ausführliche Vorwort von Ulrich Dehn in Heft 2/2020.

fentlicher Theologie (Liphan Awng Li). Diese Konzepte werden adaptiert, modifiziert, neu oder ganz anders formuliert. Ebenso vielfältig sind die Themen, mit denen sich Kirchen sowie Theologen und Theologinnen auseinandersetzen: Religionsfreiheit (Awng Li), das Verhältnis zum Islam (Abraham S. Wilar), Personenkult und ein belastendes historisches Erbe bedingt durch die Teilung Koreas (Chung) sowie christliche (öffentliche) Identität in einem kommunistisch geprägten Kontext (Ruomin) oder in der Demokratischen Republik Kongo, die nach wie vor von den heftigen politischen Konflikten der vergangenen Jahrzehnte geprägt ist (Kakule Molo).

Vermehrt haben in letzten Jahrzehnten auch charismatische und pentekostale Kirchen das Feld des Politischen betreten, mit eigenen theologischen Begründungslinien und Schwerpunktsetzungen. Die Beiträge von Risto Saarinen (in Bezug auf Finnland) und von Jörg Haustein (Äthiopien) haben diese bereits im letzten Heft erkundet. In der vorliegenden Ausgabe fragt Ebenezer Obadare diesbezüglich nicht nach theologischen Konzeptionen, sondern zeigt die in dem von nigerianischen Christ*innen häufig geäusserten Satz (»It is well«) subtil zum Ausdruck gebrachten Formen eines pentekostal geprägten Weltverhältnisses auf. Einen spannenden Einblick in »Pentecostal Strategies of Public Engagement« gibt zudem der ausführliche Bericht von Leita Ngoy zur 11. GlobPent Konferenz, die im Februar 2020 in Basel stattgefunden hat.

Die schon genannten Beiträge hat Ulrich Dehn bereits im Editorial des letzten Heftes ausführlicher vorgestellt. Zwei weitere sind noch dazugekommen, die bestens zum Themenschwerpunkt passen: Roland Spliesgart schliesst im Spektum der Beiträge eine wichtige Lücke. Am Beispiel von Kuba, das allerdings in vielerlei Hinsicht einen Sonderfall darstellt, zeichnet er die Entwicklungen der (lateinamerikanischen) Befreiungstheologie nach und damit auch das Verhältnis derselben zum Sozialismus. In Kuba, so Spliesgart, hat die Befreiungstheologie innerhalb der katholischen Kirche erstaunlicherweise weniger Beachtung gefunden als in anderen Ländern Lateinamerikas. In seinem Artikel entfaltet Spliesgart sodann seine These, dass viele der Anliegen der Befreiungstheologie nicht in den »offiziellen« Kirchen ihren Ausdruck fanden, sondern in den Praktiken der populären afrokubanischen Religionen.

Daniel Jara J. setzt mit seinem Beitrag ein gewichtiges epistemologisches Fragezeichen – auch in Bezug auf unsere beiden Themenhefte: Mithilfe der soziologischen Theorie von Boaventura de Sousa Santos fragt er kritisch, inwiefern die westliche akademische (und theologische) Dominanz immer noch den globalen wissenschaftlichen Diskurs prägt und damit auch dessen volles Potential beschneidet, indem gewisse Stimmen überhört und gewisse Phänomene nicht wahrgenommen werden (können) – dies aufgrund von methodologischen und erkenntnistheoretischen Engführungen. Diese Fragen beschäftigen freilich die interkulturelle Theologie und Missionswissenschaft schon seit längerem; innerhalb des theologischen Fächerkanons ist sie sicherlich diejenige Disziplin, die sich der genannten Schieflage am ehesten bewusst gewesen ist und versucht hat, diese in Ansätzen zu beheben. Die stetige kritische Anfrage im Sinne von de Sousa Santos und Jara ist und bleibt dennoch notwendig, auch im Blick auf die vorliegende Zeitschrift. Wer und was kommt wie zur Sprache? Wer schreibt über wen? Welche theologischen Kategorien kommen zur Anwendung – sind bspw. die Konzepte von politischer, öffentlicher oder interkultureller Theologie adäquat oder handelt es sich um Setzungen, die immer noch von einem westlichen Blick bestimmt sind? Was ist überhaupt dieser »westliche« Blick? Dies sind jedenfalls Fragen, die uns im Redaktionsteam immer wieder umtreiben. Umso mehr freut es uns, dass es für diese beiden Hefte gelungen ist, vielfältige Beiträge aus ganz verschiedenen Kontexten zu versammeln und hoffentlich so zu einem weitergehenden interkulturellen Gespräch beitragen zu können.

Dass es gar nicht so lange her ist, dass ausserwestliche theologische Stimmen überhaupt wahrgenommen wurden, und mit wie vielen Hürden dieser Weg verbunden war, zeigt im Übrigen der Beitrag von Michael Biehl zur Geschichte des Internationalen Missionsrates (IMR), der anfänglich stark von westlichen Akteuren dominiert war. Das Ungleichgewicht zwischen entsendenden Kirchen und den Kirchen in den Missionsgebieten konnte erst später – durch die Integration des IMR in den Ökumenischen Rat der Kirchen (ÖRK) und durch das selbstbewusste und bestimmte Auftreten der nun unabhängig gewordenen Kirchen – ansatzweise behoben werden. Biehl rekonstruiert die Anfänge des IMR, dessen Gründung nun 100 Jahre zurückliegt, mit einem speziellen Augenmerk auf den – ambivalenten und durch zwei Weltkriege verkomplizierten – Beitrag der deutschen Missionsgesellschaften.

Eine Institution, die sich von Beginn an dem internationalen ökumenischen Dialog verschrieben hat, ist die 1954 gegründete Missionsakademie an der Universität Hamburg. Anton Knuth zeichnet ihre Geschichte nach und bietet somit eine Gesamtschau der reichhaltigen Themen, die die Akademie als einzigartiger ökumenischer Lernort bis heute bearbeitet und in den deutschsprachigen kirchlichen Kontext hinein vermittelt hat. Diese reichen vom Anliegen, den Austausch mit Vertreter*innen von »Kirchen des Südens« zu fördern, über entwicklungspolitische Bildungsarbeit bis hin zu Angeboten im Bereich interkultureller und interreligiöser Begegnungen.

Last but not least: Mit dieser Heftnummer beginnt ein neuer Zeitabschnitt in der Geschichte der Zeitschrift: Seit 2010 hat Ulrich Dehn die *Interkulturelle Theologie* als Hauptschriftleiter bzw. Chefredaktor geprägt und mitgestaltet, nachdem er zuvor schon zwölf Jahre als Mitglied der Schriftleitung tätig war. Dabei übernahm er nicht nur mit grossem Engagement und Zeiteinsatz den Hauptteil der redaktionellen Arbeiten: die Kontakte mit den Autor*innen und Verlagen, die Schlussredaktion der Beiträge und die Abstimmung mit dem Layouter Wolfgang Neumann. Er hat zudem wichtige Neuerungen umgesetzt, wie den Wechsel vom Lembeck Verlag zur Evangelischen Verlagsanstalt oder die Umstellung auf ein zweimaliges Erscheinen pro Jahr. Ulrich Dehn hat auch die Redaktionssitzungen einberufen und geleitet und vor allem entscheidend zur freundschaftlichen, fröhlichen und herzlichen Atmosphäre derselben beigetragen. Wir werden ihn also nicht nur als unermüdlichen Arbeiter für die Sache vermissen, sondern ebenso als Kollegen im Redaktionsteam.

Neu wird die Hauptverantwortung unter den Mitgliedern des Redaktionsteams von Ausgabe zu Ausgabe wechseln. Für das vorliegende Heft habe ich diese Aufgabe übernommen. Beginnend mit dieser Ausgabe ist Frank Thiel (Erlangen) für das Layout der Zeitschrift verantwortlich. Sowohl für Redaktion als auch Layout stellt dieses Heft also die Feuerprobe dar, Abläufe und Organisation müssen neu definiert und organisiert werden. Mein Dank geht an Frank Thiel für die gute Zusammenarbeit, für Geduld und Gelassenheit in dieser Anfangsphase. Ein herzlicher Dank ergeht auch nochmals an seinen Vorgänger, Wolfgang Neumann, der das Gesicht der Interkulturellen Theologie in den letzten Jahren, bzw. Jahrzehnten mit grosser Sorgfalt entscheidend mitbestimmt hat.

Im Namen der gesamten Redaktion grüsse ich Sie herzlich und wünsche Ihnen eine anregende Lektüre,

Katrin Kusmierz

Engagement of Christians in Politics: An Alternative Way to Political Stability in Africa?

Kakule Molo

Despite the independence of many African countries that took place around the sixties, most of them have continuously experienced severe political crises which have caused so much suffering to the African populations. These crises are the result of internal as well as external factors. At the internal level, those in power are blamed for poor state leadership, corruption, injustices etc. For more than a decade, voices are being heard that a formal engagement of Christians in politics could be an alternative approach that could contribute to stability. The assumption is that Christians who have been educated in the Christian faith and remain faithful to it are better equipped with moral values that are important for a sustainable development of the African continent as it is in the case of the European and American continents with their Christian heritage. The objective of this article is therefore to contribute to this debate in reflecting on the challenges and the opportunities of the engagement of Christians in politics.

Looking back at the time of the Reformation

The starting point of the reflection is the protestant affirmation of the separation of church and state going back to the protestant Reformation in the 16th century. Despite fundamental differences on a number of theological issues that came up in the Reformation, especially between the main reformers Luther and Calvin on the one hand and the Anabaptists on the other hand, the separation of church and state is regarded as a common protestant heritage of the Reformation. We all know that even though the Reformation essentially had to do with church matters, state rulers, to a great extent, interfered into its process, especially when its spirit became the source of unprecedented social and political upheavals that swept through almost the entire European states. At the beginning, the engagement of Christians in politics was not a primary issue. Luther rather intended Reformation with the aim to bring back the church to its orthodoxy, that is to be faithful to the Gospel. But when Luther and Calvin introduced the notion of the two orders, the political and the spiritual, and along with it the idea of two citizenships, Anabaptists vehemently opposed such a structure. While they, too, accepted that the state was established by God in order to maintain law and order for the sake of humanity, they, however, held it as a lower structure in comparison to the church which is at the service of human salvation.

In this article, I will not review at length Luther's theology as such which has been so extensively and even controversially discussed in many circles. Rather, the main focus is on the issue of the engagement of Christians in politics in the African context, drawing on Luther's doctrine of the two Kingdoms based on the two orders mentioned above. In today's African context of recurring political crises, what are the lessons the church in Africa could learn from both Luther's doctrine of the two kingdoms and other theological reflections related to it, with regard to the engagement of Christians in politics being considered by many as a possible remedy? What would the implication be for the protestant tradition of separation of church and state?

In his theological reflection, Luther says that God rules over the world through the Gospel representing the church and the law representing the state.[1] This concept of two kingdoms later led to controversial interpretations, namely that he conceived the two kingdoms as two structures which were to function in an autonomous way from one another. This criticism was reinforced when the spirit of what he thought to be a religious reformation was taken over into the social and political spheres. For instance when the German peasants, in the heart of the reformation, revolted against the state rulers whom they accused of social injustices, Luther reacted by saying that social demands cannot be justified on the Gospel's ground[2]. But at the same time, he affirmed the interdependence of both kingdoms

1 Gerard Siegwalt, Les deux règnes: Concernant la relation entre Eglise et Etat, in: Revue d'Histoire et de Philosophie Religieuse, 70/2 (1990), 165–172.

2 André Biéler, La pensée économique et sociale de Calvin, Genève 2008.

in arguing that the Gospel itself cannot preserve societal peace and justice, and civil government cannot effect salvation.[3] In other words, he meant that the two kingdoms work together or they complement each other. John Calvin, also like Luther, recognized the necessity to separate church and state as well as the sovereignty of God over the two entities.

But unlike Luther who thought of interdependence in terms of each fulfilling its duty assigned by God in a complementary but autonomous manner, Calvin rather understood interdependence in a sense that whatever the state undertakes is justified on the basis of the work of salvation and earthly wellbeing of humankind given to the church. In that sense the separation of church and state implies two separated functions, but united in God's purpose for his people. Therefore, based on such an understanding, Calvin engaged in both theological and social reflections in order to contribute to reforms needed in both the church and the state. For him the church had a say in state affairs if circumstances allowed it. That is the reason why in the midst of acute protests against social injustices Calvin affirmed that there could be no genuine church Reformation without social, economic and political implications, whereas Luther thought this was beyond the primary objectives of the church Reformation. As Belier puts it: for Calvin, »social reforms prolong religious reforms«.[4] In this regard, contrary to Luther, Calvin lessened the separation between church and state in the modern sense. But one should recognize that basically both shared the belief that the state and the church ought to act, each under the sovereignty of God. This means that both recognized that the church and the state worked for the carrying out of God's will in the society, namely the church in spiritual and the state in temporal matters.

The essential nuance between the two is that Luther expected the Reformation to bring restoration into the life of the church first, including the renewal of the spiritual life of Christians – social transformations were not the ultimate goal of Luther's agenda – while Calvin held both together. Calvin, being aware of the magnitude of upheavals that the Reformation ignited at that time, was convinced that a genuine religious reformation could not be complete without addressing the social and economic injustices that prevailed in society and which caused so

3 Ibid., 60.

4 Reference taken from: Henry Van Til, Calvin on Church, State and Politics: from a Calvinistic concept of culture (21.10.2008), http://www.godandculture.com/blog/tag/henry-van-til (last access: May 6, 2020).

much suffering to the common people. Therefore for him Gods' justice was to be reflected in the political, social and economic structures of the state. For that reason he engaged not only in the development of theological reflections but also initiated practical, social and economic measures he expected to bring about practical changes and improvement in both the church and the state at his time.[5]

Church and state relation in contemporary contexts

Following the developments described above, a variety of interpretations and practices with regard to the relationship between church and state arose in churches or in church leadership around the world, sometimes with a lot of ambiguities. In the United States for instance, because of the historical background of religious persecution in Europe, religious freedom versus the rule of the state is a fundamental element of the constitution. Therefore, there is still great concern for keeping the balance in the relationship between church and state important.

Also, on the basis of Luther's theology of the two kingdoms, criticism against Lutheranism continues to be heard in a number of circles. On the one hand, namely it is being said that, unlike Calvinism, Lutheranism made little effort to »Christianize« the social and political order. Lutheranism is even accused to be at the source of secularism which has impacted so much the Western society,[6] whereas Calvinism is seen as a clear enterprise to bring the state to rule according to Christian principles. On the other hand – and despite the fact that the great reformers as well as the first Anabaptists recognized that the state is established by God – it is believed that the state is more inclined towards doing evil than good. These critiques, therefore, blame both Luther and Calvin for affirming a too positive relationship between church and state. They hold that there should be no relation between church and state and Christians were to avoid any position in politics.

Nevertheless, today, as John H. Redekop reports, modern Mennonites understand that holding a political position could be an opportunity to contribute to the common good. Yet, they insist, he adds, that this should be done in the manner

5 Biéler, La pensée, qualifies Calvin's reflections combining a theological and social agenda in the first and second parts of his book as an integral Reformation of the society.

6 Biéler, La pensée, 29.

of discipleship, that is: like Jesus Christ who served the world and fulfilled God's will in faithfulness without compromising with the evil practices that prevailed in the religious and state realms. Therefore, Mennonites today continue to ensure that in their social engagement the notion of the costs of discipleship is maintained.[7]

Furthermore, looking back at the situation of the church in the time of National Socialism in Germany, we observe that the Lutheran theological perspective of separation between church and state was so much challenged then that the theologian Dietrich Bonhoeffer felt compelled to oppose Hitler's political regime against the Jews and other races so that he even sacrificed his life as an expression of Christian discipleship. At his initiative others – mainly theologians joining him – affirmed the Barmen declaration that the church has the right to stand against rulers who do not respect God's order. These theologians underlined the responsibility of the church in society and the right and duty of the church to call the state rulers to fulfil God's will for humanity. This was seen by critics of Luther as not tallying with Luther's original affirmation that social claims cannot be justified on a biblical ground. The initiative of Bonhoeffer and other German church leaders and theologians to oppose Hitler's regime with its glaring injustices appeared as a new and decisive development in Lutheranism.

Church and state relation and the question of Christian engagement in politics in the African context

With regard to the African setting, basically Christian churches uphold the affirmation of the protestant Reformation that church and state must be separated. Also, all agree that the church has the responsibility to keep governments in check so that it may fulfil its duties in an orderly way. Therefore, the same question reformers like Luther, Calvin and even radical reformers like Anabaptists were confronted with, comes back. Whether the church should respect the autonomy of the state or intervene in its affairs when the circumstances deem it necessary, continues to be debated within church circles in Africa. Also, the majority of Christian churches in Africa are of the opinion that the church has to

7 John H. Redekop, Politique soumise à Dieu, Kinshasa 2007, 55.

intervene when governments fail to work for the common good of their respective people or when the state is responsible of flagrant injustices in the society.

The real and contested question that remains is how this should be put into practice. In the absence of a common formal agreement on the church-state-relation, in several African countries lay people and, to a lesser extent, clergy increasingly engage in politics, especially since elections have allowed people to access positions in government. The rationale often given is that: »if we do not take care of politics, politics will take care of us.« This means that if politics is left in the hands of people who are not enlightened by the Word of God, there should be little surprise when things go wrong in the society or in the state. This sounds like an attempt to »Christianize« the political and social spheres in the manner Calvin is said to have done. But the main idea is to ensure that those who hold power are impregnated by Christian values around human dignity such as peace, justice, freedom etc. It is argued that if reliable Christians get into political positions, this could become the solution to the recurrent political instability which has caused social, political and economic disintegration in many African countries. But the reality is that, on the one hand, a great number of political leaders in power also claim to be Christians but fail to live up to Christian values or Christian ethics. On the other hand, a good number of churches or church leaders have not been better models in their management. In other words, poor leadership and the mismanagement of resources that governments are accused of in Africa are also found in a number of churches.

Another approach is that churches and individual Christians should limit their role to reminding those in power to faithfully carry out their political duties and to educate citizens to keep those in politics in check. In individual churches as well as in ecumenical gatherings, the necessity of the church to play its prophetic role has always been stressed. But, on the one hand, the magnitude of political crises that in many cases have resulted in severe violence, has pushed many church leaders to remain silent. In a context of lawlessness and disorder, the few who tried paid a high price. On the other hand, the prophetic role of the church hardly bears immediate fruit, since the culture of democracy and tolerance has not yet taken roots in Africa and injustice with all its corollaries is widely practiced. Therefore, it appears that given a diversity of political contexts, no single approach seems to be applicable everywhere.

In my own experience in the parliament of the Democratic Republic of the Congo, I felt very often that some practices of the ruling majority to which my party, the Christian Democratic Party, belonged were in contradiction with my Christian belief. This put me in an awkward position not only against the ruling majority but also against my own party which I was supposed to support. It is worth mentioning that I was encouraged to join the party because its identity was founded on Christian and democratic values. After the adoption of the constitution in 2006 that prescribed democratic structures, there was much hope that the era of dictatorship had finally come to an end. But shortly thereafter, experience showed that the existence of democratic structures did not change the mind-set of many political leaders. While talking about democracy, they did not undertake much efforts to conform their style of governing to democratic values and because of that they carried on the system of ill management of the past.

The most painful experience occurred whenever I visited my voters who believed that the government was not fulfilling its duties. They held the members of the parliament, including myself, responsible for the bad management the government was accused of, because, according to the constitution, one of the responsibilities of the parliament is, in fact, to control the actions of the government. Yet, the members of the Parliament were hindered to accomplish that duty because they had the obligation to protect their respective parties which formed the ruling majority. As a consequence, several sectors of life did not improve and even worsened in some parts of the country. We were therefore taken for liars because during the electoral campaign we had promised not just to speak on behalf of the people who had elected us, but also to hold the government to account. I felt a permanent tension within me in my status as a citizen, as a member of the parliament called to serve faithfully my country and as a Christian expected to witness to righteousness. It is true, that my main motivation in running for the parliament was not to become a politician in a true sense but to become somebody who was mandated to speak on behalf of the people. In others words, I understood myself not as servant of the government but of the people who had elected me.

In addition, even though I had not officially been mandated by my church, the church prayed for me and expected my behaviour, as a pastor, to reflect the Christian witness in dealing with political matters. But the government was so much concerned about its own interest that the wellbeing of the people was not sufficiently attended to. The members of the parliament were also caught in that system and there was almost no space left for manoeuvring on behalf of the people who mandated them. Such a situation was embarrassing to me to the point that I ended up by deciding not to run for a second term. My attempt to quit before the end of the parliamentary period was repeatedly not accepted by the leadership of the party. Instead they continued to remind me that our party had the responsibility to contribute to the changes that the people awaited in the country. Unfortunately little changes occurred throughout the five years period of the parliament. Likewise, I did not sense that in the exercise of their political duties, the members of my party where conforming themselves enough to the Christian ideology of our party. They made no significant difference from other political actors.

Surprisingly, many people sensed, that my decision not to run again for parliament or for another position, carried the risk of leaving political affairs in the hands of people who had no fear of God. They felt that political changes in the Congo have more chances to occur if true believers come to power or at least are present in state structures. I was left with the understanding that despite the embarrassment and disappointment Christians may experience in their political engagement, average people who are mostly the victims of ill political structures or of misconduct of political leaders, set their hopes for a better future on engaged Christians involved in politics. They, therefore, encourage them to heed political calling but they also expect them not to compromise the essentials of their Christian identity. That was the case with my own situation when I ended up by accepting to run for parliament. Several people approached me and argued that my twelve years' experience, living in the German society and working with an international church mission, could contribute to the changes which were expected in the country after the adoption of a new constitution that was expected to lay the basis for democratic processes in the Congo.

Reflecting on my experiences and the insights of others, I finally came to the conclusion that despite my dissatisfaction, my office as member of parliament had provided me the opportunity to see with my own eyes the root-causes of the political plight that my country had been undergoing over years. I understood that my country needed a new generation of leaders with an education undergirded by both, knowledge and societal values, because, in spite of the presence of knowledgeable people in government, the lack of an ethical culture, hampered good governance. Building on this, in my current function as rector of a church related university I have engaged myself to raise the awareness of the students to become more critical of systems that logically cannot impulse positive changes in the society as a whole. In this perspective, the education at our university is now focusing on bringing together the acquisition of knowledge, know-how and leadership capacities built on moral or ethical values. With the combination of these three elements of education, we expect students to be equipped with good knowledge, the capacity and the leadership that should enable them to become actors of social transformation which can guarantee a sustainable and harmonious development of the country.

Reminiscence of Christian values in the development of Western societies

We need to be reminded that the foundation of the democratic development and, accompanying it, the economic welfare in Europe and North America has a background in Christian history. Christian values have become such an inextricable part of the European and North American general culture, that people are no longer aware of their impact on the development of their respective societies. It might be argued that Europe, with its high level of secularism, may no longer have any Christian reference. Ironically, consciously or unconsciously, the European and Western societies generally continue to be guided by Christian values. This is the case even in the midst of new interpretations of some biblical elements that used to be considered as fundamentals of Christian faith. Redekop observes that, even though Christian ethics is no longer accepted as general norm in Western societies, there is still a »sub-Christian society« with diverse levels of »sub-Christian ethics«.[8] Redekop adds that this sub-Christian ethics can be found throughout the depravation of Nazism and Stalinist communism to the more enlightened politics of many countries of our time. Despite many political tragedies that were experienced on the European and American continents and that are rooted in the Christian tradition, nevertheless, Redekop argues, a sub-Christian society bears the potential to be transformed into a more just, more human and more civilized society.

Even though Christianity in a formal sense is said to be declining in Western societies, the reminiscences of Christian values continue to play an important role in ensuring a stable development in the various areas of human life. This model of Western societies can be an inspiration for Africa. In fact, today, Africa is said to be the epicentre of Christianity. Yet, it is astonishing to observe practices which are contrary to the Christian faith such as corruption, conflicts, genocide, hate, poor leadership and many other immoral behaviours. There is a joke

8 Ibid., 23.

which depicts the essence of this reality: participation in church services and church gatherings in Africa covers one square kilometer but it is only one centimetre in depth. This means, that despite the preaching of the churches, the Christian faith is still shallow in the daily behaviour of most Christians. Since many of those who claim to be Christians are not being transformed by the message of the Gospel, it becomes natural that leaders in the society will never be able to bring about positive changes. Conversely, even though many people especially in Europe no longer attend church services, their daily life is nevertheless nurtured by the sap of Christian values. To put it in another way, Christian values or ethics are an integral part of their cultural heritage and have modelled their mind-set. This doesn't mean that Western societies are devoid of immorality. Yet, ingrained in Western culture is an awareness of the importance of law and other measures that foster morality in the society. In most African societies this culture is missing, in both church and state. Therefore, it is more difficult to reach a widened and shared understanding how church and state should complement each other in ensuring a stable continent. Members of the communities are, at the same time, members of their respective churches as well as citizens of their respective states. It is, therefore, necessary that they have a good understanding on how each of them, church and state, functions, how to relate to each of them in a balanced way and what their duties are towards both.

Even though Anabaptists opposed the idea of Luther and Calvin of the two citizenships, this double citizenship is a daily experienced reality for Christians and people of other faiths. Jesus himself recognized this reality when he had to answer the cunning question of the Herodians about taxes to be paid to Caesar: »Give to Caesar what is Caesar's and to God what is God's« (Mathew 22:21). This doesn't imply that Jesus put Caesar and God on the same level. One is to understand this to mean that Caesar represents the state – which also the Anabaptists recognized to have been established by God and therefore should be given the means it needed to fulfil its duties. Christians will continue to experience such a dualistic style of living as long as they remain in the reality of the temporal and spiritual dimensions of their existence. But despite this reality, Anabaptists rejected the two forms of ethics which Luther and Calvin attributed to the church and to the state. For Anabaptists there is only one type of ethics: the Christian ethics which should regulate the whole life of those who follow Jesus.[9]

9 Ibid., 22–23.

If the question of the relationship of church and state is less brought to the fore in Western societies, it is because in both, church and state, there are sufficient people who know what is to be done in each of the two entities. This doesn't mean that there are no more problems that affect the relation between church and state in the West. But we believe that the rules regulating both entities are well understood by most people, which helps to avoid unjustified intervention in each other's matters. One could even say that it is on the basis of such a commonly shared understanding that sound discussions can be engaged in case of conflict. The lack of a culture of law and order in Africa has been a serious hindrance to reach this objective. Generally, it is hoped that democracy is the key to establish good and stable governance in Africa. But since democracy means governing by the people, the people must be well informed about the rules of governance. Furthermore, the people – both, those who govern as well as those who are governed – have to be aware of the moral or ethical values that underlie a genuine democracy. Otherwise democracy turns into a destructive system of governing.

During a symposium held by the All Africa Conference of Churches in 1991, the issue of democracy was discussed.[10] The symposium took place in the context of both: the wave of political changes on the one hand and, on the other hand, the crises in Africa as a result of the Conference at la Baule in France in 1990 at which the then French President Francois Mitterand summoned African heads of states. At that conference, Mitterand had announced that French aid to African countries was going to be conditioned to democratic governing. But unfortunately, as most heads of states had not been prepared for such a radical political orientation, yet euphoria was triggered among African people, this resulted in all kinds of disturbances and political crises in many countries. One should remember that the terrible genocide that took place in Rwanda in 1994 was the outcome of this political development. Due to this chaos coupled with the coming to an end of the second millennium, the All Africa Conference of Churches deemed it necessary to evaluate the situation of the African continent socially, politically and economically. The participants pointed out that the crises in Africa were the result of the bankruptcy of imported ideologies. They particularly pointed

10 All Africa Conference of Churches, Problems and Promises of Africa Towards and Beyond the Year 2000. A Summary of the Proceeding of the Symposium Convened by the AACC in Mombasa in November, Nairobi 1993, 28.

out that democracy had been imposed to Africa from abroad as a ready-made structure, and pleaded, instead, for a democracy which ought to bring freedom and self-determination with dignity. In their reflections on possible solutions to the problem, the conference participants suggested that education should be strengthened. But it was also noticed that most schools were state controlled and therefore could not provide an integrated education for children. The absence of churches in the system of education in many African countries was seen to be a hindrance to education which actually should be the clue to the transformation of Africa. The conference participants also recognized that even if the church was fulfilling the duty of counselling and advising individuals as an extended family in the African society, it could not replace the nuclear family which primarily assured social education. In such a situation, it was suggested: »In the context of its training-programme-for-all, the Church has the duty to prepare parents for the irreplaceable task of educating their children«[11].

It is to be noted that despite the fact that the symposium took place at a time of such an unexpected political development in Africa, the participants did neither discuss the question how the churches had been relating to the governments of their respective countries previous to Mitterand's conference. Nor did they reflect on the church's position with regard to the new political challenge brought in by the French President, namely on the question of how an authentic democracy fit for Africa should look like or what could be the measure to achieve it. Instead they blamed democracy as an imported ideology which did not fit Africa since it was not rooted in the African cultural tradition. In his reflections on the conference Kä Mana wrote the following: »Everything happens as if we felt that today the future of our continent will depend on the way in which we shall carry out democracy of our countries and the mutations which the democratic process requires not only in the field of political institutions, but also in the setting of our culture, in the principles of our mentality and in the global system of our imagination«[12].

Though the symposium did not elaborate much on concrete steps which the church in Africa should attempt in order to help African states to deal with the consequences of the la Baule conference, at least they recognized that the edu-

11 Ibid., 24.
12 Kä Mana, Christ d'Afrique, Enjeux éthiques de la foi africaine en Jésus-Christ, Nairobi 1994, 224.

cation of the people was important. Education, it was stated, should include Christian values in order to model the general culture of the society in Africa. Furthermore, as Kä Mana puts it, a democratic system suited to Africa requires cultural transformation. This culture should surely be made up by positive elements of the African tradition and Christian values in a democratic approach where all contribute to the achievement of a better society. Unfortunately, the painful experience that has been made with democratic attempts in Africa, has allowed some critics to question its relevance in Africa in the overall. However, on the one hand, one should not lose sight of the fact that Western countries also went through very painful political processes until they achieved stability. On the other hand, democratic European countries have established different political structures. For instance, the democratic set up in France is not similar to the one in Germany or in the Netherlands. In Switzerland, they have a democratic system whereby the president is elected every year among the seven members of the federal council (the executive). While the spirit of democracy must prevail everywhere, African countries are not obliged to follow any democratic system that is not appropriated to their reality and does not respond to their needs.

The Democratic Republic of Congo is one of the African countries which have had the most troubled democratization process with devastating consequences in the political, social, economic and security areas. This situation has of course portrayed a negative image of the Congo in comparison to other countries in the region which show a relatively stable and harmonious development. But one should not underestimate the reality that, out of the instability and disorder in the Congo, something essential has been gained: in DRC it is not only the constitution that defines democratic structures. Rather, through the exercise of democracy it is being appropriated by the people so that it may, little by little, end up becoming part of the general culture of the country including the political area. Experiences have shown that political systems that on the surface appear quiet and ordered sometimes incubate loud turmoil, whereas severe but well mastered turbulences – such as those which countries in the Western world had known in their history – can produce sustainable development. If African states, like the European states, succeed to capitalize the painful experiences they have gone through in history, they will be able to shape a better future. Despite many prevailing wrongdoings in the Congo, it is no longer obvious that the government can engage in actions contrary to the expectation of the people and to the laws of the country, without facing opposition. Of course democratic leadership is needed not only for political actors but also for those who are responsible for families and schools. Indeed most schools and families use a paternalistic educational approach which lacks the notion of individual responsibility that is important for an efficient education. In other words the spirit of democracy should begin within the families and be continued in the schools. The church has a great role in assisting families and educators in schools and other educational church structures. For that purpose, as it was said before, educational measures should be undertaken to ensure that the rules are followed properly by all.

Perspective for Christian engagement in politics: Drawing from the past

From religious experiences in the history of the church – be it in the time of Reformation, during the Nazi time in Germany or in the search for religious freedom in America vis à vis the state – it has been observed that the great reformers as well as the more radical Anabaptist reformers were of a common understanding that the church and the state operated under the sovereignty of God and had a divine mandate. This assumption prepared the perspective that those who believed in God may serve him in both realms. Today, even modern Anabaptists like the Monnonites engage, Redekop reminds us, in social works as an expression of human solidarity which is an essential element of Christianity. Furthermore, as has been indicated, the circumstances of the 16th century have changed. Today, countries are facing diverse realities which call for contextualized theological paradigms, while keeping the spirit of Reformation. Therefore, in the face of the political situation in Africa where recurrent political crises are caused by leadership deficiency, it appears reasonable to envisage the engagement in politics of people with good Christian testimony as an active witness to the truth and the justice of the Gospel as it is expressed in John 8:32: »Then you will know the truth, and the truth will set you free«. The truth of the Gospel provides freedom which sets believers free from the bondage of evil practices in their respective societies. It is also said in Proverb 14:34: »Righteousness exalts a nation, but sin is a disgrace to any people.« Redekop also recognizes that the absence of Christians in the political sphere has negative effects on the society: »Despite the historical evidence, many Christians, apparently see little value in political action and tend to distance themselves from the political realm. This disturbs me because we know that when religious people distance themselves from politics, those who hold other values will have a great influence«.[13]

On the one hand – as I learned from my own experience as member of parliament – engaging in politics as a mindful Christian is surely a challenge, given the complexity of political issues. Politics is a realm where often evil lurks and power and some practices happen to be in contradiction with the ways of Christian conduct: »in the secular politics«, Redekop states, »prestige, hierarchy, popularity, power and control are well estimated; in the Christian life, service, submission, sacrifice, love and God's adoration are more important.«[14] That is why radical Anabaptists simply advise Christians not to engage in politics. But on the other hand, engaging in politics offers an opportunity for service to people, in the manner of Jesus Christ who came to the world to serve it and to offer life in abundance to it. Therefore, those to be called should be Christians who already showed an engagement for keeping a harmonious development of the communities in which they live so that they may be able to contribute to the emergence of positive changes in the political realm. Redekop expresses the same view as follows: »I maintain the point of view that is supported by historical evidence that a society intrinsically non-Christian, particularly if it is democratic, could be improved considerably by good contributions and enlightened decisions in the political arena. In particular, I believe that it can be made more just and more humanitarian through Christian influence«.[15]

The relevance of such an assumption seems to be shown in an experience made recently in the Democratic Republic of Congo after it had been discovered that designated funds for the implementation of social projects were embezzled. As a result, high ranking persons including the head of staff of the president of the republic were arrested. In order to avoid such an embarrassing situation to be repeated and to ensure good management of a special fund that was established to combat the corona virus illness, the president, as it seems, called upon the leaders of religious confessions to become members of a supervising committee. He nominated the Catholic Cardinal – who is also the vice-chairperson of the Episcopal Conference – as chairperson of the supervising committee of the fund and the president of the Protestant church as substitute chair-person. This

13 Redekop, Politique, 101.
14 Ibid., 22–23.
15 Ibid., 100.

complies with the observation made by Redekop with regard to Mennonites, that when the state is in difficulties, the church can accept to work alongside the state for the advancement of common good. However, as he points out, Mennonites always ensure that this is done in the spirit of an uncompromising Christian discipleship. Drawing from the call of the Congolese president to religious leaders, one could say that, besides the engagement of individual Christians in politics, the church can also suggest to the state punctual measures for a more efficient performance of state affairs, as in the case of the corona virus in the Congo. Also, the church can inspire more sustainable reforms that could release what Biéler – in appreciating Calvin's social and economic enterprise from a theological point of view – qualifies as »integral reformation« of the society. As Biéler indicates, Calvin understood that, in delivering his people from the Egyptian bondage, God established the Canaanite land as a common heritage where all members of the community had to live in freedom and be well nourished. Therefore, there should be no structure whereby a few accroach everything to themselves and oppress others. Life in the land is to be organized in a way that events of spiritual life must, by analogy, determine the social behaviour that modify social and political structures. These structures must be as close as possible to the spiritual realities which command human existence. According to Biéler, for Calvin the spiritual purpose of God giving land to Israel should guide the conduct and the social behaviour of the people.[16] This implies that the future of the land whether good or bad was determined by the behaviour of the people.

As we suggested already, in order to ensure a stable and effective role of Christians in politics, the church should continue to educate the people in the Christian values from their earliest age. It should also assist those who engage in politics not to »Christianize« politics but to let their behaviour be guided by the teaching of the Gospel in their political duties. In other words, the aim is not to dominate politics with Christianity but rather to make use of the Christian values that sustain humanity. Therefore political actors coming from other religions with values that foster humanity should also contribute to the shaping of sound political systems.

Furthermore, the principle of the separation of church and state should not be misused by irresponsible politicians who think that the church should have no say with regard to their political duties or that politics is not a place for Christian witness. Being part of society, the church has the right to speak to issues that may

16 Biéler, La pensée, 381–382.

have an impact not only on its function but even more on the people it serves. The fact that states recognize the social and religious mission of the churches in the society justifies the influence of churches in matters that concern the physical and spiritual wellbeing of the people. The state should not be subservient to the church and the church should not be subservient to the state. The state has to keep the public order and the church has to ensure that the people enjoy a dignified life, both physically and spiritually.

Churches in Africa should take advantage of the eagerness of their members to attend church services and other church events to provide them with the biblical teachings that can transform their minds and their lives so that they may become potential actors of positive changes in the society as a whole. We need to remain aware that the expected changes in politics will never happen if the people in the society from which political actors come do not change. To recall Calvin's theological understanding of the land as God's gift to the people of Israel and whose future depended on their conduct: Africans also, whether Christians or not, ought to look at their respective countries as a gift of God for their common good. Therefore their future, whether good or bad, shall be determined by their behaviour that translates or not God's purpose for them. Actors of social transformation committed to the achievement of such a vision are needed for all sectors of the society so that political crises in Africa may come to an end and a sustainable development in Africa may finally be triggered.

(Rev. Dr. Kakule Molo is since 2017 rector of the Université Libre des Pays des Grands Lacs, a church related university based in the city of Goma in the eastern part of the Democratic Republic of Congo. Before that he served for ten years as President of the Baptist Church in Central Africa with its headquarters in Goma, DR Congo. Before coming back in 2005, he worked as Executive Secretary for the Francophone Africa Desk of the United Evangelical Mission with its office in Wuppertal, Germany.)

ABSTRACT

Christliches Engagement in der Politik ist in Afrika aufgrund der politischen Krisen zu einem Thema ohne Ende geworden. Eine zentrale Frage dabei ist, ob Christ*innen in die Politik gehen sollten, um mehr Stabilität in Afrika zu erreichen. Kirchen und Einzelpersonen haben diesbezüglich unterschiedliche Entscheidungen getroffen und Wege eingeschlagen. Der vorliegende Artikel erörtert die genannte Frage, indem er auf Interaktionen zwischen Kirche, Gesellschaft und Staat von der Reformation an bis heute blickt. Der Artikel kommt zu dem Schluss, dass die Herausforderungen, denen die Kirchen in ihren jeweiligen Kontexten begegnen, und die Aufgabe, sowohl Gottes Heilsauftrag zu erfüllen als auch menschliches Leben in der Welt zu erhalten, dazu führen, dass Kirchen heute die Möglichkeiten dafür prüfen – bzw. prüfen sollten –, wie sich Christ*innen in ihren Kontexten politisch engagieren können, ohne ihr christliches Zeugnis zu gefährden.

»It is well«: An Essay in Pentecostal Political Semantics

Ebenezer Obadare

What do Nigerian Pentecostals mean whenever they say, »It is well«? What insights into the Pentecostal imaginary in its specific relation to the Nigerian state, society, and politics can be gained from a critical examination of those words and the discursive and material contexts in which they tend to be uttered? Advancing multiple interpretations, this essay opens a window into Nigerian Pentecostals' understanding of culture and society, and how that understanding informs their conceptions of life, politics, morality, sociality, and futurity. The very currency of the phrase is tendered as proof, both of Pentecostalism's locutionary transgressiveness, and the power of its rhetoric to inundate and capture secular language.

> »Run now, I pray thee, to meet her, and say unto her, Is it well with thee? Is it well with thy husband? Is it well with the child? And she answered, It is well:« 2 Kings 4:26.

Waiting in line

We were all standing quietly, if a bit edgily, in line when the incident which set me thinking about the theme of this paper happened. The place was Murtala Muhammed International Airport, Lagos, Nigeria; it was October 2019, and I was on my way out of the country having just participated in that year's edition of the Ake Arts and Book Festival. I was flying with United Airlines en route Washington, D.C., and as has been my wont now over the past several years, I had elected to pay for an upgrade from basic to premium economy. This was the reason I found myself in a short line in a little side office to the back of the terminal.

At any rate, there we were, prospective upgraders all, waiting our turn, when the power went out. Other than the loud hiss of frustration emitted by the middle-aged woman who was next in line for help, there was practically no reaction from the rest of us. As adult Nigerians, hence no strangers to the general instability of power supply in the country, we know very well never to take electricity (or security)[1] for granted, even at a major international airport, and in the ensuing partial darkness, all I could make out was an all too familiar shaking of heads.

And then all of a sudden, as if out of nowhere, the words rose up from behind the perforated glass curtain behind which was installed a female United Airlines staffer: »It is well.«

It was not the first time I had heard those words. Before then, I had noticed the increased frequency of their use, primarily by Nigerian Pentecostals, and generally by Nigerian Christians, but it was the first time it occurred to me that perhaps I should think more deeply about them. Why would anyone, in the face of an obviously inconvenient, not to mention unpalatable and embarrassing situation such as we were in, think that »It is well«? At that moment, I had no way of establishing the particular faith tradition, if any, that the United Airlines staffer belonged to. But not being able to does not suffice to invalidate my inquest, given my overall theorizing (more below) that contemporary Nigeria is a Pentecostal Republic, and that one of the many arenas in which Pentecostal influence manifests is in the arena of everyday language. What I find striking is how readily this, i. e. »It is well,« is offered, proof for me that, in a pentecostalized milieu, one does not have to be a card-carrying Pentecostal to begin to speak like one.

Hence, the key question I address here: What do Nigerians (Pentecostals and non-) *really* mean when they say »It is well,« and what overall insights into the Pentecostal imaginary in its specific relation to the Nigerian state, society, and politics can be accrued from a critical examination of the words and the various discursive and material contexts in which they are used? In asking this question, I am by no means assuming that the words circulate only within Pentecostal-Christian circles. On the contrary, and consistent with my overall posture on the

1 At least twice in the past couple of years, armed bandits have stormed the main terminal of the airport, robbing prospective travelers and carting away property worth millions of Naira. More spectacularly, in February 2018, at the same airport, unknown bandits had attacked an Air Peace (a Nigerian domestic airline) aircraft as it taxied for takeoff. See http://saharareporters.com/2018/02/09/robbers-attack-air-peace-aircraft-while-taxiing-take-lagos-airport (accessed March 19, 2020).

influence of Pentecostalism, its non-religious articulations constitute an ample illustration of its locutionary transgressiveness, and the power of its rhetoric to flow into and overwhelm secular language. It is possible to compare »It is well« with analogues in, say, Yoruba, »O daa« or »Ko s'iyonu« (rough translation, »it's all right«), English, »No problem«, or Pidgin, »Nothing spoil« or even »No wahala.« The essential difference with »It is well« is that it is not nearly the lackadaisical shrug that everyday life with its permanent threat of ennui sometimes engenders, which is what, in my view, these other Yoruba, English and Pidgin usages point up.

That said, the variety of contexts in which I have heard the words spoken over the past few years (whether Pentecostal or non-), disqualifies any probability that individual users may have used them with the same meaning in mind. Yet, the apparent episodicity of use in no way offers a relief from speculation, especially given my insistence on an original Pentecostal lineage; rather, the fact that the words have gained currency within a specific Nigerian-Pentecostal sociological milieu, I believe, makes critical scrutiny imperative.

On pentecostal language: A clarification

Analysis of Pentecostal language forms a key segment of the broader academic literature on Pentecostalism as a whole. Much of this subsidiary scholarship has been dominated by interest in glossolalia or speaking in tongues[2] , the semantics of sermons, and the performativity of translation. To the extent that this literature is interested in language, accepting it as a way to illuminate aspects of Pentecostal praxes, mine is an addition to this literature.

My interest is in language insofar as it helps throw a light on broader socio-economic, political and cultural phenomena. Therefore, I focus on the socially-determined and constantly shifting meaning of words (thus the semantics in the

2 See for instance Elaine J. Lawless, God's Peculiar People. Women's Voices & Folk Tradition in a Pentecostal Church, Lexington 2005 (orig. 1988); James N. Amanze/James N. et al., Glossolalia. Divine Speech or Man-Made Language? A Psychological Analysis of the Gift of Speaking in Tongues in the Pentecostal Churches in Botswana, in: Studia Historiae Ecclesiasticae 41/1 (2015), 3–19; Ogbu U. Kalu, African Pentecostalism. An Introduction, Oxford 2008; Nelson Kalombo Ngoy, Neo-Pentecostalism. A Post-Colonial Critique of the Prosperity Gospel in the Democratic Republic of the Congo, Eugene 2019.

title), rather than in the philological minutiae of their structure or arrangement. In focusing on language in this manner, I commit seriously to words in their capacity to do and undo, to found and disestablish, especially in a political sense.

More crucially, I take Pentecostalism itself as a language, that is, a structure of meaning that, in aspiring to displace the prevailing mode, proposes an alternate understanding of agency, causality, and history in Nigeria. Pentecostalism partitions Nigerian political history into a »Before« and »After,« the latter unfolding under its divinely-activated sign. In this reading, and as I have argued before[3], the Fourth Republic itself is nothing short of a miraculous fulfillment of God's promise to Nigerian Christians, an epiphany clothed in the language of political discourse. One does not overreach in concluding that Pentecostalism is the language of the Fourth Republic, or that language itself is essential to the emergence of Pentecostal power.

If the foregoing is accepted, »It is well,« beyond the different permutations plausible within various social contexts involving individual Pentecostals and other Christian agents as discussed below, emerges, in my interpretation, as Pentecostalism's grand statement of assurance. Emanating from its conceit in relation to its understanding of its place in Nigerian history, it is Pentecostalism's theological warranty that, no matter the current turmoil, things will be all right in Nigeria. Eventually.

A faith purposed for the times

To properly ground this analysis, some contextual remarks on Nigerian Pentecostalism seem necessary. The point of these remarks is to establish the ascendance of Pentecostalism as the dominant mode of Christianity in Nigeria over the past two decades, and furthermore, to show that this dominance, transgressing the boundaries of Christianity, bleeds into all aspects of daily life, including language and communication.

As I argued in my recent study (2018), the mutual enfolding of the Nigerian Fourth Republic (1999–) and the ascendance of Pentecostalism is such that the Fourth Republic is most properly described as a Pentecostal Republic. Having

3 Ebenezer Obadare, Pentecostal Republic. Religion and the Struggle for State Power in Nigeria, London 2018.

arguably, though not irreversibly, pushed past Islam in the perennial struggle for supremacy in the Nigerian political arena,[4] such is its force that, in the western part of the country at least, even Islam has been forced to significantly overhaul its devotional strategies. Pentecostalism, over the past two decades, has rapidly planted the flag of its influence in various aspects of Nigerian public life, including but not limited to education, entertainment, the media, sport, and the bureaucracy. Nothing captures the extent of Pentecostalism's reach as the *idée fixe* of the Fourth Republic more strongly than the sometimes servile scramble among the political elite and aspirants for public office for the endorsement of leading Pentecostal pastors, and the virtual beatification of the latter by a cross section of the Nigerian public.

What explains Pentecostalism's grip on the (Nigerian) mind? As I have argued elsewhere[5], Pentecostalism's success owes to a combination of factors: its ability to reduce complex social, economic and political struggles to a »personal« relationship between the believer and God; its »capacity to adapt itself to local social concerns and cosmologies«[6]; its claim, via a plethora of doctrinal affirmations, to *being the answer* to people's existential problems[7]; its appeal to the senses via rousing musical performances[8]; and finally, the fact that it grants, as a standard part of the history of conversion[9] a certain social agent the opportunity to acquire a new social identity, often times complete with a new name[10]. As I have suggested elsewhere[11], such names as Miracle, Laughter, Pray, Praise, Praise the Lord, Prayer, Success, Testimony, Living Testimony, Prosper, Prosperity, Yuletide, Independence, Worship, Answer, Favor, Jesus Is Coming, Light, Pillar, Rhapsody, Hallelujah, Good News, Divine, Ministry, Rapture, and last but definitely not least, Pentecostal, perfectly illustrate not just Pentecostalism's

4 See Ebenezer Obadare, The Muslim Response to the Pentecostal Surge in Nigeria. Prayer and the Rise of Charismatic Islam, in: Journal of Religious and Political Practice 2/1 (2016), 75–91.

5 Ibid.

6 Rosalind H. Shaw, Displacing Violence. Making Pentecostal Memory in Postwar Sierra Leone, in: Cultural Anthropology 22/1 (2007), 66–93, here: 70.

7 Paul Gifford, Ghana's New Christianity. Pentecostalism in a Globalising African Economy, Bloomington 2004.

8 See also Birgit Meyer, Aesthetics of Persuasion. Global Christianity and Pentecostalism's Sensational Forms, in: South Atlantic Quarterly 109/4 (2010), 741–763.

9 See for instance the collection of essays in Brendan Carmody, Religious Conversion. An African Perspective, Lusaka 2018.

10 Obadare, The Muslim Response, 2016.

11 Ebenezer Obadare, »The New Name? It's a Prayer!« http://forums.ssrc.org/ndsp/2013/08/29/the-new-name-its-a-prayer/, 2013.

inroads into the collective imaginary, but also the way in which it, i. e. Pentecostalism, often functions as an identity in itself. Sociologically[12], these names serve to mark the Pentecostal in-group as normatively distinct from the world out there.

Admittedly, the Pentecostalization of social life in Nigeria is never a one-way phenomenon. Even as it puts its stamp on social life on the one hand, on the other, Pentecostalism continues to absorb, and be shaped by, the peculiarities of the Nigerian condition. As a faith fashioned from the fabric of, thus intimately bound up with, Nigeria's postcolonial predicament, its doctrinal assertions and ritualistic emphases are appropriately, almost eerily, Nigerian. Not only does it draw directly on the lived experience of religious citizens in the Fourth Republic, Pentecostalism's vocabulary is a reliable guide into the desires and exasperations of daily life as endured by majority of Nigerians in this particular historical moment. Accordingly, and to take just one example, it requires no unique insight, contemplating something as seemingly ordinary as the language of Pentecostal prayer, to realize that its idioms and phraseologies constitute a subconscious commentary on the agonies and challenges of quotidian life in Nigeria.[13]

Variant meanings

Having hopefully established the pentecostalization of social life in Nigeria (and the attendant inundation of Pentecostalism by the Nigerian condition) as a material reality, I now return to the scene of the original provocation. I wish to proffer, against the backdrop of everyday Nigerian reality, different possible meanings of the phrase »It is well,« with the hope that these interpretive trajectories will, at a minimum, provide a deep insight into Nigerian Pentecostals' (and increasingly other Christian groups') understanding of social life in Nigeria, and how that understanding informs their conceptions of life, politics, morality, sociality, and futurity.

12 See for instance Janet Finch, Naming Names. Kinship, Individuality and Personal Names, in: Sociology 42/4 (2008), 709–725; Jane Pilcher, Names, Bodies and Identities, in: Sociology 50/4 (2016), 764–779.

13 If I have limited myself to the Nigerian situation here, it is not because there are no parallels in other countries, both within and outside Africa. As a matter of fact, and given how Pentecostalism has been on a tear globally, with the only difference being in the degree of penetration of the corridors of power, the existence of such parallels can be assumed.

In terms of historical comparison, the phraseology that immediately comes to mind when we contemplate the words »It is well« are the words »Insha Allah« (Arabic for »God willing«). They controversially entered the Nigerian political vocabulary after former military dictator, Ibrahim Babangida spoke them, plainly hoping to recoup some moral credit and restore popular faith in a Transition to Civil Rule program that, by the time, the media, if not the public at large, had come to perceive as an elaborate ruse. Within the historical moment, one in which Babangida was fond of playing God, »Insha Allah« was a cynical attempt on the part of the despot to make the vexed subject of his own tenure a matter of divine whim, thus closed off to everyday civic speculation. Considering what followed, Nigerians had every right to be dubious.

But does »Insha Allah« connote the same thing as »It is well«? To some extent. One thread apparently running through both is the element of resignation. For his part, the former military ruler seemed to be urging Nigerians to resign (re-sign?) themselves to a sinuous and seemingly interminable transition program going on for as long as Allah willed it. Therefore, »Insha Allah« was not just a prayer, as indeed it can be, but a diplomatic dodge by a tyrant desperate to avoid transparency. »It is well« has that hint of resignation bordering on despondency as well. When, as is often the case, uttered with a sigh, it can signal, as it did with the United Airlines staffer that fateful evening, that the utterer has had it.

But has enough of what exactly? What, precisely, is the »it« that the speaker has had enough of, but which is »well« at the same time? With the airport scene, the proximate trigger was the sudden power outage, so it is reasonable to surmise that the affirmation was uttered in response to that. But even if that is granted, we are not totally out of the woods in terms of what she meant to signify. Was she implying that the loss of power would be temporary and we would all be served and on our way as was eventually the case? Or, that no matter how unstable power supply may get (both at the airport and in the country at large), things will eventually get done? Was she »claiming,« in Pentecostal-speak,[14] that no matter what happens, all will be »well« with Nigeria? Or was she just plain frustrated, realizing how unpredictable power supply has become at the airport, how the Nigerian condition appears to have finally caught up with the airport, and how

14 Meaning, the vast fund of words and phraseologies mobilized by Nigerian Pentecostals within a specific frame of meaning, and, whether intended or not, specifying an enclosed universe of understanding.

the state of things there is a metaphor for the state of things in the country as a whole? That these readings are not mutually exclusive goes to show how elusive those three words are.

In other settings in which I have heard the words spoken, it is important to note that they were [are] not necessarily directed at a particular audience. Even at the airport, the woman who spoke them did not exactly direct them to those of us waiting in line, which is not to say that we were not meant to hear them. It was a groan from the pit of the stomach, not meant for anyone in particular, yet ineffective without the understanding of the immediate audience, who inhabit the same universe of meaning as the speaker. For such people, »It« needs no explanation. »It« was a combination of the power outage, the state of the airport, the country's degraded infrastructure, the abjectness of the leadership, and the sheer desperation of everyday life.

As emphasized by a vast body of work[15], Nigerians have devised an infinite variety of ways and means for coping with the rigors of socio-economic hardship. To the extent that Pentecostalism itself, especially in terms of its doctrinal assurances, may be said to serve as a coping strategy, it is productive of discourses and tropes that betray its insertion in the Nigerian crisis. Put differently, to analyze Nigerian Pentecostalism is to open an inlet into the larger interplay of socio-political and cultural forces that gives the country its specific sociological stamp. Unsurprisingly, then, such tropes play out in the arena of everyday language, testimony to the power of the Nigerian to transform the incongruities of daily life into the stuff of dark humor. I suggest that, being an example of such everyday usages, »It is well« both feeds off, and is contextually embedded in, multiple layers of meaning.

It can, for example, signal positive affirmation, a refusal to accept current travails as dispositive, and an insistence that, *in the end*, it *shall* be well. In this way, part of what is being affirmed by the speaker is that »God is in control,« and, »so far as he occupies the divine throne,« as Nigerian Pentecostals like to say, there is hope. This is faith expressed as philosophical serenity, a deep conviction that, notwithstanding the extant tumult, it *will* be well.

But while serenity, representing a coming to terms with, can be a coping strategy, an unperturbable anticipation of better times in a future that remains unspecified, it can also be read, legitimately I think, as acquiescence. In this mode, »It

15 For instance Ebenezer Obadare, Humor, Silence, and Civil Society in Nigeria, New York 2016.

is well« functions in the same way as *a category of* silence, particularly insofar as it means that the speaker, in seeking accommodation with (or is it looking beyond?) the current political or socio-moral order, and finding mental repose in a future dispensation, is resistant to direct engagement with, or questioning of, the existing one. As it happens, the latter reading chimes with my overall skeptical intuition that Nigerian Pentecostalism carries a reactionary potential that makes it susceptible to conservative forces in the society. Read this way, »It is well« is suggestive of political abdication, one in which the agent more or less self-incapacitates.

While I am willing to defend the latter as a legitimate inference, this does not imply that those who say »It is well« are themselves always cognizant of the political ramifications of the phrase. In any case, such a reading does not automatically nullify or delegitimize other plausible readings. My point is that as a semantic signifier, »It is well« is pregnant with interpretive possibilities, and that given the already stated affinity between Pentecostalism and politics in Nigeria, it would be remiss to overlook explicit political extrapolations.

In doing so, one should of course be careful not to discount other possible interpretations, especially at the level of interpersonal relationships, where »It is well« can be motivational as well as confessional. After all, the words are often casually invoked in everyday conversations between two or more people, and with politics presumably out of sight. Under such circumstances, saying »It is well« may be a signal of the speaker's reluctance to engage in a potentially exhausting or stressful debate, or to avoid conflict with an immediate interlocutor. It is when »It is well« becomes a generalized attitude, something like a collective shrug of the shoulders, that it becomes politically potent, or impotent as the case may be.

Conclusion: Three incisions in a politico-linguistic economy

Why does all this matter? Why does it matter what its utterers (Pentecostal and non-) mean by these three simple words? They matter, first and foremost, because of my basic attitude that words matter, not least because of their inherent capacity to do and undo, especially in the political domain. By the same token, Pentecostal language matters because of what I take to be the fact of Pentecostal dominance of the Fourth Republic, a dominance that is visible in various aspects of the Nigerian society, especially politics, sport, popular culture, and the media. Pentecostal language, I have argued, is inextricably connected to *how* the Nigerian Fourth Republic speaks. Accordingly, to take such language seriously is to take seriously broader socio-economic, political and cultural phenomena as they are impacted, rhetorically and otherwise, by Pentecostalism.

None of this is to suggest that the meanings of »It is well« are fixed, or that different users necessarily swim in the same pool of significations. On the contrary, several contending inferences can be mutually legitimate, even though my chief interest is in the ideological agendas the words are apt to serve consequent upon the agential possibilities activated, maintained, or reinforced by Pentecostalism. Put differently: I am intrigued by the possibility that »It is well,« being representative of Pentecostalism's reactionary instinct, obliges depoliticization by justifying the existing social order.

(Ebenezer Obadare is Professor at the Department of Sociology, University of Kansas, Lawrence, USA, and fellow at the University of South Africa's Institute of Theology.)

ABSTRACT

Was bedeutet es für nigerianische Pfingstler*innen, wenn sie sagen: »Es ist gut«? Der Artikel nimmt diese Aussage zum Ausgangspunkt, um sich dem pentekostalen Verständnis des gesellschaftspolitischen Kontexts in Nigeria anzunähern. Der Autor bedient sich dabei einer kritischen Untersuchung der diskursiven und realpolitischen Einbettung der besagten Formel. Davon ausgehend eröffnet der Beitrag vielschichtige Bilder und Vorstellungsräume, die in der nigerianischen Pfingstbewegung dazu dienen, um ihr Verhältnis zu Staat, Gesellschaft und Politik auszudrücken. Die Formel »Es ist gut« bietet darüber hinaus einen Ausgangspunkt, um das pentekostale Lebensverständnis überhaupt nachzuvollziehen. Sie umschließt Assoziationen von Kultur und Gesellschaft, von Gemeinschaft und Zukunft. Schlussendlich weist die Analyse dieser Aussage darauf hin, dass pentekostale Rhetorik längst über religiöse Bedeutungsinhalte hinausweist und dabei ist, säkulare Sprache zu bedienen und deren Semantik zu besetzen.

Yoruba – Santería – Jazz Batá

Lateinamerikanische Befreiungstheologie und sozialistischer Realismus in Kuba

Roland Spliesgart

Wer an der Geschichte der lateinamerikanischen *Befreiungstheologie* schreibt, begegnet zwei Ereignissen in Jahreszahlen, die höchst unterschiedliche Perspektiven auf dasselbe Geschehen eröffnen. 1968 schlossen sich die lateinamerikanischen Bischöfe auf ihrer II. Generalkonferenz in Medellín der vorrangigen Option der Kirche für die Armen an. Die Befreiungstheologie wurde daraufhin zur »Normaltheologie« in vielen Diözesen und fand auch Anhänger in einigen protestantischen Kirchen. Soweit die etwas spröde, kirchlich-katholische Lesart. In Lateinamerika selbst bedeutet jedoch ein ganz anderes Ereignis neun Jahre zuvor die Geburtsstunde eines Mythos:

> »1959 triumphiert in Kuba die erste lateinamerikanische sozialistische Revolution. Dieser Prozess bedeutet einen ›historischen Bruch‹, einen ›Anfang‹, der sich in ein Zeichen, ein Programm und eine Hoffnung für den ganzen Kontinent verwandelt […] und daher hat das Datum 1959 einen symbolischen Wert.«[1]

Mit diesem Urteil fasst der chilenische Befreiungstheologe Pablo Richard im Jahr 1981 die einzigartige Bedeutung zusammen, die dem Sieg der bärtigen Revolutionäre um Fidel Castro über das korrupte Regime des Diktators Batista am 1. Januar 1959 für die lateinamerikanische Volksbewegung und darunter viele Christ*innen zukommen sollte.

1 Pablo Richard, A igreja latino-americana entre o temor e a esperanca. Apontamentos teológicos para a decada de 80, São Paulo 1982, 65. Alle Übersetzungen aus dem Portugiesischen und Spanischen erfolgen durch den Vf.

In Folge beider Ereignisse favorisierte die Befreiungstheologie, die auch als Befreiungstheologie der ersten Generation bezeichnet werden kann, einhellig ein sozialistisches Gesellschaftsmodell.[2] Der reale Sozialismus in Kuba wurde dabei zur historischen Konfiguration der befreiungstheologischen Utopie. So schrieb der Argentinier Enrique Dussel 1971 in seiner *Geschichte der Kirche in Lateinamerika*: »In Kuba ist die Krise [der lateinamerikanischen Kirche und Gesellschaft] überwunden.«[3] Die Befreiungstheologie wurde so zum »Ausdruck eines speziellen historischen Moments, der in Lateinamerika gelebt wurde. Es handelt sich um die 1970er und 1980er Dekaden, eine Zeit des Kampfs gegen die Militärdiktaturen und des Erstarkens verschiedener politischer und sozialer Bewegungen mit der Unterstützung der christlichen Kirchen.«[4]

Bis etwa 1990 kann insofern von einer relativen Einheitlichkeit ausgegangen werden, als eine Mehrheit männlicher Theologen in großer »phallozentrischer Harmonie«[5] eine Orthodoxie etablierten, die eine Befreiung der ›Armen‹ ausschließlich in politischen und ökonomischen Kategorien dachte. Die wenigen Befreiungstheologinnen dieser Zeit hatten sich – so Ivone Gebara – dem männlichen Denken weitgehend angeschlossen.[6] Wer aus dem Jahr 2021 auf die Weltgeschichte der Befreiungstheologie blickt, muss dagegen eine Vielfalt an Nach- und Wechselwirkungen in neuen sozialen Bewegungen, spirituellen Aufbrüchen, biblischen und sozialethischen Impulsen anerkennen, die hier nicht alle in den Blick genommen werden können. Stattdessen möchte ich mich mit der speziellen Wirkungsgeschichte der Befreiungstheologie am Ursprungsort jenes Mythos befassen, der sie selbst hervorgebracht hat: in Kuba.

Rein äußerlich fällt auf, dass in Kuba das Konzept der Befreiungstheologie zunächst nur wenig Beachtung fand, obwohl 1985 die Gespräche des brasiliani-

2 Vgl. Ivone Gebara nach Maria José Rosado-Nunes, Teologia Feminista e a crítica da razão religiosa patriarcal: entrevista com Ivone Gebara, in: Estudos Feministas 14/1 (2006), 294–304, hier: 300; Leonardo Boff, Socialismo real e teologia da libertação, in: Tempo e Presença 9/224 (1987), 23–24, hier: 23.

3 Enrique Dussel, Die Geschichte der Kirche in Lateinamerika, Mainz 1988 [1971], 401.

4 Gebara, Teologia Feminista, 300.

5 Ivone Gebara, A Teologia da Libertação e as mulheres, in: Revista Sociedade e Cultura 23 (2020), https://doi.org/10.5216/sec.v23i.61023 (24.4.2020).

6 Den Grund sieht Ivone Gebara darin, dass auch die Befreiungstheolog*innen* zunächst den Vorrang des Politischen akzeptierten und in der Bewegung nicht als Imperialistinnen kritisiert werden wollten, obwohl sie spürten, dass die vielfältige Unterdrückung der Frauen in Lateinamerika ein überaus wichtiges Thema wäre. Seit etwa 1980 äußerten Frauen zunehmend Kritik am von männlichen Dominanzmustern bestimmten Denken und artikulierten eigene, feministische Befreiungstheologien. Vgl. Gebara, Teologia da Libertação.

schen Befreiungstheologen Frei Betto mit dem *máximo líder* Fidel Castro schlaglichtartig internationale Verbreitung fanden. Aber was geschah mit ihrer sozialistischen Utopie genau in jenem Land, das einen sozialistischen Realismus eigener Art mitsamt einer speziellen Lebenswirklichkeit und Kultur hervorgebracht hat?

Um diese Frage zu beantworten, soll der Blick unter Zurückstellung aller (geo-)politischen und ideologischen Fragen und Interessenlagen auf die inneren Zusammenhänge und Motive religiösen Bewusstseins gerichtet werden. Damit wird auch die psychosoziale Realität kubanischer Lebensart und Religiosität jenseits der Grenzen der Christentumsgeschichte zum Thema. Anderenfalls droht ein Rückfall in alte, dogmatische Grabenkämpfe konkurrierender Geschichtsphilosophien ohne jeden Erkenntnisgewinn. Dies zeigt das Beispiel Joseph Kardinal Ratzingers, der die Befreiungstheologie als eine »Theologie der erlösenden politischen Praxis«[7] bezeichnete, die im Gefolge der marxistischen Ideologie zu radikaler Unfreiheit führe.

Im Folgenden soll zunächst (1.) der *Mythos Kuba* und seine Bedeutung für die Befreiungstheologie näher beleuchtet werden. Dann wird (2.) der Frage nachgegangen, wo die Gründe dafür liegen, dass die lateinamerikanische Theologie der Befreiung im kubanischen Katholizismus deutlich weniger Beachtung fand als in anderen Teilen Lateinamerikas sowie (3.) inwiefern sich die protestantischen Kirchen Kubas mit der Befreiungstheologie auseinandersetzten. Schließlich wird (4.) die These untermauert, dass sich innerhalb der überaus populären afrokubanischen Religionen Praktiken etablierten, die das Anliegen der christlichen Befreiungstheologie – gleichsam in exkulturierter Gestalt – realisierten. Unter den Bedingungen einer real existierenden sozialistischen Gesellschaft ließ sich das emanzipatorische Potential für die Kubaner nur auf einer kulturellen und spirituellen Ebene ausleben.

1. Kuba als Symbol der Befreiungstheologie

Die Beziehung der Befreiungstheologie zum Modell des kubanischen Sozialismus war durchaus essentieller Natur. Dabei war das Bewusstsein, dass die Zukünf-

7 Joseph Ratzinger, Relación sobre la situación actual de la fe y la teología. Cit. p. Sergio Silva, Transformationen der lateinamerikanischen Befreiungstheologie in den ’90er Jahren, in: Klaus Koschorke (Hg.), Falling Walls. The Year 1989/90 as a Turning Point in the History of World Christianity, Wiesbaden 2009, 335–349, hier: 336.

tigkeit des Reiches Gottes nicht mit der Marxschen Idee des Reichs der Freiheit in der klassenlosen Gesellschaft gleichzusetzen sei, häufig sehr gering ausgeprägt.

Als die lateinamerikanischen Bischöfe 1968 in Medellín die Option der Kirche für die Armen beschlossen, folgten sie dem Konzept des peruanischen Befreiungstheologen Gustavo Gutiérrez und erklärten es zur Leitlinie der Arbeit in ihren Diözesen. Indem sich die katholische Kirche vorbehaltlos auf die Seite des »unterdrückten und leidenden Volkes« (pueblo) stellte, beendete sie den jahrhundertelangen Missbrauch der Religion als ideologischer Stütze der Herrschenden.[8]

Der Radikalisierung der katholischen Amtskirche waren die Forderungen der christlichen Basisbewegung vorangegangen, die seit 1960 unter Arbeiter*innen, der Jugend und Studierenden entstanden war und ökonomische, soziale, politische und ideologische Missstände anprangerte.[9] In dieser Zeit war der Gegensatz von Unterdrückung und Befreiung in den lateinamerikanischen Gesellschaften unmittelbar evident und im Gegenüber von Großgrundbesitzern und Landarbeitern bzw. Pächtern, internationalen oder nationalen Unternehmen und dem dort beschäftigten Proletariat sichtbar. Nicht zuletzt gelangten in vielen Ländern Militärregierungen an die Macht, die den Widerstand des Volkes mit Folter und Morden grausam bekämpften.

Für den Theologen Pablo Richard bedeutete der Sieg der Revolution in Kuba 1959 eine entscheidende Wende für die lateinamerikanische Kirche in einem heilsgeschichtlichen Konzept.[10] Nach diesem engagierten sich Christen nun bewusst für den Kampf gegen die neokoloniale Ausbeutung ihrer Länder durch das kapitalistische System und die mit ihm verbundene so genannte »Neochristenheit«. Für die aus dieser Bewegung entstandene »Kirche des Volkes« (igreja popular) sei – so Richard – »die ausdrückliche und bewusste Option für den Sozialismus der direkte Ausdruck des christlichen Verständnisses des Kampfes für Leben, das in den populären Mehrheiten präsent ist.«[11] Da der Sozialismus in

8 Zur Befreiungstheogie vgl. Dussel, Geschichte, 200–379; Sergio Silva, Theologiegeschichte Lateinamerikas seit 1945, in: Johannes Meier/Veit Straßner (Hg.), Kirche und Katholizismus seit 1945, Bd. 6. Lateinamerika und Karibik, Paderborn u. a. 2009, 29–58.

9 Vgl. Richard, Igreja, 52–62.

10 Dieses hatte 1492 mit der Kolonisierung und Evangelisierung Lateinamerikas begonnen und ein koloniales Christentum hervorgebracht. Mit der politischen Unabhängigkeit von Spanien bzw. Portugal geriet die Christenheit zunehmend in Abhängigkeit von England und später den USA. Vgl. Richard, Igreja, 63–66.

11 A. a. O., 93, s. auch 92–94.

Lateinamerika eine Frage von Leben oder Tod der Massen sei, benötige er keine weitere ideologische oder theologische Begründung.

Dementsprechend spricht sich Richard für die Verwendung des Marxismus als wissenschaftliche Methode im Prozess der Befreiung aus.[12] Als Philosophie sei der Marxismus dagegen abzulehnen. Dessen Atheismus sieht Richard politisch begründet: in Ablehnung der »Vergötzung« und Vergöttlichung des kapitalistischen Systems. Schließlich plädiert Richard für eine strategische Allianz von Christen und Marxisten und folgt hier der Meinung Ernesto »Che« Guevaras: »Die Christen sollten definitiv für die Revolution optieren und ganz besonders in unserem Kontinent, wo der christliche Glaube der Volksmassen so wichtig ist. [...] Sobald die Christen sich trauen, ein integrales revolutionäres Zeugnis abzulegen, wird die lateinamerikanische Revolution unbesiegbar sein.«[13]

Auch der Brasilianer Leonardo Boff betrachtet die sozialistischen Gesellschaften als konkrete Utopie für sein befreiungstheologisches Programm. Nach einer Reise in die Sowjetunion stellt er 1987 fest, dass im Sozialismus zahlreiche christliche Ideen verwirklicht seien. V. a. könnten die Menschen dort ihre Gemeinschaftlichkeit besser ausleben als im Kapitalismus. Schließlich bewertet Boff den im Sozialismus erzielten »historischen Fortschritt als in der Zeit antizipierte und konkretisierte Realisierung der Güter des Reichs Gottes«[14]. Seiner Meinung nach verträten die Sozialisten die »Sache Gottes«, auch wenn sie ihn negierten, »weil sie dem Leben dienen, und sie produzieren die Mittel für das Leben zum Nutzen der Personen, die Söhne und Töchter des himmlischen Vaters sind.«[15]

Im Anschluss an »Che« Guevara meint auch Boff, dass die Christen *innerhalb* des Sozialismus bei der Verwirklichung seiner Ideale helfen und sie als evangeliumsgemäße Ideale artikulieren sollten. Zwar sei die Ablehnung der Religion bei Marx ein Irrtum, jedoch sehe er »in Kuba [...] Zeichen [...] einer wirklichen Revision«[16]. Demgegenüber kritisiert Boff die mangelnde Partizipation des Volkes in der Sowjetunion. Er sieht die zentrale Aufgabe daher in der Entwicklung eines lateinamerikanischen Sozialismus auf der Grundlage der eigenen kulturellen Wurzeln und unter Beteiligung des gesamten Volkes. Dass Boff hier offen-

12 Vgl. Richard, Igreja, 95–109.
13 A. a. O., 106.
14 Boff, Socialismo, 24.
15 Ebd.
16 Ebd.

sichtlich das Vorbild Kubas im Blick hat, legt die Hochschätzung der »direkten, partizipativen Demokratie«[17] in Kuba im Beitrag von Paulo Schilling in derselben Ausgabe der vom ökumenischen Zentrum CEDI (*Centro Ecumenico de Informação de Documentação*) herausgegebenen Zeitschrift *Tempo e Presença* – einem wichtigen Organ der Befreiungstheologie in Brasilien – mit dem Titel »70 Jahre Sozialismus« nahe.

Der Fall der Berliner Mauer löste auch in Lateinamerika unmittelbar Diskussionen aus. Die Ausgabe von *Tempo e Presença* mit dem Titel »Ist der Sozialismus gestorben?« vom Juli 1990 dokumentiert das Festhalten der ersten Generation von Befreiungstheolog*innen am *Mythos Kuba*.

In einem programmatischen Beitrag stellt Leonardo Boff fest, dass die Befreiungstheologie vom Zusammenbruch des Sozialismus nicht betroffen sei, da ihre Option allein den Armen gelte. Dem Sozialismus komme lediglich vermittelnde Funktion zur Förderung des Lebens und der Gerechtigkeit der Unterdrückten zu. Insofern »lebe die Theologie der Befreiung [weiterhin] von ihrer ursprünglichen Intuition, die innige Verbindung zwischen dem Gott des Lebens, den Armen und der Befreiung entdeckt zu haben.«[18] Damit bleibe die Forderung nach einem revolutionären Christentum für Lateinamerika bestehen. Als Beleg dient ihm die Praxis der Christen in Nicaragua.

Frei Betto dagegen schreibt – etwas trotzig – in derselben Ausgabe: »Der Sozialismus ist gestorben – es lebe der Sozialismus«[19] und verweist auf den immanent demokratischen Charakter des sozialistischen Wirtschaftssystems. Insofern müsse das Scheitern des Stalinismus in Osteuropa von allen linken Kräften begrüßt werden. Daher »gebe es für Lateinamerika, Afrika und Asien keine Lösung außerhalb des demokratischen Sozialismus.«[20] Die Bedeutung Kubas als sozialistische Utopie für Lateinamerika beschreibt der Beitrag des aus Uruguay stammenden Schriftstellers Eduardo Galeano. Anders als der undemokratische stalinistische Staatssozialismus verfolge Kuba ein eigenständiges Modell, das

17 Paulo R. Schilling, O socialismo na América Latina, in: Tempo e Presença 12/224 (1987), 11–13, hier: 13.

18 Leonardo Boff, Implosão do socialismo e teologia da libertação, in: Tempo e Presença 12/252 (1990), 32–36, hier: 36.

19 Frei Betto, O socialismo morreu – viva o socialismo, in: Tempo e Presença 12/252 (1990), 17–20.

20 A. a. O., 20.

»weder von oben noch von außen orthopädisch eingeführt wurde, sondern von ganz innen entstanden und von unten gewachsen ist.«[21]

Das Verhältnis der Befreiungstheologie zum sozialistischen Regime in Kuba erläutert Frei Betto explizit in einem Vortrag auf einem Treffen zur Kubanischen Theologie in La Habana im April 2005.[22] Die theologische Bewertung einer Regierung solle sich ausschließlich danach richten, inwiefern diese dem Volk diene. Damit geht Betto einerseits auf vorsichtige Distanz zu den Machthabern in Kuba. Andererseits betont er, dass – anders als etwa in Brasilien, El Salvador oder Guatemala – die sozialistische Regierung das Leben für alle garantiere, indem sie »Brot teil[e]«[23]. Insofern müsse sich die Kirche auf die Seite des Regimes stellen, damit das Volk Leben in Fülle haben kann. Dies ist umso bemerkenswerter,als sich Kuba in der so genannten »Sonderperiode in Friedenszeiten« (*período especial en tiempos de paz*) befand, in der zwar kein Hunger, aber großer Mangel an Nahrungsmitteln herrschte. Gleichwohl beschließt Frei Betto seinen Vortrag mit einem Bekenntnis zur kubanischen Revolution:

> »Wenn die Revolution in diese Richtung geht, dann geht die Revolution in die Richtung von Jesus. Die Revolution trägt dazu bei, das Reich Gottes in der Geschichte aufzubauen.«[24]

Demnach änderte der Fall der Berliner Mauer bei dem stark politisierten Teil der Befreiungstheolog*innen der ersten Generation nichts an der Hochschätzung des Sozialismus in Kuba nichts. Selbst der gemäßigte chilenische Theologe Sergio Silva bestätigt, dass es auch nach dem Zusammenbruch des Sozialismus die Aufgabe der Befreiungstheologie bleibe »Zeichen der Zeit« zu identifizieren, in denen Gottes Handeln aus der Perspektive der »Option für die Armen« konkret sichtbar werde, denn der Neoliberalismus als das dominierende Weltsystem lasse sich kaum als Ort der Gegenwart Gottes behaupten.[25]

Mit der zunehmenden Schwächung der linken Volksbewegungen in Lateinamerika verloren die Sympathisanten des Sozialismus jedoch an Einfluss sowohl

21 Eduardo Galeano, Cadaveres trocados na política, in: Tempo e Presença 12/252 (1990), 5–8, hier: 7.
22 Frei Betto, Desafíos actuales de la Teología de la liberación, in: Ecaminos. Revista cubana de pensamiento socioteológico 37 (2005). https://revista.ecaminos.org/la-teologia-cubana (30.3.2020).
23 Ebd.
24 Ebd.
25 Silva, Transformationen, 336–338.

innerhalb der Gesellschaft als auch gegenüber denjenigen Theolog*innen, die eine differenzierte Betrachtung »der Armen« und »der Armut« forderten. Dies führte zu einem Richtungswechsel der Befreiungstheologie.[26]

Neue Akteure erhoben ihre Stimmen und machten sie gegen die vormals von männlichen und westlichen Parametern dominierte Theologie geltend. Indigene, Afroamerikaner*innen, PoCs, Frauen, Opfer sexueller Diskriminierung, Homosexuelle und Queere führten an, dass Unterdrückung nicht nur in ökonomischer Hinsicht, sondern auch aufgrund von Kultur (indigene Völker, Afroamerikaner), Hautfarbe, Gender und anderer Faktoren erfolge. Dementsprechend seien die jeweiligen kulturellen Werte eine unverzichtbare Voraussetzung für jede Befreiung. Frauen kritisierten den Machismus auch innerhalb der linken Bewegungen sowie dessen Rechtfertigung durch einen »Gott der Ordnung«[27] und erschlossen sich eigene Räume der Freiheit – häufig außerhalb oder an den Rändern der Institutionen. Nicht zuletzt wurden Stimmen unter den Befreiungstheolog*innen lauter, die forderten, auch die ästhetische Dimension des Lebens zu berücksichtigen, etwa die Frage des Glücks, der Lust, des Genusses »bis hin zum Genuss, den […] die schönen Künste gewähren können.«[28] Forderungen, die von der ersten Generation der Befreiungstheologie als imperialistisch und konterrevolutionär gebrandmarkt worden wären.

Insgesamt zeigen diese Entwicklungen nach 1990, dass die Befreiungstheologie bis dahin zu einseitig und dogmatisch an ihren Überzeugungen festgehalten hatte. Im Rückblick lässt sich daher kritisieren, dass »das Volk« zu sehr als monolithische Einheit gesehen und dementsprechend kollektive Lösungen avisiert worden waren.[29] Aus dieser Perspektive erklärt sich folgerichtig die Idealisierung des kubanischen Sozialismus bis in eine Zeit, in der es bereits zahlreiche Hinweise gab, die für eine kritischere Betrachtung des Regimes gesprochen hätten. In der Folgezeit wandten sich viele Theolog*innen der ersten Generation, u. a. Leonardo Boff, allgemeineren Themen wie der Ökologie und der Spiritualität zu. Zugleich führten verschiedene Impulse zu einer Differenzierung der Befreiungstheologien, die insgesamt jedoch an Verve verloren.

26 Vgl. Silva, Transformationen, 340–347; Roland Spliesgart, Befreiungstheologie im Wandel. Wird der Kollektivismus durch den Multikulturalismus abgelöst? Herausforderungen für die 90er Jahre, in: Jahrbuch für kontextuelle Theologien 3, Frankfurt a. M. 1995, 95–113.

27 Vgl. Gebara, Teologia da libertação.

28 Silva, Transformationen, 345.

29 Vgl. Spliesgart, Befreiungstheologie, 97–100.

2. Der kubanische Katholizismus in Distanz zur Befreiungstheologie

Das soziale und politische Engagement der Christen, die Entwicklung befreiungstheologischer Konzepte und die Beschlüsse der Bischofskonferenz in Medellín 1968 hatten zu einem radikalen Wandel innerhalb des lateinamerikanischen Katholizismus geführt. Nicht zuletzt setzten die Bischöfe damit den »Geist der Erneuerung« in kreativer Weise um, der vom 2. Vatikanischen Konzil (1962–1965) ausgegangen war. In der katholischen Kirche Kubas war von diesem Aufbruch wenig zu spüren. Die Befreiungstheologie stieß weder auf nennenswerte Resonanz unter Priestern und Gläubigen noch teilten sie die Hochschätzung der Theolog*innen auf dem lateinamerikanischen Festland für den Sozialismus. Dies hat mehrere Gründe.

i. *Der Katholizismus in Kuba war von den Entwicklungen im übrigen Lateinamerika weitgehend isoliert.*

Der kubanische Historiker Felipe Valencia vertritt die Ansicht, dass die Kirche in Kuba in den Jahren 1959 bis 1966 kaum Verbindung zu ihren lateinamerikanischen Schwesterkirchen hatte und daher den durch das 2. Vatikanum ausgelösten Modernisierungsschub nicht nachvollziehen konnte. Während es im übrigen Lateinamerika zu einem Dialog mit Kultur und Gesellschaft, der Enteuropäisierung des Klerus sowie zur soziopolitischen Wende kam, befand sich die Kirche in Kuba in einer Position des Rückzugs und der Bewahrung des kirchlichen Lebens. Dies sei allein dem Projekt der neuen Revolutionsregierung geschuldet, die allen Gruppen, die nicht mit dem Marxismus sympathisierten, die Teilhabe an der Rekonstruktion der Gesellschaft verwehrte.[30]

Indem der Staat den Atheismus verordnete und Religion zur Privatsache erklärte, förderte er aktiv die Entkirchlichung der Gesellschaft.[31] Die katholische Kirche Kubas war daher ganz auf ihre eigenen Probleme fokussiert, so dass sie weder Kapazitäten für einen Dialog mit ihren Schwesterkirchen noch für weitergehende theologische Reflexionen hatte. Die Beschlüsse des 2. Vatikanums

30 Vgl. Felipe P. Valencia, La iglesia catolica cubana: entre el Vaticano II y la revolution marxista (1959–1966), in: Revista Cultura & Religion 13/1 (2019), 4–23, hier: 18.

31 Vgl. Michael Huhn, Die Kirchen in Kuba und die Ereignisse von 1989/90, in: Klaus Koschorke (Hg.), Falling Walls. The Year 1989/90 as a Turning Point in the History of World Christianity, Wiesbaden 2009, 259–280, hier: 263–266.

wurden daher in Kuba kaum rezipiert und nur in geringem Umfang umgesetzt, obwohl eine Delegation von vier Bischöfen auf dem Konzil vertreten war.

Auch in den folgenden Jahren blieb die kubanische Kirche weitgehend isoliert. Als auf der 3. Generalkonferenz 1979 des lateinamerikanischen Episkopats in Puebla die Bischöfe ihre Kontroverse um die Befreiungstheologie führten, fühlten sich die anwesenden Kubaner weitgehend übergangen.[32] Zwar wurde viel über Ausbeutung und Unterdrückung, Kapitalismus und Marxismus gesprochen, jedoch vermied man offensichtlich eine Auseinandersetzung über die sozialistische Herausforderung, wie sie in Kuba längst Realität war. Die betroffenen kubanischen Bischöfe reagierten mit einer Stellungnahme, in der sie darauf verwiesen, dass nur sie Erfahrungen gelebten Glaubens in einem sozialistischen Land in Lateinamerika besäßen.

Dieselbe Diskrepanz spiegelt sich in der geringen Rezeption der Befreiungstheologie in Kuba wider. In einem offiziellen Dokument wurde sie erstmals 1986 erwähnt und ihre Bedeutung gewürdigt, nicht ohne einschränkend auf die Unterschiedlichkeit der gesellschaftlichen Kontexte hinzuweisen.[33] Umgekehrt wurden kubanische Ansätze wie die »Theologie der Versöhnung« (Teología de la Reconciliación) im restlichen Lateinamerika nicht wahrgenommen.[34]

ii. Die katholische Kirche befand sich durchgehend in Opposition zum sozialistischen Projekt.

Historisch war die katholische Kirche in Kuba in besonderer Weise mit der wirtschaftlichen und politischen Elite des Landes verbunden, die v. a. in den urbanen Zentren lebte und eine traditionelle Form des Christentums pflegte.[35] Dazu kam, dass der Klerus zu 82 % aus Ausländern – mehrheitlich Spaniern – bestand.

Trotz ihrer konservativen Prägung begrüßte die Kirche zunächst den Sieg der Revolutionäre, deren Absichten, wie die einer Landreform, durchaus den

32 Othmar Noggler, Kuba, in: Hans Jürgen Prien (Hg.), Lateinamerika. Gesellschaft – Kirche – Theologie, Bd. I, Göttingen 1981, 273–303, hier: 295f.

33 Vgl. das Abschlussdokument des *Encuentro Nacional Eclesial Cubano* (ENEC – Landesweite kubanische Kirchenversammlung) vom 17.–23.2.1986 in La Habana. Vgl. Huhn, Kuba, 269–271.

34 Diese setzte sich für Versöhnung von Christen und Marxisten, aber auch mit den Exilkubanern in den USA ein. Vgl. Valencia, Iglesia, 18f; Huhn, Kuba, 268.

35 Vgl. Noggler, Kuba, 274–278; Johannes Meier, Die Anfänge der Kirche auf den Karibischen Inseln, Immensee 1991, hier: 147.

Werten der katholischen Soziallehre entsprachen.[36] Bereits zuvor hatten sich einige Priester den Kämpfern angeschlossen, und der Erzbischof von Santiago de Cuba, Pérez Serantes, hatte sich 1953 nach der Verhaftung von Fidel Castro sogar für dessen Freilassung eingesetzt. Schon nach wenigen Wochen kam es zu ersten Spannungen, nachdem die Kirche Kritik an den Hinrichtungen von Anhängern des gestürzten Batista-Regimes äußerte. Zum Bruch kam es, als sich die Revolutionsregierung – nicht zuletzt in Reaktion auf die westliche Blockadepolitik – ideologisch an die Sowjetunion annäherte und Kuba am 1. Mai 1961 zur Sozialistisch-Demokratischen Republik erklärte.

Auch wenn sich das Verhältnis von Kirche und Staat in Kuba in verschiedene Phasen einteilen lässt, muss doch festgestellt werden, dass sich die katholische Kirche in einem strikten ideologischen Gegensatz zum sozialistischen Staat sah und diesen *durchgehend* kritisierte. Dies zeigen die folgenden Beispiele:

Bereits am 22. Mai 1960 schrieb Erzbischof Pérez Serantes in einem Hirtenwort, »daß der Kommunismus der große Feind des Christentums ist«[37]. Und die Bischöfe warnten in einem Hirtenbrief am 7. August 1960 vor der materialistischen und gottlosen Weltanschauung, die alle sozialen, karitativen, erzieherischen und apostolischen Werke der Kirche zersetze.[38] Als Reaktion darauf erklärte Fidel Castro alle gläubigen Antikommunisten zu Staatsfeinden. Das Motto, das Castro 1961 verkündete und das bis 1976 Bestand hatte, lautete: »Kein Recht gegen die Revolution«[39] (»Contra la revolución ningún derecho«).

Die Folge war eine enorme Schwächung des Katholizismus, dem der Einfluss auf die Bildung durch die Verstaatlichung der kirchlichen Schulen 1961 sowie auf Zeitungen und öffentliche Medien entzogen wurde. Zudem erfolgte die Ausweisung und Auswanderung von 600 Priestern (von ehemals 800), 1800 Ordensschwestern (von 2000) und zahlreichen engagierten Christen. Darüber hinaus distanzierten sich viele Gläubige von der Kirche, um innerhalb der atheistischen Gesellschaft am Aufbau des Sozialismus mitzuwirken.

Am 10. April 1969 wandten sich die Bischöfe direkt an Fidel Castro und beriefen sich explizit auf die Beschlüsse des Konzils von Medellín. Indem sie die

36 Vgl. zum Folgenden Johannes Meier, Kuba, in: Johannes Meier/Veit Straßner (Hg.), Kirche und Katholizismus seit 1945, Bd. 6. Lateinamerika und Karibik, Paderborn u. a. 2009, 205–228, hier: 212–219; Noggler, Kuba, 278–290; Huhn, Kuba, 262–269.

37 S. HKorr 14 (1960), 501–503. Cit. p. Noggler, Kuba, 281.

38 Vgl. HKorr 15 (1960), 126f. Cit. p. Noggler, Kuba, 284f.

39 Valencia, Iglesia, 17.

westliche Blockadepolitik gegen Kuba verurteilten, stellten sie sich einerseits auf die Seite des kubanischen Volkes und des sozialistischen Regimes; andererseits kritisierten sie, dass dieses für die moralische Entwicklung »ausschließlich auf den Gebrauch der äußeren Dinge setz[e]«[40]. Wenig später sprachen sie sich dafür aus, dass Christen auf der praktischen Ebene bei ihren irdischen Aufgaben durchaus auch mit Atheisten zusammenarbeiten sollten und diesen mit Respekt und brüderlicher Liebe begegnen.[41]

Deutlich konstruktiver formuliert das Abschlussdokument der Kubanischen Kirchenversammlung ENEC (*Encuentro Nacional Eclesial Cubano*) im Jahr 1986 die Rolle der Kirche: Diese solle »aktiv an der geschichtlichen Realität Kubas [...] mitwirken [...], d. h. in einer entsakralisierten und säkularisierten Gesellschaft marxistischer Prägung«[42]. Dabei verstand man sich als »Kirche unter dem Sozialismus« – und nicht »im Sozialismus«, wodurch man bereits begrifflich die eigene Distanz zum sozialistischen System ausdrückte. Einerseits lobte man die Errungenschaften des kubanischen Staates, andererseits erinnerte man daran, dass damit noch keinesfalls das Reich Gottes verwirklicht sei, und benannte konkrete Missstände wie Korruption, Lügen und Verschwendung von Staatseigentum.

Unterdessen hatte Fidel Castro das Gespräch mit dem Brasilianer Frei Betto dazu genutzt, um sich als Sympathisant der lateinamerikanischen Befreiungstheologie zu präsentieren.[43] Dabei wies Castro immer wieder darauf hin, dass die Kirche in Kuba vor der Revolution eine reaktionäre Kirche einer reichen Minderheit gewesen sei, die inzwischen zum großen Teil das Land verlassen habe.[44] Jetzt seien die Spannungen mit der katholischen Kirche überwunden, und die wenigen verbliebenen Christen würden – ebenso wie die Anhänger anderer Religionen[45] – in ihren Anschauungen respektiert. Der Wert der Befreiungstheologie bestehe darin, dass mit ihr das Christentum zu seinen glorreichen Wurzeln des Urchristentums zurückkehre. Die Befreiungstheologie entziehe so in der Ge-

40 Comunicado de la Conferencia Episcopal. Sobre la injusta situación del bloqueo, 10.4.1969, cit. p. Noggler, Kuba, 288.

41 Vgl. Pastoral Colectiva del Episcopado, Problemática y Crecimiento de la Fe en una Sociedad den Cambio, Mai 1970, cit. p. Noggler 1981, 291.

42 Adveniat (Hg.), Kirche in Kuba. Eine Botschaft der kubanischen Katholiken (Zeugnisse – Berichte – Kommentare 13), Essen 1986, cit. p. Huhn, Kuba, 269.

43 Zum Verhältnis von Frei Betto und Fidel Castro vgl. Theodor Herr, Kirche auf Cuba, St. Ottilien 1988 168–180.

44 Vgl. Frei Betto, Fidel e a religião. Conversas com Frei Betto, São Paulo 1985, 276f.

45 A. a. O., 203.

genwart »den Ausbeutern, den Eroberern, den Unterdrückern, den Invasoren und Plünderern unserer Völker ihr wertvollstes Instrument, über das sie verfügen, um die Massen zu verwirren, sie zu betrügen, sie zu entfremden und sie in der Ausbeutung zu halten.«[46] In ähnlicher Weise hatte Fidel Castro bereits 1970 im Gespräch mit dem nicaraguanischen Priester Ernesto Cardenal geäußert, »daß das wahre Christentum revolutionär ist. War es doch die Religion der Armen und der Sklaven im Römischen Reich.«[47] Die Grundlage des Gesprächs Frei Bettos mit Fidel Castro bildete die gemeinsame Überzeugung, dass Christentum und Marxismus in ihren Grundsätzen weitgehend übereinstimmten. Insofern blieben kontroverse Punkte bewusst außen vor. Ein Ergebnis der Gespräche mit den prominenten Vertretern der Befreiungstheologie war, dass sie dem sozialistischen *líder maximo* Fidel Castro große internationale Aufmerksamkeit verschafften und sein Bild im Ausland deutlich verbesserten.

In Kuba selbst äußerten die katholischen Bischöfe zunehmend heftige und offene Kritik am kubanischen Staat, die in ihrer Botschaft vom 8. September 1993 mit dem Titel »Die Liebe hofft alles« (El amor todo lo espera) kulminierte. In dieser stellten sie zunächst fest, dass sie als »Hirten der Kirche« keine Politiker seien und sich daher mit keiner Partei, politischen Gruppierung oder Ideologie identifizieren könnten.[48] Gleichwohl erhoben sie konkrete politische Forderungen wie das Ende der bestehenden Einschränkungen der Freiheitsrechte und der exzessiven Kontrolle durch die Sicherheitsorgane des Staates. Weiterhin kritisierten sie die hohe Zahl der Gefangenen, die Diskriminierung aufgrund philosophischer, politischer oder religiöser Vorstellungen, das Ein-Parteiensystem sowie die Zentralisierung von Presse, Radio und Fernsehen.[49] Im Januar 1988 fasste der Erzbischof von Santiago, Pedro Meurice, anlässlich des Besuchs von Papst Johannes Paul II. die Kritik in Anspielung an die Befreiungstheologie auf originelle Weise zusammen: »Die Kirche in Lateinamerika wählte in Puebla die Option für die Armen. Die Ärmsten unter uns sind jene, die nicht das geschätzte Geschenk der Freiheit haben.«[50]

46 A. a. O., 291.
47 Ernesto Cardenal, Kubanisches Tagebuch, Gütersloh [4]1983, 113.
48 Konferenz der Katholischen Bischöfe Kubas, Die Liebe hofft alles, in: Stimmen der Weltkirche 35, Bonn 1993, hier: 12.
49 A. a. O., 20, 24.
50 P. Meurice, Palabras de Bienvenido al Santo Padre. Santiago de Cuba, 24.1.1998, cit. p. Huhn, Kuba, 276f.

Insgesamt war die katholische Kirche in Kuba dem real existierenden Sozialismus gegenüber deutlich kritischer eingestellt, da sie ein wesentlich differenzierteres Bild besaß, als es den Theolog*innen der Befreiung aus der Außenperspektive möglich war. Diese wiederum idealisierten das kubanische Modell, was von der Führung in Gestalt Fidel Castros geschickt zur eigenen Propaganda genutzt wurde.

iii. Die katholische Kirche hat in Kuba keine Verwurzelung im Volk.

Weitaus gewichtiger für die nur geringe sozialpolitische Kraft der Befreiungstheologie und -praxis in Kuba ist die Tatsache, dass der Katholizismus hier weitaus weniger in den »populären Schichten« des Volkes verwurzelt ist als im übrigen Lateinamerika. An diesem Punkt muss der Analyse Fidel Castros zugestimmt werden:

> »Die Kirche in Kuba war nicht volkstümlich, sie war nicht eigentlich eine Kirche des Volkes, sie war keine Kirche der Arbeiter, der Bauern, derer, die in Hütten wohnen, der einfachen [humilde] Schichten der Bevölkerung. Hier gab es niemals Priester, die mit den Bewohnern der Armenviertel arbeiteten, mit Arbeitern oder auf dem Land, wie es schon in manchen Ländern vorkam und danach in Lateinamerika üblich wurde.«[51]

Tatsächlich stellt Kuba innerhalb der Religionsgeschichte Lateinamerikas einen Sonderfall dar.[52] Während dort der Katholizismus die Kultur und die so genannte Volksreligiosität entscheidend prägte, blieb das Christentum in Kuba eher auf die weißen Eliten beschränkt – zum einen, weil die katholischen Kleriker es vorzogen in den Städten zu wohnen, und zum anderen, weil sie offensichtlich nicht sonderlich daran interessiert waren, das Volk in den Grundzügen des christlichen Glaubens zu unterweisen.[53] Dementsprechend sieht der ehemalige Erzbischof von Havanna, Jaime Ortega y Alamino, in seiner Kirche bereits in der Zeit vor der Revolution eine religiöse Praxis

> »ohne Menschen im Gottesdienst, ohne katholisch engagierte Intellektuelle, die ihr Prestige hätten verleihen können, mit der fehlenden politischen Präsenz, wegen der schwachen Laienbewegung, in einer Situation, in der die Farbigen [sic!] am normalen kirchlichen

51 Betto, Fidel, 206f.

52 Vgl. Armando Lampe, Historia do cristianismo no Caribe, Petrópolis 1995, 147.

53 Vgl. Meier, Anfänge, 57, 145–150.

Leben kaum teilnahmen und einen Synkretismus praktizierten, der für die katholische Kirche zwar sympathisch war, aber in ethischer Hinsicht arm.«[54]

Wenn der Bischof hier vom *religiösen Synkretismus* der Kubaner spricht, dann könnte man denken, dass damit jene Mischung aus Christentum und anderen Religionen gemeint sei, mit der sich die PoC ihre alten religiösen Vorstellungen erhielten und zugleich den katholischen Glauben auf ihre Weise interpretierten – gleichsam als eine Form interkultureller Theologie. De facto herrscht unter Religionswissenschaftler*innen weitgehend Konsens darüber, dass für einen Großteil der kubanischen Bevölkerung afrikanische und spiritistische Vorstellungen prägend sind. So schreibt Armando Lampe, dass die Sklaven das Christentum nie verinnerlicht hätten und sie es in der ihnen eigenen afrikanischen Weltsicht eher als ein »Reinigungsritual gegen ›Hexerei‹«[55] betrachteten. Die so entstandene Volksreligiosität sei in erster Linie von einer »plurireligiösen Identität«[56] geprägt, die es den Kubanern erlaube, zwischen den verschiedenen religiösen Traditionen souverän zu interagieren.

Die neueren Forschungen bestätigen damit Fidel Castros Wahrnehmung: »Wirklich populär waren hier nur die afrikanischen Religionen.«[57] Schätzungen aus den 1990er Jahren gehen davon aus, dass ca. 40 % der Kubaner katholisch getauft, jedoch mindestens 70 % Anhänger afrokubanischer Religionen (*santería*) waren.[58]

54 Jaime Ortega, Festvortrag: Der Beitrag der Kirche für die kubanische Gesellschaft während der 100 Jahre des Bestehens der Republik, in: Raúl Fornet-Betancourt (Hg.), Kuba im Dialog. Kirchliche, politische und kulturelle Perspektiven der Zusammenarbeit, Aachen 2003, 17–34, hier: 30.

55 Armando Lampe, Problemas de la historiografía del cristianismo en el área del Caribe, in: Hans Jürgen Prien (Hg.), Religiosidad e historiografía, Frankfurt a. M. 1998, 147–154, hier: 152. Lampe bezieht sich in seinen Ausführungen auf den gesamten karibischen Raum, die natürlich auch für Kuba gültig sind.

56 A. a. O., 153.

57 Cardenal, Tagebuch, 1983, 113.

58 Vgl. Claudia Rauhut, Santería und ihre Globalisierung in Kuba, Würzburg 2012, 108. »Santería« bedeutet »Heiligenglaube« und wurde ursprünglich von der katholischen Kirche als abwertende Bezeichnung für alle afrokubanischen Kulte gebraucht. Heute beziehen sich deren Anhänger – die *santeros* – in positiver Weise auf die *santería* als ihre Religion. Gleichwohl wird der Begriff nicht einheitlich verwendet. Zum einen ist er ein Sammelbegriff für das gesamte Feld neo-afrikanischer Kulte in Kuba wie *espiritismo*, *regla de ocha* und *palo monte* oder *regla de congo*. Vgl. Ingrid Kummels, Grenzen über den Körper. Das Sakrale im sozialistischen Kuba, in: Shalini Randeria (Hg.), Border Crossings. Grenzverschiebungen und Grenzüberschreitungen in einer globalisierten Welt, Zürich 2016, 195–220, hier 202f. Zum anderen bezeichnet *santería* als Synonym für die *regla de ocha* diejenige Variante der afrokubanischen Religionen, deren Wurzeln in der Religion der Yoruba

Die befreiungstheologischen Konzepte waren also für Kuba unpassend, weil zum einen die katholische Kirche längst ihre soziale Basis im »Volk« verloren hatte, dessen religiöses Leben von afrikanischen Traditionen geprägt war. Zum anderen stellte sie auch für die Elite keine entscheidende Größe mehr dar. Der im übrigen Lateinamerika bestehende Konflikt zwischen einer »Kirche der Mächtigen« und einer »Kirche des Volkes« – eine zentrale Voraussetzung der Befreiungstheologie – war in Kuba also gar nicht gegeben. In diesem Sinne – so der marxistische Historiker Walterio Carbonell – »hat Afrika den Triumph der sozialen Transformation [Kubas] erleichtert«[59]. Einen Betrag der Befreiungstheologie dazu gab es nicht.

3. Protestantismus: Theologie in Revolution

Folgt man dem Urteil von Fidel Castro, dann hatten »die Protestanten [...] besseren Kontakt mit dem Volk«[60] als ihre katholischen Glaubensbrüder. Dies ist wenig verwunderlich, denn der Protestantismus stellte in Kuba Ende des 19. Jahrhunderts eine Alternative zu dem eng mit den traditionellen Eliten verbundenen Katholizismus dar und fand daher innerhalb der liberalen Unabhängigkeitsbewegung viele Anhänger.[61] Auch wandte er sich verstärkt den unteren Mittelschichten zu, die marginalisiert auf dem Land lebten und bislang von der katholischen Kirche nicht beachtet worden waren. Insofern vertraten die protestantischen Kirchen die emanzipatorischen Ideale des kubanischen Volkes.

Dies änderte sich jedoch ab 1902, als die USA die politische Vorherrschaft über Kuba erlangten. Von nun an gerieten die jungen protestantischen Kirchen ganz unter den Einfluss der Missionswerke der US-amerikanischen Denomi-

in der Region des heutigen Nigeria und Benin liegen. Vgl. Huberta von Wangenheim, BeGeisterte Wahrnehmung. Das Phänomen der médium unidad, eine besondere Form der Welterfahrung im Kontext afrokubanischer Religionen, Berlin 2009, 43–45; Miguel Barnet, Afrokubanische Kulte. Die Regla de Ocha. Die Regla de Palo Monte, Frankfurt a. M. 2000.

59 Walterio Carbonell, Crítica. Cómo surgió la cultura cubana (1961), cit. p. Mario G. Castillo Santana, Vorwort, in: Serafin (Tato) Quiñones, Afrodescendencias, Ciudad de Panama 2017, XIV.

60 Cardenal, Tagebuch, 113.

61 Vgl. Odén Marichal, El cristianismo protestante en la coyuntura cubana actual. Ecaminos. Revista cubana de pensamiento socioteológico 37: »Ser cubano« (2005). https://revista.ecaminos.org/la-teologia-cubana (30.3.2020); David Puig Jordán, Memoria subversiva, Hamburg 2013, 99–103.

nationen. 1959 gehörten 6 % der Kubaner einer protestantischen Kirche an,[62] was diesen einen gewissen Einfluss auf die unteren Schichten der Bevölkerung verschaffte.

Die Protestanten standen der revolutionären Bewegung in Teilen positiv gegenüber. Frank País, Sohn eines Baptistenpredigers, war Chef einer Einheit im revolutionären Kampf, und in der Schlacht in Santa Clara bekamen die Truppen von Ernesto »Che« Guevara logistische Unterstützung von einer adventistischen Schule. Nach der erfolgreichen Befreiung Kubas versammelten sich 15 000 Protestanten im *Parque Central* (Zentralpark) von La Habana zur Feier eines Dankgottesdienstes, und in zahlreichen Stellungnahmen sowohl in Kuba als auch im Ausland lobten Protestanten die Revolution in höchsten Tönen. So konnte man in der Januarausgabe 1959 im presbyterianischen Kirchenblatt *Heraldo Cristiano* lesen:

> »Die göttliche und die menschliche Wahrheit ist die Wahrheit Gottes, der sich nicht der feigen Menschen erfreut, sondern denen zuneigt, die zu kämpfen und zu siegen wissen. Die große Wahrheit, die uns frei macht, ist die Gotteserkenntnis und die Zusammenarbeit mit jenen Menschen, die ER ausgewählt hat, damit unser Vaterland seinen Platz unter den großen Völkern des Universums frei und unabhängig einnehmen kann.«[63]

Wenn hier die Befreiung des Volkes als Werk und Wille Gottes dargestellt wird, dann klingt dies wie ein frühes Manifest der im Entstehen begriffenen Theologie der Befreiung. Es scheint, dass im kubanischen Protestantismus die Voraussetzungen für eine positive Rezeption der Befreiungstheologie und einen konstruktiven Dialog mit ihren Vertretern eher gegeben waren als im Katholizismus. Allerdings kam sie aus folgenden Gründen nicht zustande.

i. Die Befreiungstheologie kam zu spät.

Nach der anfänglichen Begeisterung vieler kubanischer Protestanten für die Revolution setzte eine Ernüchterung ein, als einzelne Kirchen in Konflikt mit

62 Die mitgliedsstärksten protestantischen Kirchen waren die Baptisten, die Methodisten, die Pfingstkirchen, die Presbyterianer, Episkopale Kirchen, Adventisten und Quäker. Daneben waren 1 % der Kubaner Zeugen Jehovas. Vgl. Puig Jordán, Memoria, 99f.

63 Heraldo Cristiano, Januar 1959, 3, cit. p. Theo Tschuy, Hundert Jahre kubanischer Protestantismus (1868–1961), Frankfurt a. M. u. a. 1978, 361.

dem sozialistischen Regime gerieten.[64] Zudem waren die Protestanten plötzlich herausgefordert, auf die politischen und sozioökonomischen Veränderungen im Zusammenhang des Aufbaus einer sozialistischen Gesellschaft zu reagieren. Für die notwendige Reflexion fehlten ihnen jedoch die theologischen und soziologischen Ressourcen, denn bislang waren sie vollständig von ihren US-amerikanischen Mutterkirchen abhängig gewesen. Wie diese vertraten sie einen konservativen Pietismus, der großes Gewicht auf persönliche Bekehrung und individuelles Heil(-sversprechen) legte. Schon bald fielen die Protestanten wieder in eine Situation des »lethargischen Spiritualismus«[65] zurück, außer Stande, sich »zu Gunsten der sozialen Gerechtigkeit, des kollektiven Wohlergehens und des Kampfes für Fortschritt zu positionieren.«[66]

Die Folge war eine Teilung der Protestanten in drei Gruppen: Die einen verließen Kuba, weil sie keine Möglichkeit mehr sahen, hier als Christen zu leben – so 70 % der Gemeindeleiter. Andere wandten sich von den Kirchen ab, weil es ihnen Vorteile brachte. Die dritte Gruppe, die weiterhin in den Kirchen ihre Überzeugungen leben wollten, war wiederum gespalten: in die einen, die sich aus der Gesellschaft zurückzogen und aus der Kirche ein großes Ghetto machten, und in jene, die zugunsten des sozialistischen Fortschritts Partei ergriffen. Letztere begannen eine theologische Reflexion des Sozialismus. Mit Blick auf die Befreiungstheologie stellten sie jedoch fest:

> »Als uns die Texte von Gustavo Gutiérrez, José Ignacio González Faus, Jon Sobrino, Ignacio Ellacuría und Leonardo Boff neben anderen erreichten, mit […] ihren Fragestellungen bezüglich einer lateinamerikanischen Theologie, […] hatten wir Kubaner bereits mit einer Analyse unserer eigenen Realität begonnen, und, ohne sie angemessen systematisiert zu haben, […] lebten wir bereits die Interpretation Gottes, die für unsere Glaubenserfahrung notwendig war.«[67]

Mit anderen Worten: Die Befreiungstheologie kam für die in der sozialistischen Gesellschaft engagierten kubanischen Protestanten zu spät. Umgekehrt vertraten protestantische Theolog*innen in Kuba Positionen wie die der Offen-

64 Vgl. Puig Jordán, Memoria, 103–112.

65 Noel Fernandez, La Teología cubana, in: Revista cubana de pensamiento socioteológico 37: »Ser cubano« (2005). https://revista.ecaminos.org/la-teologia-cubana (30.3.2020).

66 Ebd.

67 Ebd.

barung Gottes in der Geschichte und des Primats der Orthopraxis bereits Jahre bevor ihre lateinamerikanischen katholischen Kolleg*innen diese für ihre Theologie der Befreiung reklamierten.[68]

ii. Die Befreiungstheologie war nicht passend für Kuba.

Die Texte der Befreiungstheolog*innen waren in den 1960er Jahren in einem Kontext entstanden, in dem Christen an der Seite linker Volksbewegungen gegen ökonomische Ausbeutung und autoritäre rechte Regimes kämpften. In Kuba dagegen war »die Befreiung vom Pharao, der Weg durch die Wüste, der hoffnungsvolle Gang ins gelobte Land kein Zukunftsideal mehr, sondern eine Entscheidung für die Gegenwart«[69]. Die Christen »brauchten [daher] nicht mehr die Befreiung, die die Exponenten des Südens vorschlugen, sondern die Analyse und Reflexion dessen, was einer Kirche entsprach, die von Unterdrückung, imperialer Herrschaft, den zerstörerischen Kräften des Kapitalismus und Konkurrenzdenken befreit war. Eine ›Theologie eines befreiten Volkes‹ war unverzichtbar.«[70]

Eine kontextuelle Theologie für Kuba wurde vor allem am *Seminario Evangélico de Teología* SET (Evangelisch-protestantisches Theologisches Seminar) in Matanzas von Sergio Arce, Adolfo Ham, Rafael Cepeda und anderen Professoren entwickelt. Diese rezipierten vorwiegend europäische Theologen (Dietrich Bonhoeffer, Karl Barth, Helmut Gollwitzer, Jürgen Moltmann, Johann Baptist Metz, Josef Hromádka) und nordamerikanische Theologen (Richard Shaull, Harvey Cox, Richard Niebuhr). Aus der Befreiungstheologie ließen sich die Kubaner v. a. von dem Presbyterianer Rubem Alves und dem Pädagogen Paulo Freire inspirieren.[71] Die Unterschiedlichkeit der Autoren lässt auf eine eher selektive und kreative Interpretation schließen.

Dabei legten die kubanischen Theolog*innen extremen Wert auf ihre Autonomie, auch und gerade gegenüber ihren lateinamerikanischen Kolleg*innen. Nachdem sie sich nämlich mühsam aus der neokolonialen Bevormundung durch Nordamerika und Europa befreit hatten, wollten sie nun »ein eigenes theologisches Konzept verwirklichen, weder europäisch noch südamerikanisch noch

68 So Puig Jordán, Memoria, 137.
69 Fernandez, Teología cubana.
70 Ebd.
71 Vgl. Fernandez, Teología cubana; Puig Jordán, Memoria, 127–129, 139–142, 146f., 150, 156–158 u. a.

nordamerikanisch, sondern kubanisch.«[72] Sergio Arce geht sogar so weit, die Idee der Universalität generell abzulehnen, da es keine Theologie gäbe, »die sowohl für die kubanische Kirche als auch für die amerikanischen, europäischen, asiatischen, afrikanischen, karibischen und lateinamerikanischen Kirchen angemessen ist«[73].

Zu Recht können kubanische Theolog*innen auf nationale Traditionen verweisen wie den Priester Felix Varela (1788–1853) sowie den Schriftsteller und Nationalhelden José Martí (1853–1895), der weitreichende Überlegungen zum befreierischen Potential des Christentums angestellt hat.[74] Die Theolog*innen der nachfolgenden Generation entwickelten in kreativer Weise für den kubanischen Kontext angepasste Theologien. Besonders hervorzuheben sind Ofelia Ortega Suárez, die von 1996 bis 2004 als Rektorin dem SET vorstand, und Dora Arce Valentín, die sich beide für eine biblisch orientierte, feministische Befreiungstheologie einsetzen.[75]

iii. Die Befreiungstheologie war nicht radikal genug.

1965 legte Sergio Arce mit seinem Aufsatz *La misión de la iglesia en una sociedad socialista* (Die Mission der Kirche in einer sozialistischen Gesellschaft) das Programm einer kontextuellen kubanischen Theologie vor.[76] Zusammen mit seinen Kolleg*innen vom SET betrachtete er die Revolution Fidel Castros als ein Ereignis sui generis in der Geschichte Kubas mit universaler Bedeutung. Der Theologie käme daher die Aufgabe zu, die revolutionäre Realität und deren marxistisch-leninistische Ideologie aus einer biblischen, kirchenhistorischen, ethischen und kulturellen Perspektive zu interpretieren.

Ziel der theologischen Arbeit sei es herauszufinden, wie die Kirche wirksam auf alle soziopolitischen Forderungen reagieren solle, die die Revolution den kubanischen Christen stelle. Die Theologie solle keine Angelegenheit *von* Ge-

72 Fernandez, Teología cubana.

73 Sergio Arce, La teología cubana: contexto, aportes y desafios, in: Ecaminos. Revista cubana de pensamiento socioteólogico 37: »Ser cubano« (2005). https://revista.ecaminos.org/la-teologia-cubana (30.3.2020).

74 Vgl. Rafael Cepeda Clemente, Raíces de liberación en la teología cubana, in: Raúl Suárez Ramos (Hg.), Fé por Cuba. Editorial caminos, La Habana 2016, 193–204.

75 Vgl. Ofelia Ortega Suárez, La vida es lo que cuenta. Libertad y igualtad para todas y todos, in: Suárez Ramos, Fé, 69–85; Dora Arce Valentín, La opción radical por la vida. História de dos mujeres, in: Suárez Ramos, Fé, 139–153.

76 Vgl. Arce, Teología; Puig Jordán, Memoria, 89–179.

lehrten *für* Gelehrte sein, sondern dem kirchlichen Leben des einfachen Volkes der Gläubigen dienen und ihnen »ihre Berufung als mystischer Leib Christi in einem revolutionären Kuba«[77] zeigen. Dabei ist Arce von der Vorstellung eines historischen Jesus geleitet, der als Anführer einer »antireligiösen und antiimperialistischen Rebellion«[78] auf der Seite der Zeloten stand und für die Befreiung »armer Galiläer und wehrloser Frauen«[79] kämpfte. Im Kontext Lateinamerikas verkörpere Jesus den Typus des Guerrillero und Revolutionärs, dessen Eigenschaften in der Praxis des kolumbianischen (Ex-)Priesters Camilo Torres Restrepo ein leuchtendes Beispiel fanden.[80]

In dem von Arce vorgelegten Konzept bilden Kirche, Theologie, kubanisches Volk und sozialistische Revolution eine essentielle und einzigartige Verbindung.[81] Die Bezeichnung als »Theologie in Revolution« (*Teología en revolución*) ist zugleich Programm. Sie ist weder eine »Theologie in der Revolution« – also eine Theologie unter den Bedingungen der sozialistischen Gesellschaft – noch eine »Theologie der Revolution«, die diese zum Gegenstand macht. Vielmehr war es für Arce entscheidend, »die theologische Reflexion [selbst] in eine wirklich revolutionäre zu verwandeln«[82].

Die später in Lateinamerika entstandene Befreiungstheologie sieht Arce vorwiegend kritisch.[83] Deren Rezeption des Marxismus findet er einerseits positiv, da dieser eine kritische soziologische Analyse des kapitalistischen Systems leiste. Andererseits bemängelt er, dass die Befreiungstheolog*innen nur ein theoretisches Wissen über den Marxismus hätten und zudem sehr naiv hinsichtlich dessen Atheismus seien. Die kubanische Theologie hingegen hätte die Ideologie des Marxismus-Leninismus bereits ein Jahrzehnt vor der »Theologie der kontinentalen Befreiung«[84] aus eigener Erfahrung reflektiert. Dabei habe man auch den Atheismus mitbedacht, der eine Gegenreaktion auf das verfälschte und

77 Arce, Teología.
78 Ebd.
79 Ebd. Vgl. Puig Jordán, Memoria, 156–159.
80 Ebenso vertritt Fidel Castro die Vorstellung von Jesus als Revolutionär. Vgl. Betto, Fidel, 320–326. So wie »Marx die Bergpredigt unterschrieben haben könnte« (F. Castro, cit. p. Betto, Fidel, 325), sei Jesus »der Marx seiner Zeit« (s. Arce nach Puig Jordán, Memoria, 159).
81 Arce, Teología, gebraucht das Bild der »Kirche in einer geweihten Ehe mit dem revolutionären kubanischen Volk ›verheiratet‹«, die in Kuba neben einer »Kirche, die von ihrem Volk ›geschieden‹ wurde, weil sie antikommunistisch war«, koexistiert.
82 Puig Jordán, Memoria, 162.
83 So auch Puig Jordán, Memoria, 156.
84 Arce, Teología.

manipulierte Gottesbild derjenigen Christen sei, die den Kapitalismus politisch und theologisch verklärten. Daher sollte die kubanische Kirche und Theologie die Kritik der atheistischen Marxisten aufnehmen und das falsche Gottesbild radikal in Frage stellen.

Zentral für die Theologie in Revolution ist die Überzeugung, dass die Christen in Kuba durch den Aufbau der sozialistischen Gesellschaft zusammen mit den anderen sozialen Kräften bereits in der geschichtlichen Gegenwart das Reich Gottes verwirklichen könnten.[85] Bereits 1960 hatte der reformierte Theologe Rafael Cepeda in seiner Schrift *Fidel y el Reino de Dios* (Fidel und das Gottesreich) festgestellt,

> »dass Fidel Castro ein Instrument in Händen Gottes ist für [die] Erschaffung seines Königreiches unter den Menschen [...] Ich glaube, dass Fidel Castro auf Kuba genau das erreicht, was Gott für alle vergessenen Völker will: eine neue Möglichkeit angemessen und in Würde zu leben. [...] Auch er benötigt ›Instrumente‹ [...]. Fidel Castro ist eines dieser Instrumente, ob er religiösen Glauben hat oder nicht.«[86]

Damit erklärt die kubanische Theologie in Revolution den realen Sozialismus in Kuba zu ihrer Utopie und antizipiert gleichsam die Option der späteren lateinamerikanischen Befreiungstheolog*innen. Andererseits wird die von diesen konstatierte Zukünftigkeit des Reiches Gottes als kritische Instanz gegen mögliche Verirrungen vollständig aufgehoben. Die Identifikation der revolutionären protestantischen Kirchen mit der sozialistischen Gesellschaft in Kuba wurde schließlich zum status confessionis erklärt. Die Theologie in Revolution führte zur Formulierung eines neuen *Glaubensbekenntnisses der Presbyterianisch-Reformierten Kirche in Cuba*, das 1977 auf ihrer Nationalversammlung in Matanzas verabschiedet wurde.[87]

Die Theologie in Revolution bildet bis heute den Rahmen, innerhalb dessen sich die protestantische Theologiebildung in Kuba bewegt.[88] Aus heutiger Sicht

85 Vgl. Puig Jordán, Memoria, 136–139, 167–170.

86 Rafael Cepeda, Fidel y el Reino de Dios, in: Sergio Arce u. a. (Hg.), Pensamiento cubano reformado, La Habana, 1988, 156. Cit. p. Puig Jordán, Memoria, 139.

87 Vgl. Konrad Stock (Hg.), Cubanisches Glaubensbekenntnis, München u. a. 1980.

88 Vgl. die Beiträge in Suárez Ramos, Fé, aus dem Jahr 2016.

kommen zumindest Fragen auf,[89] wenn Kubaner*innen inzwischen lateinamerikanische Befreiungstheolog*innen zitieren, die gegen autoritäre Diktaturen angetreten waren, und zur gleichen Zeit ein unverbrüchliches Bekenntnis zum kubanischen Sozialismus aussprechen.

4. Afrokubanische Religionen als Befreiungstheologie der eigenen Art

Als Merkmale der kubanischen Volksreligiosität gelten zum einen die Dominanz der afrikanischen Traditionen, zum anderen ihr plurireligiöser Charakter. Das heißt, dass die Menschen nicht einer religiösen Tradition in dogmatischer Reinheit folgen, sondern sich je nach Situation einzelner Elemente aus unterschiedlichen Religionen bedienen. Dem liegt als Strukturprinzip der afrokubanische Spiritismus zugrunde, der sich als überaus offen und flexibel gegenüber neuen Situationen erwiesen hat. Die Bedeutung des Afrikanischen für die kubanische Kultur und Religiosität zeigt sich in dem Sprichwort: »Wer keinen *congo* als Vorfahren hat, hat bestimmt einen *carabalí* in der Familie«[90].

Wenn Kubaner also ihre afrikanischen Gottheiten mit katholischen Heiligen identifizierten, dann war dies keine gleichberechtigte Vermischung der Traditionen, sondern allein »formelle Maskerade«[91]. Vielmehr integrierten die als Sklavinnen und Sklaven verschleppten Afrikaner*innen und ihre Nachkommen den Katholizismus so in ihre eigene, afrokubanische religiöse Matrix. Der Katholizismus hat »im Grunde die religiösen Ideen der Mehrheit nicht verändert«[92]. Umgekehrt konnte die schwarze kubanische Bevölkerung durch die scheinbare Annahme des Christentums ihre als primitiv und unzivilisiert geltenden afrika-

89 So Heike Walz, Wohin weht Kubas sozialistischer Geist – bei scharfem Gegenwind? In: ZMiss 43/4 (2017), 420–431, hier: 430.

90 Nach Ingrid Kummels, Popmusik und das Sakrale. Kubanische Religiosität aus der Perspektive der Forschung zu Populärkultur, in: Heike Drohtbohm/Lioba Rossbach de Olmos (Hg.), Kontrapunkte. Theoretische Transitionen und empirischer Transfer in der Afroamerikaforschung, Marburg 2009, 75–95, hier: 85. Congo und carabalí sind mit den lucumí die wichtigsten Ethnien, aus denen die Sklav*innen für Kuba rekrutiert wurden.

91 Rauhut, Santeria, 75, vgl. 75–78. Zu demselben Ergebnis kommt Stephan Palmié, Das Exil der Götter. Geschichte und Vorstellungswelt einer afro-kubanischen Religion, Frankfurt a. M. u. a. 1991, 121f.

92 Lydia Cabrera, El monte, La Habana, 2018 [= ^{5}2014], 23.

nischen Praktiken gegen die dominierende Kultur der Spanier und später gegen die der weißen Eliten bewahren.

Die sich dabei ereignenden Prozesse von *Transkulturation* lassen sich in einer christlich-theologischen Perspektive als »Konversion ins Heidentum«[93] oder *Exkulturation*[94] beschreiben. Soziologisch hingegen handelt es sich um eine »subversive gegenhegemoniale Praxis«[95] einer marginalisierten Bevölkerung, die sich auf diese Weise Freiräume religiös-kultureller Interpretation und Gestaltung innerhalb des dominierenden spanisch-christlichen Systems sicherte. Diese besondere Fähigkeit der ehemaligen Sklaven hat sich bis heute in der kubanischen Volksreligiosität erhalten. In dem multireligiösen gesellschaftlichen Feld sind die Kubaner jederzeit in der Lage, souverän zu agieren und sich aus den unterschiedlichen religiösen Traditionen eine jeweils passende Mischung zusammenzustellen. Umgekehrt ist es wenig verwunderlich, wenn für die Mehrheit der Kubaner »religiöse Alltagspraktiken und die konfessionelle Zugehörigkeit stark auseinander[fallen]«[96].

Im Folgenden wird die These vertreten, dass sich die »populären Schichten« der kubanischen Gesellschaft seit etwa 1990 wieder verstärkt den afrokubanischen Religionen zuwenden, da diese ihnen Räume von Selbstbestimmung, Emanzipation und Widerstand auf der Grundlage ihrer religiös-kulturellen Ressourcen ermöglichen. Damit werden in der Praxis der afrokubanischen Volksreligion, die über keine explizite und verschriftlichte Theologiebildung verfügt, wichtige Anliegen der lateinamerikanischen Befreiungstheologie vertreten. Diese »Selbstbefreiung des Volkes« findet jedoch außerhalb der christlichen Kirchen statt. Die politischen Ziele der klassischen Befreiungstheologie werden vorerst nicht anvisiert, da unter den Bedingungen der real existierenden sozialistischen Gesellschaft keine offene politische Praxis möglich ist. Stattdessen realisieren sich Prozesse von Befreiung in kulturellen und spirituellen Räumen.

Kubanische Religionssoziologen sprechen von einem »religiösen Boom« seit dem Beginn der »Sonderperiode in Friedenszeiten« 1989 und dem Ende der Unterstützung Kubas durch die sozialistischen Staaten Osteuropas. Im kubanischen

93 Rauhut, Santeria, 59. Ähnlich sieht es Palmié, Exil, 98f, 105, u. a.

94 Zum Begriff der Exkulturation vgl. Hermann Brandt, Die heilige Barbara in Brasilien. Kulturtransfer und Synkretismus. Erlangen 2003, 127–133.

95 Rauhut, Santeria, 59.

96 Kummels, Popmusik, 77.

Volk kursiert das Sprichwort »La religión esta de moda«[97] – die Religion ist in Mode. Von diesem Boom profitieren v. a. die afrokubanischen Religionen. Deren Anhänger zeigen sich mit ihrer weißen Kleidung und den bunten, jeweils einem bestimmten *orisha* (afrikanische Gottheit) geweihten Ketten, verstärkt in der Öffentlichkeit, was die zunehmende *Spiritualisierung* und *Re-Afrikanisierung* der Gesellschaft sichtbar werden lässt.

Bereits seit Mitte der 1980er Jahre hatte sich die sozialistische Regierung für die afrokubanischen Religionen geöffnet.[98] 1991 erkannte sie die *Asociación Cultural Yoruba* (Kulturelle Vereinigung der Yoruba/ACYC) als Zusammenschluss zahlreicher afrokubanischer Kultzentren offiziell an und beauftragte sie mit der Pflege und Verbreitung der Yoruba-Kultur in Kuba. Die Revitalisierung afrokubanischer Religionen war für den kubanischen Staat schon deswegen opportun, weil deren Anhänger vorwiegend aus den unteren Schichten stammten, die am meisten von der Revolution profitiert hatten; von ihnen war daher wenig Kritik an der Ideologie und Politik des Staates zu erwarten. Gleichwohl verstand der Staat die afrokubanische Religion und Kultur eher als Folklore.

Anhand von drei Themen soll gezeigt werden, wie afrokubanische Religiosität als wichtiger sinn- und kulturstiftender Faktor ihren Anhängern konkrete Lebenshilfe verschafft und es ihnen ermöglicht, sich bei der Deutung und Gestaltung des Alltags als selbstbestimmte Akteure zu erfahren. Auf diese Weise werden Mikrosphären des Widerstands und der Freiheit erzeugt.

i. Spiritualisierung der Lebenswelt als Alternative

Im Kontext afrokubanischer Religion gilt es als völlig normal, Stimmen zu hören, die einem ins Ohr sprechen, Vorahnungen oder Intuitionen zu haben, prophetische Träume zu empfangen, mit Geistern und Toten zu kommunizieren. Die Ethnologin Huberta von Wangenheim vertritt die These, dass die Fähigkeit zu übersinnlicher – »beGeisterter« – Wahrnehmung (*médium unidad*) als soziokulturelles Phänomen in Kuba allgegenwärtig ist und eine zentrale Rolle in der Welt- und Selbsterfahrung spielt. Die Wahrnehmungen werden als verstehbare

97 Wangenheim, Wahrnehmung, 44. Vgl. Jorge Ramírez Calzadilla, Religion, cultura y sociedad en Cuba, in: Papers. Revista de Sociologia 52 (1997), 139–153, hier: 151.

98 Vgl. zum Folgenden Rauhut, Santeria, 87–127; Ingrid Kummels, Globale Heilige. Transnationalisierungen des Religiösen in Lateinamerika, in: Zeitschrift für Ethnologie 136 (2011), 317–335, hier: 325f.

und bedeutsame Botschaften interpretiert, und sie werden schließlich zu etwas Realem, das die soziale Realität reflektiert und produziert.

Völlig verkehrt wäre es nun, die Kommunikation mit der spirituellen Welt in marxistischer Manier als »Entfremdung« des Volkes von ihren wahren politischen Interessen (»Opium«) und Vertröstung auf ein Jenseits zu bewerten. Vielmehr steht die spirituell-religiöse Weltsicht in einem historischen Kontinuum als Form des Widerstands subalterner Schichten gegen die dominierende Kultur, die in der Situation nach 1989 neue Kraft entfaltet. Diese Zeit des *período especial* lässt sich sehr gut als »Kubanischer Surrealismus«[99] charakterisieren. Einerseits hielt der Staat in politischer Hinsicht am Sozialismus als offizieller Ideologie fest und forderte ein entsprechend angepasstes Verhalten, andererseits war die ökonomische Grundlage Kubas mit dem Zusammenbruch der sozialistischen Staaten des Ostblocks angesichts der weiter bestehenden Blockadepolitik der USA schwierig geworden. De facto hatte in Kuba eine Kommerzialisierung des Lebens im Rahmen der Dollarwirtschaft – mittlerweile auf der Basis des *peso convertible* (CUC) als einer frei konvertierbaren Währung – Einzug gehalten, die jeden Kubaner und jede Kubanerin für die Besorgung überlebenswichtiger Dinge zur Erwirtschaftung von Devisen und damit zu kapitalistischem Handeln nötigt. Das Leben der Kubaner ist seitdem von einem ständigen Konflikt zwischen offizieller sozialistischer Ideologie, notwendigem kapitalistischen Verhalten und magisch-religiöser Weltsicht bestimmt.

Um ihr Überleben zu sichern, müssen die Menschen zwischen verschiedenen Systemen navigieren und vieles tun, was strikt verboten ist. Hinzu kommt die permanente Sorge vor Feinden, die einen wegen der verschiedenen – legalen und/oder illegalen – Aktivitäten denunzieren könnten. Die afrokubanischen Religionen helfen den Menschen dabei, sich in ihren verschiedenen Rollen in dieser multidimensionalen Realität zurechtzufinden. Sie bieten einen Raum existentiellen Potentials, in dem jeder und jede seine und ihre Erfahrungen in einem praktischen Ritual ausdrücken, reflektieren, interpretieren und transformieren kann. Nicht zuletzt liefern sie Orientierung und schaffen Sicherheit in dem gesellschaftlichen Verwirrspiel. In diesem gilt: »Menschen lügen, aber die Toten sagen die Wahrheit.«[100] Nur »die Toten bilden eine soziale Instanz, die Wahrheit

99 Wangenheim, Wahrnehmung, 16, vgl. 16–24.
100 A. a. O., 200.

und Sicherheit in einer Welt ausdrückt und verkörpert, die durch Widersprüche und Ungewissheiten charakterisiert ist.«[101]

Umgekehrt wird die Verdrängung übersinnlicher Wahrnehmung als problematisch und Ursache für mentale und psychische Probleme gesehen. Wer in Kuba Stimmen hört, gilt nicht automatisch als verrückt oder psychotisch, sondern als mit einer besonderen »Gabe« ausgestattet. Es entspricht mittlerweile üblicher Praxis kubanischer, nach westlichen medizinischen Standards ausgebildeter Psychiater, auch die religiösen Diskurse von Besessenheit, Verhexung etc. ihrer Patienten ernst zu nehmen und zu respektieren.[102] Vielfach kooperieren Psycholog*innen und Mediziner*innen offen mit Priestern[103] der *santería* und entscheiden gemeinsam, ob eine psychopathologische oder eine religiös-kulturelle Störung vorliegt und beraten dann über die angemessene Behandlung. Im Falle einer spirituellen Störung überlassen viele Psychiater*innen ihre Patient*innen einem Priester zur rituellen Wiederherstellung ihrer Gesundheit. Damit erkennen sie die Grenzen der eigenen »rationalen« Wissenschaft ebenso an wie die Gültigkeit traditionellen religiösen Wissens und belegen so die Bedeutung der spirituellen Wahrnehmung für die Gesundheit der kubanischen Bevölkerung. Dies ist auch notwendig, denn anderenfalls müsste die Psychiatrie die Mehrheit der Bevölkerung in Havanna für verrückt erklären.[104]

Der befreiende Charakter afrokubanischer Religionen zeigt sich auch in ihrer praktischen Ausrichtung. In den Ritualen geht es nicht um jenseitige Erlösung, sondern um eine wirksame Lösung von Alltagsproblemen.[105] Dies können Sorgen um die Gesundheit, das wirtschaftliche Wohlergehen oder Beziehungskonflikte sein. In einem Ritual wird eine direkte reziproke Beziehung zu den Heiligen hergestellt und so eine Lösung problematischer Konstellationen bewirkt. Ein Vorteil all dieser spirituellen Rituale ist, dass sich die Beteiligten damit weder in direkte Opposition zur katholischen Kirche noch zum sozialistisch-materialistischen Staat begeben müssen.

101 Huberta von Wangenheim, El discurso sobre el fenómeno de la médium unidad en las religiones afrocubanas, in: Revista Colombiana de Antropologia 45 (2009), 169–203, hier: 199.

102 Vgl. Wangenheim, Wahrnehmung, 217–262: Kapitel »Geisteskrank? beGeisterte Wahrnehmung und Psychiatrie«.

103 In den afrokubanischen Religionen werden nach wie vor keine Priesterinnen akzeptiert. Vgl. Ennis B. Edmonds/Michelle A. Gonzalez, Caribbean Religious History. An Introduction, New York 2010, 218.

104 Vgl. Wangenheim, Discurso, 173.

105 Vgl. Kummels, Heilige, 319, 333.

ii. Musik und Kunst als Räume religionskultureller Produktivität und Sinnstiftung

Afrokubanische Religion ist weder institutionalisiert noch von der Vorstellung »dogmatischer Reinheit« geprägt. Vielmehr erlaubt und ermöglicht sie den Glaubenden die Inszenierung religiöser Praxis in Festen, Tanz, Musik, Literatur und Kunst. Sie besitzt damit ein enormes Potential zur Produktion religiös-kultureller Ausdrucksformen, die für die Kubaner als sinnstiftender Faktor extrem bedeutsam sind.

In der volkstümlichen Musik Kubas ist das afrikanische Erbe bis heute lebendig. Die aus Afrika verschleppten Sklav*innen haben ihr Wissen über afrikanische Weltentstehungslehren, Rituale und damit verbundene kulturelle Praktiken über die Generationen hinweg bewahrt. Die Instrumente, der Gesang sowie der Tanz waren immer Teil eines rituellen, kollektiven Geschehens. Dabei ist die Musik das bevorzugte Mittel der Kommunikation mit den Göttern, sie ist Teil einer Welt, in der sich die Toten immer noch unter den Lebenden befinden, in der die Grenze zwischen dem Heiligen und dem Profanen verschwimmt. Das soziale Handeln der Beteiligten – Musiker*innen wie Zuhörer*innen – hat also immer eine religiöse Dimension.[106] Besonders die geweihte *batá*-Trommel gilt als Mittlerin zwischen Menschen und Göttern, ihr Gebrauch ist nur besonders initiierten Personen erlaubt. So nimmt es nicht wunder, dass viele kubanische Musiker, im Besonderen Perkussionisten, in afrokubanische Kultsysteme eingeweiht sind.

Als nach der Unabhängigkeit Kubas von der spanischen Kolonialherrschaft die weiße kreolische Oberschicht zunächst die kulturellen und ästhetischen Manifestationen der afrokubanischen Religionen als primitiv ablehnte und diskriminierte, erreichten die Schwarzen durch das Medium der Musik recht bald deren Anerkennung jenseits von »Rassen«- und Schichtgrenzen. In der Folgezeit griffen auch weiße Komponisten auf Musik, Tanz und Religion der Schwarzen zurück und eigneten sich die Afrikanismen als kulturelles Gegenmodell gegenüber Spanien und der neokolonialen Macht USA erfolgreich an.

Der Rekurs auf die eigenen afrokubanischen religiös-musikalischen Wurzeln lässt sich heute wieder verstärkt bei jüngeren, zum Teil international agierenden Jazz- und Fusion-Musikern beobachten, so bei dem Pianisten Chucho Valdés mit Irakere und seinem aktuellen Projekt »Jazz Batá 2«, der Rapperin Telmary, der Hip-Hop-Sängerin und Percussionistin Brenda Navarette und der Jazz-Sängerin

106 Vgl. Maya Roy, Buena Vista. Die Musik Kubas, Heidelberg 2000, 24.

Daymé Arocena. Damit setzen diese Musiker einerseits ihre kubanischen religiös-musikalischen Traditionen in produktiver Weise fort, andererseits spielen sie auch mit internationalen Musikern verschiedener Genres und integrieren westliche Musikstile. Indem sie diese jedoch konsequent mit afrokubanischen Rhythmen verbinden, wenden sie sich aktiv gegen die kulturell-musikalische Hegemonie des Westens und unterscheiden sich auch in ihrer persönlichen, religiösen Performance ganz wesentlich von westlichen Lebensstilen.

In analoger Weise stehen die zeitgenössischen Bildenden Künste in einer wechselseitigen Beziehung zu afrokubanischen Kulten.[107] Dieser Trend kann seit den 1980er Jahren beobachtet werden, als Künstler begannen, sich mit dem Weltbild der *santería* auseinanderzusetzen und es als Alternative zum rationalen wissenschaftlichen Weltbild zu verstehen. Indem sie ihre Alltags- und Lebenserfahrungen in religiöse Kunst übersetzen, kommt es sowohl zur Spiritualisierung der Kunstobjekte selbst als auch der Erfahrungs- und Lebenswelt der Künstler und eines Großteils der Kubaner.

Unter Künstlern ist es weit verbreitet, die *orishas*, d. h. die Gottheiten der *santería*, in Bildern und Skulpturen in großer künstlerischer Freiheit zur Darstellung zu bringen. Darüber hinaus findet man auf den Altären der *santería* zahlreiche Alltagsgegenstände, die von den Anhängern zu kultischen Objekten transformiert wurden. Die Meeresgöttin *Yemayá* erscheint auf einem Altar plötzlich als Spielzeugdampfer, das Sakrale also im Gewand des Alltäglichen.[108] Der Transfer religiöser Inhalte geschieht »vor allem in den Köpfen der Menschen«[109], wobei die Bilder eine Erinnerung, eine Imagination und ein inneres Bewusstsein auslösen. Die Identität der *orishas* als heilige Wesen ist nicht auf eine bestimmte Vorstellung festgelegt, sondern lässt sich auf unterschiedlichen Ebenen vermitteln, im Alltagsdiskurs ebenso wie in Objekten, in den alten Legenden und im Ritual.

Eine weitere wichtige Ausdrucksform sind Körperinszenierungen in Musik und Tanz. Die Körper als religiöse Medien dienen hier nicht als symbolische Realität, sondern sind selbst gelebte Realität und verweisen direkt auf eine religi-

107 Natalie Göltenboth, Kunst und Kult in Kuba heute. Kurze Revue einer lebendigen Beziehung, in: Heike Drohtbohm/Lioba Rossbach de Olmos (Hg.), Afroamerikanische Kontroversen, Marburg 2007, 73–81.

108 Vgl. Natalie Göltenboth, Yemayá und der Spielzeugdampfer. Zur Sakralität der Ready-mades auf afrokubanischen Altären. Eine Einführung in die bunte Welt der heiligen Spielzeugtiere, Puppen und Wasserschüsseln, in: Heike Drohtbohm/Lioba Rossbach de Olmos (Hg.), Ideen über Afroamerika, Marburg 2003, 127–135.

109 A. a. O., 129.

öse Bedeutungsebene jenseits aufgedrängter Essentialismen.[110] Auf diese Weise »stoßen die Künstler mit ihren Arbeiten in die Bereiche des Kultischen vor und visualisieren religiöse Inhalte nach ihrer Fasson, während die Spezialisten der afrokubanischen Religionen sich eine große Offenheit gegenüber neuen und subjektiven Formen der Darstellung bewahren.«[111]

Die kubanische Fotographin Elena Martínez versteht die künstlerische Darstellung von Körperinszenierungen verschiedener *orishas*, die jeweils von bekannten Tänzern repräsentiert werden, selbst als religiösen Akt.[112] Zum einen erzeugt sie dabei eine Manifestation des Sakralen im Medium der Körper und bringt auf diese Weise die spirituelle Schaffenskraft der Tänzer zum Ausdruck, zum anderen verarbeitet sie zugleich ihre eigenen Erfahrungen im Kontext der kubanischen Gesellschaft, die sie in der Kunst in eine »sehr mächtige Waffe der Existenz und Widerstandskraft«[113] transformiert.

Insgesamt leisten Musiker*innen und Künstler*innen einen wichtigen spirituellen Beitrag zum (Über-)Leben der Kubaner in einer gesellschaftlichen Realität des Mangels und der gegenseitigen Kontrolle, indem sie in einer ästhetischen Weise jenseits von Sprache und sogenannter Vernunft für sich und andere »Minisphären des Gegendiskurses«[114] erzeugen.

iii. Laien erobern als Akteure Deutung über ihren Alltag und das dominierende System.

Die starke Affinität von Künstler*innen und der Bevölkerung zu den Mythen der afrokubanischen Traditionen verdankt sich zum großen Teil der enormen Freiheit, die diese den einzelnen Individuen bei der persönlichen Aneignung und Gestaltung bieten. Dabei schränken die *babalawos* (Priester) als die Spezialisten ihrer Religion die Laien in keiner Weise ein, sondern zeigen sich offen gegenüber neuen und subjektiven Formen der Darstellung der *orishas* und heiliger Gegenstände. Die Ethnologin Natalie Göltenboth hält gerade dieses »Bekenntnis zur Subjektivität«[115] für den zentralen »Anknüpfungspunkt, der die Berührung

110 Vgl. Kummels, Körper, 217.
111 Vgl. Göltenboth, Kunst, 80.
112 Vgl. Elena Martínez, Facebook-Eintrag vom 21.12.2019. https:/facebook.com/elenamartinexznegrxfotografx/ (26.5.2020).
113 Ebd.
114 Kummels, Heilige, 326.
115 Göltenboth, Kunst, 80.

von Kunst und Kult in Kuba in dieser Weise möglich macht.«[116] Der offene und undogmatische Charakter der *santería* ermöglicht es allen Kreativen und Kulturschaffenden, die Besonderheit des afrikanischen Erbes zu bewahren und zugleich in unterschiedlichsten Medien (Kunst, Kultur, Musik, Tanz und Körper) in die moderne Welt und ihre persönlichen, sehr verschiedenen Lebenssituationen zu integrieren.[117]

Dazu kommt, dass die afrokubanischen Kulte jenseits institutioneller religiöser Kontexte in Privathäusern, Hinterhöfen, auf Straßen, kurzum: im Alltag, gelebt und gestaltet werden. Dabei sind es v. a. die Laien, die in ihrer Praxis ihre eigene Religiosität (*religiosidad popular*) zum Ausdruck bringen und ein Gegenmodell gegen jede Art von Dogmen, sei es religiöser Experten und Institutionen, sei es wissenschaftlicher oder staatlicher Ideologien, in einem lebendigen Prozess entwickeln. Indem sie ständig religiöse Praktiken und Diskurse entsprechend der gegebenen Bedingungen verändern, alternative Bedeutungszuschreibungen vertreten und für sie werben, konstituieren sie jeweils eigenständige Glaubensfelder. Auf diese Weise gelingt es den Kubaner*innen im Kontext ungleicher Machtverhältnisse, die hegemonialen Glaubensvorstellungen, Ideologien und Praktiken zu unterwandern und einen effizienten Gegendiskurs gegen die Akteure und Mechanismen des sie dominierenden Systems zu entwickeln.[118]

5. Fazit

Die afrokubanischen Religionen stellen ihren Anhängern eine völlig eigene Ontologie zur Verfügung, die es ihnen erlaubt, die Bedingungen und Gesetze ihres Lebens in einer neuen Weise zu interpretieren, indem sie ihre Erfahrungen mit einer spirituellen Sphäre in Beziehung setzen.[119] Zugleich leisten sie als religiöse Akteure eine eigenständige Reinterpretation und Reorganisation des Sakralen. Indem die Menschen den Mythos mit ihrem Alltag verbinden, reflektieren sie ihre aktuelle gesellschaftliche Situation in Kuba und erlangen zugleich Deutungs- und Handlungskompetenz. Nicht zuletzt werden Performances und

116 Ebd.
117 Vgl. Göltenboth, Yemayá, 133.
118 Vgl. Kummels, Heilige, 321.
119 Vgl. Wangenheim, Wahrnehmung, 185–216.

nichtsprachliche Medien dabei zu wirksamen religiös-politischen Statements im öffentlichen Raum.[120]

Insgesamt erweist sich die Identifikation mit dem magisch-religiösen Weltbild für Kubaner*innen als sinnvoll und sinnstiftend, denn es gibt ihnen eine spirituelle, außereuropäische Alternative sowohl zum westlichen Rationalismus als auch zum sozialistischen Materialismus an die Hand. Zugleich befähigt es sie, nach dem Prinzip der Collage die unterschiedlichsten Erfahrungen in einem alternativen, eigenen Kontext neu zu bestimmen und zu ordnen und macht ihnen so das Überleben zwischen alter, sozialistischer Ordnung und neuer, materialistischer Realität möglich.

Die afrokubanischen Religionen verschaffen den Menschen durch ihre vielfältigen Möglichkeiten religiös-kulturellen Ausdrucks subtile Formen des Widerstands gegen das dominierende, gleichermaßen sozialistische wie materialistische System und eröffnen Räume der persönlichen Freiheit und Gestaltung.[121] Damit realisieren die Anhänger der *santería* eine religiös motivierte Praxis der Befreiung der eigenen Art. Diese Praxis geht auf Formen des Widerstands zurück, die Afrokubaner zur Zeit der Sklaverei gegen herrschende Ideologien entwickelt hatten.

Wenn es Kubaner*innen heute gelingt, sich unter Rekurs auf die eigenen religiös-kulturellen Ressourcen Räume der Freiheit zu erobern, dann setzen sie erfolgreich zentrale Anliegen der lateinamerikanischen Praxis und Theologie der Befreiung in einer nichtchristlichen, gleichsam exkulturierten, kubanischen Variante um. Zugleich vollziehen sie den nach dem Zusammenbruch des Sozialismus in Europa geforderten »cultural turn« der Befreiungstheologie und berücksichtigen auch die ästhetischen Dimensionen von Befreiung.[122] Daneben setzen sie den stets propagierten Vorrang der Praxis und des Volkes als Akteur im Kampf der Befreiung in radikaler und kreativer Weise um.

Für die christlichen Kirchen und alle Befreiungstheolog*innen erwächst daraus die wichtige Anfrage, wie mit diesen Entwicklungen umgegangen werden soll. Die katholische Kirche in Kuba pflegt eine »antagonistische Beziehung«[123] zu den Manifestationen afrokubanischer Religiosität. Innerhalb des Protestantismus fordern einzelne Theolog*innen einen interkulturellen Dialog, stellen

120 Vgl. Kummels, Körper, 326.
121 Vgl. Wangenheim, Discurso, 198.
122 Vgl. Silva, Transformationen, 345f.
123 Edmond/Gonzalez, History, 204.

aber fest, dass es in vielen Kirchen schwierig ist, »to raise the question whether God is present in folk religion and Afro-Cuban culture«[124]. In den USA hingegen entwickeln kubanoamerikanische Theolog*innen Konzepte einer afrokubanischen interkulturellen Theologie.[125] Die entscheidende Frage für die kommenden Jahre in Kuba lautet indessen: Inwieweit wird es den Kubaner*innen gelingen, aus ihren religiösen Wurzeln auch politische Handlungen zu generieren, die zu konkreter Befreiung führen?

(PD Dr. Roland Spliesgart, Pfarrer im Schuldienst und Privatdozent für Kirchengeschichte/Weltweite Christentumsgeschichte an der Evang.-Theol. Fakultät der LMU, München)

ABSTRACT

With the resolution on the »option for the poor« at the conference in Medellín in 1968, the Catholic bishops of Latin America implemented a central demand of the theologians of liberation. They sympathised with a socialist system of government and declared Cuba, which had been liberated in 1959 by a revolution led by Fidel Castro, to be their utopia. In Cuba, the Catholic Church distanced itself from the socialist government, while Protestant theologians formulated a «theology in revolution« as their own form of «liberation theology«. The people, on the other hand, who were predominantly Afro-Cuban, developed strategies of resistance on an individual and cultural level, drawing on their own religious and cultural resources, and thus conquered spaces of freedom within the boundaries of the real socialist system.

124 Ofélia Ortega, Contextuality and Community. Challenges for Theological Education and Ecumenical Formation, in: International Review of Mission 98/1 (2009), 25–36, hier: 31. Vgl. Clara Luz Ajo Lázaro, Die Spiritualität unserer Vorfahren, in: Concilium 36/5 (2000), 568–575.

125 Vgl. Michelle A. Gonzalez, Afro-cuban Theology. Religion, Race, Culture and Identity, Gainsville 2006.

Christians Living in a Time of Islamic Resurgence: The Case of Contemporary Indonesia (2014–2020)

Abraham Silo Wilar

Introduction

Since the beginning of Islam, Christians have been continuously living with Muslims. How they live and interact with Muslims is well documented, for example, in a project led by David Thomas entitled »Christian-Muslim Relations: A Bibliographical History.« Each volume of the project contains a portrait as well as an analysis of the relations during a certain period of time.[1] However, there are areas of Christian-Muslim relations that remain beyond the scope of the project, and one of the areas is Christian-Muslim relations in Southeast Asia, including Indonesia.

Being known as the country with the world's largest Muslim-population, Indonesia had a Christian population since its beginnings along with Buddhists, Hindus, and indigenous communities. Therefore, Christians living under the domination of Muslims in this country must have certain experiences in relating to Muslims. One of the experiences that I will focus on in this paper is that of living with the Islamic Resurgence phenomenon that began to flourish after the

1 David Thomas/Barbara Rogema (eds.), Christian-Muslim Relations. A Bibliographical History, Vol. 1 (600–900), Leiden/Boston 2009; David Thomas/Alex Mallett (eds.), Christian-Muslim Relations. A Bibliographical History, Vol. 2 (900–1050), Leiden/Boston 2010; David Thomas/Alex Mallett (eds.), Christian-Muslim Relations. A Bibliographical History, Vol. 3 (1050–1200), Leiden/Boston 2011; David Thomas/Alex Mallett (eds.), Christian-Muslim Relations. A Bibliographical History, Vol. 4 (1200–1350), Leiden/Boston 2012; David Thomas/Alex Mallett (eds.), Christian-Muslim Relations. A Bibliographical History, Vol. 5 (1350–1500), Leiden/Boston 2013; David Thomas/John Chesworth (eds.), Christian-Muslim Relations. A Bibliographical History, Vol. 6 (Western Europe 1500–1600), Leiden/Boston 2014.

toppling of Suharto's New Order in 1998. More specifically, I have chosen to focus on the period of Joko Widodo's presidency. Within this setting, Islam as the dominant religion of the country has been transformed into a movement that I call the »Islamic Resurgence«. This transformation is caused by various factors, both internally and externally. These factors are very complex to describe, since it is a movement that fuses the religious tenets of Islam, a political agenda and a social movement. By joining these three aspects, the movement offers a different way of perceiving what Islam is, how to be a true Muslim, and how to live this life in a true Islamic way. This is extremely different from what has been practiced for ages by traditional Muslims of the country.

However, we might identify some of the movement's backbones. Frequently quoted examples are, *first*, campus-based Islamic preaching organizations (*jamaah tarbiyah*), *second*, political parties such as the Prosperous Justice Party, and *third*, social organizations such as *Hizbut Tahrir* and others. Also, common concerns might be noted that are often referred to in describing the Resurgence, including a rhetoric on Islamic piety in the public space as for example modesty of dress, Islamic governance such as the establishment of a Caliphate as well as Islamic finance, and an Islamic way of governing such as the application of Islamic jurisprudence.

Background

In Rifki Rosyad's research the Resurgence is described as primarily being caused by a quest for true Islam flourishing among youth.[2] Researching a similar phenomenon, Yon Machmudi indicates that islamising Indonesia is the very motivation of the movement, something which also becomes part of the agenda of its supporters.[3] Historically speaking, the internal factor helping the Resurgence to appear in public is commonly traced back to the period of Suharto's New Order. It is important to mention, however, that the independence period also played a role in its future development. For instance, the period witnessed the desire to make Islam the state's platform in 1945 as the country struggled to establish its

2 Rifki Rosyad, A Quest for True Islam. A Study of Islamic Resurgence Movement among the Youth in Bandung, Indonesia, Canberra 1995.

3 Yon Machmudi, Islamising Indonesia. The Rise of Jamaah Tarbiyah and The Prosperous Justice Party (PKS), Canberra 2006.

identity, arguing that Islam should have a privileged place in the country-to-be. An example of such a privilege is found in the 1945 Jakarta Charter, which states that it is obligatory for Muslims to practice Islamic shari'a (»dengan kewajiban menjalankan syariat Islam bagi pemeluk-pemeluknya«). On the other hand, some Indonesians wanted the country to be a republic. This objective seems to have met with the mode of the state established by the State's Independence Committee. This committee had finally made a gentle agreement to delete such privileges from the constitution in order to show that the mode of the new state would be a republic. R. E. Olsen discusses this at length and states that it is one of two failed attempts to make Indonesia an Islamic state.[4] Later on, as a response to the Nationalists who controlled the newborn state, Kartosuwiryo launched the *Darul Islam* movement in 1949 to demonstrate that Muslims were being marginalized by the Nationalists and that they should not be treated in such a way.[5] These are two internal factors allowing the country to become a fertile ground for cultivating the seeds of the Islamic Resurgence, and it is during the country's New Order era that these seeds bore fruit.

As the New Order regime carried out a political suppression of Islam, these historical events became part of the cultural memory that remains alive in the minds of many Muslims in the country. It even became more solid after the regime was toppled down on May 21, 1998 and still continues to grow and manifests its influence in the period of Joko Widodo's second term. As it grows, it takes many different forms. One of which is promoting the Islamic Khalifah that has been proposed by *Hizbut Tahrir* Indonesia. In response, in 2017, the state decided to invalidate *Hizbut Tahrir's* operational permit, hoping that this would slow down its growth.[6] However, the effectiveness of the effort to stop its influence among Indonesian Muslims is skeptically doubted.

The Resurgence has affected not only Christians, but also traditional Muslims and other communities, like Buddhists and Hindus. There have been cases related to the Resurgence occurring in many places of the country. For instance, in

4 R. E. Olsen, Another Look at the Jakarta Charter Controversy of 1945, Indonesia 88, 2009, in: https://ecommons.cornell.edu/bitstream/handle/1813/54483/INDO_88_0_1255982649_105_130.pdf (30.4.2020).

5 Chiara Formichi, Islam and the Making of the Nation. Kartosuwiryo and political Islam in 20th century Indonesia, Leiden 2012; Chiara Formichi, (Re)Writing the History of Political Islam in Indonesia, Sojourn: Journal of Social Issues in Southeast Asia, 30/1 (2015), 105–140.

6 https://nasional.kompas.com/read/2017/07/19/10180761/hti-resmi-dibubarkan-pemerintah (4.5.2020).

Bangka Barat, the regent of Bangka Barat, Markus, S. H., who is a Christian, was barred by the *Defender of Islam Front* (*Front Pembela Islam*) from attending Islamic festivals and other Islamic events due to his Christian faith.[7] In Yogyakarta, Slamet Jumiarto and his family who have been moved to Pleret, Kabupaten Bantul, to stay in their newly rented house, were rejected by the chief of the village as Jumiarto came to report himself and his family as a Catholic family.[8] Tanjung Balai, Sumatera Utara, also witnessed the Resurgence in the case of Meiliana, a Tionghoa Indonesian, who was sentenced in 2017 by the district court of Medan for her protest against the high volume of Azan coming from al-Maksum Mosque which is near to her residence.[9] Even Yogyakarta, which has been claiming to be a city of tolerance on account of its student population from all provinces of the country, is currently ranked as the second-most intolerant city in the country.

Additionally, the country has witnessed how the election of Jakarta's governorship in 2017 has been filled with Islamic rhetoric containing religious threats to Muslims who chose to support Basuki Tjahaja Purnama (popularly knownas Ahok) and Djarot Saiful Hidayat. Supporters of the Islamic Resurgence utilized such rhetoric during the campaign.[10] Examples of the rhetoric were »Muslims who choose to take side with Basuki Tjahaja Purnama and Djarot Saiful Hidayat in the government elections would not get an Islamic funeral service performed on their behalf at a mosque as if they were suddenly dead.« All of the rhetoric is rooted in the al-Maidah controversy which was started by Ahok's speech on September 30, 2016.[11] Following his speech, the controversy sprang up in the country as the supporters of the Islamic Resurgence began to exploit it for the sake of their political interest. At the end of the government campaign, Basuki Tjahaja Purnama and Djarot Saiful Hidayat were defeated by their competitor, and their defeat may be described as revealing the actual influence of the Islamic Resurgence supporters in the political arena.

7 https://tirto.id/ulah-fpi-di-bangka-sebab-pemerintah-tak-serius-tangkal-intoleransi-elmr (17.1.2020).
8 https://tirto.id/intoleransi-merebak-di-perdesaan-adakah-cara-mengatasinya-dlfq (17.1.2020).
9 https://regional.kompas.com/read/2018/08/23/15053451/kronologi-kasus-meiliana-yang-dipenjara-karena-keluhkan-pengeras-suara-azan (17.1.2020).
10 https://megapolitan.kompas.com/read/2017/12/19/08151061/kaleidoskop-2017-tahun-tumbangnya-ahok-dan-djarot (2.5.2020).
11 https://news.detik.com/berita/d-3315258/ini-video-utuh-ahok-pidato-singgung-surat-al-maidah-51-yang-jadi-polemik (16.9.2020).

In these circumstances, and having won the election for his second term, Joko Widodo is commonly believed to have become a hope and release for the country to counter the influence of the Islamic Resurgence supporters. There are two main reasons for this hope among Indonesians. First, in his first speech after winning the election, Joko Widodo stated publicly that there is no place for radicalism in the country and that it poses a serious threat to the state.[12] Second, in the campaign period, Joko Widodo was portrayed as the true nationalist compared to his competitor, Prabowo Subianto. This portrait of him was actually based on the perception that Prabowo was supported by Islamic Resurgence supporters, while Joko Widodo was supported by a group of nationalist figures. Furthermore, it was suggested that the future of the country would be bleak, should Prabowo win the election: the country would turn into an Islamic state.

During this heated political competition during the presidential election, roughly speaking, most Christians in the country preferred to describe themselves as supporters of Joko Widodo to defend the country from being turned into an Islamic state. They chose him in the first presidential election and allowed him to win his second term. One of the reasons why Christians chose Joko Widodo was his nationalist platform. In contrast, there had also been Christians on the side of his competitor, Prabowo Subianto. Christians choosing to support Prabowo were considered to be less nationalistic, since Prabowo received substantial backing from the Resurgence supporters. The supporters of Prabowo were believed to destabilize the country, turning it into an Islamic state, if Prabowo were to win the election. This sort of belief was common among Christians during the 2019 election.

This explains a lot about the current influences of the Islamic Resurgence in the country. The fact that Christians chose to be the supporters of Joko Widodo gives expression to their nationalism and their resistance aiganst the Islamic Resurgence. I further consider that their support of Joko Widodo discloses their position and perception on how they relate to and perceive the state and their Christian identity. In such a position, as I observe, Christians are blind supporters of Joko Widodo for they rarely express criticism toward him.

Despite the president's public critique of the Resurgence, the state since then has received criticism from its citizens. Their critique aimed at the state's incom-

12 https://www.liputan6.com/news/read/4014446/tindaklanjuti-pidato-visi-indonesia-jokowi-relawan-soroti-paham-radikalisme-di-bumn# (1.5.2020).

petency in law enforcement to prevent the Resurgence supporters from running their daily activities, including their educational activities. For instance, the banning of Hizbut Tahrir Indonesia in 2017 does not necessarily mean that its daily activities, including its schools, were also abandoned.

As a result of this, I consider that Joko Widodo seems to have failed to keep his commitment to protect the state's pluralism. As is well known, such pluralism is the basic tenet of the national ideology of Indonesians. This is clearly stated in the state's logo, *Burung Garuda* (the Hawk Bird), that carries a banner stating »Bhineka Tunggal Ika« (Diversity in Unity) and has five principles serving the state as its Golden Rule. The five principles are commonly translated as follows: »1. Oneness of Godship, 2. A just and Civilized Humanity, 3. The Unity of Indonesians, 4. A Citizenship that is led by inner wisdom in consultation and dialogue, and 5. Social Justice for the whole of Indonesia and its people.«

Christians have always been on the side of the Nationalist group since the beginning of the country, and they are committed to defend nationalism and make it their form of resistance against the Resurgence. Based on this political awareness, Christians prefer to choose to participate in organizing civic engagements together with other nationalists, including their Muslim fellows, in order to strengthen nationalism and patriotism. Their preference contains a missional understanding of their Christian identity as may be seen in theologians such as Rev. Zakaria Ngelow, Rev. Martin Lukito Sinaga, and Rev. Albertus Patty. While Zakaria shows the importance for the nationalist movement to work interreligiously to fight radicalization and violence coming from Islamic Resurgence supporters,[13] both Martin[14] and Albertus[15] hold a belief that it is only Pancasila which becomes the key to keep the state running. So, therefore, it is the only instrument available for Indonesians to remain citizens of the *Republic* of Indonesia. Christians are destined to keep Pancasila. In other words, the Christians position as it has been described in the aforementioned thoughts proposed by some theologians, discloses their missional presence both as Christians and Indonesians.

13 Zakaria Ngelow, Interfaith Cooperation against Radicalism and Violence in Indonesia: A Christian Perspective. Paper delivered to CCA's Workshop in Jakarta, March 9–13, 2008. This paper is a concise form originated from another paper presented at a Conference of EMS on Indonesia in Stuttgart, Germany, 2007.

14 https://www.senkom.info/2019/12/diklat-pembinaan-ideologi-pancasila-bagi-organisasi-keagamaan-dan-kepemudaan/ (30.4.2020).

15 https://www.liputan6.com/news/read/3064603/pgi-tanpa-pancasila-indonesia-bisa-bubar (30.4.2020).

Therefore, to protect the country and to keep its existing form as a state of Pancasila, is a theological calling.

In response, I would like to argue that the »missional presence« of Christians as described above has instead made the gap between nationalists and Islamists wider, and offered almost nothing to the *realpolitik* of the country. Its fundamental problem is its lack of common language binding them together. This common language would help Indonesians, including the supporters of the Resurgence, to talk to each other, to understand one another, to contribute to the *realpolitik*, and to offer a critical platform to evaluate the subtle content of the Resurgence. Such purposes cannot be accomplished by Christians by campaigning for nationalism as has been suggested by the theologians mentioned above. Rather, to support the argument, I would like to propose an alternate reading of Pancasila that offers a common language which may serve Christians to pursue the aforementioned purposes. However, it also provides me with a platform for reorienting the missional presence of Christians from blindly supporting nationalism to guarding the deeper values of Pancasila, rooted in my reading of it.

In my discussion of the topic, I will keep to the following structure: first, I will look at internal and external factors of the Islamic Resurgence in contemporary Indonesia. Secondly, I will suggest an alternate reading on Pancasila and consider its impact on the missional presence of Christians. With that structure I hope to be able to show what issues the state faces, how Christians relate to the state, and how they respond to the Resurgence. I will close by offering my critique of positions which are taken by Christians.

Internal & external factors of the Islamic Resurgence in contemporary Indonesia

Speaking of contemporary Indonesia means that it is shaped by a certain heritage that is derived from its past. Here, I use the term »contemporary Indonesia« to refer to the period that began with the first presidency of Joko Widodo in 2014. Thus, the paper will focus on the years between 2014 and 2020.

A. *Internal factor: acute corruption, transactional democracy and the cultural memory of the Islamic State*

1. Acute corruption & transactional democracy

In his address on corruption in Indonesia, Peter King stated that there is a direct connection between the New Order's centralization and the growth of corruption of in country.[16] The popularly known abbreviation »KKN« (»*Korupsi, Kolusi dan Nepotisme*«, »Corruption, collusion and nepotism«) is used by King to show that the regime has created a systemic corrupt mentality among its citizens. That kind of legacy, Maria Martini writes, has corroded many institutions existing in the country, both government institutions and social/private institutions, allowing clientelism in business, public service, and political engagement to dominate the country.[17] Those corroded institutions resulted in some legislators of DPRD Malang (the Malang Regional House of Representatives), East Java, being arrested by the KPK (*Komisi Pemberantasan Korupsi*, or the Eradication of Corruption Commission) in 2018.[18] Fortyfive legislators were seized. Only four members of the institution remained, leaving an indelible mark on that institution. Additionally, Hal Hill and Dionisius Narjoko write in their article that the acute corruption has its roots in the economic strategy adopted by the New Order regime which has caused burgeoning industrialization, a rich upper-class, and foreign debt.[19]

Such corruption has been used by proponents of the Islamic Resurgence to argue for the importance of Islam and an Islamic state as the »final solution and the only solution« to the problem.[20] This specific form of state that is proposed is intended to replace the current political system of the country. However, as I observe, it is still unclear whether this Islamic state would be limited to the territorial area of Indonesia or whether it would be part of the worldwide Caliphate

16 Peter King, Corruption Ruins Everything: Gridlock over Suharto's legacy in Indonesia (Part 1), The Asia-Pacific Journal, 6/3 (2008), Article ID 267, 1.

17 Maria Martini, Causes of Corruption in Indonesia, U4 Anti-Corruption Resource Centre, CMI, Bergen, Norway 2012, 1.

18 http://www.tribunnews.com/regional/2018/09/04/anggota-dprd-kota-malang-nyaris-habis-ditangkap-kpk-dari-45-orang-tinggal-4 (15.1.2020).

19 Hal Hill/Dionisius Narjoko, Managing Industrialization in a Globalizing Economy: Lessons from the Soeharto Era, in: Edward Aspinall/Greg Fealy (eds.), Soeharto's New Order and Its Legacy. Essays in Honour of Harold Crouch, Canberra 2010, 49–56.

20 https://mediaumat.news/khilafah-islam-adalah-solusi-tuntas-problem-bangsa-kita/ (30.4.2020). This news is an example of the rhetoric in the public sphere.

proposed by the Islamic State in Iraq and Syria, by Hizbut Tahrir, and others. Although the form is unclear, the solution is commonly believed to be divine, as it is directly rooted in God's law, Shari'a Law. This sort of religious rhetoric fills the public sphere of the country, attracts commoners to imagine a way out of the acute problems that they face daily, and gives some Muslims a religious way to purify themselves through its code of conduct. In other words, the acute corruption is a golden opportunity to turn the state's economic orientation, including its political ideology, into an Islamic economy under the principles of Shari'a law.

Another determinant factor in the emergence of the Islamic Resurgence is the nature of democratic practices in the country. After living under a totalitarian regime led by Suharto (1967–1998), Indonesians are said to live in a democratic country. For example, elections after the New Order era are believed to have practiced the values of democracy. However, many observers point out that the practices of democracy in the country are more likely procedural than substantial, and that they generate a phenomenon that is called »transactional democracy«. Within such a democracy, political parties and a set of elections function merely as tools to gain access to the state's economy and to accumulate profit from such power. This deprives the majority of Indonesians of economic equality and allows elites to control the access to the country's wealth, making them even wealthier than before. This portrait of democracy has been put forward by Koichi Kawamura. In his article, he discusses Indonesia's democracy in relation to the politics of inequality in Indonesia.[21] At the beginning of his article, Kawamura states that democracy cannot be separated from economic equality, which is one of the achievements of practicing democracy.[22] With this understanding of democracy, Kawamura identifies the politics of inequality in the country as the source of the economic inequality and discusses it in relation to democratic practices. These democratic practices have not resulted in Indonesians enjoying a prosperous life, and did not improve the quality of democracy.

The deprived condition of the country's democracy has become one of the sources to promote the Islamic Resurgence. Actually, problems have become apparent in public when Indonesia started its transition to become a democratic state after the Suharto regime had stepped down. As we all know, during the

21 Koichi Kawamura, »Politics of Inequality in Indonesia: Does democracy matter?« in: Keiichi Tsunekawa/Yasuyuki Todo (eds.), Emerging States at Crossroads, Singapore 2019, 231–254.

22 Ibid., 231.

regime the country had been known as an authoritarian/totalitarian state despite the existence of political parties, elections, and other democratic elements in the country. Stefan Eklof, for instance, discusses how Suharto's authoritarianism shaped the political culture of the country and how this culture impacted political parties during his time in office.[23] One party that experienced Suharto's authoritarianism was the Indonesian Democratic Party led by Megawati Sukarnoputri.

In 1993, the party convened its national congress in Medan, and Suharto's authoritarian power intervened by claiming that the former chairman of the party, Soerjadi, had been elected to replace the current party chairman, Megawati Sukarnoputri, his successor. The intervention caused chaos among the participants.[24] Following that congress, the party proposed to convene anew in an extraordinary meeting in Surabaya. It was held in December 1993 and ended up with discontent among the participants. The party's rise in the midst of the authoritarian regime led by Suharto ended with the incident on July 27, 1996, where the head office of the party was ambushed by unknown people, causing riots and casualties in the party.[25]

Following these events, the country began to write a new story, moving towards democracy. Marco Bunte and Andreas Ufen, addressing the process of democratization in Post-Suharto Indonesia, note that it has to face some fundamental issues relating to democracy along with acute problems that have originated during the Suharto regime.[26] For instance, decentralization is said to have become an expression of democratic values which allows for democracy being practiced in the country. Thus, it is among the top concerns of democratization following the toppling of Suharto's regime in 1998.[27]

The condition of the country's democracy has been well exploited by the proponents of the Islamic Resurgence, allowing them to gain control both in the

23 Stefan Eklof, Power and Political Culture in Suharto's Indonesia: The Indonesian Democratic Party (PDI) and the Decline of the New Order, Copenhagen 2003.

24 Ibid., 202.

25 https://nasional.kompas.com/read/2020/07/27/10170991/peristiwa-kudatuli-27-juli-1996-saat-megawati-melawan-tetapi-berakhir-diam?page=all (15.9.2020).

26 Marco Bunte/Andreas Ufen (eds.), Democratization in Post-Suharto Indonesia, London/New York 2009.

27 Marco Bunte, Indonesia's protracted decentralization: Contested reforms and their unintended consequences, in: Marco Bunte/Andreas Ufen (eds.), Democratization in Post-Suharto Indonesia, London/New York 2009, 102–123.

House of Representatives and in the public sphere. Since then, it seems ironic that democracy has been a place to cultivate the Resurgence agenda.

2. Cultural memory of the Islamic State

As mentioned earlier, the country's history has revealed a struggle between the nationalists and the Muslims. The latter advocated for a privileged position of Islam during the pre-Independence period of the country. It is clear that the nationalists won that struggle, leaving the Islamists to feel marginalized. All of this has definitely caused certain disappointments, but the most important thing that I want to emphasize is that this has become a cultural memory among Muslims. This cultural memory serves them as religious motivation allowing them to exploit it.

This cultural memory became more volatile among its proponents as they began to use the suffering of the Palestinian people under Israel, campaigning against the continuous colonialization by Western forces under the leadership of the United States, promoting the degradation of Muslims around the world such as the Afghans, Bosnians, and so forth, and exposing them to the dangerous life under a secularism practiced by the Western countries. All of this has been used to strengthen the memory and it may be said that the memory proposed by the proponents of the Resurgence is a wounded memory where hate and anger are blended with religious motivation, allowing them to express it as a religious cause.

Borrowing on Jeanette Rodriguez' and Ted Fortier's work which demonstrates how cultural memory functions as resistance, faith and identity among Mexican Americans who live traditions from one generation to another within certain specific contexts, including crises,[28] I feel the idea of the Islamic state serves its proponents as cultural memory as much as Our Lady of Guadalupe serves Mexican Americans in preserving their indigenous traditions. As cultural memory the Islamic state is resistance, faith and identity of its adherents. And both Rodriguez and Fortier agree that this cultural memory is obviously related to history, as well as to the social and political context.[29]

28 Jeanette Rodriguez/Ted Fortier, Cultural Memory. Resistance, Faith and Identity, Austin 2007.
29 Ibid., 7.

B. External factor: global politics

Being located in a strategic position, Indonesia is an open field for external factors to influence the Indonesian people. For instance, in the past the country had played a significant role in promoting the anticolonial movement among Asian and African countries,[30] but it has also become a place that gave rise to various religious ideologies of Islam such as Wahhabism, Hizbut Tahrir, the Muslim Brotherhood, ISIS and so forth. Realizing the significant influence of those external forces in constructing contemporary Indonesia, I will address those factors below.

1. The abolishment of the ottoman caliphate in 1924

Turkey's influence on Indonesia may be seen in the discourse of secularism and the abolishment of the Caliphate by Mustafa Attaturk. For instance, in his article, Al-Makin discusses its influence on Sukarno, the first president of Indonesia, who in 1940 wrote an article addressing the causes of Turkey's separation of state and religion.[31] In his article, al-Makin points out the relationship between the abolishment of the Caliphate and the effort to develop the state's foundation and it is, he believes, the only way to achieve progress in the state. In other words, Sukarno made Turkey's secularism a model for Indonesia as he imagined it. However, it does not necessarily mean that the country's foundation was based on secularism. Rather the country is neither a secular sate, nor a religion-based state. It is a state that is founded in Pancasila ideology.

Regardless the state's form and ideology that are rooted in Pancasila, the discourses on secularism and Islam have been sensitive issues in the country. Related to this, Nurcholish Madjid is among a few Muslim scholars who engaged with the discourse in 1970, promoting the importance of secularism to build the country.[32] And, following Nurcholish Madjid, al-Makin continues the discourse

30 Quynh N. Pham/Robbie Shilliam (eds.), Meanings of Bandung. Postcolonial orders and Decolonial Visions, London/New York 2016.

31 Al-Makin, Tanggalkan Khalifah di Bumi ini: Membaca Narasi Sukarno tentang Sekularisme Turki (English: Dismantling the Caliphate on earth: Reading Sukarno's narrative on Secularism of Turkey), Al-Tahrir, 16/2 (2016), 318–338, here: 318.

32 Mun'im Sirry, »Secularization in the mind of Muslim Reformists: A Case Study of Nurcholish Madjid and Fouad Zakaria«, Journal of Indonesian Islam, 1/2 (2007), 323–355, here: 324.

through his writings, pointing out that it reappears in contemporary Indonesia since Hizbut Tahrir Indonesia intensively promotes the Islamic Caliphate in the country as contrast to the present government which is believed to represent a secular state.[33]

2. The establishment of the modern state of Israel in 1948

The establishment of the state of Israel had struck the Muslim world, becoming an enigma to many Muslims around the world. Sharing the enigma, and as the country with the world's largest Muslim population, Indonesia had decided to support the Palestines and their aspiration to be free from Israel's occupation. It is within this circumstances that the fear of Zionism is paired with a deprived portrait of the Palestines, making it part of the Islamic struggle of Indonesian Muslims. Rallies or strikes are held to show their support to the Palestines, on one side, and to demonstrate their condemnation to the Israelites and its allies, on the other side.[34] »Free Gaza« or »Save al-Aqsa« are slogans often used in such rallies.

The country also witnesses the emergence of printed media such as *Sabili* to engage with the issue. It publishes pictures of dead bodies of Palestine people caused by Israeli military aggression. In short, the concern has been capitalized to attract Muslim's empathy, and to make the Islamic Resurgence greater among Indonesian Muslims. Those who are supporters of the Islamic Resurgence also utilize it to gain support from other Muslims.

However, not all Muslims are on the side of the Islamic Resurgence supporters. There have been some Muslims who prefer to be friends with the Israelis. Prominent cleric K. H. Abdurrahaman Wahid, who is also a former president of Indonesia, is among those Muslims. He even became member of the foundation of Shimon Peres.

3. The Iranian revolution in 1979

Iran's successful transformation into the Islamic Republic of Iran through the so-called 1979 Revolution also contributed to the rise of the Islamic Resurgence in

33 Al-Makin, Tanggalkan Khalifah, 318.
34 https://www.republika.co.id/berita/nasional/politik/12/11/19/mdq6uc-kecam-israelmassa-hti-demo-kedubes-as (15.9.2020).

Indonesia. It not only provided a model to the supporters of Islamic Resurgence for setting up an Islamic state in Indonesia, but also spurred on their efforts in pursuing their goal. This observation is based on my reading of some references which expose its effects beyond Iran. For instance, John L. Esposito and James Piscatori conclude in their introductory note on »The Iranian Revolution Ten Years Later: What has been its global impact?« that its impact on Indonesia is more likely an »exemplar in reverse«. However, both acknowledge that it is the success model of an Islamic political revolution that was pursued in the name of Islam, its battle cry being »Allahu Akbar« which was shouted during the revolution.[35]

4. The expansion of Saudi Arabian wahhabism

Martin van Bruinessen's article on Wahhabi influences in Indonesia, real and imagined, states that its influence may be traced back to 1804 when three pilgrims returned from Mecca to West Sumatra and initiated a radical and occasionally violent movement of religious and social reform.[36] Its presence in the country, Bruinessen notes, was countered by founding *Nadlatul Ulama*, the largest organization of traditional Muslims in the country, to defend beliefs and practices that were attacked by the Wahhabis.[37] He says that its influence in the country continued in the form of antiZionist, antiSemitic, antiChristian, antiShi'a, anti Ahmadiya, and antiLiberalist discourses as Indonesia was flooded with cheap books from this group in 1980s to 1990s.[38] Its influence still continues beyond those years. For instance, its literalistic approach toward the Qur'an which is flourishing among contemporary Muslims; its infiltration into the assembly of the Muhammadiyah group in 2005, promoting people under its influence to hold strategic positions in the group,[39] and its infiltration into *Nadlatul Ulama* as it loses

35 John L. Esposito/James Piscatori (eds.), The Iranian Revolution Ten Years Later. What Has Been Its Global Impact? Washington 1989, 8.

36 Martin van Bruinessen, Wahhabi influences in Indonesia, real and imagined, Summary of paper presented at the Journée d'Etudes du CEIFR et MHS sur le Wahhabisme, Ecole des Hautes Etudes en Science Sociales/Maison des Sciences de l'Homme, Paris, June 10, 2002, 1.

37 Ibid., 1.

38 Ibid.

39 K. H. Abdurrahman Wahid, Musuh dalam Selimut (English: »Enemy in the blanket«), in: K. H. Abdurrahman Wahid (ed.), Ilusi Negara Islam. Ekspansi Gerakan Islam Transnasional di Indonesia (English: Islamic State Illusion. Expansion of Transnational Islam Movement in Indonesia), Jakarta 2009, 11–42, here: 23.

mosques associated with the group, as was the case for a mosque in Pati, Central Java.[40]

Hasbi Aswar refers to an institution that is called *Dewan Dakwah Islamiyah Indonesia* (the Council of Islamic Syi'ar Indonesia) which serves as a medium to disseminate the Wahhabi teaching and its influences in the country.[41] Additionally, he also identifies *Lembaga Ilmu Pengetahuan Islam dan dunia Arab* (the Institute of Islamic Knowledge and Arab World), founded in 1981, as another vehicle for the dissemination of Wahhabi teaching in public.[42] The country still faces its influences in the second term of Joko Widodo.

5. The expansion of transnational Islam

The expansion of transnational Islam is mainly pursued by various Islamic groups such as Hizbut Tahrir, the Muslim Brotherhood, al-Qaeda, and ISIS. I realise, however, that they all have a different *raison d'etre* for coming to Indonesia. Additionally, each group has different historical reasons for being in their own country. For instance, Hizbut Tahrir differs from ISIS, and so does the Muslim Brotherhood from alQaeda. However, all groups mentioned above are present in Indonesia. Each has its own supporters, meaning that the influence of each group in the country is real. For instance, the president of ISIS Indonesia (Islamic State in Iraq and Syria), Chep Hernawan, was a supporter of Prabowo Subianto during the 2019 presidential election.

An alternate reading of Pancasila and its impact on the missional presence of Christians

My proposal for an alternate reading of Pancasila is based primarily on an article entitled »Ada apa dengan Pancasila« (»What happens to Pancasila?«) which I wrote for a seminar in a Christian congregation in the country.[43] In this article, I

40 Ibid., 29.

41 Hasbi Aswar, Politik Luar Negeri Arab Saudi dan Ajaran Salafi-Wahhabi di Indonesia, JISIER A: The Journal of Islamic Studies and International Relations, 1 (2016), 15–30, here: 21.

42 Ibid., 21.

43 Abraham Silo Wilar, Ada apa dengan Pancasila? (English: What happens to Pancasila?), Paper presented at GKI Cinere, 23.2.2019.

propose two historical issues which play an important role in constructing Pancasila but are rarely mentioned in discussions of it. These two issues, to my understanding, are also extremely important for helping Christians to shape their missional presence living in the time of the Islamic Resurgence. One fundamental reason for this is that such a reading provides not only a theological vision for this purpose but also equips Christians with a language that can be utilized practically to respond to the *realpolitik* of the country as well as critiquing the supporters of the Resurgence. These two factors are missed in the common response of many Christians utilizing Pancasila to defend the country against the influences of the Resurgence.

1. Global colonialism

Generally speaking, the word »colonialism« often refers to Western colonialism. Yet, historically, it was, for example, also practiced toward Indonesia by the Japanese. On January 21, 1941, Japan openly declared that the *Hollandsche Indisch* (or Indonesia) was now to be a part of the Great East Asia Commonwealth.[44] The Japanese called themselves »Saudara Tua« (the eldest brother of Indonesia). Similar practices may be identified from other countries. This sort of colonialism is rarely realized by many Christians while talking about Pancasila.

With regard to the actors involved in colonialism, I would extend the understanding of colonialism to include knowledge domination and its basic ways of operation. Within this particular type of colonialism, one group seeks to implant its own type of knowledge on others to control people through such knowledge. Thus, colonialism is not only about the physical aggression of one country against other countries, nor is it limited to certain countries. My approach is deeply rooted in Edward Said's work, *Orientalism*. His monumental book has been praised for showing how Europeans constructed what the term »orient« means.[45] Additionally, Henry Schwarz's article reiterates what Said has written in *Orientalism*, namely, that European knowledge is colonialism,[46] and he further takes Said's work as one of the starting points for a postcolonialist approach within the aca-

44 Muhammad Abdul Aziz, Japan's colonialism and Indonesia, The Hague 1955, 117.

45 Edward Said, Orientalism. Western Conception of the Orient, London 1979.

46 Henry Schwarz, Mission Impossible. Introducing Postcolonial Studies in the US academy, in: Henry Schwarz/Sangeeta Ray (eds.), A Companion to Postcolonial Studies, Oxford 2005, 1–12, here: 4.

demic context. With Said's and Schwarz's work in the background, the extension that I propose here is plausible. In its plausibility, colonialism becomes more epistemological, as a means of colonializing the way people approach and understand themselves and others.

This new frame of colonialism allows us to identify unspoken colonialism coming from things that are familiar to us but whose aim is to colonize on a subconscious level. In connection to this, I suggest that we need to start to examine ideologies that are familiar to us in order to identify their underlying colonialist potential. For instance, the following questions may be raised in the context of the present study: is Pan-Islamism an example of colonialism? Is an Islamic caliphate another example of colonialism in the name of Islam? Answers to these questions might spark controversies but are important to disclose the substance of the ideologies.

2. Establishment of new states

When the United States of America gained independence from Great Britain in 1776, or Canada in 1867, new, independent states were established. Hence, the emergence of new countries as independent states was often related to colonial practices and it came into being in waves which were sweeping the Asian and African continents. The foundation of Indonesia is part of these waves, attempting to acquire independence from the colonial power. In the waves I can see a certain imagination and awareness of what humans are and what has driven the colonialized people to resist their colonial master: to be equal and just. This spirit of equality and justice is obviously decisive in the establishment of the new states in the above mentioned countries. And these two values are important for talking about Pancasila, for they are substantial elements of it. Therefore, Christians speaking about nationalism must not exclude these elements.

In my view, both global colonialism and the establishment of the new states form the background of making Pancasila the foundation of the Indonesian state. And I am certain that the founding fathers of the country were aware of these events as they began to struggle to decide what form of the state they would choose, what foundation would help it stand firm, and what spirit it would breathe in. With such background I am confident to state that Pancasila as the foundation of the state did not arise in service of colonialism, nor will it become the ground for committing injustice or fostering inequality as it was commonly practiced by the colonial master. Instead, it intends to safeguard Indonesia as a newborn state from duplicating what the colonial masters did, installing justice and equality as a national language for the people.

So, therefore, I believe that the imagined country which the founding fathers had in mind was a country that would not follow the Japanese and the Western countries, nor would it allow for an Islamic form of colonialism to be implemented in the new born country. Rather, the founding fathers preferred to absorb the spirit of anti-colonialism, equality and justice to make that spirit the content of the imagined state.

These two values lying behind the making of Pancasila are fundamental for Christians in constructing their missional presence in the country. Rather than supporting a sheer nationalism which is often presented in the following slogan: *NKRI Harga Mati* (»the Republic of Indonesia is not negotiable«) or defending nationalism, I suggest Christians to look behind the making of Pancasila, to discover its substantial values (anticolonialism, equality, and justice), to adopt these values, and to make them part of their language determining their missional presence. By adopting these values, Christians supporting Joko Widodo are not allowed to become blind supporters, nor to hate or to be afraid of the supporters of Islamic Resurgence. Rather, they are called to bring anti-colonialism, egalitarianism and justice into the dialogue with the supporters, discussing whether their proposal contains those values or not. Similarly, they are also called upon to bring the spirit of egalitarianism and justice to the government to examine how nationalism is being used by the government.

In doing so, I consider that it is a substantial call to understand the specific background of Pancasila as intentionally pursuing justice and egalitarianism for the common and greater good. So, instead of pronouncing a dead slogan such as »NKRI Harga Mati«, which cannot bind people together, Christians adopting the values of Pancasila will directly deal with the *realpolitik* of the country, offering some breakthrough acts and bringing justice and equality to Indonesians while presenting their missional presence. In doing so, those values are turned into a common language for Indonesians to speak to one another, and a measure for Christians to specifically find out how missional they are, how just and egalitarian the government is running its affairs, and how liberating the Islamic Resurgence's agenda is.

Closing remarks

With the alternate reading of Pancasila that I propose, Christians are called to make a substantial contribution by evaluating what the government has offered to Indonesians and by promoting the suggestion to pursue the values of Pancasila. Such a contribution would include mobilizing networks and resources to tackle corruption issues in order to foster equality and justice among Indonesians, and starting a conversation and potential collaboration with the Islamic Resurgence supporters to work on the ideal values they promote and to find out how these values accommodate the presence of those who are not Muslims.

(Rev. Dr. Abraham Silo Wilar, M. Th., M. A., Lecturer in Inter-Religious Studies, Jakarta Theological Seminary)

ABSTRACT

Dieser Beitrag beschreibt, wie indonesische Christen und Christinnen in einer Zeit islamischen Erwachens (»Islamic Resurgence«) leben. Im Allgemeinen identifizieren sie sich als Anhänger*innen des Nationalismus und nutzen ihn als Mittel, um den Einflüssen des islamischen Erwachens zu begegnen. Diese Art und Weise, wie Christen und Christinnen auf die Einflüsse reagieren, wird als nicht sehr hilfreich angesehen, denn sie führt dazu, dass die indonesische Gesellschaft immer stärker segmentiert wird. Um eine solche Segmentierung zu umgehen, wird hier eine alternative Lesart der Pancasila vorgeschlagen. In dieser alternativen Lesart werden der globale Kolonialismus, die darauf folgenden Unabhängigkeitsbestrebungen sowie die Werte, die der Pancasila zu Grunde liegen, in den Blick genommen. Es wird argumentiert, dass diese Art der Relektüre für beide Seiten eine Sprache anbietet, die verbinden kann. So wird es beiden Parteien ermöglicht, miteinander ins Gespräch zu kommen und ihre Kluft zu überbrücken.

Religious Freedom and the State in Myanmar

A Call for a Public Theological Response[1]

Lahphai Awng Li

1. Restrictions on minority ethnic religious freedom

Since 1960, all missionaries of non-Buddhist religions have been expelled from Myanmar and almost all private schools and hospitals owned by non-Buddhist groups have been nationalized. Christian and Islamic groups have had difficulties in importing religious literature into the country. The Government's censorship office has controlled all publications, religious and secular. The Bible in indigenous languages has to be printed abroad and imported into the country illegally. Local printing for limited circulation or photocopying of a limited number of copies of religious materials are possible without getting the approval from the government censor, but it is also illegal. Bamars (Burmans), a majority ethnic group, usually claim that »the Bamars are Buddhists and the Buddhists are Bamars« because Buddhism has become firmly rooted and played a key role in the lives of Bamars in Myanmar. They usually assume that »if a person is not a Buddhist, he is not a real Bamar.«[2] Ashin Addga Dhama, one of the nationalistic Buddhist monks, strongly refuses to allow Christians to use the Pali words such as Phaya (god), Thawara (eternal), Thama (truth), Ngaye (hell), etc., in the Burmese Christian Bible because they are Buddhist sacred words.[3]

1 *A preliminary note by the editors:* The following paper has been written and handed in prior to the latest political developments in Burma since February 2021. Therefore it makes no reference to those developments, but rather focuses on the question of religious freedom – a pressing issue especially for members of non-buddhist religions, but also for society as a whole.

2 R. Grant Brown, Burma As I Saw It. 1889–1917, London 1962, 102.

3 A presentation paper of Ashin Addga Dhama submitted to U Thein Sein, President of Union of Myanmar, on 12.6.2012 (in Burmese language).

Most of the ethnic Bamars (Burmans) see non-Buddhism as the religion of foreigners or the religion brought by the colonialists, even though Buddhism itself is imported from a foreign land. In the thinking of Bamars (Burmans), Christianity is suspected to be neo-colonialist or pro-Western even today, because of its keeping in touch with the West.[4]

2. Christianity as a religion of foreigners

Since the early days of Christian mission in Myanmar, Buddhists have perceived Christianity as a religion of foreigners and the Christian missionaries as invaders dividing Bamars. Besides, Buddhist society, backed by the government, also treats non-Buddhists as outsiders or guests, not as people like themselves. Bamars who become Christians or Muslims are looked down upon as traitors to the country because religion and nationality are so closely related in Burmese nationalist ideology. Many contemporary Bamar Christians or Muslims still experience alienation from families and friends in many instances.

Religious minority groups were occasionally employed as forced laborers to destroy mosques, churches or graveyards, in order to build Buddhist pagodas or to carry bricks and other supplies for the construction of the pagodas. In many cases, non-Buddhists had to pay bribes to the authorities to obtain the necessary permits to erect a religious building and to observe the religious ceremonies inside or outside their religious compound.

Thus, non-Buddhists are facing various restrictions in obtaining a permit to celebrate religious ceremonies, own a place of worship, and build religious buildings, etc. There was a significant political turning point in 2015, because the National League of Democracy (NLD) took the leading role as the first democratically elected government. Political freedom is starting to set foot on the soil of Myanmar again. The NLD, led by Aung San Suu Kyi, has become the ruling party since 2016, and 55 Christian members of Parliament (MPs) have been elected to the Union parliament. Ethnic Chin Christian Henrey Van Thio has been appointed as vice-president, and five other Christians were appointed as chief

4 For more information see also: Nyi Nyi Kyaw, Freedom of Religion, the Role of the State, and Interreligious Relations in Myanmar, Colombo, Sri Lanka 2018, 19.

ministers in ethnic states. It is the first time Christians have held such high offices in Myanmar in decades. However, even though they are given such positions, their responsibility in political affairs is very limited or restricted. Apart from that, religious discrimination in Myanmar has much to do with the idea of favor-*ism* or *favoritism* of the majority's religion. Since 1948 the successive governments – democratic or military – have been promoting Buddhism in the nation building process. The 2008 constitution, the latest constitution of Myanmar, not only grants limited rights to freedom of religion, but also grants a special position and privilege to Buddhism. Although the 2008 constitution forbids discrimination on ethnic or religious grounds, the successive governments directly or indirectly supported the policy of Burmanization which is to assimilate all ethnic minorities into the dominant ethnic Burman group and non-Buddhists into Buddhism. Only in Article 362 of the Constitution are other minor religions recognized as existing religions. Although the constitution from 2008 speaks of religious freedom, Christianity and other religions do not have equal rights to religious freedom in Myanmar. Even some Buddhist monks who do not support or agree with the religious policy of the government and the government's military arm do not have equal rights of religious freedom, compared to those who support or agree with the religious policy of the ruling government and the armed forces. They are very often persecuted in many ways for preaching the essence of Buddha's teaching to promote peace and justice including religious freedom.

After Aung San Suu Kyi's government had taken the leading position in the country, ethnic minorities hoped that there would be no more human rights violations and a good solution to Myanmar's longest running civil wars. However, they still face human rights violations as usual and have to struggle for their existence, for dignity, peace, and human rights. It is undeniable that religious freedom is still a long way away from this political change. The NLD led by Aung San Suu Kyi has launched a peace process by inviting the ethnic armed opposition groups to sign a Nationwide Ceasefire Agreement and initiating the »Panglong 21« conference. The Government of Myanmar and eight ethnic Armed Organizations signed a National Ceasefire Agreement (NCA) in October 2015, but at least ten armed groups did not sign it. The situation is not improving and serious violations continue to take place off and on in marginalized communities in Myanmar. Religious discrimination is still going on in every way in the country. It seems that the ideology of Burmanization continues to influence the mindset of the majority of Burman ethnic groups. Until today, the NLD, the ruling party, has received mounting criticism for the lack of government action to thwart hate speech based on religiosity and rising religious nationalism.

3. Theological response: A public theological perspective

Myanmar Christian Theology has itself been active in dispensing with the discussion on and the fight for the realization of Human Rights. The reasons might be found in fear, anxiety, ethnicity, grievances and exclusive theological thinking for decades under the military dictatorships or in the constitution of the country which gives a special position to Buddhism. While the citizens are faced with problems, including the violation of religious freedom, most of the churches in Myanmar keep silent or practice a non-engagement policy in the socio-political affairs of the country. Without taking responsibility for defending and promoting human dignity and rights at all costs, how can Christians be the salt of the earth and the light of the world? Theologically, Christians in Myanmar are challenged not only to engage in active opposition to religio-socio-political injustices and oppression, but also to take responsibility for defending and promoting human dignity and rights at all costs.

3.1 Basic biblical views on freedom of religion

God created humankind in His image giving them the gift of freedom of choice (Genesis 1,26; Joshua 24,15). The very nature of God's creation and of humankind is to be free – to make decisions of their own including their religion. Thus freedom of religion, the very nature of humankind, is rooted in biblical principles. Human life, the greatest gift of God, is sacred, unique, precious, worthy, valuable, and meaningful. As God gives dignity, freedom and equality to the human being, all human beings, regardless of color, race, nationality, culture or sex, have equal and inherent worth. Hence, all of the God-given gifts of volitions in humanity, including religious freedom, must be protected and respected. According to Genesis 1,27, being created in the image of God means not only having fellowship between God and humanity, male and female, and humanity and creation, but also living according to the will and design of God. In Genesis 1,28f, the creation of human beings is followed by the blessing of God and the human calling to be fruitful and to rule over the earth according to the will and command of the creator who loves his creation. Therefore, an attempt to live a life of disharmony among the creatures or amidst a religiously pluralistic society is sin. To deny humanity freedom of religion is to debase the creation of God.

The Baptist World Alliance has stated that »religious freedom is a civil freedom, a freedom from any compulsion and coercion by the state or national church in matters of religious faith and practice.«[5] It is the right of freedom to have or adopt any religion, to change one's religion or beliefs, to practice worship, manifest and observe one's religion, and to abstain as atheist. Freedom of religion does not merely provide unity for those with the same faith. It not only prevents certain religious teachings which can be a divisive factor in society, but also conflicts between opposing religious groups.

Religious freedom, »a cornerstone of human rights«[6], is for all, not for a selected religion or a certain group of people whether they form the majority or minority in a community. As religious freedom is part of their identity, »Baptists have always pleaded for full religious freedom not only for themselves but for others, whatever their religion.«[7] No one, including the state authorities, should have a say in dictating a particular religion for its citizens. However, that does not mean that religious freedom gives people the license to do anything they want, i. e., harm or kill others physically or mentally. Freedom of religion is a crucial human right and must be coupled with responsibility – to love our neighbours by promoting a spirit of peaceful coexistence and an overall wellbeing of society. Violation of religious freedom can create instability and insecurity in the daily lives of individuals, families, communities and nations. Therefore, to preserve religious freedom handed down by our Creator to every human being is everybody's duty, for Christians and non-Christians alike. Mutual recognition and interrelationship of different religions, affirmation of the beauty and richness of diversity, and the fulfillment of human obligations of sharing, caring and responsibility in the world can cherish and increase its fullness. Today, Christians are called to promote religious freedom in Myanmar in the midst of an unjust structural system and human rights violations along with non-Christians brothers and sisters.

5 Baptist World Alliance, We Baptists, Franklin, Tennessee 1999, 32.
6 Ibid., 32.
7 Ibid., 31–32.

3.2 Exclusivistic attitude

Christianity was first introduced to Burma in the middle of the 16th century by Roman Catholic Portuguese merchants and mercenaries. In the late 17th century Roman Catholic missionaries were sent to Burma, and in 1813 Protestant Christianity was introduced to Burma through the arrival of American Baptist Missionaries, led by Adoniram Judson. As already mentioned before, Christianity came through the western colonial powers. Therefore, Adoniram Judson, one of the Baptist missionaries, declared that »it is more difficult for a Bamar to become a Christian than it is to extract a tooth from a tiger's mouth.«[8] In the present time, the President's office of Myanmar repeatedly claims that religious freedom is one of the fundamental rights and there is no religious discrimination in Myanmar.[9] Nevertheless, the present Myanmar government also tries to promote Buddhism all over the country by many means and strategies. There are still restrictions on the construction or renovation of churches and activites outside the church compound.

In mission history, Christians in Myanmar practiced »a confrontational or competitive attitude towards other religions.«[10] Most of the members of the churches of Myanmar are only concerned with the other-worldly spiritual realm of their lives. To prevent backsliding, missionaries encouraged the new converts or the faithful to avoid close friendships/relationships with non-Christians. This mentality and attitude has led Christians to isolate themselves from the community where they live in. The missionaries and some preachers only emphasize the salvation of the individual soul. They only focus on a vision of life after death, where all suffering, pain, and sorrow will no longer exist. They ignore the physical realm which is related to the life upon this earth. Hence, Mary Dun stated:

> »they (most of the members of the churches of Myanmar) have failed to relate their lives to the realities of the historical, social, economic and cultural problems that are occurring in their own country. They have failed in their actual calling by God to participate in

8 Paul D. Clasper, Christianity and Buddhism (lecture notes), Rangoon 1960, 10.

9 Briefing Room, Old News, http://www.president-office.gov.mm/en/briefing-room/news/2013/06/25/id-2257 (20.8.2020).

10 Simon Pau Khan En, The Quest for Authentic Myanmar Contextual Theology, in: Ray. MIT Journal of Theology 2 (2001), 31–48, here: 38.

God's holistic mission – a mission which concerns both heaven and earth.«[11]

Besides, most missionaries and Christians in Myanmar look upon Buddhists and people of other faiths as inferior or the children of Satan. Some churches do not allow Burmese traditional melodies in songs of praise in the worship services, but only western or modern tunes. Some pastors and evangelists usually teach the young generation that Buddhism is false and Buddhists will go to hell. Because of such exclusivistic attitudes, Christianity is still alien to Myanmar Buddhists and has been suffering from various forms of political suspicion and religious discrimination.

In fact, both Christianity and Buddhism are basically religions of peace, compassion, and life-reverence. Nonetheless, Buddhists and Christians are encountering each other in the fields of their mission with their exclusive claims of superiority over another. The Buddhists wish all Christians to change to Buddhist religion, and the Christians have the specific aim that Myanmar will be a Christian State. Although some academics of both religions practice interfaith dialogue to some extent, the majority of both Christians and Buddhists see each other as rivals or as an alternative community. Therefore, in general, there is no positive intimate relationship or religious interaction between Christians and Buddhists, but they attend their own religious rites regularly and try to build up their own religious society. Instead of building a good relationship, Christian and Buddhist missions are competing, especially among the people of ethnic minorities. Such an exclusive understanding and attitude can lead to the disintegration of the nation where different religions and people are living together. Actually, both religions ought to take an active interest in human welfare. Now, therefore, the time has come to overcome religious exclusivism and discrimination and establish better relationships between Buddhists and Christians.

3.3 *The separation of church and state*

Since the missionaries' days, the idea of the separation of church and state already exists among the churches of Myanmar. There are several reasons why Myanmar churches avoid active participation in the realm of political affairs. The first one

11 Mary Dun, Inter-Faith Dialogue. Christians Initiative for Dialogue with Buddhists in Myanmar. Th. D. Dissertation, SEAGST 1997, 230.

is the dichotomized theology of sacred and secular. This theological concept is founded on the traditional theological understanding that the kingdom of God is not of this world (John 18,36) or that this world is not a Christian's home. According to this theological stance, the church is sacred (holy) and the world outside the church or Christianity is secular (evil or unholy). What is holy (the church) must not interact with what is unholy (the world). The state or the realm of political affairs is a worldly one, broken or evil beyond redemption. The churches, the body of Christ and being under the Lordship of Christ, must be free from the secular affairs of this world outside the church or Christianity in matters relating to their spiritual life. They enjoy a vision of life-after-death where all suffering, pain, and sorrow will no longer exist. Such an understanding leads some Christians/churches to have nothing to do with this evil world or to seek total separation from the state or the realm of political affairs, including noninvolvement in social and societal activities.

In fact, God is not only at work through the gospel, offering new life to human beings, but also at work through the law and order to form a peaceful world where His will be done. Therefore, the »secular« world is also God's world where God is at work. God calls His people to work in and for the world. In John 17 Jesus prayed, »My prayer is not that you take them out of the world, but that you protect them from the evil one« (17,15); »they are not of the world« (17,16); »As you sent me into the world, I have sent them into the world« (17,18). This says that the churches or Christians are expected neither to withdraw from the world nor to conform to it. But they are sent into the world »to be responsibly in the world to oppose evil, work towards the elimination of all that corrupts or degrades the life of people, bring mutual respect, sisterhood and brotherhood, justice, and peace in all relationships of people and races and nations.«[12] Christians are members of the church and citizens of a particular nation on earth. As they are part of the nation, they are not supposed to withdraw from the nation (the world) but rather to engage it with the gospel for the common good and welfare of every citizen of the nation.

The second reason for political restraint is, for example in the case of the Baptist church, its traditional teaching that »the state must not exercise direct control over the church, interfere with its free self-government under Christ, or bring legal pressure to bear upon the individual in matters of religious faith and

12 Walter B. Shurden, The Baptist Identity. Four Fragile Freedoms, Macon 1993, 110.

practice«.[13] The traditional Baptist teaching is that a Christian needs to denounce the mundane world which is outside the church. That is why many Christians hold that ministers or full-time pastors of the churches must avoid participating in the political affairs of the state. As a majority of Christians in Myanmar are Baptists, Baptist beliefs affect the lives of the churches of Myanmar and direct the ways of Christians in socio-political, economic, religious and cultural contexts. That is also one of the reasons why the churches keep silent in any issues governed by the state in Myanmar or avoid participation in the affairs of religious policy.

Because of the above-mentioned misunderstanding of the theology of separation of church and state, most Christians (and churches) in Myanmar are silent in the face of social and political oppression, religious persecution, ethnic genocide, public issues, and human rights abuses.

In fact, church and state are distinct, but both are ordained by God to fulfill the divine purpose on earth. The separation of church and state means that »the church refrains from any attempt to use the power of government to enhance the power or programs of a church and the state refrains from any attempt to govern the affairs of churches or from supporting any particular religious activity.«[14] Under the Lordship and guidance of Jesus Christ, the church has »a mandate to represent the ideal community to society at large where the virtues of love, justice, and peace become normative for every conceivable relationship.«[15] As the obligation of the state is to exercise civil authority to maintain rules and order in the country and promote public welfare, it has a responsibility to protect the church to pursue its spiritual ends. Likewise, the church has to promote the morality and spirituality of the people to be good citizens who respect the law and order of the state for the sake of the common welfare of everybody in the country. The obligation of the church and the state is to defend and promote human dignity and rights at all costs, and to resist all evils, including abuses of the power of the state and an evil religio-socio-political system.

Therefore, although they are distinct, they must have a proper relationship under God to fulfill the divine purpose on earth. They must have mutual understanding, mutual recognition, mutual respect, mutual enrichment, and they must cooperate to oppose evil, to work toward the elimination of all that corrupts or

13 Shurden, Baptist Identity, 76.
14 Everett C. Goodwin, Down by the riverside. A brief history of Baptist Faith, Valley Forge 2002, 102.
15 Luther D. Ivory, Toward a Theology of Radical Involvement. The Theological Legacy of Martin Luther King Jr., Nashville 1997, 46.

degrades the life of people, to maintain basic human rights, and to promote public welfare. In other words, both church and state must work together in building a nation where the virtues of love, justice, equality, freedom and peace become normative for everybody.

3.4 The subordination of the church to the political authority

As already mentioned, Myanmar is notorious as one of the most religiously discriminating countries. Religious minorities, including Hindus, Christians, and Muslims, continue to face threats and persecution in the country. In such a situation, Christians have to work out their response to the authorities prayerfully and practically. However, the concept of the subordination of the church to political authority or state power without questioning, based on Roman 13, exercises great influence on some churches. Some Christians and churches that adhere to the subordination of the church to the state interpret Romans 13 in a way that the church must submit to and obey the state uncritically because it has been instituted by God. Therefore, they are determined to obey the government without any involvement in the realm of political affairs. They never raise their voice against their government's evil acts regarding the right of religious freedom. We have to notice that there is a diversity of biblical teachings on the relation of church and state based on the respective context. For instance, Romans 13 appreciates the civil government (the state) because the government in the context of Romans 13 fulfills to some degree God's plan for them, but Revelation 13 opposes the government (the state) because the government in the context of Revelation 13 was very brutal. Therefore, if the government becomes brutal and violates basic human rights or the right to religious freedom of its citizens, the churches need to raise their voice against it and actively engage in promoting the basic human rights of the citizens by all means.

The second reason why the churches of Myanmar have to submit to and obey the government is their concern that if they get involved in public affairs they may face more discrimination or persecution than before. Such fear leads them to keep silent and to remain subject to the unjust political leadership. The leaders of the churches also try to design Christianity in Myanmar as a form of ritualistic religion, rather than as a politically explicit prophetic religion raising its voice against its government's evil acts denying the right of religious freedom and persuading the state to give just treatment to every citizen in the country.

Most Christians in Myanmar are too submissive to the state, even though they know that their government has violated the basic human rights of its citizens or committed inhumane evils and atrocities in the country.

In reality, as citizens of a certain country, Christians are supposed to obey the law and order of that country because they are imposed for the equality and the common welfare of its citizens. Christians, as good citizens, need to honor and serve the state which always tries to safeguard the rights and equality of all its citizens, and the well-being of everybody in the country. Nevertheless, if the political authorities become thoroughly corrupt, brutal and treat their civilians unjustly, citizens, including Christians, must raise their voice against their evil government, and engage actively in the amendment of the evil things done by the political authorities.

3.5 Christian involvement in nation building in Myanmar

Although the majority of the traditional, conservative Christians have practiced noninvolvement in state affairs, we have it on record that some Christians have very actively raised their voice, demanding fair and open participation in state affairs for every citizen in Myanmar. For instance, in 1935, Rev. Lahpai Zau Tu, a 100-year-old Kachin Baptist pastor and chief, led 56 Kachin chiefs to Rangoon and demanded from the English colonial governor of Burma, Sir Spencer Harcourt Butler, political freedom and rights (self-governing status: self-rule or home rule) for the Kachin Ethnics of Myanmar.[16] When U Nu, the prime minister of independent Myanmar, once again confirmed Buddhism as the State religion in August 1961, many ethnic Christians, especially Kachin and Karen Christians opposed it, and some Kachin Christian youth took up arms to fight the government for religious freedom and self-determination. In recent decades, because of the enormously evil impact of drugs on the lives of individuals and the community, Kachin Christian communities in Kachin State and Northern Shan State, Myanmar, along with civil society groups, have led an anti-drug campaign, offering drug education seminars and information to raise public awareness of the dangers of drug abuse. Ethnic youth activists launched an anti-war movement and called on the government to free the Internally Displaced Persons, to provide them with humanitarian assistance and to establish new Internally Displaced Per-

16 Lanang Bawk, Becoming Kachin State in Myanmar, Laiza Muklung 2012, 38.

sons' camps in affected areas[17] whenever civilians face a critical situation in the war zones. The Kachin Christian youths, however, perceived their participation in the movement as a revolutionary action for Kachin ethnic identity and dignity, not as a fruit of Christian spirituality.

In the foreign missionaries' days, Christian mission hospitals, schools, social development trainings, and social development programs for the community were very well-known and highly regarded. Nevertheless, all foreign Christian missionaries were driven out of Myanmar in the mid-1960s and all Christian mission hospitals and schools nationalized. That is why the contribution of Christian mission hospitals and schools was diminished for several decades. But now some ethnic Christian churches have again started Christian clinics, hospitals, schools, development trainings, and social development programs for the community. Therefore, human rights activist Benedict Rogers stated that:

> Although numerically a small minority, Christians have long been at the very center of Myanmar's social development, building and running hospitals and schools, providing aid to the displaced, fighting drug addiction, speaking up for the rights of religious and ethnic minorities and promoting peace. While perhaps more engaged in social development rather than explicitly »political« activities, at least at an institutional level, Christianity has contributed to the social and political fabric of Myanmar throughout the past century or more, and in recent years has seen resurgence in impact. Christianity is particularly influential among a number of Myanmar's ethnic nationalities, where religion and cultural identity are tightly intertwined.[18]

As an interdenominational body, the Myanmar Council of Churches (MCC) needs, as expected by some, to be actively involved in pursuing religious freedom for everybody in every circumstance which is directly related to the peace and stability of the country. In 2007, in the Saffron Revolution, a series of economic and political protests and demonstrations broke out during August, September and October 2007 in Myanmar. Tens of thousands of Buddhist monks led massive non-violent and peaceful demonstrations all over the country in order to end

17 Steve Tickner et al, Kachin youth activists launch potent anti-war movement, in: https://www.frontiermyanmar.net/en/kachin-youth-activists-launch-potent-anti-war-movement/ (16.5.2020).

18 Benedict Rogers, The Contribution of Christianity to Myanmar's social and political development, in: The Review of Faith & International Affairs 13/4 (2015), 60–70, here: 60.

military dictatorship, political repression and political corruption, and human rights violations. Civilians from all walks of life joined the protests for the common welfare of everybody in the country. The Myanmar Council of Churches did not publicly support it or get actively involved in it, while some non-Buddhist organizations or associations provided support or active involvement, especially Muslim Youth Groups which distributed purified drinking water to the participants of the revolution. The Myanmar Council of Churches, along with the Catholic Bishops Conference of Myanmar (CBCM), merely issued a statement requesting the government to find a peaceful way of resolving the problems of the country. MCC usually worries that their action or involvement may negatively affect their good relationship with the government or their entity as a Christian interdenominational body in Myanmar. Christians in Myanmar enjoy celebrating a prayer week in September every year for the better future of the country without engaging in action in public life for the common good and welfare.

Concerning »why Christians should not keep silent in today's Myanmar political milieu«, the Myanmar Baptist Convention, the largest Christian Convention in number, issued several resolutions from their conference titled »The Role of Baptist Churches in Nation Building« held in the capital (Nay Pyi Taw) in 2016. They are as follows:

(a) The Baptist churches (about 5000) and Baptist Theological Schools (45) are encouraged to promote competent church leadership so that the churches know how to play a role in nation building under the federal system that is expected to come to ethnic regions in the near future.

(b) Baptist churches and theological institutions are encouraged to take more and more critical involvement in nation building in the future. Theological and Bible schools are to be encouraged to allow study courses in subjects such as political theology, public theology, church and society, and must also be encouraged to conduct academic workshops/seminars for church leaders and theological educators, especially on the awareness of church-state relations, human rights issues, peacemaking, conflict transformation, and other church-related sociopolitical issues in Myanmar.

(c) The churches in Myanmar are encouraged to be in solidarity with each other in raising a common voice, especially on various socio-political issues such as social injustice, religious oppression, racial and gender discrimination, and various other kinds of moral corruption that are rampant in Myanmar.

(d) The churches or religious leaders must be educated to know that any religion can be manipulated by its leaders in many ways when it is used by the authorities and also by the rich as a tool for covering up what they have done wrong, and for showing their faces to the public for personal gains and favors. This issue is to be tackled at the national level.
(e) All Christian churches must encourage and support enhancement of interfaith cooperation, interfaith dialogue, and peace building between and among religious communities, so that all people regardless of religion, race, and culture may work together for the common good of Myanmar and Asia.[19]

The resolutions issued by the conference are an encouragement to active participation in politics and nation building. However, the leaders of the Myanmar Baptist Convention had never been actively involved in demonstrations with civilians when the government practiced oppression and actions of injustice. The Myanmar Baptist Convention and some Christian organizations usually send letters to the government to indicate their stance, and some Christian activists have been privately involved in demonstrations. In reality, Christian organizations, conventions and churches never lead the demonstrations or any activities to oppose the evil policy and action of the state. There has been no collective Christian movement for the transformation of the socio-political setting in Myanmar. Most ecumenical seminaries have taught political theology, liberation theology, Asian theology, Third World theology and public theology for several decades, training students to be the leaders of prophetic churches which participate in promoting peace and justice in our community and our country. However, most of the Christian leaders were not yet able to train their church members to be mature Christians who love God and their neighbors as themselves. Most Christians in Myanmar strongly hold to the traditional conservative theology which dichotomizes the sacred and the secular, only longing for the other-world where there is no pain, sorrow, suffering and death.

A few of the advanced Christian theologians and scholars, along with non-Christian religious leaders, have already started interreligious or interfaith dialogue programs in Myanmar several years ago. Interreligious dialogues can be

19 Samuel Ngun Ling, Minority Issues. Ethnic Diversity in Myanmar, Paper presented at the joint project of Myanmar Institute of Theology and Norwegian School of Theology MF, Myanmar, January 17, 2019.

the best way to reduce tension amidst communal and religious conflicts, to promote mutuality among people of different religions, and to enhance peace and tranquility among different ethnic and religious groups. Nevertheless, we cannot yet see any good fruits from their programs, because most of the adherents of all religions are not yet mature enough in their spirituality.

In Myanmar, therefore, a small number of Christians and churches are convinced that the religious/church community is called to be the servant of the entire community in Myanmar society. Some Christians and churches raise their voice against the unjust structure and the state of the social and political system of the country. Some Christians actively participate in demonstrations against the evil social-political system privately, but not as representatives of any churches or Christian organizations. But most Christians in Myanmar do not participate in any civic affairs, based on their classical understanding of spirituality and the separation of church and state which prohibits them from doing so.

3.6 Challenges to public theology

Since public theology engages with public issues and questions, the question of religious freedom in Myanmar is part of the theological agenda of public theology both in Myanmar and in the world today. Although the constitution guarantees religious freedom, the provision of special favors to Buddhism both constitutionally and socio-politically is a violation of universal human rights and creates social disintegration among the citizens in Myanmar, where diverse faiths have lived together. On the other hand, some successive government leaders, nationalist monks and authoritarian military leaders use Buddhism as a tool to achieve their political goal to promote unity without embracing diversity in building a unitary state. To be sure, Buddhism itself is good and not the problem. However, the way it has come to be used as a state-favored religion in Myanmar's political history has made it unacceptable for non-Buddhists groups, because it has a pejorative or discriminating sense. Nowadays, Myanmar has democracy as the form of government. But in practice, there is a lack of true religious freedom and equal rights of the religions. The lack of true religious freedom and equal rights of religions is a sign of a lack of democratic practice in Myanmar. In such a public context, every Myanmar citizen, including Christians, needs to defend religious freedom because »religious freedom is the right of all persons to believe, speak, and act – individually and in community with others, in private and in public – in accord with their understanding of ultimate truth. It includes the right of religious individuals, institutions, and communities to express religious truths in their private lives, and to bring those truths into political life through their respective claims about justice, peace, equality, and freedom, and to seek the agreement of their fellow citizens on a basis equal to all others in society.«[20] Hence, promoting the rights of religious freedom is the most fundamental factor in nation building for a peaceful co-existence in Myanmar. On the other hand, Myanmar citizens are struggling for good governance creating the necessary conditions for the practice of justice in society, and for a good constitution which will guarantee the equality of every citizen and religion. In other words, Myanmar is urgently in need of good governance and a good constitution emphasizing the role of political processes for the good and the common welfare of every citizen in equality, justice, and without exclusion. To set up good governance and a good constitution that guarantees the equal rights of every religion is also one of the most challenging issues for Myanmar public theology. In such a situation, Myanmar Christianity as part of the community of Myanmar should not ignore the significance of these public issues and questions in Myanmar theological reflection.

Promoting and protecting religious freedom means upholding human dignity and the human rights of every individual. When freedom of religion, which strengthens the spirituality of humanity, is violated, it will directly fuel hatred or pessimism against diversity and negatively affect the peace and order of the country. Promoting and protecting religious freedom in Myanmar, therefore, is a crucial responsibility of every Myanmar and global citizen. As Christians living in God's spiritual kingdom, which includes God's physical created world, Myanmar Christians are part of Myanmar society. They are called not only to serve in the church and Christian community but also to stand along with people from a certain community to serve the needs of people and help to solve the common problems of all. As God so loves the world (John 3,16) and engages in the public space for the common good and welfare of the people, churches/Christians are called to love the world and to engage in the public space for the common good and welfare of the people. Since Christians are called to live and witness in the world as the salt of the earth and light of the world, they are »responsible for defending and promoting human dignity and rights at all costs, and [it] must boldly

20 Thomas Farr, What in the World is Religious Freedom, in: https://www.religiousfreedominstitute.org/blog/what-in-the-world-is-religious-freedom (29.12.2020).

resist all human evils, including state power, at any cost.«[21] They are called from the world and sent into the world to be transformative agents in the world. The role of Christianity/the churches must be to function as an agent to empower the weak, to serve the needy, to protect the vulnerable, to build the community that transcends deep-rooted and inherited differences, to promote the rule of law and good governance which guarantees peace and harmony in society, and to encourage all citizens together to move towards the future in conversation with each other's religious traditions, worldviews and value-systems, etc.

Therefore, the contextual condition of the right to religious freedom in Myanmar reminds and challenges the churches of Myanmar to rethink and refashion their role, responsibilities and accountabilities in the religio-socio-political setting of Myanmar. The main challenge is to develop a theology which encourages Christians to be strongly based on Christian faith and to engage the public realm in an effective and responsible way as salt and light of the world. In other words, in the context of a slow and ambivalent process towards democracy, and a continuation of religious persecution, ethnic cleansing, massive human rights violations and political oppression, Myanmar Christians or churches are challenged to play a significant role in the public life of the state by defending human rights, equality, freedom, and by cultivating a culture of peace and justice for all in the public sphere of Myanmar and beyond.

As the responsibility of religions is directed towards the healing of humanity and the world from suffering under the evil that exists in the world, Christians and non-Christians can build a just and sustainable interreligious community, in which peaceful means are employed to resolve not only the problems of misunderstanding, mistrust and alienation but also the problem of the unjust relations and structure of the society, including the constitution of the country. In so doing, gradually, both Christians and non-Christians may gain the conviction that inter-religious understanding and interaction can create solidarity among them, transcending religious borders. However, in reality, Christians in Myanmar have not yet fulfilled »a mandate to represent the ideal community to society at large where the virtues of love, justice, and peace become normative for every conceivable relationship«.[22]

21 Yeow Choo Lak, Time for Action. Theological Education for Asia, Singapore 1988, 140.
22 Ivory, Theology, 46.

Practically, Myanmar churches need to cultivate the spirituality of our church members which recognizes that »God works through humans, not only through individual efforts but also through their social and political structures«[23], and encourages people to actively participate in civic affairs as the salt of the earth and the light of the world. Christians are called to follow Jesus and walk in his footsteps here on earth. In virtue of the incarnation, Jesus identified himself as a part of society in the midst of its political and power conflicts. Although Jesus did not belong to any political party or religious leaders or political officers, His proclamation of the kingdom of God through words and deeds generated a dynamism of socio-political change for the common welfare of society. Likewise, Myanmar Christians, as a representation of the people of God in the world, are to respond willingly to God's call not only to put an end to poverty, injustice, oppression, exploitation, and discrimination, but also to try to set up reconciliation, justice, equality, non-discrimination and the common good and welfare of the society in Myanmar.

Since the second half of the 20th century, Myanmar theologians have recognized the inadequacy of the direct use of imported western theologies and they have been trying to re-conceptualize the Christian message within the Myanmar context. Nevertheless, the process of Myanmar Christian theology is only in its infancy when it comes to preaching from the pulpit, teaching in training courses, and writing articles. Some ecumenical theologians have attempted to conceptualize the Christian message in response to the theological challenges of socio-political and religio-cultural issues of Myanmar without encouraging Myanmar Christians to engage prophetically in the public sphere. Some of them engage in translating the Western theological concepts into Myanmar languages and thought patterns. Some theologians overemphasize philosophical theology as they accommodate their hospitality to their Buddhist neighbors. Some just relate the Christian message to other religious traditions, beliefs, and practices. That is why contemporary Myanmar theologies could not provide enough inspiration and motivation for Myanmar Christians to engage in the socio-political transformation and in the process of promoting religious freedom in Myanmar.

Consequently, Myanmar Christians themselves, in practice, did not identify with people who suffered poverty, oppression, discrimination, and human rights

23 Kathryn Kleinhans, The Work of a Christian. Vocation in Lutheran Perspective, in: Word & World 25/4 (2005), 394–402, here: 399.

violations as Jesus did. Most of the time, their theological contributions are also applied only in teaching, discussing and writing academic papers in theological seminaries and colleges. Thus, Myanmar Christianity and Myanmar theologies have no influence on the socio-political life and the policy making of the political agenda in Myanmar. In fact, the task of Myanmar public theology is to bring a new theological perspective which motivates Christians and non-Christians to live together in peaceful co-existence in a pluralistic society, to engage together in building the common good and welfare of every citizen and to solve together the questions and causes that affect everyone in the public sphere.

Therefore, it is imperative for Christians in Myanmar to overcome the theological deadlock that makes them unable to engage or co-operate with people outside the church in order to transform our society on the basis of freedom, justice and equality. We have to develop a public theology that equips Christians to demonstrate what faith means in the secular arena, to get involved in activities that contribute to the welfare of society, to find the political milieu in which God assigned them to live and act, to engage in the public and political sphere for the common good of everybody, to participate wholeheartedly in the nation building venture as a good citizen, and to promote human dignity and rights at all costs.

4. Conclusion

Today religious minorities are confronted with abuses of the right to religious freedom at home in Myanmar. In Myanmar, religious oppression not only targets other religions but also the monks and Buddhists who oppose policies of the government or the authoritarian military leaders. Factors which have caused a violation of religious freedom in Myanmar are religious nationalism, religious favoritism, the constitution of the country and the practice to use religious teaching as a tool to oppress others, etc. The right to religious freedom, one of the most fundamental of universal human rights, is directly related to socio-political rights. Consequently, the violation of religious freedom has negatively affected the socio-political affairs of the country in Myanmar.

The history of Myanmar has proved that giving Buddhism a special position and violating the right to religious freedom has led to religious conflicts, civil war, and tensions between Buddhists and non-Buddhists; it is the cause of the failure to unify Burma and even hinders the return of the spirit of the Union of

Burma. To be a better country, or a peaceful and harmonious country, citizens of Myanmar, including Myanmar Christians, are individually and collectively obligated to develop religious freedom which can promote love, justice, equality, reconciliation, harmony, and peace in Myanmar.

In His incarnation and mission, Jesus identified Himself as part of society in the midst of religious and political tensions and conflicts. Our theology, our understanding of Christian faith and work or spirituality, our responsibilities and accountability to contribute to the community and the country need to be redefined or remodelled in the light of the virtue of Jesus Christ's incarnation and mission. Likewise, Myanmar theology must be a theology that equips people to be more faithful to the Christian faith and actively engage in the public realm in an effective and responsible way as good citizens. Myanmar churches must not only nurture their members to be spiritually mature, actively proclaiming the Word of God in words and deeds in the midst of rapid social-political changes, but also encourage their members to become involved in public affairs by peaceful means. The life of the Myanmar Christians, individually or collectively, must identify with the people of the whole community and cooperate with all religious communities for liberation from the demonic power which has destroyed the common good and the common welfare of society. In doing so, Christians in Myanmar will be known as true patriots by their way of life in engaging in the peaceful struggle for religious freedom and in nation building, and Christianity will be rooted in the national life of the country. Consequently, various public issues, especially religio-socio-political matters, facing the people of Myanmar collectively will be healed and the virtue of love, justice, harmony and peace will become normative for the daily life of every person in Myanmar.

(Rev. Dr. Lahphai Awng Li, Professor & Head of Theological Studies Department, Myanmar Institute of Theology)

ABSTRACT

Die Frage der Religionsfreiheit ist in Myanmar seit der Bildung der Union Myanmar ein grosses Thema, weil die meisten Regierenden Religion als ein politisches Werkzeug benutzen, um ihre Macht zu erhalten. Daher ist die gemeinsame Sicherstellung der Religionsfreiheit der verschiedenen Gemeinschaften Myanmars dringend notwendig für den Aufbau einer friedlichen und harmonischen Gesellschaft. Die herausforderndste Aufgabe für die Bürger*innen Myanmars, einschließlich der Christen und Christinnen, ist es, gemeinsam dafür zu kämpfen, eine konfrontative oder konkurrierende Haltung gegenüber anderen Religionen zu beenden, die Menschenrechte und die Religionsfreiheit im öffentlichen Raum zu fördern und die Situation des Landes zu verbessern, um ein föderales demokratisches Land zu werden, in dem ethnisch und religiös unterschiedliche Menschen friedlich und harmonisch zusammenleben.

Christen sind, als Bürger und Bürgerinnen von Myanmar, dazu verpflichtet, Religionsfreiheit dahingehend zu entwickeln, dass Liebe, Gerechtigkeit, Gleichheit, Versöhnung und Harmonie möglich werden. Dadurch werden auch verschiedene gesellschaftliche Probleme, besonders religiös-soziale und politische Angelegenheiten, mit denen die Menschen in Myanmar kollektiv konfrontiert sind, gelöst werden können.

Kontextuelle Situierung der evangelischen Theologie in Korea[1]

Meehyun Chung

Einleitung

Ich bin in einer Kirchgemeinde in den 1960er und 1970er Jahren aufgewachsen, zu einer Zeit, in der der Fokus der Demokratiebewegung auf der Opposition gegen die Militärdiktatur lag. Für mich hatte deshalb die politische Theologie primär eine linksorientierte sozialkritische Dimension. Aber seit sich in Südkorea eine funktionierende Zivilgesellschaft etabliert hat, ist die politische Szene komplexer geworden. Sie spannt sich in einem Spektrum zwischen dem linken Flügel, repräsentiert durch die so genannten *candlelight rallies*, und dem rechts orientierten Flügel, dessen Symbol die koreanische Nationalflagge (*Taeggki*) ist. Daher meine ich heutzutage politisch eine ideologische Prägung zu erkennen, die einerseits links, aber auch rechtskonservativ-evangelikal orientiert ist.

Jede Theologie ist kontextgebunden. Dieser Kontext bezieht sich nicht nur auf die individuelle Ebene, sondern auch auf die gesellschaftspolitische. In diesem Aufsatz gehe ich auf meine eigene biographische Erfahrung ein, um auf diesem Wege die Beziehung von Theologie und Politik zu erläutern. Vorrangig habe ich in westlichen Sprachen zugängliche Texte verwendet, während die zahlreich vorhandene koreanische Literatur auf wenige Beispiele begrenzt wurde.

1 Diese Forschung wurde durch das *International Research & Development Program* der *National Research Foundation of Korea (NRF)* gefördert, die vom *Ministry of Education* (2019S1B2A1A011134) finanziert wird.

Der Koreanische Kontext in Bezug auf Christentum und Kirche in Geschichte und Gesellschaft

Wenn auch die allererste koreanische Kirche von einem Koreaner, der das Evangelium in China empfangen hatte, im heutigen Nordkorea gegründet wurde – eine Tatsache, auf die koreanische Christen stolz sind –, so ist die Verbreitung des Christentums hauptsächlich durch amerikanische Missionstätigkeit erfolgt. Erst durch sie bekam die presbyterianische oder evangelisch-reformierte Kirche ihre Gestalt. So lässt sich sagen, dass die systematische Einführung der Kirche durch nordamerikanische Missionare erfolgreich war.

Die katholische Kirche in Korea ist ebenfalls durch Eigeninitiative von koreanischen Wissenschaftlern entstanden und verbreitete sich, bevor die Missionstätigkeit verboten wurde, und zahlreiche katholische Christ*innen zu Märtyrern wurden. Während viele Katholiken im Zuge der koreanischen Mission unterdrückt wurden, gab es kaum Schwierigkeiten für die protestantische Mission. Erst unter der japanischen Herrschaft wurden auch Protestant*innen zu Märtyrer*innen, weil sie die Ehrerweisung vor Shinto-Schreinen verweigert hatten. Nach der katholischen Missionstätigkeit im 18. Jahrhundert begann seit 1885 der ungehinderte Großeinsatz der Protestanten von außen: zunächst der Presbyterianer, der Methodisten, später der Baptisten und Anglikaner etc.[2] Westliche protestantische Missionare und Missionarinnen kamen auch in Korea zeitgleich mit der expansionsgierigen imperialistischen Macht und mit dem aufgezwungenen Handel mit kapitalistischen Ausländern. Die dabei vollzogene Aufteilung des Missionsgebietes hat die jetzige Spaltung in die vielen protestantischen Kirchen hauptsächlich verursacht. Dennoch müssen die Leistungen der Mission differenziert bewertet werden.

Im Gegensatz zu vielen Missionaren des 19. Jahrhunderts im Globalen Süden, die einer höheren Bildung nicht oberste Priorität eingeräumt haben, haben sich einige nordamerikanische Missionare bemüht, eine solche in Korea zu ermöglichen. Dazu zählen Horace Grant Underwood, Lillias Horton Underwood und Oliver Avison u. a. Sie haben zur Bildung durch die Einrichtung von Colleges, zur Verkündigung des Evangeliums durch die Kirche und zur Heilung durch me-

2 Der erste presbyterianische Missionar war Horace Grant Underwood (1859–1916) aus den USA mit britischem Hintergrund, der zusammen mit seinem methodistischen Freund und Missionar Henry Gerhard Appenzeller (1858–1902) mit schweizerischem Hintergrund am 5. April 1885 Korea betrat.

dizinische Einrichtungen beigetragen. Daraus folgte die Gründung der heutigen Yonsei-Universität mit ihren medizinischen Einrichtungen sowie der protestantischen Kirchen.[3]

Seit Beginn des 20. Jahrhunderts lassen sich soziopolitisch drei Phasen unterscheiden, anhand derer gesellschaftliche Phänomena beschrieben werden können: die erste Phase bezieht sich auf die japanische Besatzungszeit zwischen 1910 und 1945. Die zweite Phase umfasst die militärische und diktatorische Herrschaft zwischen 1946 und 1992. Die dritte Phase ist mit der demokratischen Regierung seit 1993 angebrochen.

In der ersten Phase kam es zu politischen Einschränkungen, weil Korea die Unabhängigkeit als souveränes Land verloren hatte. Der japanische Imperialismus bestimmte nicht nur das politische System, sondern auch alle anderen Bereiche, wie etwa Erziehung und Kultur. Der Gebrauch der koreanischen Sprache wurde verboten. Seit dem 1. März 1919 gab es eine landesweite organisierte Unabhängigkeitsbewegung. Dabei spielten religiöse Führungsfiguren eine grosse Rolle. Donghak, die indigene Religion in Korea, Buddhisten und Christen waren dabei federführend. Als diese Unabhängigkeitsbewegung brutal niedergeschlagen wurde, verlagerte sie sich ins Ausland. Aufgrund der Kolonialherrschaft gab es eine provisorische koreanische Regierung in China, die seit 1919 als Zentrum der Unabhängigkeitsbestrebungen fungierte.

Das Wachstum des Christentums hat in der ersten Phase mit der japanischen Kolonialisierungsperiode zu tun. Es ist nicht einfach, allgemein etwas dazu zu sagen, wie die Kirche sich in jener Zeit gegenüber der Politik verhalten hat. Wenn auch die Verhaltensweisen von Missionar*innen jeweils sehr unterschiedlich waren, wurde die Haltung, dass auf die japanische Regierung nicht reagiert werden sollte, von einem grossen Teil der Missionar*innen geteilt. Die Kirche sollte apolitisch bleiben. Die Zwei-Reiche-Lehre wurde wortwörtlich genommen. Von der Politik Distanz zu halten wurde eine Tugend unter Christ*innen und die Trennung zwischen Politik und Kirche war allgemeingültig geworden.

Trotz zahlreicher Unabhängigkeitsbewegungen und -bemühungen ist die Befreiung des Landes leider nicht von innen, sondern von aussen durch die UdSSR und die USA erfolgt. Als diese grossen Länder den 2. Weltkrieg zu einem Ende bringen wollten, hatten sie in den *Yalta Agreements* Korea einfach zweigeteilt.

3 Vgl. Meehyun Chung, Die Werke des Dichters Dong-Ju Yun und der Einfluss der christlichen Bildung an der Yonsei Universität, in: Interkulturelle Theologie 40/4 (2014), 40. Jg., 303–345.

Aufgrund dieser willkürlichen Teilung des Landes durch die UdSSR und die USA war die Spannung im Kontext des Kalten Krieges vorprogrammiert und hatte sich bald verschärft. Insofern ist die Befreiung des Landes nicht vollkommen erfüllt. Das Joch für Korea war nach wie vor schwer, es war von der japanischen Herrschaft in andere Hände übergegangen. Die Opfer der japanischen Herrschaft waren nun Opfer des Kalten Kriegs geworden, während Japan vom Täter zum Opfer der nuklearen Bombardierung in Hiroshima und Nagasaki geworden ist.

Der Koreakrieg als Stellvertreterkrieg der beiden Grossmächte wurde im Jahr 1953 durch eine Waffenstillstandsvereinbarung provisorisch beendet. Sie beinhaltet, dass der Krieg jederzeit neu ausbrechen kann. Diese Unsicherheit konnte als Legitimation der Dominanz des Militärs dienen. Dem Sicherheitsgesetz des Landes wurde grosser Wert beigemessen, um angeblich das Land zu schützen, aber es fungierte auch als Mechanismus der Unterdrückung, um Oppositionelle zu kontrollieren und bei Gelegenheit zu erpressen. Die Demonstrationen von Student*innen und Bürger*innen für eine gerechte Demokratie wurden brutal niedergeschlagen, so beispielsweise jene zwischen dem 19. April 1960 und dem 18. Mai 1980 sowie am 10. Juni 1987. Trotz der unmenschlichen Unterdrückung durch das Militär haben die Bürger*inneninitiativen durch Zivilcourage der Demokratie zum Sieg verholfen.

Die vom Volk direkt gewählte Regierung ist seit Februar 1993 im Amt. Das heißt, die Geschichte der Demokratie ist relativ kurz. Eine Praxis der demokratischen Verwirklichung fehlt in der geschichtlichen Entwicklung, wenn auch die diktatorische Herrschaft zu Ende ging. Das schnelle wirtschaftliche Wachstum hatte viele Nebenwirkungen. Das Wirtschaftssystem ist von Mega-Konglomeraten beherrscht, während Mittel- und Kleinunternehmen wenig Chancen haben. Der Schock, 1997 unter die Kontrolle des *International Monetary Fund* zu geraten, und die ökonomische Krise von 2008 führten zu einer noch größeren Kluft zwischen Armen und Reichen. Während dieser Krisenzeit sind zahlreiche Menschen in Konkurs geraten.

Die kirchliche Szene stellt sich nicht viel anders dar und ist ähnlich wie das Wirtschaftssystem strukturiert. Die grossen Kirchen sind sehr gross, während die kleinen Kirchen nicht viel Chance zum Überleben hatten. Wie in einem grossen Wirtschaftskonglomerat wurden die Megakirchen als Familienbetrieb geführt.

Was das kirchliche Wirken in die Politik hinein betrifft, hat sich die Szene seit den 1990er Jahren verändert. Unter der Diktatur waren die Mehrheitskirchen eher schweigsam. Die sozialkritischen Kirchen hingegen sind zahlenmässig nicht stark gewachsen. Die numerisch grossen Kirchen sind in Bezug auf gesellschaftliche Stellungnahmen nach wie vor eher konservativ. Dies zeigte sich in der Amtsenthebungsanklage gegen die frühere Staatspräsidentin, als die Demonstrant*innen in zwei Flügel gespalten waren: zum einen hat die Nationalflagge (*Taeggki*) denjenigen Flügel symbolisiert, der mehr mit den USA alliiert ist und den konservativen Kirchen nahe steht. Zum anderen sind die kerzenhaltenden Demonstranten (*candlelight-rallies*) für die Demokratie eingetreten. Es zeigt sich ein Kontrast zwischen sich von der Gesellschaft abschottenden Christ*innen und gesellschaftsoffenen.

Mein theologisches Konzept als Selbstpositionierung[4]

Ich bin in eine christliche Familie hinein geboren. Das ist keine selbstverständliche Sache in Korea, aber auch keine Seltenheit. Mein Grossvater väterlicherseits hat während der japanischen Besatzungszeit am 15. April 1930 eine Kirche auf dem Land gestiftet, während meine Grossmutter mütterlicherseits eine konvertierte Christin war. In meiner Kindheit habe ich nichts anderes als christliche Kultur innerhalb meiner Familie erlebt, hingegen war die Umgebung und Nachbarschaft von anderen Religionen wie Schamanismus, Buddhismus und Konfuzianismus geprägt.

Dank meinem Pfarrer, der meine Eltern getraut und mich und meine Geschwister getauft und konfirmiert hat, gab es in meiner Gemeinde viele Gäste aus Europa, da er Zentralausschussmitglied des Ökumenischen Rates der Kirchen war. Viele europäische Theologen besuchten meine Gemeinde, die zugleich als ein ökumenisches Zentrum galt. Dadurch konnte ich mich frühzeitig für deutschsprachige Theologie interessieren. Einer dieser Besucher aus Europa war mein späterer Doktorvater Professor Jan Milič Lochman.

Seine Predigt hat mich dazu inspiriert, seine Schriften zu studieren. Danach habe ich mich entschlossen, bei ihm in Basel meine Kenntnisse der reformierten Theologie zu vertiefen. Sein Bezug zur (damaligen) Tschechoslowakei, bzw. zum

4 Diesen Teil entnehme ich in leicht revidierter Fassung aus dem folgenden Aufsatz: Meehyun Chung, Von den koreanischen Gebetsbergen in die Schweizer Alpen, in: Bärbel Fünfsinn/Gabriele Mayer (Hg.), Gender und religiöse Bildung weltweit, Frankfurt a. M. 2009, 33–35.

heutigen Tschechien, war für mich besonders interessant, denn Südkorea hatte bis dahin keine diplomatischen Beziehungen zu seinem Vaterland. Die osteuropäischen Länder galten für uns als Feinde, weil sie im Koreakrieg mit Nordkorea alliiert waren. In meiner Schulausbilung, die sehr einseitig antikommunistisch orientiert war, gab es immer Vorurteile und Fehlinformationen zu diesen Ostblockländern, als ob sie Monster mit Hörnern wären.

Das Thema meiner Dissertation lautete »Karl Barth, Josef Lukl Hromádka und Korea«.[5] Dabei ging es um das Verständnis von Offenbarung und Geschichte im Denken Karl Barths im Vergleich mit dem Offenbarungs- und Geschichtsverständnis Josef Lukl Hromádkas in Bezug auf ihre jeweilige theologische und politische Tätigkeit.

Der Inhalt meiner Forschung hat mit meinen Kindheitserfahrungen zu tun. In Korea war und ist immer wieder die Rede von privaten Offenbarungserfahrungen. Nicht nur das Christentum, auch die koreanische indigene Religion wie Donghak oder die buddhistische Maitreya-Ideologie haben mit Offenbarung im allgemeinen Sinne zu tun. Die Gründer der vielen Mythen und Religionen sehen sich als Erscheinungen des göttlichen Wesens. »Offenbarung« wird deshalb sehr häufig gebraucht, und wurde in vielen sektiererischen Bewegungen auf pervertierte Weise auch missbraucht.

Die Legitimation der Gründer und Führer durch den Verweis auf die geoffenbarte und sie beauftragende Gottheit führte zu Abhängigkeitsverhältnissen bei ihren Anhänger*innen. Der Ursprung meines Interesses am Begriff der Offenbarung lag in den Erfahrungen meiner Großmutter auf den Gebetsbergen in Korea, wo sich überwiegend Frauen zum intensiven Gebet versammelten. Wenn sie innerfamiliäre Probleme oder Anliegen hatten, beteten sie inbrünstig. Im Traum oder in mystischen Erfahrungen meinten sie, von der Gottheit geoffenbarte Antworten zu erhalten.

Zuerst setzte ich mich in meiner Dissertation mit den großen männlichen Theologen und ihrer Rezeption auseinander. Während des Studiums in Basel lernte ich durch meinen Ko-Referenten Martin Anton Schmidt auch die Frauenmystik des Mittelalters, bspw. von Hildegard von Bingen, kennen. Später habe ich mich vertieft mit der Interpretation von Dorothee Sölle in »Mystik und Widerstand« befasst. Ohne meine eigene Richtung und Linie, die von Karl Barth geprägt ist, zu verlieren, habe ich die Ansätze von Rudolf Bultmann und Sölle

5 Meehyun Chung, Karl Barth, Josef Lukl Hromádka, Korea, Berlin 1995.

adaptiert. So sah ich mich mit der Grundsatzfrage konfrontiert, wie man am besten mit Offenbarungserfahrungen umgehen darf und kann. Was heißt Offenbarung im biblischen und theologischen Sinne? Inwiefern sind mystische Erfahrungen legitim? Wie kann man die Beliebigkeit solcher Erfahrungen beurteilen?

Um meine Schlussfolgerung vorwegzunehmen: Individuelle Erfahrungen und besonders Frauen-Erfahrungen sind hoch zu schätzen, aber m. E. darf es nicht übertrieben werden. Auch die koreanische feministische Theologie ist von Frauenerfahrungen ausgehend entwickelt worden. Aber Erfahrung ist relativ. Wegen dieser Beliebigkeit sollte die Erfahrung nicht verabsolutiert werden.

Mit diesem Hintergrund habe ich mich in Basel bei Lochman vertieft mit Karl Barth befasst, über den ich schon in Korea bei meiner Professorin Soonkyung Park viel gelernt hatte. Als ich nach fast siebenjährigem Studium der Theologie Barths 1995 die Stadt Basel verliess, warnte mich einer meiner europäischen Kollegen: »Du brauchst doch nicht Karl Barths Theologie zu verteidigen!«[6] Ohne den koreanischen Kontext zu kennen, wusste er, was passieren würde. Seine Warnung war berechtigt. Als ich heimkam, wurde ich von feministischen Kreisen kritisiert, ich sei nicht feministisch genug, denn ich hatte die Theologie des weißen männlichen Europäers Karl Barth, der als Misogynist galt, studiert. Vermutlich glaubten sie, ich sei durch Barths Theologie »getauft« und negativ beeinflusst worden. Es war für mich am Anfang in Korea fast nicht möglich, etwas über die Barthsche Theologie zu sagen, denn es herrschte vor allem bei Theologinnen ein sehr negatives Bild derselben vor. Woher kam dieses Vorurteil, das mich, noch bevor ich den Mund aufgemacht hatte, als »Barthianerin« abstempelte und ich somit keine »Feministin« sein konnte?

Kritische Stimmen zur Barthschen Theologie kamen nicht nur von Theologinnen, sondern auch von den anderen Gruppierungen. Ein negatives Vorurteil zu korrigieren ist schwieriger als eine völlig neue Idee einzubringen. Es war schwierig, über Barth zu diskutieren, denn Barth wird, aus gewissen Gründen, in Korea weithin negativ gesehen, auch wenn seine Bücher nicht gelesen werden. Die konservativen Theologen, die politisch rechts orientiert sind, sind der Meinung, Barth sei sehr politisch gewesen, und seine Theologie sei so liberal und radikal, dass sie die Kirchen Europas in den Ruin geführt habe. Die politisch und theologisch linksradikal progressiven Theologen hingegen finden Barths Gedanken

6 Vgl. Meehyun Chung, Mein Verständnis der Theologie Karl Barths, in: Dies., Reis und Wasser. Eine Feministische Theologie in Korea, Berlin 2012, 211.

und Methoden so konservativ, dass sie geradezu die Orthodoxie wieder aufleben liessen, bzw. eine neue Orthodoxie einführten. Sie kritisierten Barths Lehre über Gott als das »totaliter aliter – das ganz andere«. Er sehe Gott als einen, der allein im Himmel throne und sich nicht um die Probleme der Welt kümmere. Nach Ansicht der Feministinnen wiederum ist Barths Theologie misogynisch, wie oben erwähnt. Für Theologinnen allgemein ist Barth keine besonders sympathische Figur. Sie sind der Ansicht, die autoritäre Struktur seiner Theologie lasse keinen Raum für die Würde der Frauen. Die meisten feministischen Theologinnen erinnern sich nur an bestimmte wiederholt zitierte Sätze zur formalen Ordnung zwischen Mann und Frau aus Barths Kirchlicher Dogmatik (III/4), ohne den Zusammenhang zu erkennen.[7] Über diese Passage äussern sie sich sehr sarkastisch.[8] Weitere Diskussionen werden dadurch gleichzeitig blockiert.

Meine theologische Position hat ihre Basis in der schweizerisch reformierten Tradition, die ich mit feministischen Ansätzen verbinde. Barth ist derjenige, der das reformatorische Erbe im 20. Jahrhundert am effizientesten neu konzipiert hat. Es geht darum, dass Gott von Gott her erkannt werden kann. Die relative Sache darf nicht verabsolutiert werden, um die Gefahr des Götzendienstes zu bannen. Die Offenbarung ist das Subjekt der Geschichte und die Geschichte ist das Prädikat der Offenbarung. »Offenbarung ist nicht ein Prädikat der Geschichte, sondern Geschichte ist ein Prädikat der Offenbarung.«[9] Viele Dinge könnten an der Stelle des Prädikats eingesetzt werden, aber nicht umgekehrt.

Mein theologisches Axiom und andere Konzepte im koreanischen Kontext[10]

Korea hatte bereits eine sehr lange Tradition von Schriftreligionen wie Buddhismus und Konfuzianismus. Dies war ein Grund, warum die Bibel als Kanon akzeptiert wurde, als das Christentum zunächst als westliche Wissenschaft ins

7 Karl Barth, Die Kirchliche Dogmatik, III/4, Zürich 1993, 188ff.

8 Vgl. Chung, Mein Verständnis, 211.

9 Karl Barth, Die Kirchliche Dogmatik I/2, Zürich 1987, 64.

10 Diesen Teil habe ich mit Änderungen übernommen aus: Meehyun Chung, Calvinism in Korea without Calvin. A women's perspective, in: Christoph Stückelberger/Reinhold Bernhardt (Hg.), Calvin Global. How Faith Influences Societies (Globethics.net Series No. 3), Geneva 2009, 195–204, siehe https://www.globethics.net/documents/4289936/13403236/GlobalSeries_3_CalvinGlobal_text.pdf/ (12.4.2021).

Land kam. Das Lesen der Bibel hat wesentlich zur Alphabetisierung der Bevölkerung v. a. der Frauen beigetragen, als die Geschichten der Bibel mündlich durch Bibel-Frauen verbreitet wurden.

In einer sozial und politisch durch imperialistische Expansionsmächte bedrohten, hoffnungslosen Situation im 19. Jahrhundert begann die protestantische Mission. Diese Missionstätigkeit bot mit der Verkündigung des Evangeliums neue Hoffnung, nämlich jene auf das Reich Gottes. Sie brachte eine gewisse Befreiung von der Unterwerfung unter die alten gesellschaftlichen und kulturellen Konventionen und war eine Quelle der Kraft in einer Situation der Resignation. Eine klare Änderung der Lebenspraxis und der Lebensorientierung bei den Christ*innen war spürbar. In diesem Sinne hat die Mission in Korea die Modernisierung beschleunigt. Die dreifache konventionelle Missionstätigkeit in den Bereichen Bildung, Evangelisation und Heilung/Gesundheit funktionierte ausserordentlich gut. Zahlreiche christliche Schulen, Krankenhäuser sowie die Frauenbewegungen sind einige positive Beispiele von aus der Missionstätigkeit hervorgegangenen Neuerungen. Deshalb muss das Ergebnis der Missionstätigkeit differenziert bewertet werden.

Was die theologische Prägung betrifft, lässt sich weniger Positives sagen. Auf dem Hintergrund der Missionstätigkeit entstand eine »made-in-USA-Kirche«. Damit meine ich ein puritanisch und fundamentalistisch geprägtes Christentum. Der Presbyterianismus, der in Korea mit etwa 69 % die grosse Mehrheit der protestantischen Kirchen stellt, und der bei Huldrych Zwingli und Jean Calvin eigentlich theologisch im Mittelpunkt steht, ist – in vielen Punkten pervertiert – von der Schweiz über Holland, Schottland und die USA nach Korea gekommen. Martin Luther ist allgemein viel bekannter als die Schweizer Reformatoren. Calvin ist dabei differenzierter vorgestellt worden als Zwingli. Es wäre wichtig, den Ursprung der schweizerischen Reformation direkt zu erforschen und die Kenntnis Zwinglis und Calvins auch von den Urtexten her und mit Blick auf das historische Umfeld zu vertiefen, anstatt einfach den amerikanischen Calvinismus zu adaptieren. Mit amerikanischem Calvinismus meine ich den puritanisch geprägten Fundamentalismus, der auf der *Westminster Confession* gründet. Diese Confession wurde von der ersten koreanischen presbyterianischen Synode 1907 als Grundlage der Kirche anerkannt.

Calvin und der Calvinismus wurden sehr gegensätzlich gesehen. Die calvinistische Lehre von der doppelten Prädestination hat in Korea verhängnisvolle Auswirkungen gehabt. Dies hat mit der Moralisierung zu tun, die mit der traditionellen Denkweise, in der das Gute gefördert und das Böse bestraft wird, verbunden wurde. Sie wurde gegenüber ideologisch Andersdenkenden und religiös Andersgläubigen immer als dualistisches Modell mit Freund- und Feindbild gebraucht. »Glaube an Jesus führt zum Himmel, Nichtglaube an Jesus führt zur Hölle«. Dieses Motto, das mit Calvin inhaltlich nichts zu tun hat, wurde dennoch als der Segen-Verfluchung-Mechanismus aus Calvins Einfluss verstanden. Er wurde bei Strassenevangelisationen sehr häufig gepredigt und war auch zwischen den Denominationen von Bedeutung. Wer von der Angst vor der Hölle ausgeht, kann vom Gefühl der Sünde und von der Furcht vor Strafe nie befreit werden. Dieser Gedanke hat die blinde Akzeptanz eines ungerechten sozialen Systems, blinden Antikommunismus und die Bereitschaft, andere zu diffamieren, innerhalb des Christentums tendenziell gefördert. Strukturelle Sünde wurde beschränkt wahrgenommen, während Reichtum verherrlicht und Armut verflucht wurde.

Die schweizerische reformierte Theologie und ihren grundlegenden Texte vertieft zu lesen und kontextgemäss zu interpretieren bleibt unsere Aufgabe, wie Karl Barth es zu seiner Zeit getan hat. Dies hiesse z. B. die Erwählungslehre zu erneuern, anstatt sie kritiklos zu repetieren. Aufgrund der kulturellen Prägung, die sich aus der koreanischen Religiosität ergeben hat, ist das lutherische Schema von Gesetz und Evangelium einfacher zu akzeptieren als der reformierte Ansatz vom Evangelium zum Gesetz. Das Sich-ans-Gesetz-Halten und die Kumulation der guten Werke ist ein Grundschema des religiösen Kontextes, das nicht das Evangelium als befreiende Kraft unterstreicht.

Zuversicht in Gott hat mit Unterwürfigkeit vor grosser weltlicher Macht eigentlich nichts zu tun. Aber durch die amerikanische Missionswelle wurde Amerika als solches an die Stelle von grosser Macht gesetzt. Das nordamerikanisch orientierte Christentum wird als Gottes Segen verstanden, und das Evangelium und Segen werden mit materiellem Wohlstand gleichgesetzt. Die Angst vor der Strafe Gottes ist mit der Angst vor der grossen Macht Amerikas verbunden. So ist auch die Unterwürfigkeit gegenüber Gott an die Unterwürfigkeit des Christentums gegenüber Amerika gebunden. Fundamentalistisch orientierte konservative Christen haben diese Tendenz, sodass politische Selbstbestimmung und politisches Selbstbewusstsein nicht gefördert werden. Die Tendenz, sich an Gott anzulehnen, um von der eigenen Angst und von den eigenen Problemen wegzukommen, ist von der Anlehnungs- und Abhängigkeitstendenz gegenüber Amerika nicht zu trennen. Damit wird wirtschaftliche und politische Unabhängigkeit Koreas von Amerika nicht gefördert.

Das Christentum brachte einerseits Befreiung für die Frauen, welche in frauenverachtenden Traditionen und Religionen in Korea lebten. Aber andererseits ist eine andere und neue Unterdrückung der Frauen innerhalb des Christentums und der christlichen Kirchen entstanden. Daher zeigen sich Gegensätze und Widersprüche, wenn man die Folgen der Einführung des Christentums näher betrachtet: Zwar war die Emanzipation der Frauen eine gewisse positive Folge derselben, doch blieb diese Befreiung leider unvollendet und einseitig. Männerherrschaft in der Kirche und Theologie ist nach wie vor viel dominanter.[11]

Westlicher Patriarchalismus und calvinistisch geprägter Puritanismus konnten gut an den koreanischem Patriarchalismus anschliessen. Die patriarchalische koreanische Tradition und die patriarchalische Prägung der Missionstätigkeit sind mit Formen des koreanischen Christentums vermischt und dadurch gefestigt worden. Dies hatte innerhalb des Christentums sehr starke Auswirkungen, sodass ein neues patriarchales System verankert wurde.

Wie die Weltkirchengeschichte gezeigt hat, haben die Frauen bei der Etablierung der Kirche in Korea eine ungeheuer wichtige Rolle gespielt. Die Hingabe der koreanischen Christinnen, die »Bibel-Frauen« oder »Evangelistinnen« genannt wurden, zum kirchlichen Engagement war für die Ausbreitung des Christentums wichtiger als der Erfolg der sogenannten Neviusmethode (self-propagation, self-goverment, self-support).[12] Sie haben mit grosser Leidenschaft Häuser besucht, um das Evangelium auf ganz einfache Weise zu verkündigen und kirchliche Lieder sowie die biblische Geschichte bekannt zu machen.

Diese Frauen haben viel zum Aufbau der Gemeinde beigetragen. Aber sie wurden im Vergleich zu den Pfarrern gesellschaftlich nicht sehr hoch angesehen und bekamen viel weniger Anerkennung und Lohn, obwohl sie viel härter gearbeitet hatten als die Pfarrer. Schon damals wurden die Frauen innerhalb der Kirche nicht gleichwertig behandelt. Nach der Etablierung der Kirchen wurden die Frauen von Leitungsfunktion ausgeschlossen. Es war ihnen nur erlaubt, arbeitsam, gehorsam, bibelkundig und grosszügig für freiwillige Arbeit in der Diakonie da zu sein.

11 Vgl. Meehyun Chung, Mission Impossible!? Zwischen Evangelisation und Emanzipation in Südkorea, ZMiss, 1–2 (2006), 147–148.

12 Yung-Jae Kim, Der Protestantismus in Korea und die calvinistische Tradition. Eine geschichtliche Untersuchung über Entstehung und Entwicklung der Presbyterianischen Kirche in Korea, Frankfurt am Main 1981, 43–47.

In die Kirchenordnung wurden einfach der Calvinismus und die Ämterlehre Calvins wörtlich übernommen, ohne dass man sich mit deren historischem oder kontextuellem Hintergrund befasst hätte. Dabei spielte die konfuzianische Tradition mit, in der einfach die Meinungen und die Lehren der grossen Lehrer auswendig gelernt werden. So wurde calvinistische Lehre einfach, ohne kritisches Hinterfragen, übernommen. Wenn man unter Calvinismus amerikanischen Puritanismus versteht, der ja durch US-Missionar*innen fundamentalistischer Prägung ins Land eingepflanzt worden ist, so ist er sehr gut in die konfuzianische Struktur integriert worden. Die von Calvin vorgegebene Ämter-Struktur wurde nicht funktional, sondern als Stufenleiter verstanden. Diese Hierarchisierung hat dazu geführt, dass Frauen von höheren Leitungspositionen mit Entscheidungsmacht ausgeschlossen sind und nur in dienenden Sektoren eingesetzt werden. Und so ist ein besonderes Amt geschaffen worden, eingeschoben zwischen Ältesten und Diakonen, für Frauen, die sich mit hingebungsvoller, treuer Arbeit zu Gotteslohn hervorgetan haben. Darüber hinaus hat auch die Tendenz, die Bibel wortwörtlich literarisch zu akzeptieren, ohne sie textkritisch, kulturkritisch oder historisch-kritisch zu hinterfragen, mit dieser religiösen Kultur zu tun. Viele frauenfeindliche Bibelstellen, die kontextgebunden sind, wurden wortwörtlich repetiert und direkt zitiert. Dadurch hat die Bibel ideologisch zur Ungleichheit der Geschlechter beigetragen.

All diese Dinge haben mit dem Verständnis der Allmacht Gottes zu tun, welches verhindert hat, dass Gott als Gott in Beziehung verstanden werden kann. Der Pfarrer hat als Verkündiger von Gottes Wort Autorität. Daher ist die Kirche pfarrerzentriert geworden und in den Gemeinden konnte sich keine Basisdemokratie entwickeln. Die Gefahr der Ruhmsucht eines Menschen und des Personenkultes ist ziemlich hoch. Ein Pfarrer, der selber eine Gemeinde gegründet und zahlenmässig Erfolg hat, wird hoch geehrt, obwohl Calvin selber ja sogar die Lage seines Grabes geheim gehalten wissen wollte, um sich vor der Verehrung durch Menschen zu schützen. Die calvinistische hierarchische Kirchenordnung hat mit dem Calvinismus zu tun, nicht mit Calvin selbst.[13] Das zeigt dieses Beispiel einer einseitigen und unzureichenden Interpretation der reformierten Theologie.

Wo befinden sich nun die Frauen in der Gesellschaft und der Kirche in Korea? Tendenziell spielen die Frauen mittlerweile wichtige Rollen in Gesellschaft

13 Vgl. Chung, Calvinism in Korea, 202–203.

und Politk, wenn auch die Quote noch immer nicht ausreichend ist. Hingegen übernehmen sie in der Kirche nicht die entscheidenden Rollen. Die Kirche oder religiöse Gemeinschaften bleiben die letzte Bastion des Patriarchalismus. Persönlich orientierte Frömmigkeit und jenseitsorientierte Haltung des Glaubens sind immer noch allgemeiner Stil im kirchlichen Umfeld. Was sagt die Minjung-Theologie dazu, wie solche gesellschaftlichen Probleme zu lösen sind?

Minjung-Theologie hat weltweit eine Art der koreanischen Befreiungstheologie bekannt gemacht.[14] Hingegen ist die Akzeptanz innerhalb des Landes nicht so signifikant. Wenn ich die koreanische Kirche in aller Kürze vorstellen würde, würde ich drei Richtungen erwähnen: Die eine Gruppe orientiert sich an Gott dem Vater, eine andere an Jesus Christus als Befreier und die letzte an der Heiligen Geistkraft. Die erste Gruppe – sie bildet die Mehrheit unter den Protestanten – ist religiös stark nordostasiatisch, d. h. konfuzianisch und taoistisch geprägt. Die zweite Gruppe tendiert zu sozio-politischem Engagement, indem sie Jesus als gegenüber dem römischen Imperialismus politisch handelnde Person versteht. Bei der dritten Gruppe steht die Heilige Geistkraft, als Heiler und Glücksbringer verstanden, im Mittelpunkt. Ihre Theologie ist primär die Theologie der Prosperität.[15]

Der Minjung-Theologe[16] Byungmu Ahn hebt die Wichtigkeit der koreanischen Schriftsprache hervor. Während die führende Schicht mehr an chinesischer Schrift und Literalität orientiert war, hatte das einfache Volk – Minjung – mit der koreanischen Schriftsprache und Oralität zu tun. Das koreanische Alphabet wurde Minjungschrift.[17] In der traditionellen sozialen Minjung-Bewegung wird diese »mündliche Schrift« viel gebraucht, weil es durch sie möglich ist, formlos, rasch und unauffällig die Stimmen von unten zum Ausdruck zu bringen. Im

14 Zum neusten Stand der Minjung Theologie siehe Sangchul Lee et al., Minjung Theology. Reading the Age of Pain, Seoul 2018; Jinkwan Kwon, Minjung Theology and Arts, Seoul 2018; Hiheon Kim, For a Minjung Theology as Political Panentheism, Seoul 2014.

15 Vgl. Chung, Reis und Wasser, 23.

16 Innerhalb der Minjung-Theologie existiert auch ein Werteunterschied zwischen geschriebener Theologie und theologisch orientierter Bewegung. Dies zeigt, dass die Schriftlichkeit in der Minjung-Theologie nicht immer die gleiche Bedeutung hat. Die Texte können je nach angelegten Maß und Deutung einen performativen Effekt haben. Die Theologie wird überwiegend von Männern betrieben, während die Bewegung überwiegend von Frauen und im diakonischen Bereich Tätigen getragen ist. Über minjungdiakonische Arbeit und Bewegung siehe https://m.cafe.daum.net/kordiakonia/_rec?boardType=M (29. März, 2020).

17 Vgl. Byungmu Ahn, Draußen vor dem Tor: Kirche und Minjung in Korea. Theologische Beiträge und Reflexionen (hg. v. Winfried Glüer), Göttingen 1986, 87.

Unterschied zu den Gelehrten, die die chinesische Schrift beherrschten und sich der chinesischen Kultur anpassten, hat die Minjung-Schicht daher mehr von der eigenen koreanischen Kulturidentität bewahrt.[18]

Byungmu Ahn unterstreicht die Bedeutung der »mündlichen Schrift« für das Leben der Kirche und sieht eine Parallele mit der Sprache Jesu. Er macht deutlich, dass die Sprache Jesu, besonders die der Gleichnisse, typische Minjungsprache ist. Der Ursprung dieser Sprache basiert nicht auf der Kirche oder der Schule, sondern im gemeinsamen Leben Jesu mit dem »*ochlos* (dem einfachen Volk)«, in der Identifikation Jesu mit dem Minjung.[19]

In der Realität haben sich jedoch viele Minjungkirchen – Kirchen, die sich mit Minjung identifizieren wollten – nicht an Minjung-Theologie orientiert, sondern an der Prosperitätstheologie. Minjung hat sich nicht sehr für strukturelle Sünde interessiert, weil das alltägliche Management des Lebens viel dringender war als soziopolitische Belange. Für diejenigen, die leiden und in Armut leben, würde es nicht ausreichen, einfach über das Kreuz und die Erlösung von der Sünde zu predigen. Prosperität im Blick auf den materiellen Erfolg ist viel wichtiger zum Leben, wenn dies auch manchmal wie ein Opium wirkte. Deshalb ist die Prosperitätstheologie viel attraktiver als die trockenen Dogmen der Mainline-Kirchen. Optimistische Trostworte als dreifaches Segenswort für seelische Heilung, körperliche Gesundheit und materiellen Wohlstand in einem vielfältig schwierigen Umfeld sind akzeptabler als theologische Überlegungen und Reflexionen. Diese Menschen sehnen sich nach Wundern im wortwörtlichen Sinne.[20] Young-Hoon Lee, Yonggi Chos Nachfolger bei der Yoido Full Gospel Gemeinde, macht es plausibel:

> »The Minjung theology movement is so concerned about the poor and the oppressed. However, the social activities of the Minjung movement and the Yoido Full Gospel Church are quite different. The former focuses on social participation and the reform of society like the liberation movement, while the Yoido Full Gospel Church is more concerned about charity and the direct relief for the poor.«[21]

18 Vgl. a. a. O., 88–89.

19 Vgl. Byungmu Ahn, History and Interpretation, Chunan 1998, 34, 304.

20 Young-Hoon Lee ist nicht der leibliche Sohn von David Cho, dem Begründer der Full Gospel Church. Er ist sein »spiritueller« Sohn. Wie in vielen anderen Kirchen in Korea ist er als eine dem Gründer sehr nahestehende Person sein Nachfolger geworden.

21 Young-Hoon Lee, The Holy Spirit Movement in Korea. Its Historical and Doctrinal Development, Oxford 2009, 115.

Die pentekostale Kirche hat materiell arme Menschen stärker angezogen und konkrete Hilfe einschließlich einer optimistischen Denkweise angeboten, während die Minjungtheologie und die daraus entstandene Bewegung eher eine NGO-artige Bewegung geblieben ist. Die letztere hat sich zwar um die strukturelle Sünde gekümmert, aber es hat nicht dazu ausgereicht, das numerische Wachstum der Mitgliederzahl der christlichen Gemeinde zu erhöhen.

Hingegen sind die pentekostal orientierten Kirchen zahlenmässig gewachsen, aber nicht im Geist der sozial gemeinnützigen Orientierung. Das Bewusstsein im Blick auf soziale Belange hat sich deshalb nicht stark verändert.[22] Individuelle Erlösung und Seelenheil sind wichtiger als gemeinschaftliche Orientierung. Deshalb wird die Beziehung zu Gott nur als private Angelegenheit verstanden. Ökumenische Weite oder horizontale Erweiterung werden nicht stark gewichtet.[23]

Minjung hat mit den sozioökonomischen Klassen zu tun. Inzwischen hat sich die wirtschaftliche Lage geändert. Diejenigen, die früher zu den Unterdrückten gehörten, sind inzwischen Unterdrücker geworden, wenn auch nicht alle. Klassenwechsel passiert ständig. Die sozialen Verhältnisse ändern sich je nach Kontext. Das beinhaltet Beliebigkeit und Relativität von Minjung. Jesus ist Minjung. Aber Minjung darf nicht als Jesus definiert sein. Das Verhältnis zwischen Subjekt und Prädikat sollte in diesem Sinne bestehen bleiben.

Eine Schwäche der Minjungtheologie ist, dass sie das Genderthema ausser Acht gelassen hat. Minjungtheologie hat sich mit dem Thema der Ungleichheit befasst. Dennoch blieb sie einseitig, weil das Geschlechtsverhältnis nicht berücksichtigt wurde. Minjung ist ein genderneutraler Begriff. Frauen unter den Minjung sind die Unterdrücktesten unter den Unterdrückten.

Der Ausgangspunkt der feministischen Theologie in Korea war eine Bewegung unter theologisch gebildeten Frauen, die einen Theologinnenverein gegründet hatten, um die Ungleichheit der Geschlechter kritisch zu hinterfragen und ins Bewusstsein zu rufen. Zunächst ging es um die Rezeption der europäischen und nordamerikanischen feministischen Theologie. Bald danach konzentrierten sie sich auf die eigene indigene Sache und den eigenen Kontext; u. a. Wiedervereinigung, Trostfrauen, Koreanische Kultur und Religiosität wie Schamanismus,

22 Siehe Allan H. Anderson, Global Pentecostalism in the New Millennium, in: Ders./Walter J. Hollenweger, Pentecostals After a Century. Global Perspectives on a Movement in Transition, London 1999, 210.

23 Vgl. Meehyun Chung, Korean Pentecostalism and the Preaching of Prosperity, in: Religionswissenschaft. Die Zeitschrift für Missionswissenschaft und Religionswissenschaft, 99 (2015), 286–287.

Buddhismus und Konfuzianismus, Migration, um nur einige Stichworte zu nennen. In diesem Sinne versucht feministische Reflexion kollektiv gesellschaftlichen Zusammenhängen Aufmerksamkeit zu schenken; allerdings ist sie bis jetzt nicht weit verbreitet.

Die dritte Generation der Minjungtheologie versucht, sich erneut mit anderen Themen auseinanderzusetzen, wie Geschlechtergerechtigkeit, mit dem Thema der Prozesstheologie, der Umweltethik usw. In der ersten Generation der Minjungtheologie wurde die sozioökonomische Situation eher eindimensional bewältigt. Inzwischen ist der Kontext viel komplexer geworden, sodass man Themen multidimensional angehen muss. Diese kontextgebundene Theologie ist als praxisorientierte Bewegung zu verstehen, die mit NGOs und verschiedenen diakonischen Aufgaben in Verbindung steht, anstatt nur als Theorie zu wirken.

Schlussfolgerung: Die Überwindung des dualistischen Ansatzes und der Verabsolutierung der menschlichen Belange

Nach dem 2. Weltkrieg haben viele Länder unter dem kolonialen Imperialismus gelitten, und viele Länder im globalen Süden wurden von internen Kriegen erschüttert, die mit dem kolonialen Erbe zusammenhingen. Dies war auch in Korea der Fall. Der ideologische Konflikt zwischen den grossen Mächten und dem Kommunismus und Antikommunismus im Kalten Krieg hat den Koreakrieg verursacht. Der Koreakrieg hat in vieler Hinsicht Spuren hinterlassen. Unter anderem wurden eine dualistische Denkweise und ein Schwarz-Weiss-Denken verbreitet. Das Freund-Feind-Schema ist in der Gesellschaft weit verbreitet. Die Kirche, die zahlenmässig überwiegend politisch rechts-konservativ orientiert ist, folgt diesem Muster. Dieser Dualismus wurde durch den Expansionseifer der Kirchen, die militant nach zahlenmäßigem Wachstum strebten, verbreitet.

Aufgrund der militärischen Spannungen zwischen den beiden Koreas gibt es immer wieder viele politische Vorfälle und Ereignisse. Sie stehen äusserlich immer noch hauptsächlich im Zusammenhang mit militaristischen Einrichtungen wie der US-Militärbasis in Pyeongtaek[24], der US-Marinenbasis im Dorf Gang-

24 Vgl. Chung, Reis und Wasser, 163.

jeong auf der Insel Jeju,[25] dem THAAD-Waffensystem (Terminal High Altitude Area Defense) in Sungju, um nur die wichtigsten Beispiele zu nennen.[26] Psychologisch wird damit das Feind-Freundschema zementiert – eine innere Dimension dieser Konflikte, die unsichtbar ist, aber dennoch gefährlich werden könnte. Feindschaft zu säen ist stärker und einfacher als Frieden zu stiften. Im evangelischen Kirchengesangbuch stehen beispielsweise viele militärisch geprägte Verse, weil der Sieg Jesu Christi über das Böse wortwörtlich verstanden wird. Solche Tendenzen beeinflussen die Kultur der Mehrheitskirchen allgemein.

Die progressiven Kirchen, die kleine Minderheiten sind, arbeiteten mit anderen Glaubensgemeinschaften zusammen und konzentrierten sich nicht auf militärische Lösungen, sondern auf die Herausforderung, wie Frieden gepflegt und das Leben gefördert werden kann. Um den Status quo der weltpolitischen Linie in Verbindung mit der Tendenz der koreanischen Abhängigkeit von der militaristischen Politik der USA aufrechtzuerhalten, bleibt Koreas tiefe Spaltung des Landes bestehen. Wenn der derzeitige Status eines »Waffenstillstandsabkommens« weder in ein Nichtangriffsabkommen noch in ein »dauerhaftes Friedensabkommen« geändert wird, bleibt die ständige Angst vor einem möglichen Krieg in Korea und einer Kultur der dualistischen Zerstörung bestehen.

Diese dominante Kultur der Feindschaft verhindert die Friedensförderung inklusive einer versöhnungsorientierten Verhaltensweise gegenüber anders denkenden, anders aussehenden und allgemein anderen Mitgeschöpfen auf der koreanischen Halbinsel. Diese besondere politische Krise und dieser besondere politische Kontext fördern eine Kultur des Militarismus und der ständigen Feindschaft. Aus Gründen der nationalen Sicherheit bleiben die demokratische Bewegung oder Fragen der ökologischen und ökonomischen Gerechtigkeit immer wieder zurück, wenn auch ein gewisser Fortschritt im Vergleich zu den 1970er und 1980er Jahren zu beobachten ist. Dennoch dominieren nach wie vor ein von Gier getriebenes Wirtschaftswachstum, Militärausgaben und Militärgeschäfte.

Die Spannung und der ideologische Konflikt zwischen Kommunismus und Antikommunismus ist sowohl in der Gesellschaft als auch bei den Kirchen immer noch vorhanden. Was ich heute in diesem politischen Kontext als die Bedeu-

25 Vgl. Meehyun Chung, Seeking the Lost Three fold Thoughts: Relationships with God, Earth and Human Beings, in: Madang. International Journal of Contextual Theology, 22/12 (2014), 128.

26 Vgl. Meehyun Chung, Regional approaches to eco-theology in Korea: Different Focuses and Emphasis, in: Dietrich Werner (Hg.), Kairos for Creation – Confessing Hope for the Earth, Solingen 2020, 152.

tung Zwinglis und Calvins für die Kirchen und die Christenheit hervorheben möchte, ist vor allem ihre christliche Sozialethik und ihre Betonung der Gemeinschaft mit Hilfe der Heiligen Geistkraft. Hier geht es nicht nur um die für Protestanten typischen emsig tüchtigen Lebensmuster, sondern um das Wirtschaftssystem. Calvins Lehre hat gewiss im positiven Sinne zu wirtschaftlichem Wachstum beigetragen. Insofern wurde bestätigt, was Max Weber in seiner These zu Calvinismus und Kapitalismus geschrieben hat. Aber die andere Wirtschaftsethik Calvins, wie sie seinerzeit Max Geiger hervorgehoben hat,[27] nämlich das Erkennen struktureller Sünde, die Parteinahme für die Armen und die starke Solidarität mit den sozial Schwachen sowie die Achtsamkeit auf den Gemeinnutz, sollen mehr unterstrichen werden. Die koreanischen Christ*innen stehen immer noch vor der Aufgabe, die Inkulturation, die Erweiterung des Glaubenshorizontes, d. h. eine über menschenzentrierten Heilsegoismus, Ego- und Familienzentrismus hinausschauende Perspektive und christliche Ethik in der Gesellschaft sowie eine Horizonterweiterung hin zur Ökumene zu vertreten. Dabei würde helfen, die reformierte Lehre und deren sozialen Hintergrund genauer anzuschauen und differenzierter zu interpretieren. Es geht nicht darum, ein allzeit gültiges Rezept zu finden zu versuchen, sondern sie in unsere Zeit und unseren Sitz im Leben zu übertragen und zu verwenden.

Durch weltweite Vernetzung könnten wir voneinander lernen und dabei eigene Schwächen und Stärken neu wahrnehmen, wenn auch verschiedene Formen und Normen nie eins zu eins verglichen oder übernommen werden könnten. Ein wichtiges Ziel der Begegnung ist doch, das gelebte Evangelium in anderen Kulturen kennen zu lernen. Dadurch könnten ökumenische Werte und Horizonte erweitert werden.

Aufgrund von Covid-19 wurden zudem die verborgenen Probleme der Sekten aufgedeckt. In der modernen Geschichte gab es viele verschiedene Sekten, die synkretistisch aus verschiedenen religiösen Komponenten geformt sind. Hier ist vor allem im Kontext von Covid-19 die Sekte Shinchongi zu nennen, die Neuer Himmel und neue Erde heisst. Sekten dieser Art, die inzwischen mehr als 300 000 Mitglieder zählen und sich als medizinisch beratungsresistent erwiesen, wurden in Südkorea zu Super-Spreadern. So auch eine andere Sekte, die Guwonpa heisst, und die 2014 mit dem Schiffsunglück der Fähre Sewol in

27 Max Geiger, Calvin, Calvinismus und Kapitalismus, in: Ders. (Hg.), Gottesreich und Menschenreich, Ernst Staehelin zum 80. Geburtstag, Stuttgart 1969, 231–286.

Verbindung stand und dabei fehlende ethische Verantwortung gezeigt hat. Diejenigen, die zu solchen geschlossenen Sekten gehören, glauben fest daran und halten nur ihre Mitgliedschaft und Zugehörigkeit für wichtig. Nur sie werden zu den Menschen gehören, die erlöst werden. Eines der grossen Probleme, die solche Sekten verursacht haben, ist die Machtdominanz der Hauptfigur, die einem Personenkult gleichkommt. Solche Systeme haben nicht nur zu Machtkorruption inklusive sexuellem Missbrauch geführt, sondern auch zu ökonomischer Korruption. Die Konzentration auf einzelne Machthabende hat wiederum mit dem Verständnis von Offenbarung zu tun, weil die führende Figur allgemein als Offenbarung einer Gottheit betrachtet wird. Es geht darum, mehr die Deifikation, als die Inkarnation Gottes als Quelle der Kraft zu betonen, mit der man sich mit weltlichen Problemen auseinandersetzen kann. Die absurde Behauptung und immer wiederholte Vorstellung, der zweite und dritte Jesus zu sein, ist ein zentrales Problem, das sich bei vielen Sektenbewegungen findet. Darüber hinaus geht es darum, ins jenseitsorientiere Reich Gottes eingehen zu wollen. Es zieht die einfachen Leute an, zur festgelegten Zahl von Menschen, die in der Johannesapokalypse genannt wird, zu gehören. Dieses Phänomen, ihre Mitglieder an sich zu binden, hat mit einem hierarchischen Kontroll-System zu tun. Zahlreiche Familien und Ehen wurden dadurch auseinandergetrieben und zerstört. In einer pluralistischen Gesellschaft und in sozioökonomisch instabilen Verhältnissen fühlt man sich unsicher. Dann ist ein Abhängigkeitsverhältnis einfacher zu akzeptieren, ohne kritisch nachzudenken, einschließlich des Gehorsams im Rahmen des Personenkults.

Zusammenfassend ist zu sagen, dass das Verständnis von Offenbarung als beliebigem Prädikat und die Haltung der Jenseitsorientierung, die an die Stelle von sozialer Verantwortung im irdischen Leben tritt, direkt und indirekt Personenkult und Korruption unterstützen. Fluch und Segen Gottes dürfen nicht von Menschen beliebig beurteilt werden. Sie sind letzten Endes Gottes Sache. Ich strebe danach, verwurzelt in den reformierten Traditionen Gotteserkenntnis von Gott her zu definieren, nicht vom Menschen her. Darüber hinaus versuche ich, sensibel für Gerechtigkeit im Kontext von Intersektionalität zu sein. Es geht darum, kirchenverbunden zu sein und zugleich sozial engagiert. Die Kirche soll theologisch reflektiert und gleichzeitig weltoffen sein, anstatt Feindschaft zu festigen und Andersdenkende – beispielsweise in Bezug auf sexuelle Orientierung – oder Andersgläubige zu diffamieren. Genau darin gründen die biblischen Vorstellungen von der Notwendigkeit der Nächstenliebe; es gilt also, der Frage

Raum zu geben, ob die reformierte Tradition und feministische Ansätze in Konflikt geraten oder Synergien geschaffen werden können.

Die Befreiung von den Fesseln des Patriarchalismus ist notwendig, aber ebenso die Befreiung von den Fesseln des Matriarchalismus, um den Teufelskreis zu durchbrechen. Geschlechtergerechtigkeit wurde inzwischen erweitert um das Thema der Benachteiligung aufgrund der sexuellen Orientierung. Die reformorientierte Theologie, die ihre Legitimität mit feministischen Ansätzen hinterfragt, verfolgt keine politische Strategie, aber ihr orthopraktisches Handeln ist politisch folgenreich. Sie ist sicher kein politisches Instrument zur Korrektur politischer Defizite, sondern motiviert dazu, gesellschaftliche Belange ins Auge zu fassen, um die staatlichen Lösungsroutinen und ihre unter Umständen prekären Folgen zu unterbrechen.

(Meehyun Chung ist Professorin für Systematische Theologie an der United Graduate School of Theology der Yonsei University, Seoul, und zugleich erste weibliche Chaplain der Yonsei University. Sie ist ordinierte Pfarrerin der Presbyterian Church in the Republic of Korea und hat an der Theologischen Fakultät der Universität Basel promoviert. Vgl. www.credo.or.kr)

ABSTRACT

This article introduces the development of Korean Christianity and its Churches in relation to the Korean socio-political and historical context. The goal is to elaborate on Korean protestant theology and particularly my theological concept of it. The article is comprised of four parts: firstly, the Korean context of Christianity and theology in relation to historical developments and society is sketched. Secondly, I introduce my theological concept as self-positioning and relate it, thirdly, to other concepts within the Korean context. Fourthly, I argue for overcoming dualistic approaches and those that make human matters absolute. Methodologically, this article is descriptive because it is based on my own experience, observations and hermeneutics. Overall, I claim that the Swiss Reformed tradition could be adapted to the Korean socio-political context. The main point is, that God could and should be interpreted by God's own revelation. Human history is the predicate. The arbitrariness of human experience, including dualistic arguments and thoughts, should be relativized.

Vom Christentum in China zum chinesischen Christentum

Die Sinisierung und ihr gesellschaftliches Ziel

Ruomin Liu

1. Sinisierung: die offizielle Bewegung und ihre Strategie

1.1 Die offizielle Ankündigung

Eine wichtige Voraussetzung zum Verständnis chinesischer Religionspolitik ist die Kenntnis von Theorie und Praxis der »Einheitsfrontpolitik« der Kommunistischen Partei Chinas. Diese Beobachtung bzw. dieser Hinweis von Monika Gänßbauer und Bob Whyte ist richtig[1] und weiterhin gültig. Darum möchte ich an den Anfang meiner Betrachtungen eine kurze Einführung in die Konzepte der gegenwärtigen Religionspolitik der Volksrepublik China stellen.

Am 18.5.2015 hat Xi Jinping, der seit 2012 Generalsekretär der Kommunistischen Partei Chinas sowie Vorsitzender der Zentralen Militärkommission und seit 2013 Staatspräsident der Volksrepublik China ist, offiziell die Kampagne zur Sinisierung der Religionen in China lanciert. Im wörtlichen Sinne meint Sinisierung »Chinesischwerdung« – theologisch könnte der Begriff als Inkulturation oder Kontextualisierung verstanden werden. Bei der nationalen Konferenz der Zentralabteilung der Einheitsfront des Zentralkomitees der KPCh hat Xi Jinping die Kampagne folgendermassen angekündigt:

1 Siehe: Monika Gänßbauer, Parteistaat und Protestantische Kirche. Religionspolitik im nachmaoistischen China, Frankfurt am Main 2004, 286. Siehe auch: Bob Whyte, Unfinished Encounter. China and Christianity, London 1988, 160ff und 341ff.

> »Religiöse Arbeit ist im Wesentlichen Massenarbeit. [...] Um die Religionen aktiv bei der Anpassung an die sozialistische Gesellschaft zu unterstützen, müssen wir den Kurs der Sinisierung einschlagen und daran festhalten, den Grad der Legalisierung der religiösen Arbeit erhöhen, und die Rolle der Religion dialektisch behandeln. Wir müssen auf die Rolle religiöser Leitfiguren achten und religiöse Bemühungen zur Förderung der wirtschaftlichen Entwicklung und der sozialen Harmonie einleiten. Kultureller Wohlstand, nationale Einheit und einheitliche Dienste für das Vaterland sollen gemeinsame Ziele werden.«[2]

Am 23.4.2016 hat Xi anlässlich der Nationalen Konferenz für religiöse Arbeit die »Sinisierung der Religionen in China« ein weiteres Mal hervorgehoben, um die Religionen aktiv zur Anpassung an die sozialistische Gesellschaft hinzuführen.[3]

Seitdem haben die Jahresberichte des Zentralkomitees der KPCh und des nationalen Volkskongresses, bzw. der nationalen politischen Konsultativkonferenz des chinesischen Volkes, immer wieder die Sinisierung der Religionen in China betont. Und gleichzeitig gehen alle religiösen Behörden und Institute in China mit Nachdruck die Implementierung der Sinisierungskampagne an. Die Abteilungen der Einheitsfront- und Religionsarbeit haben nämlich überall im Land in Kooperation mit Religionsvertretern und gemäß den Vorgaben zum »Festhalten am Sinisierungskurs der Religionen« gewissenhaft Studien- und Diskussionsworkshops veranstaltet und tatkräftig Pilotprojekte realisiert, sodass sich inzwischen ein breiter Konsens zwischen der Einheitsfront-Abteilung der Partei und den nationalen religiösen Organisationen in China über die Sinisierungskampagne abzeichnet. Ebenso wurden auch schon einige Erfahrungen mit der Umsetzung der Richtlinien zur Sinisierung gesammelt. Wang Zuo-an, Vizeminister der Einheitsfrontabteilung der KPCh und Direktor der nationalen Religionsbehörde, betonte mehrfach, dass die Sinisierung »die wichtigste Mission der Religionsarbeit« der Partei im neuen Zeitalter darstellt.[4]

2 http://www.xinhuanet.com//politics/2015-05/20/c_1115351358.htm (12.11.2020), Übersetzung durch den Autor.

3 http://www.xinhuanet.com/politics/2016-04/23/c_1118716540.htm (12.11.2020).

4 Zuo-an Wang, Religionspolitisches Strategiepapier der chinesischen Regierung, Original 29.3.2019. Übersetzung aus dem Chinesischen: Zhongguo Minzubao, Isabel Friemann 3.12.2019. https://www.chinainfostelle.de/aktuelles/religionspolitisches-strategiepapier-der-chinesischen-regierung (12.11.2020).

1.2 Zweck und Aufgabe

In einem religionspolitischen Strategiepapier der chinesischen Regierung formulierte Wang Zuo-an im März 2019 die Orientierung an nationalen Werten bzw. die Anpassung von Religion an die heutige sozialistische Gesellschaft als das Ziel der Sinisierung. Er äußert sich folgendermaßen:

> »Die Einhaltung des Sinisierungskurses ist nicht nur eine wichtige Forderung unserer Partei im Umgang mit nationalen religiösen Belangen, es ist auch eine wichtige Aufgabe der Religionsarbeit im neuen Zeitalter. Nur das Festhalten an der Führung durch die Partei, ermöglicht eine Vereinheitlichung des Denkens und eine Festigung des Bewusstseins. Es allein ermöglicht eine gemeinsame Orientierung an nationalen Werten [wörtlich »am Hissen der Flagge«] und eine umfassend strategische Herangehensweise.«[5]

Dazu weitet Wang Zuo-an die Aufgaben der Kampagne und ihrer Ziele noch weiter aus: die Veränderung bzw. Reformation der Religionen in China:

> »Dabei geht es um Fragen wie ›wer soll sich ändern?‹, ›was soll sich ändern?‹ und ›wie soll es sich ändern?‹. Diesbezügliche Regeln müssen sorgfältig formuliert und verfeinert werden, sodass eindeutig klar wird, was vorgeschlagen und ermutigt werden soll, was eingeschränkt und verboten werden muss, um einen guten politischen, legalen und gesellschaftlichen Rahmen zur Umsetzung der Sinisierung der Religionen zu schaffen.«[6]

Warum müssen die Religionen, darunter sogar auch der Daoismus, der als Chinas eigene und authentische Religion angesehen wird, und der chinesische Buddhismus, eine Religion, bei der »Sinisierung« schon lange erfolgt ist, die Einhaltung des Sinisierungskurses annehmen? Die Religionen stehen vor der Herausforderung, sich aktiv an die heutige sozialistische Gesellschaft anzupassen und in ihren Botschaften allgemein zur Anpassung an die sozialistische Gesellschaft beizutragen. Der Leiter der Religionsbehörde hat dies direkt benannt:

> »Wir müssen unser Problembewusstsein schärfen, grundlegende Denkweisen erfassen, in die Lebenswirklichkeiten eintauchen und eingehende Untersuchungen anstellen. Nur so können wir zeitnah

5 Zuo-an Wang, Religionspolitisches Strategiepapier.
6 Ebd.

> problematische Tendenzen aufdecken und entkräften, dem Auftauchen problematischer Trends entgegenwirken, gemäß den Gesetzen illegalen Aktivitäten begegnen, die unter dem Deckmantel Religion durchgeführt werden, und signifikanten Gefahren Einhalt gebieten, die im religiösen Bereich verborgen sind.«[7]

Anlässlich der Tagung »Erhaltung der Sinisierung der Religionen in China« am 26.9.2016 hat Wang Zuo-an schon diese Herausforderungen weiter analysiert.[8] Mit den »*tiefgreifenden Veränderungen in der nationalen und internationalen Situation*« seien viele neue Probleme im religiösen Bereich aufgetreten und seither auf dem Vormarsch: 1. Einige Religionen tendierten dazu, kommerzialisiert zu werden. Es trete das Phänomen auf, »Geld von der Religion zu leihen«. Religion werde zum Mittel, sich zu bereichern; 2. Einige Religionen zeigen Anzeichen einer »Entsinisierung« (gemeint ist: Opposition gegen Sinisierung) und orientierten sich an fremden Religionen; 3. Einige lokale Kulte und religiöse Gruppierungen entwickelten sich ungeordnet, illegale religiöse Aktivitäten spielten eine herausragende Rolle, und der Missbrauch von Religionen für Infiltrationsaktivitäten aus Übersee habe zugenommen; 4. Religiöser Extremismus habe sich an einigen Orten verbreitet und sogar gewalttätige und terroristische Vorfälle zur Folge gehabt.[9]

Gemäss Wangs Ausführungen zeigt sich, dass die Religionen in China »ungesund« sind. Wegen der tiefgreifenden Veränderungen im In- und Ausland haben die Religionen Probleme: Kommerzialisierung, illegale religiöse Aktivitäten, religiöser Extremismus, Abhängigkeit von ausländischer Unterstützung werden als Gegenspieler der Sinisierung wahrgenommen. Man kann daraus lesen, dass diese Opposition gegen Sinisierung existiert und eine große Herausforderung für die Gesellschaft bzw. die KPCh ist. Wenn diese Probleme nicht gelöst werden, wird gemäss Wang dies nicht nur die gesunde Entwicklung der Religionen im Land ernsthaft behindern, sondern auch negative Auswirkungen auf Wirtschaft und Gesellschaft haben.[10]

Der Vorschlag, alle Religionen bei der Ausrichtung auf die Sinisierung zu unterstützen, ist eine langfristige strategische Maßnahme zur Lösung dieser

7 Zuo-an Wang, Religionspolitisches Strategiepapier.
8 Zuo-an Wang, Einhaltung des Sinisierungskurses der Religionen in China, http://www.cppcc.gov.cn/zxww/2019/01/07/ARTI1546822684077333.shtml (12.11.2020).
9 Zuo-an Wang, Einhaltung des Sinisierungskurses.
10 Zuo-an Wang, Einhaltung des Sinisierungskurses.

noch offenen Probleme. Insbesondere die Maßgabe, sich religiösem Einfluss aus dem Ausland zu widersetzen, richtet sich gegen Infiltration, zielt darauf ab, die Ausbreitung von religiösem Extremismus einzudämmen und das Phänomen der »umgekehrten Sinisierung« zu kontrollieren.[11]

1.3 Die Notwendigkeit

Xi Jinping und Wang Zuo-an sind die beiden Vertreter der Forderung zur Sinisierung der Religionen auf höchster Ebene. Die Bewegung spielt also eine Rolle in der Religionspolitik und in der gesamten politischen Strategie des Landes. Bereits vor Implementierung der Sinisierungs-Kampagne wurde schon längere Zeit über das Thema von Wissenschaftler*innen aus Gesellschafts- und Religionswissenschaften diskutiert und geforscht. Nach Analyse der betreffenden Publikationen wird deutlich, dass es in der Bewegung in besonderer Weise um das Christentum in China geht.

Zhang Zhigang, Professor für Religionswissenschaft an der Beijing Universität und sein Kollege Zuo Xinping, Vorsitzender der Religionsgesellschaft in China, Direktor des Instituts für Weltreligionen und Professor für Religionswissenschaft an der Chinesischen Akademie der Sozialwissenschaften in Beijing, haben bereits am 31.3.2012 den Begriff »Sinisierung der christlichen Kirche in China«, bei einer Tagung mit demselben Titel verwendet und die Bewegung damit angekündigt bzw. eingeleitet.[12]

Zhang Zhigang schließt sich der Meinung von Luo Guangzhong (1920–2011) an, dem ehemaligen Vorsitzenden der Nationalen Drei-Selbst-Bewegung der evangelischen Kirche in China. Er zitiert: »Das moderne Christentum wurde im 19. Jahrhundert in China eingeführt und hatte gewisse Beiträge zur chinesischen Gesellschaft geleistet. Leider war die Einführung des Christentums untrennbar mit der Invasion Chinas durch den Imperialismus verbunden und wurde durch den Kolonialismus verursacht und vom Imperialismus benutzt.«[13] Nach Vergleichen der Situation der Kirche in China mit derjenigen der Kirchen in Südkorea kommt Zhang in seinem Artikel »Nachdenken über die Sinisierung der christli-

11 Zuo-an Wang, Einhaltung des Sinisierungskurses.
12 http://www.cssn.cn/ddzg/2013xsdt/201204/t20120424_812029.shtml (12.11.2020).
13 Guangzhong Luo, Qianshi Buwan Houshi Zhishi (Nicht zu vergessen die Vergangenheit, ein Leitfaden für die Zukunft – Ein Rückblick auf historische Fakten über Imperialisten, die das Christentum nutzen, um in China einzudringen), Zhongguo Zongjiao Wenhu Chubanshe: Beijing 2003, 2.

chen Kirchen in China«[14] zu dem Schluss, dass die Kirche in China noch keine eigene chinesische gesellschaftliche Identität hat und die Vision der Drei-Selbst-Bewegung der evangelischen Kirche in China tatsächlich noch nicht erfüllt ist, obwohl sie seit 1950 gefordert wurde. Er äußert sich so:

> »Der starke Kontrast zwischen beiden (Kirchen in Südkorea und Kirche in China, R. L.) reicht aus, um uns das Gefühl zu geben, dass dies ein historisches und soziologisches Problem ist, über das man nachdenken sollte: China und Südkorea sind enge Verwandte, was ihre Geschichte und ihre kulturellen Traditionen anbelangt [...]. Aber warum spielt das Christentum – eine fremde Religion in beiden Ländern – unterschiedliche soziale Rollen und erzeugt unterschiedliche soziale Eindrücke [...] Nach Ansicht des Autors liegt der Hauptgrund wahrscheinlich nicht in den christlichen Klassikern, Lehren und der Theologie selbst, sondern in den sozialen Auswirkungen von Missionaren und einheimischen Gläubigen [...] Positive Einflüsse haben zu positiven und historischen Effekten geführt, negative Einflüsse haben zu negativen sozialen und historischen Effektiven geführt.«[15]

Zhang ist hier in dem Aspekt Recht zu geben, dass das Christentum in Südkorea eine große positive Rolle in der Gesellschaft bzw. im politischen System spielt. Aber er hat vergessen und außer Acht gelassen, dass die politischen Systeme der beiden Länder unterschiedlich sind. Dazu spielen natürlich unterschiedliche Lehren und Theologien eine große Rolle für das Leben der Christ*innen in beiden Ländern.

Zhang greift den Begriff, »das Ungleichgewicht der religiösen Ökologie«, von Professorin Duan Qi auf, einer Expertin für die Geschichte des chinesischen Christentums. Auf dem »Hochrangigen Forum 2008 zu ethnischen und religiösen Fragen – Chinesische Religion im Kontext der Globalisierung« hielt sie eine Rede mit dem Titel »Das Ungleichgewicht der religiösen Ökologie ist die Hauptursache für die rasche Entwicklung des Christentums in China heute«.[16] Basierend auf Feldforschungsdaten wies sie darauf hin, dass sich die sogenannte »religiöse Ökologie« auf die soziale Existenz verschiedener Religionen bezieht, ähnlich der

14 Zhigang Zhang, Nachdenken über die Sinisierung der christlichen Kirchen in China«, http://www.aisixiang.com/data/83049.html (12.11.2020).

15 Übersetzung aus dem Chinesischen durch den Autor.

16 Qi Duan, Das Ungleichgewicht der religiösen Ökologie ist die Hauptursache für die rasche Entwicklung des Christentums in China heute, Gansu renminchubanshe: Quanzhou 2009, 140ff.

Naturökologie, und dass ihr normaler Zustand aufeinander beschränkt werden sollte, um ein Gesamtgleichgewicht zu erreichen, d. h. jede Religion hat ihren Platz, sofern es einen Markt gibt, der den Glaubensbedürfnissen verschiedener Personengruppen gerecht wird. Wenn jedoch unangemessene künstliche Eingriffe vorgenommen werden, wird ihr Gleichgewicht zerstört, was dazu führt, dass sich einige Religionen in einigen Gebieten überproportional schnell entwickeln, während andere verkümmern. Die rasche Entwicklung des Christentums nach der Reform und Öffnung hängt demnach mit einem Ungleichgewicht in der religiösen Ökologie zusammen.[17]

Zhang hat in seinem Aufsatz die gegenwärtigen Herausforderungen des Christentums in China aufgelistet. Die übermäßige Entwicklung des Christentums in China wird nach seiner Prognose eine Reihe unerwünschter Konsequenzen nach sich ziehen: Erstens fördere es das Bestreben ausländischer feindlicher Kräfte, in China Fuß zu fassen und ihren Einfluss auszudehnen und spiele ihrer Strategie, eine konstant zunehmende Christianisierung Chinas voranzutreiben, in die Hände. Infolgedessen werde es einen Kampf zwischen Kontrolle und Anti-Kontrolle geben. Konflikte und sogar Konfrontationen zwischen sozialistischen Überzeugungen und anderen traditionellen Überzeugungen in China werden, so Zhang, folglich die Stabilität und Harmonie der Gesellschaft untergraben. Eine zweite Konsequenz sei die Entwicklung einer christlichen Bewegung, die zu großen Anteilen im Untergrund stattfinde, bei der die Qualität von Lehre und Glaubenspraxis im Umgang mit Gläubigen nicht in Ruhe verbessert werden könne. Die Reinheit bzw. die Orthodoxie des Glaubens könne nicht garantiert werden. Darüber hinaus wäre es schwierig, normal mit der Gesellschaft zu kommunizieren. Es gab eine Vielzahl kirchlicher Organisationen, die nicht Teil des bekannten normalen Christentums waren und sich jeder Kontrolle entzogen. Solche Gemeinden und Kirchen können leicht von verschiedenen negativen sozialen Kräften benutzt werden und sind der »gesunden« Entwicklung eines Christentums unter dem Banner des Patriotismus nicht förderlich. Eine dritte Konsequenz und Gefahr besteht laut Zhang darin, dass der Nationalstolz und das Bewusstsein für die eigene chinesische Kultur zerstört würden, was auch das Wertesystem des Konfuzianismus schädigen würde. Der durch Buddhismus und Daoismus geschaffene menschenorientierte, sich selbst verbessernde, tugendhafte, wohlwollende und harmonische Nationalgeist werde von einer christlichen Lehre bedroht,

17 Qi Duan, Das Ungleichgewicht, 143–144.

die in ihrem Ursprung als Monotheismus Exklusivität beansprucht und aggressiv andere Religionen bekämpft.[18]

Die Gründe für eine solche Bewegung liegen nach Zhang und Zuo darin, dass es der Kirche in China an einer eigenen chinesischen politischen Identität mangle. Dazu wächst die christliche Kirche in manchen Gebieten Chinas zu schnell. Deswegen verloren nach Ansicht der beiden Wissenschaftler viele Gebiete ihr »religiöses ökologisches Gleichgewicht«. Daraus folgt: ohne Sinisierung kann man die Kirche nicht gut verwalten bzw. kontrollieren. Außerdem stellt das unproportionale Wachstum der Kirche eine Irritation für die Gesellschaft dar. Es klingt die Alarmglocke: »Dies erlaubt nicht den friedlichen Aufstieg der chinesischen Nation und steht einer Entwicklung zur harmonischen Welt im Wege.«[19]

2. Theologie als eine akribische Politik

Obwohl die heutige Bewegung zur Sinisierung der Religionen wie die Drei-Selbst-Bewegung und die Bewegung, »vereinigter Gottesdienst«[20], als Kampagne des chinesischen Parteistaates ausgefochten werden,[21] ist anzumerken, dass Theologen in China bereits seit Jahrhunderten die Kontextualisierung der Kirche bzw. Sinisierung der Theologie forderten.[22] Im vorliegenden Beitrag sollen einige Überlegungen zur möglichen Verwendung des Begriffs »Sinisierung« angestellt werden. Sinisierung hat das Potential, ein positives Konzept nicht nur für die Kirche in China, sondern auch für die große Familie der interkulturellen Theologie zu werden, wenn es sich als Fortsetzung der Bewegung zur Kontextualisierung

18 Zhigang Zhang, Nachdenken über die Sinisierung.
19 Ebd.
20 Siehe unter 3.1 und 3.2.
21 Xiaofeng Tang, Warum muss das Christentum sinisiert werden? In: Minzubao, 19. August 2014. http://gb.oversea.cnki.net/KCMS/detail/detail.aspx?filename=CMZB201408190060&dbcode=CCND&dbname=CCND2014 (12.4.2021). 0150 – Ein deutliches Zeichen dafür sind die »Verhaltensregeln für protestantische kirchliche Amtsträger« vom 23.22.2019, erstellt von den Dachverbänden der Protestantischen Kirche. Übersetzung aus dem Chinesischen Isabel Friemann. https://www.chinainfostelle.de/aktuelles/verhaltensregeln-fuer-protestantische-kirchliche-amtstraeger (28.02.2020).
22 Qi Duan, Fenjin de Licheng (Eine mutig angetretene Reise), The Commercial Press: Beijing 2004. Antony E. Clark, China's Christianity: From Missionary to Indigenous Church, Leiden/Boston 2017.

der Theologie bzw. der Bewegung zur »Verstärkung der theologischen Reflexion« (*theological renewal*) in China erweist.[23]

Bischof K. H. Ting (1915–2012), der von 1952 bis 2010 Vorsitzender des Nanjing Union Theological Seminary, des nationalen theologischen Seminars in Nanjing war, außerdem von 1981 bis 1996 in Personalunion Vorsitzender des Nationalen Christenrates und der Nationalen Drei-Selbst-Bewegung, den höchsten Dachverbänden der protestantischen Kirche in China, initiierte eine Bewegung zur »Verstärkung der theologischen Reflexion«. Ziel der Bewegung war die Weiterentwicklung der Kirche in China (»running the church well«) und das *Aggiornamento*, in diesem Fall eine Anpassung an die sozialistische Gesellschaft. Dadurch sollte also die Kirche mit dem Zeitgeist in Einklang gebracht werden. Ting äußerte sich im Jahr 2000 über die Notwendigkeit und die Ziele der Bewegung und beschreibt das in seinem letzten Artikel:

> »We are beginning to realize that theological renewal is a necessary and fundamental issue for running the church well, a crucial among many weighty issues facing the church. We live in a socialist society. This being the case, how will our students adapt if we keep to the status quo of the 19th and 20th centuries, mechanically copying all the traditional ways received by the Western missionary movement? […] Our future vision of the Chinese church is one that is rich in a theology that respects reason and is more suited to Chinese socialist society. It will be one that can help believers to establish a more harmonious and reasonable faith and witness.«[24]

23 Gänßbauer, Parteistaat und Protestantische Kirche, 146–173.

24 K. H. Ting, »My View of These Fifty Years«, in: Janice and Philip Wickeri (Hg.), A Chinese Contribution to Ecumenical Theology, WCC Publications, Geneva 2002, 112–113. K. H. Ting, »Über die letzten 10 Jahre«, in: Tianfeng, Nr. 23 (2008), 1. – Wickeri äußert sich in einem Kommentar dazu: »In Tings's understanding, theological reconstruction has been an extension of running the church well, for a well-run church should have its own theology, one that enables it to respond to the times. That theology should bear witness to God's love, confront Christian fundamentalism, play down the differences between believers and nonbelievers and give greater attention to social involvement. There is also a need for »mutual adaption« between Christianity and Chinese society in order to facilitate the mission of the church and contribute to society. Ting's own theology has been a useful corrective to the narrow one-sidedness of Chinese evangelicalism, which has tended to close the church off from its social and cultural milieu.« Philip Wickeri, Reconstructing Christianity in China. K. H. Ting and the Chinese Church, Maryknoll/New York 2007, 376.

In seinem Vortrag beim 90-jährigen Jubiläum der 4.-Mai-Bewegung[25] am 4.5.1999 am *Nanjing Union Theological Seminary*, bei dem der Autor als Student bzw. Zuhörer dabei war, betonte Ting, die Theologie sei nicht nur eine reine Wissenschaft für die Pastor*innen der Kirche, sondern auch eine Politik, eine akribische Politik. Die Theologie, bzw. die Predigten in China seien aber zutiefst westlich geprägt und wirkten stark ausgrenzend. Aus diesem Grund sei es notwendig, dass Theologen und Theologinnen die Situation tiefgreifend reflektierten und eine kritische Grundhaltung einnähmen.

»*Theologie ist eine akribische Politik.*« Man kann es mit dem berühmten Motto Dietrich Bonhoeffers verstehen: »Theologie als ein Hilfsmittel zum Kampf«.[26] Sie ist also im extremen Fall ein Mittel, die falschen, bzw. ungepflegten Gedanken oder eine ungesunde Theologie innerhalb der Kirche zu identifizieren und die Kirche in ihrem geistlichen Kampf zu unterstützen.[27] Sie ist zudem auch ein Instrument, irrende Kirchen zur Wahrheit aufzurufen. Darüber hinaus kann Theologie die menschliche Selbstkritik am guten Willen Gottes schulen und die Verantwortung und Stellvertretung für die Menschen anerkennen und tragen.

In diesem Zusammenhang stellen sich zwei Fragen: Theologie als Hilfsmittel wofür und als Kampfmittel wogegen? Ting schreibt: die Bewegung richte sich »gegen absurde fundamentalistische Strömungen« in der chinesischen Kirche, um sie an die sozialistische Gesellschaft anzupassen. Was sind absurde fundamentalistische Strömungen nach Tings Auffassung? Gemeint sind eine Theologie der Furcht und eine starke Abgrenzung der Christen gegenüber Nichtchristen.

25 Die Bewegung des 4. Mai fand ihren Ursprung in den Studentenprotesten in China gegen den Versailler Vertrag am 4. Mai 1919. China stand im Ersten Weltkrieg auf Seiten der Alliierten und hoffte auf Aufhebung der Ungleichen Verträge und Nichtanerkennung der Einundzwanzig Forderungen Japans von 1915. Diese Hoffnungen wurden von den Verträgen nicht erfüllt. Die Bewegung des Vierten Mai gilt als erste politische Massenbewegung der chinesischen Geschichte und dient damit bis heute vielen politischen Strömungen als Bezugspunkt zur Identifikation und Legitimation. Siehe Dewang Zhang, Die Geschichte der 4. Mai-Bewegung, Harbin 2011. (Chinesisch)

26 So bezeichnet Bonhoeffer auch selbst die Theologie als »ein Hilfsmittel, ein Kampfmittel, nicht Selbstzweck«. Dietrich Bonhoeffer, Theologie und Gemeinde, in: Dietrich Bonhoeffer Werke Band 16, Gütersloh 1996, 496.

27 »Bonhoeffers Verständnis von Theologie stellt, wenn wir das vorherige kurz zusammenfassen, das theoretische Bemühen in den Dienst kirchlicher Praxis. Verkündigung und glaubens-gehorsame Nachfolge Christi können als Eckpfeiler seiner Theologie gesehen werden, die sich in den sich anschließenden Einzelaspekten ebenso wiederfinden lassen wie in der Beschreibung der Theologie als reflexives und deskriptives Nachzeichnen der vorgegebenen Glaubensinhalte.« Gerhard Ludwig Müller, Bonhoeffers Theologie. Ein Ort katholischer Theologie heute, in: J. Außermeier/G. Maria Hoff (Hg.), Dietrich Bonhoeffer – Orte seiner Theologie, Ferdinand Schöningh: Paderborn/München/Wien/Zürich 2008, 36.

Monika Gänßbauer hat in ihrem Buch, *Parteistaat und Protestantische Kirche*, darauf hingewiesen: »[Ting] begründete die Notwendigkeit der Bewegung damit, dass viele Christen in China, vor allem auf dem Land, noch immer stark konservative theologische Ansichten verträten, die teilweise auf die Verkündigung westlicher Missionare zurückgingen. Auf dem Land herrsche oft noch eine Theologie der Furcht und eine starke Abgrenzung der Christen gegenüber Nichtchristen. Ein solches Christentum sei unfähig, mit Religionswissenschaftlern und Intellektuellen Chinas in einen Dialog zu treten. Er selbst verstehe sich als »liberalen Theologen« und seine Vision sei es, dass die chinesische Kirche einst über eine »wundervolle, liberale Theologie« verfüge.[28]

Seit den 1950er Jahren kritisierte Ting immer wieder diese »absurden« fundamentalistischen Strömungen der Theologie in China.[29] In den 1980er Jahren erweiterte er seine Kritik zudem auf das Missverhältnis in der Kompetenzteilung zwischen Drei-Selbst-Bewegung und chinesischer Kirche und auf die mangelhafte kircheninterne Umsetzung theologischer Einsichten.[30]

3. Die Besonderheiten bzw. die unvollendete Vision der Kirche

Der Theologe und langjährige Professor des nationalen theologischen Seminars in Nanjing, Chen Zemin (1917–2018), schreibt im Jahr 2009 in seinem letzten Vortrag, *Ich habe noch ein Wort*, den er am Seminar hält:

> »Ich hoffe, dass durch die gemeinsamen Bemühungen aller theologisch Versierten, die eine direkte oder indirekte Beziehung zu Jinling [unserem Seminar] haben, eine Gruppe theologischer Forscher*innen entsteht, die sich der Kirche anschließen, sich auf die Gesellschaft konzentrieren und in die Zukunft schauen. Sie mögen in sich die aufrichtige Bereitschaft entwickeln, zu erforschen und die Wahrheit zu suchen. Die Jinling-Schule des chinesischen Christentums, die von der Wahrheit zeugt, der sie sich verpflichtet hat. Diese christlichen und akademischen theologischen Wissenschaftler*innen mögen aufrichtig wohlwollend, wahr, gerecht, demütig und dienend sein.«[31]

28 Gänßbauer, Parteistaat und Protestantische Kirche, 147–148.
29 Chloë Starr, Chinese Theology: Text and Context, New Haven 2016, 185ff.
30 Gänßbauer, Parteistaat und Protestantische Kirche, 132ff.
31 Zemin Chen, »Ich habe noch ein Wort« (wo hai you hua yao shuo, Vortrag am 10.6.2009) in: Jinling Shenxue zhi (Theologische Zeitschrift des Jinling-Seminars) 2 (2003), 15. (Chinesisch).

Meines Erachtens wollten Ting und Chen durch die Bewegung zur »Verstärkung der theologischen Reflexion« eine Vision verwirklichen, konkret: den Aufbau einer »gepflegten« Religion unterstützen – im Gegensatz zu der tyrannischen Variante »ungepflegter Religion«, nämlich dem Fundamentalismus als einer chaotischen Variante von Religion, wie Michael Welker im Vorwort für die chinesische Auflage seines Buches, *Kirche im Pluralismus*, schrieb.[32]

Die Kirche und ihre Theologie in China sind noch nicht gut »gepflegt«, oder mit dem Wort von Wang Zuo-an »ungesund«, da die Vision einer Anpassung der Gesellschaft noch nicht erfüllt ist. Hier sind einige besondere Merkmale der chinesischen christlichen Spiritualität und ihre noch nicht erfüllten Visionen zu erwähnen.

3.1 Unabhängigkeit der Kirche

Jahrhundertelang ist es dem Christentum nicht gelungen, in China wirklich Fuß zu fassen. Zu Beginn der christlichen Mission wurde großer Wert auf Inkulturation gelegt. Die Missionare haben in Sprache, Kleidung, Namensgebung etc. so weit wie möglich versucht, sich der chinesischen Kultur anzupassen. Als nach den Opiumkriegen (1840 und 1860) die Abschottung des Landes gelockert

32 »In den letzten Jahrzehnten des 20. Jahrhunderts ging unter vielen führenden Intellektuellen im Westen die Frage um: ›Geht die Menschheit in eine Zukunft mit Religion oder ohne Religion?‹ Diese Frage hat sich zu Beginn des 21. Jahrhunderts verschoben. Sie lautet heute: ›Geht die Menschheit in eine Zukunft mit gepflegter Religion oder mit ungepflegter Religion?‹ Was förderte diesen Umbruch, und was ist mit der neuen Frage gemeint? Ein wichtiger Auslöser für das Umdenken war ›9/11‹, die Zerstörung der beiden Türme des New Yorker World Trade Center am 11. September 2001 durch islamische Fundamentalisten und Terroristen. Weitere Faktoren für die Veränderung der Fragestellung waren aber auch die christlich-fundamentalistisch gefärbte dualistische Weltanschauung der Bush II Regierung in den USA, die entsprechend primitive Hegemonial-Politik des Präsidenten und seiner Administration und, damit einhergehend, der schnelle Verfall des Ansehens der Vereinigten Staaten in aller Welt. Fundamentalistische Religiosität in ihrem ganzen Spektrum bis hin zum blutigen Terrorismus ist aber nur die eine Seite von ›ungepflegter Religion‹ – ihre tyrannische Variante. Die zweite Seite, die chaotische Variante ungepflegter Religion, müssen wir in Form von verfallenden Religionen erleiden, die inhaltlich entleert, dumm und albern werden. Diese Formen von Religiosität lösen sich von historischen und rationalen Orientierungen und damit von der Bildung und der Wissenschaft. Sie verlieren den Respekt für die in lange lebendigen Religionen gespeicherte Weisheit und das in ihnen aufbewahrte Menschheitswissen. Sie neigen zu beständigen Veränderungen des religiösen Kults und der religiösen Riten – wobei sie oft planlos vorgehen oder nur an augenblicklichen Moden und Resonanzen interessiert sind – weil sie deren Sinngehalte nicht mehr verstehen. Und sie verkennen und verlieren die sozialen und kulturellen Gestaltungskräfte, die aus tragfähigen Religionen erwachsen.« Michael Welker, Vorwort zur erweiterten chinesischen Ausgabe von Kirche im Pluralismus, Beijing 2010, 10f.

wurde, gründeten die Missionsgesellschaften eigene Stationen. Das führte zunehmend dazu, dass die Chines*innen, die Christen wurden, ihren kulturellen Rahmen verließen. »Ein Christ mehr – ein Chinese weniger«. Dadurch aber blieb das Christentum eine Fremdreligion in starker Abhängigkeit von den Missionsgesellschaften.

Chen Zemin hat im Jahr 1981 auf die Problematik der Theologie vor 1950 in China hingewiesen:

> »Prior to 1950 there was hardly any theology that the Protestant Church in China could claim to be characteristically her own. For almost a century, the »Chinese Churches« were never anything other than outposts of Western missionary societies. [...] theology of this sort could never take root, and means very little to the grassroots Chinese Christians, because they [sic] did not grow out of the real experience of the Chinese Christians.«[33]

Im Jahr 1949 gab es etwa eine Million protestantische Christen in China. Über ganz China verteilt existierten 322 christliche Krankenhäuser, mehr als 240 Schulen, 13 christliche Colleges sowie 210 Seminare und Bibelschulen, die von verschiedenen Denominationen betrieben wurden.[34] So schrieb Gänßbauer: »Die Situation des protestantischen Christentums war damit äußerst komplex.«[35] Es war allerdings deutlich, dass alle kirchlichen Institutionen ausländischen Missionsgesellschaften unterstellt waren.

Aus politischen Gründen wurden zwischen 1950 und 1952 alle ausländischen Missionare aus China ausgewiesen. Es handelte sich dabei um ungefähr 6200 Personen. Zusätzlich wurde staatlicherseits den Kirchen der Kontakt zu ausländischen Institutionen und Vereinigungen vollständig verboten. Nach den positiven Erfahrungen der in den 1950er Jahren durchgeführten Bewegung unter dem Motto: »Widerstand gegen die USA – Hilfe für Korea – patriotische Drei-Selbst-Bewegung der Christlichen Kirche in China«, die von Nanjing aus gestartet wurde, fand von Juli bis August 1954 die erste Nationalsynode protestantischer

33 Zemin Chen, Reconciliation with the People (1981), in: Richard Mouw/Ruomin Liu (ed.), The Church in China in the 20th Century, Eugene 2019, 121.

34 Revised Directory of the Protestant Christian Movement in China, National Christian Council in China, Shanghai 1949. III-10ff.

35 Gänßbauer, Parteistaat und Protestantische Kirche, 112.

Kirchen in Beijing statt. Dort wurde ein Komitee zur Leitung der Drei-Selbst-Bewegung eingesetzt und eine entsprechende Satzung erlassen.[36]

Die staatlich anerkannte protestantische Kirche in China wird seither von der »Patriotischen Drei-Selbst-Bewegung« repräsentiert, seit 1980 allerdings ergänzt um den Chinesischen Christenrat als zweite Dachorganisation, mit der es eine enge Zusammenarbeit gibt. Der Name Drei-Selbst bezieht sich auf das Prinzip der Selbständigkeit gegenüber westlichen Missionsgesellschaften, die sich auf folgenden drei Ebenen erweist: eigener Verkündigung, eigener Finanzierung, eigener Ausbildung.

Es ist auch deutlich, dass der große Anteil der Kirchen in China, die nicht zu der offiziellen protestantischen Kirche in China gehören, zumindest inhaltlich auch von der »Drei-Selbst-Bewegung« repräsentiert werden. Denn diese sind seit den 1950er Jahren ebenso unabhängig von ausländischen Missionsgesellschaften. Sie wollen sich aber nicht der sog. patriotischen Politik der Partei unterstellen, die diese Bewegung repräsentiert. Denn »die Drei-Selbst-Bewegung wurde als politische Massenorganisation immer wieder von Seiten des Parteistaates für Eingriffe in innerkirchliche Angelegenheiten missbraucht.«[37] Kirchen außerhalb des Dachverbandes streben nicht nur nach der Unabhängigkeit von ausländischer Beeinflussung, sondern auch nach einer angemessenen Trennung von Kirche und Staat.

Auch wenn die Prinzipien der Drei-Selbst-Bewegung, bzw. der Unabhängigkeit keine Erfindung der kommunistischen Machthaber sind, sondern schon vorher innerkirchlich vertreten wurden, so hat die Führung sie doch für ihre Zwecke der Kontrolle der Religion zu instrumentalisieren gewusst. Auf eine Beschwerde über die Behandlung von Christen im neuen China vom Mai 1950 hin wurde ein

36 Rulei Xu, Der Anfang der Drei-Selbst-Bewegung, in Zongjiao (Religion), Nanjing Universität, 12 (2002), 12 (Chinesisch).

37 Gänßbauer, Partiestaat und Protestantische Kirche, 132. – Am 31.3.2004 kritisierte K. H. Ting in seinem letzten öffentlichen Vortrag am *Nanjing Union Theological Seminary* in Nanjing die ungenügende Trennung von Kirche und Staat, bzw. den Missbrauch der Macht von einem Teil der Beamt*innen der chinesischen Religionsbehörde. »... Daher erscheinen Opiumtheorie und Kampftheorie wie Zwillinge immer zusammen. Dies ist meine Meinung zu dem Satz, dass ›Religion Opium ist‹. Obwohl es viele Tatsachen gibt, die uns sagen, dass wir Religion nicht als Opium betrachten können, wie es im Marxismus behauptet wurde, ist diese Ansicht in unserem Land immer noch weit verbreitet und wurde beibehalten. Obwohl auch in China die Theorie, dass ›Religion Opium für das Volk‹ sei, in den Hintergrund getreten ist, gibt es immer noch viele Menschen, die, obwohl sie es nicht sagen, immer noch denken, dass Religion Opium sei. Religion ist also das Gespenst des Opiums und das Gespenst des Kampfes gegen die Religion. Das hat gleichzeitig einen großen Einfluss auf die Welt.« (unveröffentlicht)

Manifest verfasst, das die Prinzipien der Drei-Selbst-Bewegung allen Christen verpflichtend auferlegte und deren Zustimmung mittels Unterschrift einforderte. Die Drei-Selbst-Bewegung wurde mit allen kirchenleitenden Funktionen betraut, und es begann eine Hetzjagd auf alle, die das Manifest nicht unterzeichnen wollten. Das betraf auch eine Reihe von Kirchen, die schon lange zuvor unabhängig von den Missionsgesellschaften waren. Diese waren nie »Laufhunde des Imperialismus«, aber wehrten sich gegen die Bevormundung durch den Staat. Sie bilden die Wurzel der sogenannten Hauskirchen.[38]

3.2 Die post-denominationelle Kirche

Eine der Grundlagen des chinesischen protestantischen Geisteslebens im Festland Chinas ist die sechzigjährige Erfahrung der so genannten postkonfessionellen Kirche. Fast alle Kirchen in Taiwan, Hong Kong, Macao und den chinesischen Überseegemeinden sind konfessionell gebunden und orientieren sich an den entsprechenden Traditionen. Die denominationellen Trennungen sind auf den Einfluss der Mission im 19. Jahrhundert zurückzuführen.

Unter dem Eindruck des schärfer werdenden politischen Drucks und der Trennung der Kirchen in Festland-China von den ausländischen konfessionellen (Mutter-)Kirchen und ihren Missionswerken (aus den erwähnten politischen Gründen von 1949 bis 1980), sind die Kirchen in Festland-China unter dem Stichwort »vereinigter Gottesdienst« (*lianhe libai*) einen eigenen post-denominationellen Weg gegangen.[39]

Für theologische Fragen ist der Chinesische Christenrat zuständig, der 1980 u. a. auf Betreiben von Bischof Ting als kirchlicher Gegenpol zur Drei-Selbst-Bewegung gegründet wurde, der sich aber in der Tat wenig von der Drei-Selbst-Bewegung unterscheidet und aufs engste mit dieser verflochten ist. Die eigene

38 Siehe: unter 4.1 Versöhnung zwischen Hauskirchen und Kirche im politischen System.

39 Miikka Ruokanen/Ruomin Liu/Yongtao Chen, Is »Postdenominational Christianity« Possible? Ecclesiology in the Protestant Church of China, The Ecumenical Review, 67/1, (2015), 77–95, 78: »The period of denominational Protestant churches in China was, after all, relatively short, being only about one hundred years. Protestant missionaries entered China in the beginning of the 19th century, proper church growth and the formation of Christian congregations in China started around 1860; in 1950s the Three-Self-led church abolished the right for denominations to exist. Another story involves those Christians who never recognized the leadership of the TSPM. Today they are called home ‹church› or ‹house church› Christians. A closer study of that movement is out of the scope of this paper.«

Geschichte wurde bisher nicht systematisch reflektiert. Die Drei-Selbst-Bewegung hat noch nicht ihre eigene Ekklesiologie entwickelt. Sie hat auch noch keine einheitliche Liturgie oder Theologie hervorgebracht. Die Gemeinden bringen ihre jeweilige frühere denominationelle Prägung mit ein. Aiming Wang und Fedrik Fällman haben darauf hingewiesen: »Es gibt auch viele Tendenzen in Richtung einer Rückkehr zum Denominationalismus und zu weniger Einheit« der Kirchen in China.[40]

3.3 Effizienter Dienst der Laien bzw. Mangel an ausgebildeten Theolog*innen

In dem Parteistaat ist neben der Predigt das persönliche Zeugnis der Gläubigen eine weitere effektive Möglichkeit, Gottes Wort den Chines*innen von heute zu vermitteln. In einer Situation, in der Aktivitäten der Kirche auf den semiöffentlichen Raum innerhalb der eigenen Gebäude beschränkt sind, ist die Kommunikation von Menschen zu Menschen von entscheidender Bedeutung. Chinesische Christ*innen sehen es als ihre Berufung an, das Wort Gottes und ihre eigene Glaubenserfahrung mit ihren Familienmitgliedern, Freunden, Kollegen, Nachbarn usw. zu teilen. Das Wachstum der Kirche basiert auf dieser Art von Evangelisation.

Die protestantische Kirche Chinas ist im Wesen eine Kirche, die von Laien geführt wird. In China kommt etwa eine ordinierte Pastorin, ein ordinierter Pastor, auf zehntausend Gläubige (1:10 000).[41] Die meisten Pastor*innen arbeiten in den Städten. Auf dem Land kann es Gemeinden mit Zehntausenden von Gläubigen geben, die überhaupt keine ordinierte Leitungsperson haben. Selbst die Zahl der s. g. Ältesten,[42] die fast dieselben Rechte wie Pastoren*innen und eine vergleichbare spirituelle Autorität haben, ist sehr begrenzt. Folglich liegen in großen Gebieten Gottesdienst, Predigt, Beratung, Kirchenleitung usw. in der Verantwortung von Laienprediger*innen und Laiengläubigen. Laienprediger*innen haben

40 Fredrik Fällman, Evangelisierung in der evangelischen Kirche in China – Reflexionen eines westlichen Sinologen, in China Heute XXXVI/2 (2017), China-Zentrum, Sankt Augustin, 97.

41 Ende 2016 gab es insgesamt 36177 Pastor*innen, Älteste und Prediger*innen in China. Davon waren 4149 ordinierte Pastor*innen. Siehe: Ruomin Liu, Ein geschichtlicher Überblick über die Entstehung und gegenwärtige Lage der Kirche in China, in: Theologische Stimme aus China. TIMA 14, Missionsakademie an Universität Hamburg: Hamburg 2018, 21ff.

42 Wegen der früheren denominationellen Prägung in China haben manche Gemeinden, z. B. Ortsgemeinden (Little Flock) in einigen Gebieten in China Älteste. Diese haben auch Theologie studiert und werden mit einer Zeremonie in ihr Amt eingeführt.

möglicherweise eine theologische Ausbildung, deren akademischer Grad sehr unterschiedlich ausfallen kann.

4. Versöhnung und Verantwortung

4.1 Versöhnung zwischen Hauskirche und Kirche im politischen System

Sowohl die Geschichte der Gesellschaft als auch die Geschichte der Kirche in China sind gepflastert mit Konflikten und Streit. Führt man sich bspw. die Geschichte der Kirche in China zwischen 1949 und 1979 vor Augen,[43] öffnet sich damit ein Kontext, in dem abendländisch-christliche Traditionen keinerlei Verankerung haben und von religiöser Freiheit nur schwerlich die Rede sein kann. Unter diesen extremen Umständen muss auch dem Hauskirchenwesen mit seinen geheimen Gottesdiensten und häuslichen Versammlungen eine neue Bedeutung zugeschrieben werden. Für die Kirche in China spielten diese Versammlungen mit häufig privatem Charakter eine entscheidende Rolle. In der Zeit der Kulturrevolution war jede öffentliche Religionsausübung verboten. Wollten Kirchen in dieser Periode extremer Einschränkungen weiterhin Bestand haben, mussten sie sich auf Formen des Hauskirchenwesens beschränken. So besuchten Christen in China auch während der Kulturrevolution weiterhin Gottesdienste, die nun allerdings geheim sowohl in den Städten als auch auf dem Land stattfanden. Weder die Orte noch die Zeiten der Gottesdienste waren institutionalisiert. Sie fanden in verschiedenen Häusern oft auch um Mitternacht statt. Die versammelten Christen lasen gemeinsam in der Bibel und beteten. Diese Formen von Kirche ermöglichten die unglaubliche Zahl von vier Millionen Protestanten in China

43 »In der Kulturrevolution geriet die pragmatische Haltung der Partei den Religionen gegenüber unter den Beschuss der Roten Garden. Sie versuchten, die ›Vier Alten‹ (Ideen, Kultur, Sitten, Gebräuche) auszulöschen, und in diesem Zusammenhang zerstörten sie einfach alles, was mit Religion zu tun hatte. Harte Verfolgung wurde zur Regel. Die wenigen noch geöffneten Kirchen und Tempel wurden gestürmt und geplündert, Kultgegenstände geraubt und vernichtet. Die katholischen Laien, Ordensfrauen, Mönche und Geistlichen wurden verhöhnt, geschlagen, bespuckt, Moslems gezwungen, in Kommunen mit Nicht-Moslems zu leben und zu arbeiten und die gleiche Nahrung (Schweinefleisch) zu sich zu nehmen. Die systematische Ausrottung des lamaistischen Buddhismus in Tibet zu dieser Zeit ist ein weiteres Beispiel für die Erfahrungen, die Gläubige jedweder Konfession gemacht haben. Selbst das Büro für religiöse Angelegenheiten wurde geschlossen. Keine andere Religion scheint aber auf so systematische Art eliminiert worden zu sein wie das Christentum.« R. Malek, Das Tao des Himmels, Freiburg 1996, 201f.

bereits nach Ende der Kulturrevolution im Jahre 1976 (im Vergleich zu 750 000 Protestanten im Jahre 1958).[44] Das Hauskirchenwesen ermöglichte den Christen während der Zeit der chinesischen Kulturrevolution also nicht nur weiterhin ein Leben des Glaubens, sondern trug dazu bei, den Leib Christi zu vergrößern und die Kirche für viele Menschen zu öffnen. Hier kam es gerade nicht zu individualistischen Abgrenzungen, zum Ausschluss und zur Privatisierung des Christentums. Vielmehr war das Hauskirchenwesen die einzig mögliche Form einer christlichen Kirche zur Zeit der Kulturrevolution. Die in diesem extremen Kontext angelegten Formen von Gemeinde leben bis heute in der christlichen Tradition Chinas weiter, indem sich viele Christen auch heute noch mit anderen Christen zu Gebet, Bibelkreis und Gottesdienst in ihren eigenen Häusern treffen.

Öffentliche gottesdienstliche Versammlungen und christliche Hauskirche spielen beide eine bedeutende Rolle und wirken gegenseitig aufeinander ein. Dass dabei vor allem die öffentlichen gottesdienstlichen Versammlungen sowohl nach außen als auch nach innen eine bedeutende Rolle spielen, bleibt unbestritten. Dennoch zeigt das Beispiel der chinesischen protestantischen Kirche während der extremen Situation der chinesischen Kulturrevolution, wie auch durch das Hauskirchenwesen Kirche nicht nur am Leben erhalten, sondern zugleich noch vergrößert werden kann. So können die privaten gottesdienstlichen Haussitten chinesischer Christen in dieser Zeit als Beispiel für offene und auf weitere Teile der Menschheit ausgerichtete Versammlungen gelten, die trotz ihres privaten Charakters in einer Extremsituation nicht zu einer Individualisierung der Kirche, sondern zu einer sich vergrößernden Gemeinschaft geführt haben.

4.2 Verantwortung

Indem sowohl der extreme Kollektivismus als auch gleichzeitig der extreme Individualismus unterjochende Auswirkungen haben können, treten diese beiden Spielarten häufig zusammen auf. Beide ermöglichen die Verbreitung von Korruption, richten sich gegen die Menschenrechte und unterstützen die Herrschaft von Tyrannen. Während diese Gefahren im Fall des Kollektivismus deutlicher vor Augen stehen dürften, ist zum radikalen Individualismus zu bemerken, dass auch er die effiziente Abwehr von Gefahren für Gemeinschaft und Freiheit unter-

44 M. Ruokannen, u. a., Is »Post-denominational« Christianity possible? Ecclesiology in the Protestant Church of China«, Ecumenical Review 67/1, (2015), 77ff.

graben kann. Beide Formen können sich sowohl kirchliche als auch politische Systeme zu eigen machen und in ihren Dienst stellen. So herrscht in Festland-China als offizielles, staatlich legitimiertes politisches System der Kollektivismus. Ausgerichtet ist dieser Kollektivismus, der jedes Menschenleben nur als Teil der »Organisation« begreift, auf die »Chinesische Kommunistische Partei«.[45] Und gleichzeitig blüht inmitten dieses Kollektivismus, wie oben gezeigt, der Individualismus durch Korruption in unfassbaren Ausmaßen. Viele wichtige Stellen des Systems sind mit Beamten besetzt, die im Volksmund als »die einsamen Beamten« (naked officials) bezeichnet werden: Ihre Familien haben zumeist ausländische Staatsangehörigkeit, und durch Korruption und Kollaboration wird von diesen Beamten ein Vermögen angesammelt, das sogleich im Ausland in Sicherheit gebracht wird. Dieser Individualismus geschieht hinter dem Schutzschild des Kollektivismus, der nach außen offiziell nach einer geschlossenen harmonischen Gesellschaft strebt, der sich jedes Individuum unterzuordnen hat und nach innen von individualistischem Machtstreben zerfressen ist. So wird China zu einem typischen Beispiel für das Paradoxon von Kollektivismus und Individualismus.

Gerade aber für die christliche Gemeinschaft, die in einer solchen Gesellschaft lebt, die sich des kollektiven Zwangs bedient, hat die Balance von christlicher Kollektivperson und Individuum eine außergewöhnlich große Bedeutung. Der Bestand dieser dialektischen Bestimmung ihrer Gemeinschaft inmitten von Korruption und Zwang zum Kollektiv kann so zur tragenden Hoffnung werden – zunächst für jeden einzelnen Christen, schließlich aber auch für die ganze Gesellschaft in ihrem Kampf gegen Kollektivismus und Individualismus.

Obwohl die protestantische Kirche in China sogar während der Extremsituation der Kulturrevolution wachsen konnte, ist ihre Situation heute vor allem unübersichtlich und verworren.[46] Hier gilt es, die protestantische Kirche auch in

45 In China finden sich schon im alltäglichen Leben viele Beispiele für die Schwierigkeiten und Entbehrungen, die Folgen des extremen Kollektivismus sind. So besitzt prinzipiell niemand wirkliches Eigentum. Die Einzelkind-Politik bis 2016 erforderte es, verschiedene Genehmigungen von ganz unterschiedlichen Behörden zu besorgen, wenn man sich für die Gründung einer Familie entschied. Ein zweites Kind zu bekommen, war auf Grund des großen bürokratischen Aufwandes fast unmöglich. Bezeichnenderweise lassen sich zu diesen Schwierigkeiten keine öffentlichen Dokumente finden, da eine Behandlung dieser Themen in China verboten ist.

46 Die offiziellen Dachorganisationen haben auf die Gemeinden selbst aber nur beschränkten Einfluss. Jede lokale Gemeinde ist, auch finanziell, für sich selbst verantwortlich. Einen Einfluss haben die staatlichen Kirchenorganisationen bei der Ausbildung der Geistlichen und bei der Bereitstellung von Arbeitsmaterialien. Religiöse Amtsträger dürfen religiöse Aktivitäten nur nach

China zu einer »gepflegten«[47] Gemeinschaft aufzubauen, die sowohl die Bibel als ihre Grundlage ernst nimmt, als auch die Tradition ihrer Theologie pflegt und nicht zuletzt ihre Verantwortung in der gegenwärtigen Welt nach innen und auch außen wahrnimmt. Im Mittelpunkt müssen dabei ebenso gottesdienstliche und kirchliche Versammlungen stehen wie die Aufgaben der Diakonie. Dabei gilt es, auch die Aufgabe der Mission wahrzunehmen und in der Öffentlichkeit Position zu beziehen.

Wenn öffentliche gesellschaftliche Ereignisse stattfinden, schweigt das Christentum in China. Selbst unter Beteiligung christlicher sozialer Dienste und bei finanziellem Engagement gibt es in den meisten Fällen keine angemessene Stimme. Im Hintergrund kann dabei eine wichtige Bemerkung Bonhoeffers paraphrasiert werden: Es gibt nicht nur eine Schuld der einzelnen Chinesen, der einzelnen Christen, sondern es gibt eine Schuld Chinas und eine Schuld der Kirche vor Gott, dem Schöpfer. Hier schaffen nicht die Bußfertigkeit und Rechtfertigung der Einzelnen Abhilfe, sondern China und die Kirche müssen Buße tun und Rechtfertigung erfahren.[48] Dieser Satz macht jedem Christen seine Verantwortung und seine Stellvertretung für die Welt deutlich bewusst. Die Kraft Christi und des Heiligen Geistes aber sind es, die es jedem Einzelnen ermöglichen, in der Welt als Zeuge und Zeugin Christi verantwortlich zu leben. Wie Chen in seinem letzten

der Bestätigung durch die staatlich anerkannten religiösen Organisationen und nach Registrierung bei den staatlichen Abteilungen für religiöse Angelegenheiten ausüben. – Auf evangelischer Seite gibt es die Gemeinden und »Versammlungsstätten«, die zum Chinesischen Christenrat und der Drei-Selbst-Bewegung gehören. Außerdem bestehen halb-unabhängige Gemeinden, die in loser Verbindung zum Chinesischen Christenrat und der Drei-Selbst-Bewegung stehen. Daneben gibt es völlig selbständige, sogenannte Hauskirchen. – Die Kirchen der Drei-Selbst-Bewegung und ihre Versammlungsstätten sind offiziell anerkannt und staatlich registriert. Ihre religiösen Versammlungsstätten befinden sich meist in den Städten beziehungsweise in deren Nähe. Die halb unabhängigen ländlichen Kirchen sind nur teilweise staatlich registriert, gehören aber nicht zur Drei-Selbst-Bewegung.

47 Welker, Vorwort, 10.

48 Dietrich Bonhoeffer, Sanctorum Communio, München 1986, 74. – Verschiedene Gruppen haben auch in der Zeit der chinesischen Kulturrevolution das politische Herrschaftssystem und dessen gesellschaftliche Auswirkungen kritisiert. Darunter befanden sich fast alle anderen religiösen Gruppen, auch die katholische Kirche. Protestantische Gruppierungen traten dagegen in diesem Zusammenhang nicht hervor. – Bonhoeffer schreibt in seiner *Ethik*: »Sie [sc. die Kirche] war stumm, wo sie hätte schreien müssen. [...] Die Kirche bekennt, an dem Zusammenbruch der elterlichen Autorität schuldig zu sein. [...] Die Kirche bekennt, die willkürliche Anwendung brutaler Gewalt, das leibliche und seelische Leiden unzähliger Unschuldiger, Unterdrückung, Hass, Mord, gesehen zu haben ohne ihre Stimme für sie zu erheben, ohne Wege gefunden zu haben, ihnen zu Hilfe zu eilen. Sie ist schuldig geworden am Leben der schwächsten und wehrlosesten Brüder Jesu Christi.« Bonhoeffer, *Ethik*, 129f.

Vortrag im Jahr 2009 betonte: Die christlichen und akademischen theologischen Wissenschaftler*innen der Jinling-Schule des chinesischen Christentums, die von der Wahrheit zeugt, der er sich verpflichtet hat, »mögen aufrichtig wohlwollend, wahr, gerecht, demütig und dienend sein.«[49]

5. Ein Wort zum Schluss

Will heute noch jemand neue sichtbare oder unsichtbare Mauern bauen? Wird die Chinesische Mauer, die das Reich der Mitte einst vor der übrigen Welt geheimnisvoll verbarg, heute nicht von Millionen ausländischer Touristen überwunden, die China besuchen? Und auch Millionen Chinesinnen und Chinesen überwinden von der anderen Seite her die abschirmende Mauer, sodass es kaum einen Ort auf dieser Erde gibt, an dem nicht auch Menschen aus China zu finden sind. Die Chinesische Mauer hat ihre trennende Kraft verloren! Besonders heute, im Zeitalter der Weiterentwicklung von Digitalisierung und künstlicher Intelligenz, kann niemand eine Mauer, weder eine sichtbare noch eine unsichtbare, die Menschen trennt, aufrechterhalten.

Luis Gutheinz hat am Ende seines Buches, *Chinesische Theologie im Werden. Ein Blick in die Werkstatt der christlichen-chinesischen Theologie*, einen Wunsch formuliert: »Wie im säkularen Bereich das ›Reich der Mitte‹ (China) sich anschickt, einen angemessenen Platz innerhalb der großen Völkerfamilie zu erobern, so beginnt auch das chinesische Christentum seine theologische Stimme zu erheben. Diese Stimme wird den Chor des weltweiten theologischen Denkens bereichern.«[50]

Wunsch und Ziel des vorliegenden Aufsatzes sind es, mit chinesischen Christ*innen und Christen weltweit in Kontakt zu kommen, ihre Lebenswirklichkeit kennen zu lernen und von ihren Wünschen und Hoffnungen zu erfahren: Die theologische Stimme aus China bzw. die Sinisierung der Theologie könnte einen wichtigen Beitrag zur Polyphonie der Theologien leisten.

(Dr. Ruomin Liu ist Studienleiter an Missionsakademie an der Universität Hamburg.)

49 Zemin Chen, »Ich habe noch ein Wort« (Vortrag am 10.6.2009), Jinling Shenxue zhi (Theologische Zeitschrift des Jinling-Seminars), 2013-02, Nanjing 2003, 15. (Chinesisch)
50 L. Gutheinz, Chinesische Theologie im Werden. Ein Blick in die Werkstatt der christlich-chinesischen Theologie, Ostfildern 2012, 127.

ABSTRACT

Since 2014 the Chinese Communist Party has adhered to the goal of »sinicizing religions« in China and has made »socialist core values« play a leading role in the religious community. The Leaders of the Country, the United Front Work Department and various scholars have claimed its necessity, task and aim.
The paper tries to offer some reflections about the potential use of the term »sinicization« (sinonization) according to the perspective of contextual theology. This is a positive concept not only for the church of China, but also for intercultural theology, when related to the context of the Church in the party state and it's search for its role. The movement of theological renewal of the Protestant Church in Mainland China since 1998 was one of the pioneers of sinicization.
Here the aim has been to show that the concept of »sinicization«, being political and cultural in its origin, could be applied to analyzing and reflecting the situation, challenges and social tasks of the Protestant Church in Mainland China. Moreover, the churches in China have many unique characteristics and peculiarities which could offer some source material for further reflections on the contextualization and inculturation of Christian theology.

Christian Knowings from the Global South

A Theological Approximation to De Sousa Santos' »Epistemologies of the South«

Daniel Jara J.

Considering the work of Dussel and others, who affirm that for centuries the theological reflections of the global South have been referred to as inferior to academic theology from European (and more recently from US American) background[1], in this article I relate key elements of the sociological theory of Boaventura De Sousa Santos (* 1940 in Coimbra) to central issues in the field of Intercultural Theology. De Sousa Santos is a Portuguese epistemologist and sociologist who holds a doctorate in Sociology of Law from Yale University. Nowadays, he is emeritus professor of Economy and Sociology at the University of Coimbra, director emeritus of its Centre for Social Studies, Global legal scholar at Warwick University, and Distinguished Legal Scholar at the University of Wisconsin-Madison. Between 2011 and 2016, De Sousa Santos directed the research project *ALICE – Strange mirrors, unforeseen lessons: defining for Europe a new way of sharing experiences around the world*, a project funded by the European Research Council (ERC). De Sousa Santos is a referential figure of the Iberoamerican political progressive wing and is one of the main promoters of the World Social Forum. His academic posture can be described as militant and is well summarized in the title of his latest book: *The End of the Cognitive Empire:*

1 See: Enrique Dussel, Flujo y reflujo del Evangelio. Cuando evangelizados se tornan evangelizadores, in: Concilium 207 (1986), 265–275; Daniel Jara J., Enrique Dussel's »Otherness« and the Problem of the Eurocentric Totalized Epistemological System in Academic Theology, in: Teología 133 (2020), 159–182.

The Coming Age of Epistemologies of the South[2]. Thereby, his publications focus on such themes as globalization, sociology of law, epistemology, democracy, and human rights[3]. His approximations to theology and religious studies are specially oriented to his social activism through publications such as *If God were a Human Rights Activist*[4]. His theory is mainly popular among Latin American social scholars and, to a lesser extent, theologians who are starting to use it as a resource for post-colonial religious research[5].

The work of the De Sousa Santos is vast. Nevertheless, he summarizes the main points of his theory as follows:

> »There is no global justice without global cognitive justice, that is to say, that there has to be equity between different ways of knowing and different kinds of knowledge. I offer this argument in conjunction with two other arguments: first, the understanding of the world by far exceeds the Western understanding of the world; second, the emancipatory transformation in the world may follow grammars and scripts other than those developed by Western-centric critical theory, and such diversity must be valorized.«[6]

This aim for global cognitive justice naturally includes epistemological justice in social sciences and humanities, and therefore in academic theology.

His research is the result of reflection on a major issue: »like never before, the most important problems of each one of the social sciences, far from being specifics, match with those that social sciences face in general« and this is: »Why did it become so difficult to create a critical social theory?« This author understands by »critical social theory« one which »does not reduce ›reality‹ to what already exists«[7]. On a theological level, this reduction points to most of the old promises made by both missiology and contextual theology, and whose fulfillment is still

2 Boaventura De Sousa Santos, The End of the Cognitive Empire. The Coming of Age of Epistemologies of the South, Durham/London 2020.

3 Centre for Social Studies University of Coimbra: Boaventura de Sousa Santos [website], https://ces.uc.pt/en/ces/pessoas/investigadoras-es/boaventura-de-sousa-santos (28.1.2018).

4 Boaventura De Sousa Santos, If God Were a Human Rights Activist, Stanford 2015.

5 See: Nicolás Panotto, Razón pública, religiones y contra-públicos, in: Religión e incidencia pública 7 (2019), 65–90; Pedro Acevedo, El Foro Mundial de Teología y Liberación. Una mirada panorámica, in: Revista CLAR 4 (2005). 45–53.

6 Boaventura De Sousa Santos, Epistemologies of the South. Justice Against Epistemicide, London/New York 2016, 237.

7 Boaventura De Sousa Santos, Conocer Desde el Sur. Para Una Política Emancipatoria, Lima 2006, 17.

a pending task. Among the most important are: first, the promise of an egalitarian status between theological reflections from the global North and the global South, in the current situation where southern theologies are still exotic guests at the theological table, as Sugirtharajah asserts in the 25th-anniversary edition of his book *Voices from the margin*: »Biblical scholarship continues to be managed and controlled by the West. There has been no perceptible improvement since I raised this issue in the fifteenth-anniversary edition of *Voices*. Of all the disciplines in the humanities, biblical studies was the creation of the West and remains unabashedly Eurocentric.«[8]

A second unfulfilled promise refers to the still pending methodological freedom among scholars in nowadays polycentric Christendom, considering that European-made methods, such as historical criticism, are far from abandoning their position of academic prevalence. In this sense, Horkheimer's definition of a critical theory is fully applicable to theology: »The modern critical theory is, above all, a theory epistemologically founded on the need to overcome the bourgeois dualism between the individual scientist [European theologian] as the autonomous creator of knowledge and the *totality* of the social activity [religious experience]«[9].

De Sousa Santos' analysis usually deploys a radical approach that seems to fall in reductionist generalizations regarding the intellectual work in the global North and South. Nevertheless, it should not be overlooked that his discursive style follows the line of many other notorious Latin American polemicists in the modernity/coloniality tradition, such as Enrique Dussel, Walter Mignolo, and Aníbal Quijano. In this sense, the scientific rigorousness of his academic reflection frequently fades before the urgency and vigor of his political and social engagement. Nonetheless, several of De Sousa Santos' vindications are incisive critiques to common practices of European academic thinking. To make a theological extrapolation, I can mention for example its tendency to reduce all the enigmatic richness of the religious experience and God's revelation to a series of rational doctrines of global validity; and how the excessive parceling of the theological knowledge ended up by creating theologians who fit very well to De Sousa Santo's epithet of »specialized ignorants.«[10]

8 S. R. Sugirtharajah, Voices from the Margin: Interpreting the Bible in the Third World, New York 2016, 315.
9 Max Horkheimer, Critical Theory. Selected Essays, New York 1972, 98.
10 Boaventura De Sousa Santos, Una Epistemología del Sur, México 2009, 48.

In De Sousa Santos' theory, the global North and South are two categories that are mainly used as metaphors to differentiate between styles of knowing, their methods, backgrounds, and the power relations existing among them:

> »The South is used here as a metaphor for the human suffering which is systematically caused by colonialism and capitalism. It is a South that exists as well in the geographic global North, the so-called interior third world of the hegemonic countries. At the same time, the global South contains in itself [...] the local practices of complicity with them.«[11]

Thus, although both global North and global South overlap in a significant degree with their geographical correspondents, there exist several »Norths« in the geographical southern hemisphere, as is the case of mainstream academic theology in the metropolis of New Zealand and Australia. Likewise, several »Souths« emerge as a response to different situations of structural oppression in the geographical North, as occurs among religious communities in Belarus, Mongolia, or Mexico. In this sense, at the very center of this categorization lies a profound paradox: De Sousa Santos claims the richly diverse epistemological nature of human reflections, at the same time dividing them on the basis of a dualistic North/South classification. Hence the deeply metaphorical nature of these categories is an indication of relations of power and validation among knowing styles rather than static categories.

To address these issues, the current article is divided into five main parts. The first one analyzes the self-placed position of privilege of academic western theology, the common features of the epistemological systems that support it, and its normative role over global theological knowledge. The second part studies the constitutive differences between the knowledges and the *ways of knowing* involved in global theological reflection. The third part analyzes the »absent« condition of southern theological *ways of knowing*, the ruling status that »metonymic reason« possess over the metropolitan knowledge, and the character of emptiness or absence it reserves for the *ways of knowing* from the global South. Fourth, the article states the crucial role that the *Sociology of the emergences* can play to facilitate the outbreak of theological *ways of knowing* from the global South in intercultural ecumenical exchange, and it refers to three kinds of emergences that

11 De Sousa Santos, Una Epistemología del Sur, 2.

deserve to be mentioned and analyzed according to this methodology: seed ruins, counter-hegemonic appropriations, and liberated zones. Finally, as a conclusion, it evaluates the theoretical and methodological significance of De Sousa Santos' sociological theory for current Intercultural Theology.

On the one side of the abyssal line: the self-placed position of privilege of academic western theology

One of the main theses of De Sousa Santos is that the »unique vision [of western scientific knowledge], far from being a natural phenomenon, is the consubstantial or original product of the creative destruction of modern science«[12]. In this sense, though controversial, it is necessary to explore to what extent the normative position of western theology is in part the result of a centuries-long active effort to eliminate any alternative knowledge or reflection that could menace such a position. A modern example that could sustain this hypothesis is the canonical process in 1984 carried out against Leonardo Boff's book *Church: Charism and Power*, and the entire Latin American Liberation Theology by extension. It is highly relevant to our discussion that the Notification of the *Congregation for the Doctrine of the Faith* about this process stated: »When examined in the light of the criteria of an authentic theological method – which has just been briefly outlined – certain options in L. Boff's book appear to be unsustainable.«[13] This »criteria of an authentic theological method« is obviously Latin-Germanic methodology, all outside of it results by exclusion as inauthentic, spurious, or illicit. About this canonical process, Dussel controversially reflects: »The center fearfully protects itself [...] It feels under attack, humiliated, demanded to change [...] and it resists.«[14]

For De Sousa Santos' radical and militant black and white view, the epistemologies of the global North behave as a massive inexorable force that seems to eliminate everything in its way, and he is willing to make use of rhetoric exacerbations to illustrate his point. To his argument for the *creative destruction* of modern science, he adds: »the epistemological privilege of modern science

12 De Sousa Santos, Una epistemología del Sur, 81.

13 The Holy See – Congregation for the Doctrine of Faith, Notification on the book »Church: Charism and Power« by Father Leonardo Boff O.F.M. AAS 77, Vatican 1985, 756–762.

14 Dussel, Flujo y reflujo del Evangelio, 271.

is the consequence of an *epistemicide* [which] implies the destruction of social practices and the disqualification of the social agents which act according to the defendant knowledge«[15]. For the author, it would result paradigmatically that Boff's first punishment was to remain silent (silencing), and the second one – which caused his resignation from the Franciscan clergy – was the attempt to send him to a country in South East Asia with the prohibition to teach (elimination).

According to the Portuguese sociologist, western academy placed itself in a position of epistemological privilege, ignoring at the same time the fact that its methodology, study objects, aims, and assumptions depend »on a complex mix of science and non-science constructs«[16], which makes evident its cultural embeddedness and non-»objective« character (precisely what it rejects from alien non-scientific methodologies). Some of these constructs are for example the arbitrary selection of relevant research topics and problematics to explore, suitable theoretical models, »authentic« study methodologies, specific kinds of language and metaphors to be used, etc. Thereby, the author scrutinizes the instrumental dialectic between knowledge and the agent that produces it, to refute the claimed objectivity of western scientific knowledge:

> »There is no knowledge that is not known by someone for some purpose. All forms of knowledge are testimonial since what they know of reality (their active dimension) is always reflected back in what they reveal about the subject of this knowledge (their subjective dimension).«[17]

De Sousa Santos' polemic style ends up falling (voluntarily or not) in a reductionist position regarding the fact that there is not only one monolithic and invariable epistemological system in the global North; on the contrary, many of them have coexisted or competed for centuries. However, his theory is especially useful in Intercultural Theology because it highlights that, from a comparative perspective, most of these epistemological systems share to a greater or lesser extent some of the following features: the priority of scientific knowledge over any other knowledge or way of knowing; a deterministic scientific rigor; an almost absolute Cartesian differentiation between nature (or creation in theological

15 De Sousa Santos, Una Epistemología del Sur, 81
16 De Sousa Santos, Epistemologies of the South, 194.
17 Ibid., 201.

language) as *res extensa* and human beings as *res cogitans*; the presupposition that the linear time is the only temporal possible option; the tendency for parcelling and sub-parcelling academic disciplines in an infinite specialization trend as the natural via for knowledge's development; an almost general preference for experimentation of the world over experiencing it; a claim for supra-cultural and supra-contextual validity of their conclusions; the search for truth as the right and unique representation of reality; a clear distinction between 1) subject and object – and the reluctance to connect them in any ontological dimension – and 2) knowledge and its subject – which supported western dissociation between systematic and practical theologies –, and a deterministic search for regularities and laws which govern nature, and whose syntheses allow the condensation of the infinite complexity of the world into synthesized principles.

In conclusion, an almost general characteristic of these epistemologies of the North is the use of scientific rationality as the only means for achieving »valid« knowledge. In this sense, De Sousa Santos describes academic scientificism as a quasi-totalitarian model to the extent in which »it refuses the rational character of any way of knowing that does not follow its epistemological principles or its methodological rules«[18]. Nevertheless, on a theological level, this model conflicts with the reality of a study object (the sacred, its revelation, and the religious experience it entails) that because of its own mysterious and multi-dimensional nature refuses to be addressed based on purely rational-scientific methods.

Western theology is a suitable example showing how De Sousa Santos' theory, though useful and for the most part valid, seems to overlook the wide epistemological diversity within the global North. For example, this theory describes in an adequate manner rationally influenced theological systems such as Schleiermacher's *Kulturprotestantismus* and most liberal theologies. Nevertheless, it is an inadequate approach for the study of non-rational approaches to the divine such as the Pietist countermovement against the penetration of ideas of the Enlightenment into ecclesial life, and the so-called Spanish mystic-ascetic school of Saint Ignacio de Loyola, Teresa de Jesús, and Saint Teresa de Cepeda. In reality, mainstream European theology moves mainly within the tension between these two poles. Thereby, western theology shares with positivistic sciences the aim of examining its study object in a systematic and normative way: it explores

18 De Sousa Santos, Una Epistemología del Sur, 48.

its reasons to be, its validity and justification by employing reason and rational reflection; nevertheless, it manifests its own epistemological peculiarity when using not a simple kind of reason, but a reason which is enlightened by faith, and in the case of the Roman Catholic theology under the guidance of the Magisterium of the Church.[19]

Nonetheless, we can affirm with De Sousa Santos, that most theology from the global North is based upon meta-theoretical assumptions that include the notions of static order and stability in the world (expressed through methodological rules and doctrines of universal validity). To this, the Portuguese scholar adds: »the recognition of cultural diversity in the world does not necessarily signify recognition of the epistemological diversity of the world«[20]. Because of both, the tendency to universalize its knowledge and the lack of recognition of epistemological global diversity, theological faculties and seminaries in the global South performed for decades a constant exercise of repetition, which Dussel calls »the spirit of pure imitation«[21], of western academic theology. It merely adopted »folkloric« local aspects (such as language, dress codes, or similar native elements) while ignoring novel expressions and reflections of Christian faith and the *ways of knowing* that embody them.

Constitutive differences between the knowledges and the *ways of knowing* involved in global theological reflection

Two especially useful concepts for Intercultural Theology from De Sousa Santos' theory refer to the differentiation he makes between *knowledges* (*conocimientos* in Spanish or *connaissances* in French) and *ways of knowing* (*saberes* in Spanish or *savoirs* in French). These *ways of knowing* are characterized by their collective authorship and because they are not developed by an academic »elite« of theologians and exegetes but by common non-theologically trained believers. Unlike scientific, theological, and philosophical knowledges, the *ways of knowing* openly assert their contextual and culturally embedded character, and redefine the »relation between the knowing subject and the object of knowledge [because

19 Manuel Guerra Gómez, Historia de las Religiones, Madrid 1999, 45–46.
20 De Sousa Santos, Epistemologies of the South, 192.
21 Enrique Dussel, Philosophy of Liberation, New York 1985, 10.

they are] lived performatively«[22]. This performative nature refers to the fact that they are both technically and culturally embodied in social practices. In the religious context, these *ways of knowing* are embodied in rituals, celebrations, prayers, dances, physical ecstasy, visions, or dreams. They have an intimate relation with their subject of knowledge, because while knowledges *appropriate* reality, the ways of knowing *embody* it.[23]

These *ways of knowing* that are primarily developed in De Sousa Santos' metaphorical global South, include: ancestral knowledges, local spiritualities, syncretic religious systems, time visions that exceed the lineal western conception of temporality, a collective understanding of the religious experience, a non-dualist differentiation between the world of the living and the spiritual one in which ancestors, good and bad spirits coexist, a much more diffuse differentiation between creator and creation than in western classical theology, the role of the »motherland« and what inhabits her in religious affairs, and the role of the body as *locus* and receptacle, where humans meet the divine and this experience is archived.

Due to the non-western epistemological matrix of these religious beliefs, artifacts, and practices that are performed in Christian communities around the world, it is vain (and sometimes counterproductive) to examine all of them based on a purely rational epistemological and theological framework (as many theologians of the »accommodation« and »inculturation« models tried for decades) or by the use of methodological tools which simply overlook the most salient characteristics of these expressions of faith. For example, overlooking the role of corporal performances during the liturgy, or the strong ties of camaraderie and belonging among pentecostal *hermanos* (brothers) from South America.

To study these theological *ways of knowing*, it will be necessary to perform an interdisciplinary movement to integrate into our methodological repertoire approaches and techniques that have been traditionally related to non-theological fields. De Sousa Santos is right when adding that »the issue becomes even more complex once the *novelty* looks at the future pointing to the past, and even to the

22 Boaventura De Sousa Santos, Introducción a las Epistemologías del Sur, in: María Meneses/Karina Bidaseca, Epistemologías del Sur/Epistemologias do Sul. Buenos Aires 2018, 25–61, 30.
23 De Sousa Santos, The End of the Cognitive Empire, 3.

old past«[24]. This *novelty* does not presuppose that the past does not exist, but that it is silenced, absent, and not yet explored.

Unfortunately, the current theological practice around the world finds us in a situation in which most of the relations between *knowledges* and *ways of knowing* are characterized by an almost general indifference from believers and religious leaders who make use of contextual *ways of knowing* – most of them from pentecostal, evangelical or charismatic affiliation regarding the rich and vast academic theological tradition of the so-called »historic« churches. There are all kinds of reasons for this, for example pious suspicion of critical approaches to the Bible, old prejudices against »historic« denominations and traditions, a precarious theological educative system, or simple academic disdain. On the other hand, several theologians, scholars and ecclesial leaders from this metaphorical global North hold to a position that can be cataloged as conservative (as resistant to the new), lacking interest, or simply arrogant regarding any theological reflection or experience of faith which is not based on rational or systematic approaches. For example, beyond the natural differences regarding the dissimilar contexts of discussion, only a few theologians from the global North have been able to recognize the role that *popular* (as inherent to common people) practices, knowledges, and beliefs play in the configuration of Christian spiritualities and identities in the global South.

This apparent gap responds also to the fact that while most of the modern academic theological tradition was developed in a few European nations (Germany, Italy, Switzerland, Netherlands, the United Kingdom, etc.), most of the highest innovative and transformative theological developments in the Christian tradition during the last decades have mainly occurred in the global South (such as Liberation Theology or Pentecostal spirituality). Furthermore, these *knowledges* and *ways of knowing* respond to local historical circumstances and needs of specific Christian groups, which can make them simply irrelevant for other contexts.

Nevertheless, as stated before, De Sousa Santos' dichotomous and radical theory seems not to do justice to the fact that from a historical perspective, Christian groups do not correspond statically to one of these two knowing styles, on the contrary, even the most mystical Christian traditions have developed incipient attempts for systematic and rational reflection on the sacred and its revelation.

24 Boaventura De Sousa Santos, Epistemologías del Sur, in: Utopía y Praxis Latinoamericana 16/54 (2011), 17–39, 20.

Thereby, the richness of applying his theory to theological issues lies in the openness it promotes for different *ways of knowing* from dissimilar epistemological models to be part of theological discussions, rather than in the categorization or classification of Christian knowings according to those models, or in the creation of absolute correspondences between these models and geographical regions.

On the other side of the abyssal line: the absent condition of theological *ways of knowing*

Analogous to Fanon's theory of dissociation between metropolis and colonies[25], De Sousa Santos postulates the existence of an *abyssal line* in the human understanding of the world as a result of modern thought, which makes any equalitarian relation between knowings from both sides of the line impossible. On a theological level, what lies on the (metaphorical) southern side of the line is understood as local, alternative, post-colonial, contextual, third-world, indigenous, informal, unofficial, particular, oral, etc. Meanwhile, at the dominant side of the abyssal line, there is modern, urban, academic, formal, global, systematic, scientific, published, and written theology. This abyssal line creates a radical disjunction between the great diversity of religious experiences around the globe and the very few methodologies that are legitimized to interpret them and give them sense. In his theory, the abyssal line fulfills a regulatory function, creating a power imbalance that separates the state of ignorance which is characterized by chaos, and the state of knowledge whose major characteristic is order.

The author gives the term *Sociology of the absences* to the active cartography work around the abyssal line. This sociology makes it possible to identify the ways and means by which the abyssal line produces non-existence, absence, and irrelevance of diverse *ways of knowing*. Its central idea is that »there is no ignorance or knowledge in general. All ignorance is ignorant of certain kind of knowledge, and all knowledge is the overcoming of a particular ignorance«[26]. Underlying the formulation of the abyssal line is the awareness that there is a vast social experience that is ignored and hence »wasted« because it is not ac-

25 Frantz Fanon, The Wretched of the Earth, New York 1968, 37.
26 De Sousa Santos, Epistemologies of the South, 188.

knowledged by academic researchers[27]. In this sense, the main objective of the sociology of the absences is:

> »To show that what does not exist is, in fact, actively produced as non-existent, that is, as a non-credible alternative to what exists. Its empirical object [cannot be studied] from the point of view of the conventional social sciences. It is about transforming impossible objects into possible objects, objects that are absent in present objects. Non-existence is produced whenever a certain entity is disqualified and considered invisible, non-intelligible or disposable.«[28]

De Sousa Santos affirms that metropolitan knowledge is ruled by a kind of reason which he qualifies as *metonymic*. This term illustrates that through this reason there is a homogeneous logic that rules between the whole and its parts and they cannot exist outside its relation with the totality. The metonymic reason has been developed since the epoch of the classic Greek philosophers, and it considers dichotomy as »the most complete form of totality [...] since it combines, in the most elegant way, symmetry with hierarchy«[29]. This kind of reason renders impossible the existence of alternative knowings which are not linked by a relation of dependence with the totality of the rational system or lay claim to their independent condition as novel autonomous emergences. Its dichotomous nature is expressed in theology by the formulation of dual categories as local/global, indigenous/universal, oral/written and published, practical/systematic, periphery/center, traditional/modern, collective/individual, informal/formal, popular academic, empiric/scientific, etc. Each duality engenders a relation of ontological hierarchy depending on its location in the abyssal fracture.

As result, the metonymic reason reserves for the global South the character of emptiness and absence due to its alleged ontological inferiority. For this reason, it supposedly lacks history, philosophy, technological development, theological reflection, scientific knowledge, prosperity, progress, and more. As Hegel eloquently explains: »Africa is, in general, a closed land [...]. It is characteristic of the blacks that their consciousness has not yet even arrived at the intuition of any objectivity, for example, of God or the law, in which humanity relates to the world and intuits its essence [...] What we understand properly of Africa is something

27 De Sousa Santos, Conocer desde el Sur, 66.
28 De Sousa Santos, Epistemologías del Sur, 30.
29 De Sousa Santos, Conocer desde el Sur, 70.

isolated and lacking in history«[30]. On a theological level, for centuries it lacked reflection, historic revelation from God, spiritual authority, dogmatic systematization, or any other criteria related to what the Congregation for the Doctrine of the Faith would call »an authentic theological method«.

Making present the »absent« theological *ways of knowing* by means of De Sousa Santos' Sociology of the Emergences

To transgress the epistemological borders which are grounded by the metonymic reason in the form of an abyssal fracture, De Sousa Santos' theory proposes the Sociology of the Emergences, which is:

> »A procedure aimed at showing that, given the resilience of the abyssal line, many practices, knowledges, and agents existing on its other side […] are in fact actively produced as nonexistent by the dominant ways of knowing on this side of the abyssal line, and all the more so when they are engaged in resistance against the abyssal exclusions […] Identifying the abyssal line is the first step towards overcoming it, […] denouncing [it] allows for the opening of new horizons regarding the cultural and epistemological diversity of the world.«[31]

This sociology looks for the symbolic extension of religious meanings, practices, knowledges, and the actors that embody them. Hence, its objective is to make present or to promote the »emergence« of those knowledges that have been intentionally invisibilized and to include them in the repertoire of available theological knowledges.

The sociology of the emergences can become a crucial methodological tool for intercultural theological exchange in the sense that it does not try to *accommodate* or to *inculturate* the theological message to a specific culture as was the purpose of missiology or contextual theologies during the XX century. This sociology aims to track the diversity of global theological production, looking for emergences of the Christian faith and elevating them to an equalitarian epistemological level with western academic theology.

30 Georg Wilhelm Friedrich Hegel, Sämtliche Werke, Appendix C., Hamburg 1995, 171.
31 De Sousa Santos, The End of the Cognitive Empire, 8.

There are at least three kinds of emergences that deserve to be mentioned and analyzed according to this methodology: seed ruins, counter-hegemonic appropriations, and liberated zones. De Sousa Santos explains the first concept:

> »The seed ruins are an absent present, they are memory and alternative future at the same time. They represent everything that social groups recognize as original and authentic conceptions, philosophies, and practices that, despite having been historically [suppressed] they are still alive in their memory and in the most remote recesses of their alienated daily lives.«[32]

These seed ruins are present in those communities where Christian spiritualities and practices have been crushed by totalitarian religious persecution, dictatorial political regimes, ethnic cleansings, or similar practices. These are a special kind of emergences because their future possibilities rest on many occasions in the far past, as is the case of the descendants of those who survived the French persecution against Anabaptist communities or Catholic and Orthodox persecution in the Middle East and Africa. This is even more delicate when it is a Christian tradition that oppressed and persecuted another one, as in the case of those Protestant congregations which had to close down their churches in Latin America due to the pressure and political influence of the Roman Catholic Church. These are »living ruins« because they are embedded in the mind of communities who resist being exterminated. Because of their past nature and future possibilities they are »ruins and seeds at the same time«[33]. Just by existing, these »ruins« testify that their destruction was not definitive and they can inspire and guide alternative futures.

The second kind of emergences are the counter-hegemonic appropriations. By this concept, De Sousa Santos refers to:

> »The philosophies, concepts, and practices developed by the dominant social groups to reproduce domination, but which are appropriated by the oppressed social groups and, resignified, reconfigured, refounded, subverted, and transformed selectively and creatively to transform them into tools for the struggles against domination.«[34]

32 De Sousa Santos, Introducción a las Epistemologías del Sur, 52.
33 Ibid.
34 Ibid., 53.

As has been extensively documented, the Christian faith was one of the main instruments for the subjugation of countless cultures and people in the Middle Ages and modern history. Either by missionary action or by providing theological justification and support to colonial enterprises around the world, this faith was imposed as a general practice upon subjugated individuals and societies. This instrumentalization demanded the priests' or missionaries' accommodation of the evangelical message to correspond with these interests, as occurred with one of the most shameful episodes in Christian history by the publication of the *Parts of the Holy Bible – Selected for the use of the Negro Slaves in the British West-India Islands,* better known as the »Slave Bible«. This version of the Bible was used to highlight themes related to submission and obedience, in which the entire book of the Revelations was left out in order to eradicate the notions of any new Kingdom, any new coming world, or any project of hope for the oppressed. These efforts to use the Christian faith as an instrument of subjugation often led to re-signification by slave communities that used the same faith as a means for resistance, as Wash Wilson, a former North American slave, declared:

> »When de niggers go round singin' ›Steal Away to Jesus,‹ dat mean dere gwine be a 'ligious meetin' dat night. De masters … didn't like dem 'ligious meetin's so us natcherly slips off at night, down in de bottoms or somewhere. Sometimes us sing and pray all night.«[35]

Dr. Albert Roboteau dedicated a significant part of his academic career to recovering these counter-hegemonic appropriations that occurred in most of the cotton fields of North America. He affirms:

> »Drawing from the Bible, Protestant hymns, sermons, and African styles of singing and dancing, the slaves fashioned a religious music which expressed their faith in moving, immediate, colloquial, and, often, magnificently dramatic terms. […] That some slaves maintained their identity as persons, despite a system bent on reducing them to a subhuman level, was certainly due in part to their religious life. In the midst of slavery, religion was for slaves a space of meaning, freedom, and transcendence.«[36]

35 Albert Raboteau, Slave Religion. The Invisible Institution in the Antebellum South, Oxford/New York 2004, 244.

36 Raboteau, Slave Religion, 318.

Another case of counter-hegemonic appropriations can be traced back to the colonial *Latin American Christs,* example of Latin American *tremendism* as an expression of the grotesque and popular (as related to low classes). In the art schools of colonial Lima and Quito, *mestizos* like Baltazar Gavilán, and indigenous like Manuel Chili »*Caspicara*« (kichwa for *Wood Face*) subverted the art of the colonizers by recreating scenes of the Passion in the form of Christs with countless terrible wounds, huge blood clots, profound sadness in the face, immense thorns, and almost entirely covered in blood. According to Dussel:

> »The popular religious sculptor envisages the crucified Christ as a sublimation of his ancient vanquished gods by an also defeated Christ. In the double defeat that it is not just morbid masochism, hope is affirmed – always postponed, but firmer than life itself – of liberation.«[37]

Christ of the Mercy[38]
José Olmos »Pampite«
XVIII Century, first third
Church of Saint Roque
Quito – Ecuador

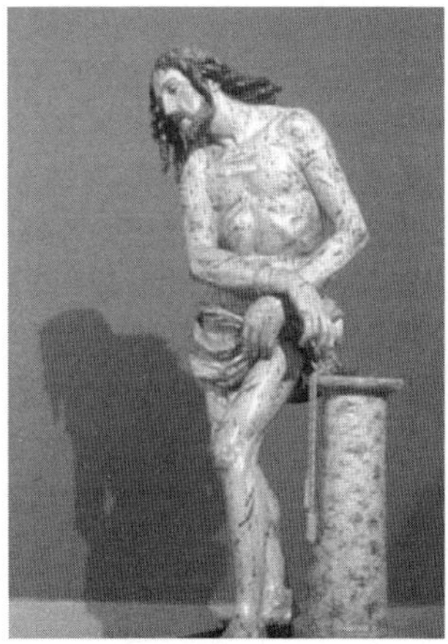

Christ of the Column[39]
Baltazar Gavilán
Middle XVIII Century, first third
Church of Saint Augustin
Lima – Peru

37 Enrique Dussel, Filosofía de la cultura y la liberación, México DF 2006, 241.
38 Unknown gallery. Public domain Creative Commons.
39 Unknown gallery. Public domain Creative Commons.

These counter-hegemonic appropriations exemplify appropriately the kind of traditions and practices that the sociology of the emergences aims to recover and to bring into discussion with hegemonic interpretations of the Bible.

The third kind of emergences which the sociology of the emergences deals with are the so-called *liberated zones*. These are self-organized spaces that are not ruled by the metonymic reason, and because of this, they are free of its hierarchical and purely rational influence. These are democratic spaces that survive because of the active participation of their partakers. These zones are »performative, prefigurative and educational in nature. They are considered as realistic utopias, or better yet, *heterotopies*«[40]. These zones are aware of their own epistemological incompleteness and constitute spaces for intercultural interaction and mutual learning. Their diasporic presence around the world makes evident the metaphoric conception of categories as the global North and South, insomuch as it is possible to find many »Souths« (liberated zones) in the geographical North and vice-versa. In the XXI century the *liberated zones* are indispensable partakers in meaningful intercultural and ecumenical dialogues and even when their participation presupposes major logistic problems, the fact that similar efforts have been carried out by groups and nets such as the *Ecclesial Base Communities* in Brazil and Mexico; and the *Small Christian Communities Network* in Africa, makes evident its plausibility.

Theoretical significance of De Sousa Santos' sociological theory for current intercultural theology

The problem that De Sousa Santos' sociological theory addresses is not new for theology. Already in 1976, the Ecumenical Association of Third World Theologians (EATWOT) published its famous Final Declaration, by which, as a voice of the so-called *Third World,* it condemned the indisputable dominance of western theological and epistemological tradition over theological reflections from the global South. As the document states:

> »The theologies from Europe and North America are dominant today in our churches and represent one form of cultural domination. They must be understood to have arisen out of situations related

40 De Sousa Santos, Introducción a las Epistemologías del Sur, 54.

> to those countries, and therefore must not be uncritically adopted without our raising the question of their relevance in the context of our countries. Indeed, we must, in order to be faithful to the gospel and to our peoples, reflect on the realities of our own situations and interpret the word of God in relation to these realities. [...] We are prepared for the radical break in epistemology, which makes commitment the first act of theology and engages in critical reflection on praxis of the reality of the Third World.«[41]

Nonetheless, after almost 50 years, the incompleteness of this postcolonial enterprise can lead us to conclude, to a greater or lesser degree, with Sugirtharajah: »Biblical scholarship continues to be managed and controlled by the West«[42]. Nowadays, authors like Fernando Segovia, Mayra Rivera Rivera, Namsoon Kang, Kwabena Asamoah-Gyadu, and Moses Mlenga continue, in De Sousa Santos' terms, to turn »impossible objects into possible objects, objects that are absent in present objects«, by mapping the theological emergences and absences around the abyssal line.

Furthermore, key elements of De Sousa Santos' theory have already been analyzed by postcolonial theologians. For example, De Sousa Santos' *monoculture of the lineal time,* by which »history has a unique and known sense and direction«[43] is contradicted by the Aymara theologian Sofía Chipana Quispe, by means of Andean ancestral temporal cosmovisions in her work *Apocalyptic: stories for the recreation of life*[44], or by Kabasele Lumbala's Christological model, which identifies Jesus Christ as a present ancestor of the African people[45]. Likewise, De Sousa Santos' argument for the embodiment of the *ways of knowing* resonates well with current research on rituals, liturgies, and religious performances.

The value of De Sousa Santos' theory concerning theological discussion lies in its capacity to formulate the imbalance problem among global theological knowings, employing new concepts and categories which unveil novel nuances and scopes of this complex reality. Furthermore, it offers theoretical support for the development of a new intercultural theological paradigm that is able to deal with the existing tension between the local religious reflections which are »con-

41 Gerald West, The Bible and the Poor. A New Way of Doing Theology, Cambridge 1999, 130.

42 Sugirtharajah, Voices from the Margin, 315.

43 De Sousa Santos, Epistemologías del Sur, 30.

44 Sofía Chipana Quispe, Apocalíptica. Relatos para la recreación de la Vida, La Paz 2012.

45 Francois Kabasele Lumbala, Celebrating Jesus Christ in Africa. Liturgy & Inculturation, New York 1998.

stituted around topics which are adopted by concrete social groups with local living projects«[46] and the totality of global theological knowledge in which they take part. During the last decades, the processes of globalization, improvements in communication technologies, and the increasing dynamism of contemporary migratory flows have transformed the world into a much vaster scenario, in which new actors with their own living realities from previously ignored regions and cultures demand active participation in global discussions. This has brought much more attention to the global/local discussion on theological matters.

The main objective of this new intercultural paradigm must be to set a creative and fruitful distance from western theological tradition and its main methodologies and postulates, which will open analytic spaces for the emergence of absent or silenced theological practices and beliefs that are developed every day around the world. At the same time, it must leave space to surprise, to enable the rise of the new, challenging the temptation to close our »theological canon«. De Sousa Santos expresses himself as a professional theologian when using a quasi-eschatological logic to explain this: »the bet on the new must be followed by the bet on the non-conclusion, on the *Not-Yet.*«[47] In this sense, »the consciousness of our own blindness must occupy the center of our epistemological attitude […] which invites to 1. a wise move as it cannot guarantee that all movements are in the intended direction […] 2. a plurality of knowledges and practices [and] 3. an uplifting and socially responsible application of the science, rather than a *technical* one«[48].

(Dr. theol. Cand. Daniel Jara J., researcher and lecturer of Intercultural Theology and Corporeality at the Protestant Faculty of Ruhr-Universität Bochum)

46 De Sousa Santos, Una Epistemología del Sur, 48–49.
47 De Sousa Santos, Epistemologías del Sur, 21.
48 De Sousa Santos, Una Epistemología del Sur, 61.

ABSTRACT

Der Artikel setzt Schlüssel-Aspekte der soziologischen Theorie von Boaventura de Sousa Santos mit zentralen Fragestellungen der Interkulturellen Theologie in Beziehung. Dabei bedient er sich der Kritik von De Sousa Santos am »kognitiven Imperium« der westlichen akademischen Reflexion, um die selbstverständliche Privilegierung der akademischen westlichen Theologie gegenüber anderen christlichen Reflexionen der ganzen Welt anzuprangern und die Hauptunterschiede zwischen dem theologischen Wissen aus dem globalen Norden und den Wissensweisen aus dem globalen Süden zu skizzieren. Der Artikel schlägt De Sousa Santos' Soziologie der Abwesenheiten und Emergenzen als eine geeignete Methode vor, um diese Abwesenheiten des Wissens aus dem globalen Süden präsent zu machen oder »emergieren« zu lassen, damit sie den gleichen epistemologischen Status wie ihre Gegenstücke aus dem globalen Norden haben. Anschließend werden drei Arten von Emergenzen benannt: Saatgut-Ruinen, gegenhegemoniale Aneignungen und befreite Zonen. Ferner wird erläutert, welche Rolle diese Emergenzen im interkulturellen theologischen Austausch spielen könnten. Abschließend wird die theoretische Bedeutung von De Sousa Santos' soziologischer Theorie für die aktuelle Interkulturelle Theologie vertieft.

»What is Mission?«[1]

Der ambivalente Beitrag deutscher Missionsgesellschaften zur Gründung des Internationalen Missionsrates 1921

Michael Biehl

Über den Jahreswechsel 1957–1958 trat der Internationale Missionsrat (IMR) zu seiner vorletzten Sitzung in Achimota, Ghana, zusammen. Kontrovers wurde der Vorschlag diskutiert, den Rat in den Ökumenischen Rat der Kirchen zu integrieren. Theologisch sprach dafür die gewachsene Einsicht, dass Einheit und Zeugnis zum Wesen der Kirche gehören. Aus dem gleichen Grund wurden Einwände erhoben, denn diskutiert werde der Zusammenschluss zweier Organisationen, von denen die eine keine Kirche sei – der Rat der Kirchen – und die andere nicht Mission – der Internationale Rat nationaler Missionsorganisationen.[2] Die Mehrheit der Mitglieder des Rates sprach sich dennoch für eine Integration aus, besonders die vertretenen Nationalen Kirchen- und Missionsräte in Asien, die ihr Entstehen auf Bewegungen zur Einheit in der Mission zurückführten.[3] Erik Nielsen, einer der Sekretäre des Rates, reflektierte im Berichtsband zu Achimota die Geschichte und die Erfahrungen des Rates seit seiner Gründung. Für ihn lief es auf die Frage zu: Was ist Mission heute, angesichts der Weltsituation und

1 Erik W. Nielsen, The Role of the I. M. C. Some Reflections on the Nature and the Task of the I. M. C. in the Present Situation, in: Ronald K. Orchard, The Ghana Assembly of the International Missionary Council, 28th December, 1957 to 8th January, 1958. Selected papers, with an Essay on the Role of the I. M. C., London 1958, 185–239, hier: 189.

2 Proposed Integration of the World Council of Churches and the International Missionary Council. (a) Summary of the Discussion in Plenary Session of the Proposed Integration of the I. M. C. and the W. C. C. by the Editor, in: Orchard, Ghana Assembly, 156–164, hier: 158.

3 Proposed Integration, 165, 167. Vgl. dazu auch die Diskussionen auf der Weltmissionskonferenz in Willingen, Walter Freytag (Hg.), Mission zwischen Gestern und Morgen. Vom Gestaltwandel der Weltmission der Christenheit im Licht der Konferenz des Internationalen Missionsrates in Willingen, Stuttgart 1952.

derjenigen der Kirchen? Diese Frage müsse von der ganzen Kirche und weltweit beantwortet werden, und das fordere ein Nachdenken über das Forum heraus, in dem sie angemessen bearbeitet werden könne.[4] Fast auf den Tag genau 40 Jahre nach seiner Gründung wurde der Rat 1961 auf der Dritten Vollversammlung des ÖRK in eine Kommission für Weltmission und Evangelisation und eine gleichnamige Abteilung im ÖRK umgewandelt. Das kann als Ergebnis des Nachdenkens über diese Frage interpretiert werden: An die Stelle eines Rates von hauptsächlich Missionsorganisationen tritt eine Kommission von überwiegend Kirchen.[5]

Mit dem Blick vom Ende her wird in diesem Beitrag die Gründung eines Internationalen Rates nationaler Missionsgesellschaften und -räte in eine komplexe Ereignisgeschichte und die in sie eingewobenen Deutungen der Beteiligten eingeordnet. Ähnlich wie die Umwandlung des IMR in eine ÖRK-Kommission war seine Gründung im Jahr 1921 in Lake Mohonk (USA) von kontroversen Diskussionen und mancherlei Bedenken begleitet. Nicht die Geschichte einer Organisation wird hier vorgestellt, sondern wer sie und warum für so wichtig hielt, dass sie trotz äußert widriger Umstände und dramatischer historischer Umbrüche nach langen Debatten gegründet wurde, um eine gemeinsame Antwort darauf zu formulieren, was Mission zu der Zeit war. In dieser Perspektive wird die Gründung des IMR in den Übergang vom langen 19. Missionsjahrhundert[6] zu der sich abzeichnenden neuen Weltordnung der Zwischenkriegszeit eingezeichnet. Dabei hängt es von der Perspektive ab, wo und wie in der vorhandenen Literatur ein Anfang dafür gesetzt wird. In diesem Beitrag wird eine solche chronologische Darstellung durchbrochen und der Rat als von diesen Entwicklungen geprägte Organisation, und gleichzeitig als Plattform für die nationalen Gesellschaften und Räte untersucht, auf der sie ihre Deutungen der Ereignisse und Entwicklungen berieten, um ihre Rolle und Aufgaben darin zu definieren. Um das nachzuzeichnen greift der Beitrag immer wieder einzelne Fäden heraus und bezieht sie auf einzelne Aspekte und auf die Arbeit des später gegründeten Missionsrates. Der Fokus des Beitrags liegt dabei auf der Rolle der deutschen Missionsgesellschaften. Ihre Aktivitäten und Haltungen spielten für das Zustandekommen des Rates eine wichtige Rolle, obwohl sie an der Gründungsversammlung nicht teilnahmen.

4 Nielsen, The Role of the I. M. C., 189.

5 Willem A. Visser't Hooft (Hg.), Neu-Delhi 1961. Dokumentarbericht über die Dritte Vollversammlung des Ökumenischen Rates der Kirchen, Stuttgart/Basel 1962, 63–67.

6 Gustav Warneck, Warum ist das 19. Jahrhundert ein Missionsjahrhundert? Halle 1880.

Kooperation in der Mission und Edinburgh 1910

Als ein erster möglicher Einstiegspunkt in die Gründung des IRM wird oft der Plan von Gustav Warneck für ein ständiges Komitee von Delegierten von nationalen Missionskonferenzen genannt. Es sollte Kooperation organisieren, zwischen Missionsgesellschaften in strittigen Fragen vermitteln und alle zehn Jahre eine internationale Missionskonferenz organisieren. Der Vorschlag wurde zwar im Konferenzbericht der internationalen Missionskonferenz 1888 in London abgedruckt, aber es gibt keinen Beleg dafür, ob er diskutiert wurde.[7] Dass damals kein entsprechender Ausschuss gegründet wurde, mag mit daran gelegen haben, dass zu der Zeit außer in Deutschland und den USA kaum nationale Missionsorganisationen existierten, die Delegierte hätten entsenden können.

Ein anderer möglicher Einstiegspunkt ist die Weltmissionskonferenz in Edinburgh 1910. »Co-Operation and the Promotion of Unity« war Gegenstand der Kommission 8, deren Bericht auf der Konferenz diskutiert wurde.[8] Entgegen dem Kommissionstitel durfte die Konferenz keine Fragen von Doktrin oder Kirchenverfassung berühren, in denen die Kirchen oder teilnehmende Missionsgesellschaften untereinander uneinig waren, was ihr Zustandekommen gefährdet hätte.[9] Dennoch erhielt der Kommissionsbericht ein längeres Kapitel über Bewegungen zu Kirchenunionen besonders in Asien.[10] Das ist einer der Hinweise darauf, wie weit die Bewegungen auf den als Missionsfelder charakterisierten Ländern in Asien den Verhandlungen in Edinburgh voraus waren.[11] Stanley vertritt in seiner Untersuchung der Konferenz von 1910 die Auffassung, dass gerade diese Kommission einen sehr viel größeren Einfluss auf die folgende ökumenische Geschichte hatte als alle anderen gemeinsam. Die auf ihr aufbauende Einsetzung des Fortsetzungsausschusses führte dazu, dass in Großbritannien eine Struktur der Kooperation von Missionsgesellschaften geschaffen wurde, wie es

7 Brian Stanley, The World Missionary Conference, Edinburgh 1910 (Studies in the History of Christian Missions) Grand Rapids, Mi/Cambridge, UK 2009, 282.

8 Report of Commission 8: Co-operation and the Promotion of Unity. World Missionary Conference 1910, Edinburgh and London o. J.

9 Stanley, World Missionary Conference, 277.

10 Vgl. Kapitel 5 »Federation and Union« in: Report of Commission 8, 83–118. Dazu Stanley, World Missionary Conference, 278.

11 Vgl. z. B. J. H. MacLean, Unity and Co-operation in the Indian Mission Field, in: IRM 1 (1912), 202–225. Ausführlicher William Richey Hogg, Ecumenical Foundations. A History of the International Missionary Council and its Nineteenth Century Background, New York 1952, 15–35.

sie auf dem Kontinent und in den USA bereits gab, die Conference of Missionary Societies in Britain and Ireland (CMSBI): »What broke new ground at Edinburgh was the decision to embody missionary co-operation in a structured form and on a global scale which imposed on wholly autonomous voluntary missionary agencies an obligation to take much more seriously than hitherto a broader ecumenical review of the missionary task.«[12]

Da die Einsetzung dieses Fortsetzungsausschusses im Rückblick meist als Beginn einer Entwicklung betrachtet wird, die letztlich zur Gründung des ÖRK geführt hat, sollte vermerkt werden, dass ein solcher Beschluss noch während der letzten Sitzungen der Weltmissionskonferenz als äußerst gefährdet betrachtet wurde. Die Gespräche im Hintergrund und im Plenum der Konferenz belegen die Sorgen der Missionsorganisationen, dass ihre Autonomie durch eine neue internationale Organisation beeinträchtigt werden könnte. Das wirft noch einmal ein mögliches Licht darauf, warum Warnecks Vorschlag zwölf Jahre zuvor nicht diskutiert wurde.

Brian Stanley hat in seiner umfassenden Studie die Missionskonferenz in Edinburgh 1910 wegen ihrer Studienarbeit als eine »Evangelical Crusade founded on a ›Science of Mission‹« charakterisiert. [13] Dabei ging es präziser um eine wissenschaftliche Sammlung von Daten, wie erschlossen ein Missionsfeld war, welche besonderen Bedürfnisse sich dort ergaben, und welche Kräfte den Missionsgesellschaften zur Verfügung standen, um die Hindernisse, die sich aus ihrer Sicht der Evangelisation der als nicht-christlich definierten Welt stellten, zu überwinden. Stanley betont, dass der in der letzten Sitzung doch noch beschlossene Fortsetzungsausschuss der einzige Beschluss war, den die Konferenz getroffen hat.[14] Der Ausschuss führte das Prinzip der Konferenz fort und setzte auf seiner ersten Sitzung acht internationale Kommissionen ein, deren Mitglieder persönlich berufen und nicht delegiert waren. Die Kommissionen sollten Themen weiterbearbeiten, zu denen teilweise bereits in Edinburgh Kommissionsberichte diskutiert worden waren.[15] Auch der Fortsetzungsausschuss wollte mit seinen Kommissionen zu einer »real science of missionary occupation which will in-

12 Stanley, World Missionary Conference, 278.
13 A. a. O., 4f.
14 A. a. O., 30f.
15 Eine ausführliche Beschreibung gibt der Vorsitzende des Ausschusses, vgl. John R. Mott, The Continuation Committee, in: IRM 1 (1912), 62–78.

fluence the policy of missionary societies« beitragen. Bekanntlich hat John Mott als Vorsitzender des Edinburgher Fortsetzungsausschusses 1912 und 1913 Asien besucht und Konferenzen organisiert. Die erste Frage der in den für deren Vorbereitung versandten Fragebögen galt der Erhebung von Daten über die Besetzung des Feldes.[16] Dem Wunsch nach verlässlichen Informationen und Studien entsprach auch die Arbeit von Kommissionen im Fortsetzungsausschuss über christliche Erziehung, Literatur und theologische Ausbildung.[17]

Das Thema »Kooperation und Einheit« wurde in einem Unterkomitee des Ausschusses behandelt, das hauptsächlich Informationen über existierende Bemühungen in dieser Richtung sammeln sollte.[18] Mit Blick auf die Bedenken während der Weltmissionskonferenz fühlte sich der Fortsetzungsausschuss offensichtlich genötigt zu betonen, dass die Aufgabe des Unterkomitees sei, für »a better common understanding, a closer co-ordination, and a more vital relationship between the missionary agencies on the home fields and the leaders of the Church in the mission fields« zu arbeiten.[19] Dass der Vorsitzende des Ausschusses, John Mott, einer der wichtigsten internationalen Akteure, außerdem ausführlich darlegt, dass der Fortsetzungsausschuss keine legislative oder verpflichtende Macht habe, lässt ahnen, wie groß die Zurückhaltung gegenüber einer internationalen Organisation von Gesellschaften war. Mott schreibt in diesem Zusammenhang: »The value of its recommendations will depend upon the experience, reality, and truth behind them.«[20]

Der spätere IMR versammelte Delegierte von nationalen Organisationen, was ihn deutlich vom Fortsetzungsausschuss unterscheidet. In der Perspektive, dass er beraten und koordinieren, aber keine Beschlüsse fassen sollte, kann er hingegen durchaus als Fortsetzung des Ausschusses gesehen werden. In der Verfassung des IMR von 1921 findet sich ein ähnlicher Gedanke wie der von Mott beschriebene: »It is recognized that the successful working of the International

16 Syllabus of questions, in: The Continuation Committee Conference in Asia 1912–1913. A Brief Account of the Conferences together with their Findings and Lists of Members, New York 1913, 471–474. Vgl. dazu Klaus Koschorke, The World Missionary Conference Edinburgh 1910 and the Rise of National Church Movements in Asia and Africa, in: Ders. (Hg.), Transkontinentale Beziehungen in der Geschichte des Außereuropäischen Christentums, Wiesbaden 2002, 203–218.

17 Mott, Continuation Committee, 66, 68.

18 A. a. O., 71.

19 A. a. O., 73.

20 A. a. O., 74.

Missionary Council is entirely dependent on the gift from God of the spirit of fellowship, mutual understanding and desire to co-operate.«[21]

Das deutsche Memorandum von 1909

Der Fortsetzungsausschuss sollte die Autonomie der Gesellschaften und der nationalen Räte nicht in Frage stellen. Stattdessen wollte er durch gemeinsame Beratungen und durch als verlässlich eingeschätzte Daten zum Stand der Organisation von Mission auf den »Missionsfeldern« zu vereinten Anstrengungen und Verabredungen über eine Arbeitsteilung motivieren. Angesichts dieses Ziels ist erstaunlich, was Hogg später in seiner Geschichte des IMR in Bezug auf dessen erste beiden Dekaden feststellt: »Indeed, it is interesting to note during how much of its course the council was directly occupied with the problems of German missions: from 1914 through World War I and until 1930 when the last of the German mission properties were returned; during 1934–35 when, with Hitler's rise, German societies could scarcely transmit money overseas; and from 1939 on in into an unseen future.«[22] Der Rat hat offensichtlich unter den Bedingungen der Nachkriegszeit über seine Beratungen und Studien hinaus mehr internationale Aktivität und Vermittlung entwickelt als sein Vorläufer.

In dieser Perspektive wird ein anderer möglicher Ansatzpunkt für die Gründung des IMR interessant. 1909 hatte der 1885 gegründete Deutsche Ausschuss der Missionsgesellschaften ein formales Memorandum an die Edinburgher Weltmissionskonferenz mit einem erneuerten Vorschlag für ein internationales Gremium gerichtet. Es wurde begleitet von einem ausführlichen Brief des damaligen Vorsitzenden des Ausschusses, Oehler, Direktor der Basler Mission. In seinem Begleitbrief bezog er sich dabei auf Antworten auf den Fragebogen, der von der Kommission 1 der Edinburgher Konferenz versandt worden war. Er hatte sie von Julius Richter, Mitglied des Deutschen Ausschusses und stellvertretendem Vorsitzenden der Kommission 1, erhalten. Oehler betonte in seinem Schreiben

21 Minutes of the International Missionary Council. Lake Mohonk, New York, U. S. A., October 1–6, 1921, Edinburgh o. J., 34. Aufgenommen wurde in den Anhang der Verfassung auch der Grundsatz, der schon Edinburgh definiert hatte: »No decision shall be sought from the Council, and no statement shall be issued by it on any matter involving an ecclesiastical or doctrinal question, on which the members of the Council or the bodies constituting the Council may differ among themselves« (40). Vgl. dazu Stanley, World Missionary Conference, 38f.

22 Hogg, Ecumenical Foundations, 361.

an die Weltmissionskonferenz, dass die Antworten in verschiedener Form die Forderung nach einer stärkeren Kooperation in der Mission erheben, und zitierte dabei drei Beispiele aus Indien.[23]

Laut dem Memorandum war das primäre Motiv, die Gründung einer internationalen Kommission zur Behandlung missionarischer Fragen zu fordern, in Zukunft zu verhindern, was deutsche Missionsgesellschaften im Zusammenhang des Krieges 1899–1902 im südlichen Afrika erlebt hatten. Das Memorandum unterstrich die schweren Verluste der Berliner Mission und der Hermannsburger Mission in diesem Krieg sowie die Weigerung der britischen Regierung, eine Kompensationszahlung an die deutschen Missionen in Erwägung zu ziehen. Die einzige Hoffnung, die britische Regierung dazu zu überreden, ihre Haltung zu ändern, sah das Memorandum in der Bildung einer internationalen Kommission, die, wie es ausgedrückt wurde, intelligenten Einfluss und Expertenwissen zum Tragen bringen würde – eine Formulierung, die der Aufgabe des späteren Fortsetzungsausschusses nahekommt. Die Edinburgher Konferenz wurde aufgefordert, die Errichtung einer internationalen Kommission mit zwei Aufgaben zu befürworten: Missionsgesellschaften in ihren Verhandlungen mit fremden Regierungen zu repräsentieren und zu unterstützen, und die Vereinten protestantischen Missionsgesellschaften bei internationalen Konferenzen zu vertreten, die sich mit Punkten wie dem Opium- oder Alkohol-Handel oder den Gräueln im Kongo beschäftigten, Ereignisse, die damals die Missionswelt empörten. Sie sollte aus aktiven Missionaren und Staatsmännern mit Erfahrung in der Mission gebildet werden. Eine Beteiligung der aus der Mission hervorgegangenen Kirchen war nicht vorgesehen, und es gibt keinen Hinweis darauf, dass Kooperation in der Evangelisierung durch diese Kommission vorangetrieben werden sollte. Gustav Warneck sollte als Mitglied der Kommission 8 der Edinburgher Konferenz das Memorandum dort vorbringen. Laut Stanley gibt es wiederum keine Hinweise darauf, ob es dort diskutiert wurde. Clements, der Biograph von John Oldham, einer weiteren zentralen Figur der Edinburgher Konferenz, vermerkt, dass die Erwartung, dass sie im Interesse ausländischer Gesellschaften bei der britischen Regierung vorstellig werden sollten, bei den britischen Missionsgesellschaften auf starke Zurückhaltung traf.[24]

23 Stanley, World Missionary Conference, 284f.

24 Keith Clements, Faith on the Frontier. A Life of J. H. Oldham, Edinburgh/Geneva 1999, 96. Stanley, World Missionary Conference, 286. Julius Richter hatte bei einem Besuch 1909 das Committee of Reference and Council des Foreign Mission Board in den USA anregen können, einen eigenen Brief

Indirekt bringt der Vorschlag die Erfahrung des Deutschen Ausschusses zum Tragen, der als gemeinsame Vertretung der Gesellschaften gegenüber dem deutschen Kolonialamt gegründet worden war. Der tatsächlich eingesetzte Fortsetzungsausschuss blieb weit davon entfernt, was hier als internationale Kooperation eingefordert wurde. Der zitierte Rückblick von Hogg auf die Arbeit des späteren IMR belegt, dass der Rat durch den ersten Weltkrieg und seine Folgen zum Handeln herausgefordert wurde. Allerdings übertrug er das anwaltliche Eintreten auf nationale Missionsorganisationen.[25] So war es nach dem Ersten Weltkrieg vor allem John Oldham, der in Bezug auf die Wiederzulassung deutscher Missionare in von Großbritannien regierten Gebieten bei den Behörden in London offensichtlich mit einigem Erfolg vorsprach.[26]

Kriegswirren

Der Fortsetzungsausschuss trat vor dem Ausbruch des Weltkriegs das letzte Mal 1913 zusammen, wurde formal jedoch erst in Lake Mohonk aufgelöst.[27] Unter Christinnen und Christen der verschiedenen Länder gab es angesichts eines drohenden Krieges in Europa Bemühungen, sich zu verbünden und die Beziehungen zwischen den Kirchen für den Erhalt des Friedens zu nutzen. Das blieb die Ausnahme. Frieder Ludwig zitiert den Aufruf von 1914 von führenden deutschen Theologen und leitenden Missionsvertretern wie Julius Richter, A. W. Schreiber, Johannes Warneck und dem Herrnhuter Bischof Henning, der ein Jahr später Vorsitzender des Deutschen Ausschusses der Missionsgesellschaften wurde. Der Aufruf stellt den Krieg als unvermeidbar dar und wirft den Regierungen der feindlichen Mächte vor, Unheil über die Welt zu bringen, indem

an die Edinburgher Konferenz zu schreiben, vgl. Clements, Faith on the Frontier, 95. Im Februar 1910 hatte sich auch die Vereinigung der Londoner Sekretäre der Missionsgesellschaften dafür ausgesprochen, dass ein solches Gremium geschaffen werden sollte, und dass Kommission 8 darüber beraten solle. Stanley ist der Meinung, dass der amerikanische, der deutsche Vorschlag und ihre wachsende Überzeugung die Mitglieder der Kommission dazu bewog, zuzustimmen, den Vorschlag für eine ständige Kooperation auf der Weltmissionskonferenz vorzubringen. Stanley, World Missionary Conference, 289.

25 Vgl. Minutes of the Committee of the International Missionary Council. Canterbury, England, July 27–30, 1922, London o. J., 16, Punkte 30, und 39, 43.

26 Clements, Faith on the Frontier, 152–154.

27 Charles R. Watson, The Fourth Meeting of the Continuation Committee. The Hague, November 14th to 20th, 1913, in: IRM 3 (1914), 157–169.

»die Beteiligung von Eingeborenen, die erst seit wenigen Jahren pazifisiert [sic] sind, an einem Krieg von weiß gegen weiß die furchtbare Gefahr des Eingeborenenaufstandes heraufbeschwört.« Dem deutschen Volk komme keine Schuld am Krieg zu, der Aufruf an die Christen in anderen Ländern erfolge im Interesse der »einzigartigen Weltaufgabe der christlichen Völker in der Entscheidungsstunde der Weltmission«[28]. In der deutschen Presse wurde in der Zeit immer wieder kritisiert, dass der Einsatz »der anderen Völker für die kolonisierten Völker heuchlerisch und unanständig sei, der eigene ehrlich und aufrichtig«[29].

Martin Greschat hat in seiner weltweiten Untersuchung herausgearbeitet, wie sich diese Amalgamierung von Nationalismus, Volk, Kirche und christlichem Glauben in praktisch allen kriegsbeteiligten Ländern vollzog und zur religiösen Legitimierung der eigenen Kriegsbeteiligung genutzt wurde. Besonders auffällig ist, dass praktisch in allen Ländern das eigene als das wahre christliche Volk stilisiert wird, das von Gott beauftragt wurde, die Welt von Gottes Gegnern zu befreien. Nicht Friedensbemühungen, sondern allein die Vernichtung des zum Antichristen stilisierten Gegners werde Frieden, Gerechtigkeit und eine sichere Welt bringen.[30] Greschat berichtet dabei von einem Brief, der Christ*innen in Deutschland, England, Österreich, Frankreich, Belgien und Serbien gegen den Krieg einen wollte. Die Antwort aus Berlin, an der Karl Axenfeld, Mitglied des Deutschen Ausschusses der Missionsgesellschaften für die Berliner Mission, beteiligt war, betont, dass die Christen in Deutschland sich einig seien, dass der Krieg durch ein gottloses Verbrechen außerhalb Deutschlands heraufbeschworen wurde, dass die deutsche Kriegsbeteiligung gerecht wäre und man durch den Kampf »am Aufbau einer Menschheit« mitwirke, die »Gott in Gerechtigkeit« diene.[31]

Die Vertreter der Missionsgesellschaften in den verschiedenen Ländern, die mit dem Fortsetzungsausschuss die sogenannte Supranationalität der Mission betonten, waren in unterschiedlicher Weise in diese Schlachten auf dem Feld der christlichen Legitimierung des Kriegs und des eigenen Handelns verstrickt.[32]

28 Frieder Ludwig, Der Erste Weltkrieg als Einschnitt in der Missions- und Kirchengeschichte (Berliner Beiträge zur Missionsgeschichte 4), Berlin 2003.

29 Ludwig, Der Erste Weltkrieg, 11.

30 Vgl. Martin Greschat, Der Erste Weltkrieg und die Christenheit: Ein globaler Überblick (Urban Akademie), Stuttgart 2014.

31 Greschat, Der Erste Weltkrieg, 76.

32 Vgl. z. B. zu Großbritannien und den USA: Greschat, Der Erste Weltkrieg, 74–77, 92–105.

Das ist umso bemerkenswerter, als es sich dabei um freie Assoziationen und Gesellschaften handelte, die von den Regierungen unabhängig waren. Allerdings waren sie abhängig von den Stimmungen in ihren jeweiligen Unterstützerkreisen, die sie in weiten Teilen teilten. 1917 kam es dadurch zu einem Höhepunkt im Disput zwischen deutschen und englischen Missionsvertretern. Die Leitung des Deutschen Ausschusses verurteilte in einer öffentlichen Erklärung Äußerungen von J. M. Ogilvie, mit dem sie im Fortsetzungsausschuss zusammen gearbeitet hatte, nach denen er in Großbritannien die »Beraubung der deutschen Missionen« in britischen Kolonialgebieten mit dem Vorwurf der Megalomanie deutscher Missionare gerechtfertigt habe.[33] Mott und Oldham wurde vorgeworfen, die notwendige politische Neutralität aufgegeben zu haben, die für die Leitung internationaler christlicher Verbände, die sich für die Ziele des »überweltlichen Reiches Christi« einsetzen, nötig wäre.[34] Die deutschen Mitglieder des Fortsetzungsausschusses könnten sie daher nicht mehr als Vorsitzenden und Sekretär des internationalen Ausschusses akzeptieren. Sie betonten, dass sie dagegen das »Grundgesetz der Supranationalität der christlichen Mission und der Kirche Christi überhaupt« weiter verteidigten.[35] Oldham argumentierte angesichts der Ereignisse und der antideutschen Stimmung in England in persönlicher Korrespondenz mit den deutschen Vertretern, dass in diesen Kriegszeiten niemand aus seiner nationalen »Haut« springen könne. Supranationalität bedeute gegenwärtig, zu einer realistischen Einschätzung der Grenzen zu kommen, die die nationale Eingebundenheit der Mission auferlege.[36]

In weiteren Äußerungen deutscher Missionsvertreter treten vergleichbare Argumente wie in der deutschen »Erklärung« auf.[37] Der schon genannte Karl Axenfeld hatte bereits 1917 dazu eine Schrift verfasst, die mit Unterstützung der Deutschen Evangelischen Missionshilfe 1919 ins Englische übersetzt und damit auch einer außerdeutschen Öffentlichkeit bekannt wurde.[38] Die deutschen Gesell-

33 Erklärung, in: AMZ 43 (1916), 305–308.

34 Vgl. dazu die ausführliche Behandlung bei Clements, Faith on the Frontier, 143–145.

35 Erklärung, AMZ, 308.

36 Clements, Faith on the Frontier, 146f.

37 Vgl. dazu auch den Sammelband Ulrich van der Heyden/Helge Wendt (Hg.), Mission und dekoloniale Perspektive. Der Erste Weltkrieg als Auslöser eines globalen Prozesses (Missionsgeschichtliches Archiv 30), Stuttgart 2020.

38 Karl Axenfeld, Germany's Battle for the freedom of the Christian Missions. Published by the German Evangelical Mission Aid, Berlin 1919. Ders., Deutschlands Kampf für die Freiheit der christlichen Mission, Berlin 1919, 5. verbesserte Auflage.

schaften seien nur zögerlich in die deutsche Kolonialmission eingestiegen. Es sei immer eine Eigenart der deutschen Mission gewesen, dass sie in Gebieten gearbeitet habe, die von fremden Regierungen beherrscht wurden. Nirgendwo hätten deutsche Missionare es an Loyalität gegenüber der Regierung fehlen lassen oder gar zum Widerstand gegen sie aufgerufen. Die deutsche Mission sei schon immer supranationalistisch eingestellt.[39] Hingegen wären es besonders die Briten gewesen, die die beherrschten Völker mit in den Konflikt hineingezogen hätten. Ihr Verbrechen wie das anderer Nationen sei, den Krieg nicht nur zwischen den beteiligten Völkern in Europa geführt zu haben, sondern ihn auf die ganze Welt auszudehnen und ihre kolonialen Untertanen in den Krieg gezerrt zu haben. Die deutsche Mission kämpfe weiter für die Freiheit der Mission, während die Feinde Deutschlands die deutsche Mission ihrer Besitzungen berauben und stehlen wollten, was eine treue Missionsgemeinde über Jahrzehnte geopfert und investiert habe.

Noch 1921, als deutsche und anglosächsische Missionsvertreter schon wieder in Gesprächen miteinander waren, griff Martin Schlunk, damals Sekretär des Deutschen Ausschusses, diese Argumente in einem Artikel auf. Zwar hält er den britischen und amerikanischen Missionsfreunden zu Gute, dass sie sich bei ihren Regierungen für die Wiederzulassung der deutschen Mission einsetzten und die verwaisten deutschen Missionsgemeinden unterstützten. Doch der englischen Regierung wirft er »die Gewissenlosigkeit« vor, »mit der man Glieder deutscher Missionsgemeinden aus Südafrika und Indien nach Frankreich auf die Kriegsschauplätze schleppte, daß [sic] sie helfen sollten, dem Volk, dass ihnen das ewige Leben brachte, den Lebensnerv zu zerschneiden.«[40] Der Missionsparagraph 438 des »sogenannten Friedensvertrags« von Versailles werde von den deutschen Missionen als »widergöttliche Vergewaltigung empfunden«[41]. Für die Mission war mit dem Friedensvertrag der theologische Kampf um die Deutung der Kriegsereignisse offensichtlich noch lange nicht beendet.

39 Vgl. neben Axenfeld z. B. ähnlich: In Schwerer Zeit, in: Die evangelischen Missionen. Illustriertes Familienblatt 25 (1919), 1–6, hier: 2, der von der »Übervolklichkeit« der christlichen Mission spricht, 4. Oder Carl Mirbt, Die Eigenart der Deutschen Mission. Vortrag auf der Weltmissionskonferenz Edinburgh, Juni 1910, Basel 1910.

40 Martin Schlunk, Die Lage der deutschen Mission auf dem Missionsfelde und daheim, in AMZ 48 (1921), 151–160, hier: 152.

41 Schlunk, Lage der deutschen Mission, 153.

Missionsgesellschaften und erwachendes Nationalbewusstsein

Bereits vor der entsprechenden Kommission der Edinburgher Konferenz 1910 war das Verhältnis von Mission und Regierungen besonders auf den sogenannten Missionsfeldern virulent.[42] Die protestantischen Missionsgesellschaften, die sich im Fortsetzungsausschuss zusammengetan hatten, waren mit ganz wenigen Ausnahmen freie Assoziationen, und die Berechtigung ihres Handelns im Herrschaftsbereich von Regierungen war immer wieder umstritten. In den Jahren um Edinburgh 1910 herum und denen des Fortsetzungsausschusses wurde das Verhältnis in nationalen Perspektiven, nicht von Imperialismus oder einer kolonialen Weltordnung her diskutiert.[43]

Nach dem Krieg und in der sich herausbildenden neuen Weltordnung wurde der Wunsch, eine internationale Missionskonferenz zusammenzurufen, immer stärker. Es war zwar gelungen, mit dem Art. 438 frühere koloniale Vereinbarungen aus der Berliner Kongoakte zur Freiheit von Mission, Forschung und Wissenschaft in Kolonialgebieten in den Versailler Vertrag einzubringen. Sippel erkennt in dem Artikel die Saat einer Dekolonisierung: Der Möglichkeit, dass die deutsche Missionsarbeit auch von anderen übernommen werden konnte, beinhalte den Gedanken, dass christliche Mission keiner Nationalität und nicht der Kolonisierung bedürfe.[44] Ein solcher Gedanke lag den deutschen Missionsvertretern fern, die auf ihre Felder zurückwollten. Doch in der Nachkriegsordnung ging es nicht nur um die Wiederzulassung der deutschen Missionen. Die siegreichen Kolonial- und Mandatsmächte planten insgesamt eine stärkere Kontrolle der Mission, aber auch philanthropischer, bildungsbezogener und medizinischer Aktivitäten in ihren Kolonien.[45]

Wirkmächtiger und diskursprägend waren allerdings andere Entwicklungen. Der vernichtende Krieg zwischen den als christlich betrachteten Nationen desavouierte für eine Mehrheit in deren Kolonien das Christentum. Auch für Christ*innen in Afrika und Asien zerbrach das »Christianity-Civilisation-Modell«,

42 Report of Commission 7: Missions and Governments. World Missionary Conference 1910, Edinburgh and London o. J.

43 Brief Oldham vom 17. November 1919 an Julius Richter, in: Rundschreiben des DEMBundes/Ausschusses an Missionsgesellschaften, 1915–1933. DEMR1/Nr. 0343, Fiche # 2, Blatt 40.

44 Harald Sippelt, Der Beitrag des Friedensvertrags von Versailles zur Dekolonisation am Beispiel deutscher christlicher Missionen, in: van der Heyden/Wendt, Mission und dekoloniale Perspektive, 89–104, hier: 103.

45 Vgl. Clements, Faith on the Frontier, 152f.

wie Koschorke herausarbeitet.[46] Für die indigen-christlichen Eliten hatte sich der christliche Glaube mit dem Versprechen von Gleichheit und Partizipation verbunden. Sie wollten durch die verändernde Kraft des Evangeliums zu Bildung, sozialen Veränderungen, Fortschritt und politischer Freiheit beitragen.[47] Die Rhetorik der deutschen Missionsgesellschaften von den treuen Gemeinden, die auf die Rückkehr ihrer Missionare warteten, wurde durch den wachsenden Ruf nach der Drei-Selbst-Kirche besonders in den asiatischen Ländern konterkariert. Ursprünglich ein Modell für die Mission, wurde sie nun gegen das missionsgesellschaftliche Establishment gewendet.[48]

Die zweite Entwicklung war, dass außereuropäische Christ*innen das Stichwort Selbstbestimmung aus dem 14-Punkte-Plan des amerikanischen Präsidenten Wilson für eine Friedensordnung auf sich bezogen und nationale Bewegungen neuen Zeiten entgegenfieberten. Stattdessen kam die Fortführung des Kolonialismus und die Mandatszeit unter dem Völkerbund. Das führte zu großer Enttäuschung und trug dazu bei, dass das westliche Demokratiemodell besonders in Asien an Attraktivität verlor.[49] Unter dem Eindruck, wie sich die westlichen Nationen im Krieg zerfleischten, und angesichts der Erfahrungen einer großen Zahl an Menschen aus den Kolonien in den Schützengräben und Versorgungsstationen in Europa konnten Nicht-Christen zu der Auffassung kommen, dass Christentum für sie Bajonette und Maschinengewehre bedeute.[50]

Dem stand in den westlichen Nationen weiterhin eine Verbindung des Überlegenheitsgefühls in Kultur und Technik mit dem christlichen Glauben gegenüber, mit welchem schon in der Vorkriegszeit Selbständigkeitsbewegungen in den Kolonien als aufmüpfig oder aufrührerisch herabwürdigt wurden.[51] Vergleichbares findet sich in Schriften deutscher Missionsvertreter im und nach dem Krieg. Martin Schlunk schrieb in den Auseinandersetzungen über eine Rückkehr der deutschen Gesellschaften, dass besonders die Missionsarbeit der dritten,

46 Klaus Koschorke, »Isn't Germany a Christian Country?« Der erste Weltkrieg als moralische Katastrophe und Ende des Christianity-Civilization-Modells in den Debatten asiatischer und afrikanischer Christen, in: van der Heyden/Wendt, Mission und dekoloniale Perspektive, 123–141, hier: 124.

47 A. a. O., 127.

48 A. a. O., 140.

49 Ebd.

50 Zitiert in Clements, Faith on the Frontier, 190.

51 Gunter Pakendorf, Die Christliche Mission und der Untergang des Abendlandes, in: van der Heyden/Wendt, Mission und dekoloniale Perspektive, 155–167, hier: 161.

vierten Generation entscheidend sei, um die Gemeinden »sittlich bei der Reinhaltung der unbedingten Forderungen des Evangeliums, dogmatisch in der Sicherung des Glaubensgehaltes vor heidnischer Beimischung, vor allen Dingen in der Abwehr einer neuen heidnischen Gesetzlichkeit, verwaltungstechnisch endlich in der Auffindung einer der Volksart angepassten Kirchenreform« zu begleiten.[52] Der Vorwurf: Die Vertreibung der deutschen Missionare beschwöre hier Gefahren herauf; der Subtext: Solche zivilisatorischen Rückfälle können nicht im Interesse einer Kolonialmacht sein.

In diesem Kontext wurde mit Briefen und durch persönliche Kontakte zwischen Missionsvertretern daran gearbeitet, eine internationale Konferenz zu organisieren. Oldham schrieb in der Vorbereitung dazu an den Deutschen Ausschuss, dass er auf der für 1920 geplanten Konferenz in Crans, Schweiz, die Situation der vertriebenen deutschen Missionen im Komplex dreier Fragen bearbeitet sehen wolle: Welchen Grad an Freiheit können Gesellschaften von Regierungen, in deren Bereich sie arbeiten, erwarten? Welchen Verpflichtungen unterliegen ausländische Missionare? Ausländische Missionare müssten sich zu dem »national spirit« in den Ländern verhalten, in denen sie tätig waren. Deshalb müssten Vertreter aus Japan, China, Indien und aus Afrika an dieser Konferenz teilnehmen. In Crans waren die ersten drei Länder vertreten – durch weiße Missionare.[53]

Aus dem internen Bericht der deutschen Beteiligten an der Konferenz geht hervor, dass es anlässlich dieser Diskussion zu einem Gesprächsgang kam, der von ihnen so charakterisiert wird: Nachdem die angelsächsischen Missionsfreunde sich weit auf deutsche Forderungen bezüglich einer Rückkehr eingelassen hatten, habe bei ihnen offenbar der Eindruck geherrscht, man müsse eine Gegenforderung stellen. Bischof Westcott, Indien, habe daher darauf gedrängt, dass die deutsche Mission bei einer Rückkehr auf die nationalen Bestrebungen zugehe. Dazu der Bericht: »es ist wahr, wir Deutschen seien zu langsam; die Angelsachsen aber seien zu schnell in der Gabe der Freiheit und Selbstständigkeit für die Missionsobjekte gewesen«[54].

Das ist einer der Punkte, an denen ansichtig wird, wie die Vertreter der Missionsgesellschaften diese heraufkommenden Veränderungen wahrnehmen. Sie

52 Schlunk, Lage der deutschen Mission, 154f.

53 Hogg, Ecumenical Foundations, 195f.

54 Internationale Missionskonferenz zu Crans, 22. bis 28. Juni 1920, in: Rundschreiben des DEM-Bundes/Ausschuss an Missionsgesellschaften, 1915–1933. DEMR1/Nr. 0343, Fiche#2, Blatt 47–53, hier: 11, Blatt 52.

sind sich einig, dass die westlichen Gesellschaften hier weiterhin eine Aufgabe haben, doch wie sie aussieht, wird zum Anlass für Auseinandersetzungen über unterschiedliche Vorstellungen dessen, was Mission ist. Auf den Konferenzen, die Mott für den Fortsetzungsausschuss in Asien 1912–1913 organisiert hatte, war die Rolle der »einheimisch« genannten Kirche bereits intensiv diskutiert worden, überwiegend von Missionaren aus Europa und den USA. Dazu hatte z. B. die nationale Konferenz in Indien festgestellt: »It is the conviction of this Conference that the stage has been reached when every effort should be made to make the Indian Church in reality the most efficient factor in the Christian propaganda in this land. To this end, it is essential that the Church in the Western lands should continue to co-operate in the further development of the Indian Church, that it may most effectively accomplish its provisional mission in the regeneration of India.« Das schien auch 1920 noch so gesehen zu werden.

Gemessen an den damaligen Entwicklungen und Diskursen darüber[55] findet sich wenig über eine veränderte Rolle der Gesellschaften in den deutschen Diskussionen über die Gründung des Internationalen Missionsrates. Sie waren vor allem mit ihrem Ausschluss von den Missionsfeldern und dem Bemühen beschäftigt, zurückkehren zu können. Das betrachteten sie als ihren Einsatz für die Freiheit der Mission und für die Völker, in denen sie Missionsgemeinden gegründet haben.[56] Dass Gemeinden und Kirchen besonders in Indien, China und Japan mit nationalen Missionsräten, nationalen Kirchenräten in Bezug auf Selbständigkeit den Entwicklungen in Deutschland und England weit voraus waren, wurde kritisch gesehen.

In der Verfassung des Internationalen Missionsrates wird später festgehalten, dass die Vertreter des japanischen Fortsetzungsausschusses, des chinesischen Ausschusses und des indischen nationalen Missionsrates je drei Delegierte haben, von denen mindestens zwei indigene Christ*innen sein müssen.[57] Zu den bisher zitierten Einschätzungen passt, was Lenwood in seinem Bericht über die

55 Vgl. dazu die Beschreibung der Interaktion indigen-christlicher Eliten aus Afrika und Asien in Tambaran 1938 mit der deutschen Erklärung an die Weltmissionskonferenz: Frieder Ludwig, Zwischen Kolonialismuskritik und Kirchenkampf. Interaktion afrikanischer, indischer und europäischer Christen während der Weltmissionskonferenz Tambaran 1938 (StAECG, 5), Göttingen 2000, 236.

56 Auch Lenwood, Mitglied im Fortsetzungsausschuss, warnte die Deutschen, ihr früherer Paternalismus werde sich bei einer Rückkehr verheerend auswirken. Vgl. Frank Lenwood, The International Missionary Council at Lake Mohonk, October 1921, in: IRM 1 (1922), 30–43, hier: 38.

57 Minutes IMC, 1921, 30.

Gründungsversammlung über diese Vertreter sagt. Er beobachtet, dass manche Bemerkungen über die Kirche in Indien nachlässig dahergesagt wären, aber ein Dr. Data, einer der indischen Vertreter, nehme sie nicht einfach hin! Auch ihre Berichte über die Konflikte, in denen sich die Kirchen in den werdenden Nationen vorfinden, seien trefflich – was sie sagen, erwähnt er mit keinem Wort. Dann gleitet seine Anerkennung in eine rassistische Charakterisierung ab: »the contribution reached its climax in the negroes, the poorest in spirit, the meekest of the races on this little, noisy earth«, die wie Jesus in Gleichnissen sprächen.[58]

Von Crans nach Lake Mohonk

Damit sind Entwicklungen benannt, die für die Einbettung der Entstehung des IMR wichtig sind. Der hehre Gedanken einer Supranationalität der Mission wurde vorgebracht, aber in den Auseinandersetzungen und Verfeindungen des Ersten Weltkriegs zerrieben. Die Missionsgesellschaften hielten dieses »Grundgesetz« (s. o.) in dem Moment hoch, in dem sie sich am nachdrücklichsten in ihrer Nationalität verfangen fanden. Von deutscher Seite wurde zudem noch der Gegensatz zwischen der angelsächsischen Mission und deren Ideal von werdenden Nationalkirchen und dem deutschen Ansatz von organischen Volkskirchen eingetragen[59] – ein Weg, der durch die Betonung des Völkischen in der Mission wenige Jahre danach in die Nähe des Nationalsozialismus führte.[60] In dieser Perspektive kann das vielgerühmte Hague-Prinzip des Fortsetzungsausschusses, nach dem alle Autorität bei den Missionsgesellschaften alleine lag, auch als nationale Abwehr von Internationalisierung verstanden werden. Durch die oben genannte Wahrnehmung des Ersten Weltkriegs in asiatischen und afrikanischen Ländern wurde auch dort die Verbindung von Nationalbewusstsein und christlichem Glauben befeuert.

58 Lenwood, International Missionary Council at Lake Mohonk, 41.

59 Martin Schlunk, Die werdenden Nationalkirchen, in: AMZ 1925, 1–6, hier: 5.

60 Vgl. Werner Ustorf, Sailing on the Next Tide. Missions, Missiology and the Third Reich (Studien zur Interkulturellen Geschichte des Christentums 125), Frankfurt/Main u. a., 2000, 10: »a revival of the Volk's deep emotions and a breakthrough of the archaic spirituality they had long been waiting for«. Vgl. dazu auch die bereits zitierte deutsche Erklärung in Tambaran, Ludwig, Zwischen Kolonialismuskritik und Kirchenkampf, 236.

Die nationale Verwurzelung war der Hintergrund für die Sorge aller Beteiligten in Europa und den USA, dass sie den Rückhalt in ihren Unterstützungskreisen verlieren, wenn bekannt würde, dass man mit dem (ehemaligen) Feind rede. Das bewegte nicht nur, aber besonders die deutschen Vertreter, sich als Individuen und unter dem Radar der Öffentlichkeit an der Konferenz 1920 in Crans zur Bildung eines Internationalen Missionsausschusses zu beteiligen. Es bedurfte vorsichtiger Sondierungen und der Einladung in die neutralen Niederlande, damit sich die deutschen Mitglieder des Fortsetzungsausschusses und englische Vertreter zuvor in Oegstgeest treffen konnten.[61] Die Briten befürchteten, dass ohne die Teilnahme der Deutschen die Konferenz in Crans nicht zustande komme. Die zu den Vorgesprächen in den Niederlanden eingeladene französische Mission wollte mit den Deutschen nicht an einem Tisch sitzen, solange Deutschland die Schuld am Krieg von sich wies.[62] Selbst für die Briten war die Teilnahme nicht ohne Risiko, denn nach ihrer Einschätzung hätte eine Fürsprache für die deutschen Missionen für sie zuhause politisch gefährlich werden können. Die deutschen Vertreter schlossen eine offizielle Teilnahme an der geplanten Konferenz kategorisch aus, da sie den Verlust ihrer Unterstützerkreise befürchteten.[63] Ihre Berichterstattung in Deutschland zeigt, was ihrer Meinung nach auf dem Spiel stand. Zu behaupten, dass Crans »die erste internationale Missionszusammenkunft nach dem Kriege« war, verschweigt das vorausgegangene Treffen in den Niederlanden, ohne das Deutsche nicht an Crans teilgenommen hätten. Zu schreiben, »Crans am Genfer See hatte einen privaten und vertraulichen Charakter« sowie der Hinweis, dass aus Deutschland »auf Grund sorgfältig erwogener Beschlüsse der Vertreterkonferenz und des Ausschusses der deutschen Missionsgesellschaften« niemand ein Jahr später in Lake Mohonk anwesend war, können nur aus der Sorge um einen möglichen Aufruhr in den nationalen Unterstützerkreisen verstanden werden.[64]

61 Matthias Feigk, Die transnationalen Netzwerke protestantischer Missionsgesellschaften nach dem Ersten Weltkrieg und das Missionstreffen von Oegstgeest 1920, in: Themenportal Europäische Geschichte, 2017, www.europa.clio-online.de/essay/id/fdae-1707 (29.4.2021). Vgl. dazu das Foto des Treffens in Oegstgeest 1920. First meeting with Germans after the war (16. bis 18. April 1920), in: Themenportal Europäische Geschichte, 2017, www.europa.clio-online.de/quelle/id/q63-28562 (29.4.2021).

62 Hogg, Ecumenical Foundations, 194–196, der einen Brief von Schlunk zitiert.

63 Feigk, Die transnationalen Netzwerke, 7.

64 Tagung des Internationalen Missionsrates (International Missionary Council) in Lake Mohonk, New York, 30.9. bis 6. Oktober 1921, in: AMZ 48 (1921), 304–311, hier 304.

Tatsächlich nahmen die vier deutschen Mitglieder des Fortsetzungsausschusses Henning, Haussleiter, Richter und Würz, auch alle Mitglieder des Deutschen Ausschusses, an der Tagung in Crans teil.[65] Hier kamen Delegierte der Missionsgesellschaften, Mitglieder des Fortsetzungsausschusses und des sogenannten Emergency Committee zusammen und beschlossen die Gründung eines Internationalen Missionsausschusses.[66] Die »Minutes« der Gründungsveranstaltung am Lake Mohonk ein Jahr später lassen erkennen, wie wichtig die Konferenz in Crans war. Hier war eine Verfassung erarbeitet und zusammen mit Namen für ein Gründungskomitee den nationalen Missionsorganisationen zur Zustimmung zugesandt worden. Dem Deutschen Evangelischen Ausschuss wurden sechs Plätze von insgesamt 70 in dem neuen Rat zugesprochen. Er bildete damit die drittgrößte Gruppe nach Amerikanern und Briten.[67] In der Anwesenheitsliste für Lake Mohonk werden Gründe genannt, warum einzelne Gesellschaften nicht anwesend sein konnten. Warum trotz der reservierten Plätze niemand vom Deutschen Ausschuss anwesend war, wird nicht vermerkt.

Dagegen gipfelte eine Sitzung über »Restrictions upon German Missions« in einer ausführlichen Erklärung des Rates.[68] Der wahrscheinlich wichtigste Punkt 5 benennt das, was Schreiber in seinem Bericht über die Gründungsveranstaltung die »Ehrenerklärung für die deutsche Mission« nennt. Der Rat erklärt, dass er aufgrund seiner Informationen folgendes festhalten kann: die Ausweisung und Vertreibung von Deutschen Missionaren »was due to general political considerations«[69]. Illoyalen Verhaltens oder gar der Aufstachelung der Völker gegen eine andere Regierung hätten sie sich nicht schuldig gemacht, sollte das doch vorgekommen sein, sei es nicht in »accordance with the policy of German missionary societies« gewesen.[70] Für Schreiber hatte die internationale Missionsgemeinschaft damit vorbehaltlos anerkannt, dass die Deutschen keine Kriegsschuld treffe, und dass deutsche Missionare sich keinerlei feindlicher oder aufrühreri-

65 Hogg, Ecumenical Foundations, 195–198; John Oldham, New Beginnings of International Missionary Cooperation, in: IRM 9 (1920), 481–494, hier 483.

66 Zur Konferenz in Crans, vgl. außerdem Clements, Faith on the Frontier, 172–175. Dort finden sich auch ein Foto und eine Namensliste. Lenwood, International Missionary Council at Lake Mohonk, 36.

67 Minutes IMC, 1921, 34f. Der deutsche Bericht kommt auf 68 Delegierte, weil die beiden Plätze für Norwegen nicht aufgeführt werden, 307.

68 A. a. O., 51f.

69 A. a. O., 55.

70 A. a. O., 52.

schen Taten schuldig gemacht hätten, und dass insgesamt das Mandat der Supranationalität für die Mission gelte.

Diese Einschätzung wurde offensichtlich geteilt. Der Arbeitsausschuss des neugegründeten Rates hielt im Juli 1922 fest, dass der Deutsche Ausschuss zwei Vertreter benannt habe, ohne den Anspruch auf die sechs Plätze im Rat aufzugeben: »The Committee resolved to record its hearty satisfaction to the decision of the German Missionary Societies.«[71] Aus der Sicht des Deutschen Ausschusses ist damit die Gründung des Internationalen Missionsrates beendet. Bei der zweiten Sitzung des Rates 1923 in Oxford wird die Anwesenheit von Martin Schlunk als Sekretär des Deutschen Evangelischen Missionsbundes und von Fritz Würz, Basler Mission, Deutscher Zweig, festgehalten.[72]

Schluss

Dieser Beitrag hat die Gründung des IMR in die Veränderungen der Welt am Ausgang des 19. Jahrhunderts eingeordnet. Dabei wurde auf Aspekte hingewiesen, in denen die unterschiedlichen Kooperationsformen von den Ereignissen und deren Einschätzungen durch die Beteiligten geprägt waren, von denen sich manche dem Neuen entgegenstemmten. Blickt man von Lake Mohonk auf die früheren Vorschläge zur Gründung eines internationalen Gremiums von nationalen Missionsgesellschaften zurück, lag die Hauptaufgabe des neuen Rates auf der Linie der Edinburgher Konferenz von 1910 und ihres Fortsetzungsausschusses: »To stimulate thinking and investigation on missionary questions, to enlist in the solution of these questions the best knowledge and experience to be found in all countries, and to make the results available for all missionary societies and missions.«[73] An zweiter Stelle steht »to help to coordinate the activities« und »to bring about united action where necessary«, Ziele, in die die Erfahrung der Kriegsjahre eingeflossen sind. In der 4. Aufgabe des Rates könnte man ein fernes Echo von Warnecks Vorschlag für eine Einmischung in internationale Ausein-

71 Minutes IMC, 1922, 6.

72 Minutes of the International Missionary Council. Oxford, England, July 9–16, 1923, London o. J. Vgl. die knappe Notiz, aus der nur hervorgeht, dass die Situation der »Deutschen Missionen« besprochen wurde, und der Bericht von Würz und Schlunk »with deep sympathy« aufgenommen wurde, 24.

73 Minutes IMC, 1921, 36.

andersetzungen erkennen. »To help to unite the Christian forces of the World in seeking justice in international and inter-racial relations.« Doch es war eine Reaktion darauf, wie sich die Weltordnung durch und nach dem Ersten Weltkrieg verändert hatte. Es zeigt sich, wie unterschiedlich sich die Frage, was Mission ist, jeweils gestellt hat, was zu unterschiedlichen Formen der Kooperation geführt hat. Letztlich haben die Antworten darauf vom Handeln nationaler Gesellschaften auf ihren Feldern hin zu internationalen Aufgaben geführt. Das wäre durch die weiteren 40 Jahre des IMR zu verfolgen. Die Integration in den ÖRK muss auch als Folge der Verschiebung des Schwerpunktes der Christenheit und der Aufbrüche im globalen Süden in Kirche und Mission verstanden werden, was wiederum nach anderen Antworten auf die Frage »Was ist Mission« verlangte, als ein Rat von nationalen Missionsorganisationen geben konnte.

(Dr. Michael Biehl ist Theologischer Referent in der »Evangelischen Mission Weltweit« [EMW], Hamburg.)

ABSTRACT

This article situates the founding of the International Missionary Council (IMC) within a complex history of events in which the interpretations of those involved are embedded. Its founding in 1921 in Lake Mohonk (USA) was preceeded by controversies. In the paper it is described who considered it so important, and why, that the IMC was founded – despite of extremely adverse circumstances and dramatic upheavals and after long debates to formulate a common response to what mission should be at that time. In this perspective, the debates on the founding of the IMR are traced throughout the transition from the long 19th century of mission to the emerging new world order of the interwar period. This paper studies the Council as shaped by these developments, and as a platform for National Mission Societies and Councils to deliberate their interpretations of the events and developments in order to define their roles and tasks within them. The article focuses on the role of the German mission societies. Their activities and attitudes played an important role in the establishment of the Council, although they did not participate in the founding assembly.

Eine kleine ökumenische Lerngeschichte der Missionsakademie an der Universität Hamburg

Anton Knuth

I. Die Notwendigkeit einer akademischen Ausbildung für Missionare

Die Missionsakademie wurde 1954 in der Hochphase der Dekolonisierung gegründet, um die Dialektik der christlichen *Mission zwischen Kolonialismus und Ökumene*[1] theologisch zu reflektieren und ein neues Verständnis des globalen Christentums zu ermöglichen. Angesichts der Selbstständigwerdung der aus den Tätigkeiten der Missionsgesellschaften hervorgegangenen Kirchen wurde ein neues Verständnis von Mission und Ökumene notwendig. Hatte die Mission dem Kolonialismus vorgearbeitet und war somit mit seiner Überwindung obsolet geworden? Oder kann Mission vielmehr als eine Aushandlungsgeschichte verstanden werden, in der der christliche Glaube eine Antwort bietet auf die Umwandlungskrise, in die der Kolonialismus die jeweiligen Sozialordnungen gestürzt hatte? Und was bedeutet es für die deutschen Kirchen, wenn »Mission in der *situation coloniale* niemals eine Einbahnstraße war, die gleichsam ausschließlich vom ›aktiv‹ Missionierenden auf den ›passiv‹ Missionierten wirkte […], sondern dass die Akteure beider Seiten in der Situation der Kulturbegegnung häufig in einem Spannungsfeld von Aktionismus, Abhängigkeit und Anpassung lebten

1 Stephen Neill, Mission zwischen Kolonialismus und Ökumene. Die Aufgabe der Kirche in der sich wandelnden Welt, Stuttgart 1962. Neill war von 1962–1967 Gastprofessor für Missionswissenschaft an der Universität Hamburg und Historiker der Ökumenischen Bewegung, vgl.: Stephen Charles Neill/Ruth Rose, Geschichte der Ökumenischen Bewegung 1517–1948. [2 Bände], Göttingen 1957.

und dabei Teil einer spezifischen transkulturellen Konstellation waren«?[2] Welches ökumenische Verständnis von Mission folgte aus diesem interkulturellen Aushandlungsgeschehen für das neue postkoloniale Zeitalter?

Während die Missionare und Missionarinnen mit ihrem europäischen Weltbild immer auch als *agents of secularisation* wirkten, wurden die Empfänger und Empfängerinnen selbst zu kreativen »Entdeckern und Entdeckerinnen« einer Botschaft, die ihrer Lebenssituation nahestand und im Rahmen der Entstehung eines globalen Christentums Relevanz für die Kirchen in Deutschland bekam. Dabei wurde absehbar, dass die protestantischen Missionsgesellschaften, die im 19. Jahrhundert im Kontext der wirtschaftlich-politischen Kolonialaktivitäten der Europäischen Industrieländer gewirkt hatten, mit der Unabhängigkeit der betreffenden Länder grundlegenden Veränderungen unterworfen würden.[3]

Die Geschichte der Missionsakademie lässt sich so als eine bis heute aktuelle ökumenische Lerngeschichte verstehen, die mit diesen Spannungen und Umbrüchen verbunden ist, zumal sich ihre Vorgeschichte auf das bereits vor dem 1. Weltkrieg existierende Hamburger Kolonialinstitut und den Missionswissenschaftlichen Lehrstuhl an der Philosophischen Fakultät der Universität Hamburg zurückführen lässt.[4] Das Kolonialinstitut wurde aus kolonialreformerischen Motiven 1908 gegründet, die aufgrund des Protestes der katholischen Zentrumspartei gegen die gewaltsamen Missstände und Fehlreaktionen der Kolonialverwaltung in Süd-West Afrika, Togo und Ostafrika im Reichstag ausgelöst worden waren.[5] Es sollte der Ausbildung von Kolonialbeamten und auch von Kaufleuten

2 Thorsten Altena, Methoden und Quellen der Missionsgeschichtsschreibung heute, in: Christoph Dahling-Sander/Andrea Schultze u. a. (Hg.), Leitfaden Ökumenische Missionstheologie, Gütersloh 2003, 63–78, hier: 66. Vgl. Anton Knuth, Who is the Subject of Mission? The Need to Decolonize Mission from the Perspective of the »Margins«, in: Transformation: An International Journal of Holistic Mission. 37/2 (2020), 131–139.

3 Dies galt trotz der Konflikte zwischen Missionen und Kolonialregierungen, wie es Friedrich Zahn deutlich gemacht hatte: »Ich bin überhaupt gegen Kolonien und das ist natürlich heute genug, um uns zu Vaterlandsfeinden zu machen. Aber wenn ein Missionar in Politik sich hineinbegibt und die deutschen Kolonialerwerbungen durch seinen Einfluss fördert – so halte ich das, was auch seine Meinungen sonst sind, für einen großen Fehler, um nicht zu sagen ein Verbrechen.« Friedrich W. Zahn, Die Verweltlichung, eine neue Missionsgefahr (1886), zit. nach: Klaus J. Bade, Imperialismus und Kolonialmission. Kaiserliches Deutschland und koloniales Imperium, Wiesbaden 1982, 70.

4 Vgl. Theodor Ahrens, Missionswissenschaft als Zeitansage. Carl Mirbt – Walter Freytag – Hans Jochen Margull, in: Ders., Gegebenheiten. Missionswissenschaftliche Studien, Frankfurt a. M. 2005, 9–80.

5 Vgl. Rebekka Habermas, Skandal in Togo. Ein Kapitel deutscher Kolonialherrschaft, Frankfurt a. M. 2016.

dienen, um eine Befriedung zu ermöglichen und die politische Legitimität der Kolonialherrschaft zu verbessern.

Auch wenn zunächst Berlin als Standort für das Kolonialinstitut naheliegend gewesen wäre, entschied man sich aufgrund der Kolonialwirtschaft für die Hamburger Hafenstadt. So spendete etwa der Reeder Edmund Sieveking erhebliche Beträge für das 1911 errichtete Hauptgebäude der heutigen Universität. Hamburg bot sich nun auch als ein Studienort für angehende Missionare an, da hier seit 1908 Sprachen, Ethnologie, und Tropenhygiene[6] und ab 1909 durch den Göttinger Kirchenhistoriker Carl Mirbt auch Missionstheologie unterrichtet wurde.[7] Mirbt forderte 1909 angesichts der »neuen Weltlage der Christenheit« eine über die seminaristisch-erweckliche Schulung hinausgehende zusätzliche »Ausrüstung für das spezielle (künftige Arbeits-)Gebiet«[8] der jeweiligen Missionare.

Während im 19. Jahrhundert viele Missionsgesellschaften bewusst auf eine akademische Qualifizierung ihrer Überseemitarbeitenden verzichtet hatten, obwohl sie sie nicht selten in einen lebenslangen Auslandsdienst entsandten, wurde auf der Weltmissionskonferenz von Edinburgh (1910) zur Verbesserung der missionarischen Arbeit die Einrichtung von »Global Study Centres« gefordert.[9] Die Delegierten folgten dem Vorschlag der Kommission V (Preparation of Missionaries), zentrale Missionshochschulen einzurichten, um den Erwerb der Sprachen und die Ausbildung in Religionssoziologie, Pädagogik, Medizin und Missionsmethoden zu verbessern. Carl Meinhof, erster Afrikanist Deutschlands, empfahl

6 Im Jahre 1927 wurden Äthiopisch, Amharisch, Tigrinya, Tigré, Somali, Galla, Berberisch, Hausa, Ful, Nama, Suaheli, Zulu, Herero, Mbundu, Bangala, Duala, Ewe und Vai und neun Südseesprachen unterrichtet. Das Asien-Afrika-Institut der Universität Hamburg stellt den größten Verbund der Asien- und Afrikawissenschaften in Deutschland dar. Vgl. https://www.aai.uni-hamburg.de/ueber-den-fachbereich/ geschichte.html (8.3.2021). Vgl. zu den kolonialreformerischen Ansprüchen des Kolonialinstituts: Jens Ruppenthal, Das Hamburgische Kolonialinstitut und die Kolonialwissenschaften, in: Jürgen Zimmerer (Hg.), Kein Platz an der Sonne. Erinnerungsorte der deutschen Kolonialgeschichte, Frankfurt a. M. 2013, 257–269, hier: 262f.

7 Vgl. Carl Mirbt, Die Evangelische Mission. Eine Einführung in ihre Geschichte und Gegenwart, Leipzig 1919. Mirbt, seit 1889 Prof. für Kirchengeschichte in Marburg, seit 1911 in Göttingen, war 1918 Gründer der Deutschen Gesellschaft für Missionswissenschaft (DGMW).

8 Vgl. Ahrens, Zeitansage, 17.

9 Günter Volz, Die Missionsakademie an der Universität Hamburg – die Geschichte ihrer Entstehung (1961), in: Werner Kahl/Michael Biehl u. a. (Hg.), Mission Interkulturell. Festschrift zum Fünfzigjährigen Bestehen der Missionsakademie, Aachen 2008, 149–172, hier: 151. Die Weltmissionskonferenz in Tambaram 1938 betonte, dass die Ausbildung unter besonderer Verantwortung der »receiving church« stehen müsste.

in Edinburgh das Hamburger Kolonialinstitut als Ausbildungsort.[10] Der ehemalige Pastor, der die Bedeutung der Übersetzung von Bibeln in die Sprachen der Menschen vor Ort betonte,[11] wurde Mentor für die Missionsanwärter, die ab 1911 im ehemaligen Wohnhaus Wicherns, dem Haus »Grüne Tanne«, auf dem Gelände des Rauen Hauses, einen Konvikt bildeten.

Da die von der Edinburger Missionskonferenz geforderte Kooperation verschiedener Missionsgesellschaften zur Etablierung einer wissenschaftlich-theologischen Ausbildungsstätte nicht verwirklicht werden konnte, wurde das Hamburger Kolonialinstitut zu einem Zentrum der akademischen Missionarsausbildung. In der Nachfolge von Carl Mirbt versah ab 1914 Martin Schlunk, Vorsitzender des Deutschen Evangelischen Missionstages und Missionsdirektor der Norddeutschen Missionsgesellschaft[12], die missionswissenschaftlichen Lehraufträge am Kolonialinstitut und veranstaltete hauseigene Seminare. Der Schüler Gustav Warnecks, dessen Publikationen missionsapologetisch ausgerichtet waren, betonte die Relevanz der Bibel für die Mission, sowie der Schulpolitik als Voraussetzung für die Evangelisierung der nicht-christlichen Bevölkerung.[13] Der in Ostindien aufgewachsene Schlunk, der aus einer Kaufmannsfamilie der Handelsgesellschaft der Basler Mission stammte, bezog sich auf das von Missionsgesellschaften seit dem 19. Jahrhundert eingeführte Bildungswesen, welches sich

10 Vgl. Carl Meinhof, Eine einzigartige Versammlung, in: A. W. Schreiber (Hg.), Die Edinburger Welt-Missions-Konferenz. Bilder und Berichte von Vertretern deutscher Missionsgesellschaften, Basel 1910, 20–22. Meinhof, Vorsitzender des Deutsch-Evangelischen Laienmissionsbundes, wurde in Edinburgh 1910 die Ehrendoktorwürde verliehen. Vgl. Carl Meinhof, Die Pflicht der Laien zur Mitarbeit an der Mission, Berlin 1908. Vgl. Rainer Hering, Die Missionswissenschaft in Hamburg 1909–1959, in: Ders., Theologische Wissenschaft und »Drittes Reich«. Studien zur Hamburger Wissenschafts- und Kirchengeschichte im 20. Jahrhundert, Pfaffenweiler 1990, 35–85, hier: 37.

11 Vgl. Carl Meinhof, Die Christianisierung der Sprachen Afrikas, Basel 1905; Ders., Die sprachliche Ausbildung des Missionars, in: Allgemeine Missionszeitschrift 38 (1911), 44–46; Ders., Afrikanische Bibelübersetzungen. Ein kurzer Überblick für die Freunde der Bibel und der Mission, Basel/Stuttgart 1926.

12 Vgl. Matin Schlunk, Die Norddeutsche Mission in Togo I. Meine Reise durchs Eweland, Bremen 1912 und Ders., Die Norddeutsche Mission in Togo II. Probleme und Aufgaben, Bremen 1912. Als katholischer Lehrbeauftragter wirkte Josef Schmidlin aus Münster. Vgl. Hering, Die Missionswissenschaft, 45.

13 Vgl. Martin Schlunk, Die Schulen für Eingeborene in den deutschen Schutzgebieten am 1. Juni 1911 (Abhandlungen des Hamburgischen Kolonialinstituts Bd. XVIII), Hamburg 1914.

»in seiner doppelten Funktion als Wegbereiter für die Einführung westlicher Kulturnormen und als Mittel des sozialen Aufstiegs«[14] charakterisieren lässt.[15]

Schlunk wurde von der 1919 aus dem Kolonialinstitut entstandenen Hamburger Universität, die aber ohne theologische Fakultät blieb, in die philosophische Fakultät übernommen. Er wirkte bis zu seinem Wechsel an die Universität Tübingen 1928 auch im allgemeinen Vorlesungswesen der Hansestadt. Bereits 1910 hatte er die deutsche Delegation auf der Weltmissionskonferenz in Edinburgh geleitet und wirkte ab 1922 als Vorsitzender des Deutschen Evangelischen Missionsbundes, in dessen Funktion er rege Kontakte zu John Mott und dem Internationalen Missionsrat (IMR) hielt, um die Isolierung der auch finanziell in schwierige Fahrwasser geratenen Missionen nach dem 1. Weltkrieg zu überwinden. Er war ab 1927 Hanseatischer Missionsdirektor und ab 1933 Vorsitzender des Deutschen Evangelischen Missionstages. Gemeinsam mit Walter Freytag, seinem Nachfolger als Missionswissenschaftler an der Philosophischen Fakultät und seit 1929 Hanseatischer Missionsdirektor für Bremen, Lübeck und Hamburg,[16] verantwortete Schlunk in Tambaram das Sondervotum der deutschen Delegation. Darin wurde in Aufnahme der Missionsmethoden von Christian Keysser und Bruno Gutmann[17] die theologische Bedeutung der Volksmission und der »natürlichen Ordnungen« unterstrichen.[18] Obwohl die Rassenideologie jeglichem missionstheologischen Universalismus entgegengesetzt war, offenbarte

14 Renate Nestvogel, Mission und Kolonialherrschaft in Kamerun, in: Klaus J. Bade (Hg.), Imperialismus und Kolonialmission. Kaiserliches Deutschland und koloniales Imperium, Wiesbaden 1982, 205–225, hier: 222.

15 Die Norddeutsche Mission etwa war anfänglich die einzige Trägerin von Schulen im heutigen Togo und engagierte sich für die Einführung der Schulpflicht sowie der Beibehaltung der Unterrichtssprache Ewe. Vgl. Arthur J. Knoll, Die Norddeutsche Missionsgesellschaft in Togo 1890–1914, in: Bade, Kolonialmission, 165–185.

16 Freytag war 1928 mit Schlunk auf der Weltmissionskonferenz in Jerusalem, die im Vergleich mit Edinburgh 1910 eine weniger optimistische Haltung einnahm. Er war zunächst Honorarprofessor an der Universität Hamburg und Kiel, ab 1953 Professor für Missionswissenschaft und ökumenische Beziehungen in Hamburg.

17 Vgl. Martin Schlunk, The Relations of Missions to Native Society, in: International Review of Missions 16 (1927), 350–363. Der missionstheologische Bezug auf die »Volkskirche« stand in Kontinuität zu Warneck, wurde aber zunehmend nazifiziert.

18 Martin Schlunk (Hg.), Das Wunder der Kirche unter den Völkern der Erde. Bericht über die Weltmissions-Konferenz in Tambaram (Südindien) 1938, Stuttgart/Basel 1939, 206–209. Vgl. zu den Hintergründen Frieder Ludwig, Zwischen Kolonialismuskritik und Kirchenkampf. Interaktionen afrikanischer, indischer und europäischer Christen während der Weltmissionskonferenz in Tambaram 1938, Göttingen 2000.

die apologetische Strategie des Deutschen Evangelischen Missionsrates (DEMR) gegenüber dem nationalsozialistischen Staat gravierende theologische Defizite.[19]

Freytag, nach dem Krieg einer der ersten deutschen Mitglieder des Internationalen Missionsrates (IMR), bekannte am 14.11.1945 in einer Erklärung des DEMR »den Brüdern anderer Missionen« die Schuld »unserer Nation, die auch unsere Schuld ist«.[20] Er war sich bewusst, dass die deutschen Missionen ihre traditionellen Gebiete nur zurückerhielten, wenn sie sich ökumenisch öffnen würden. Angesichts der notwendig gewordenen Integration der Missionen in die verstärkt nach Unabhängigkeit strebenden »Jungen Kirchen«, betonte Freytag die Notwendigkeit sowohl einer qualifizierten Ausbildung von Missionaren als auch der neuen Kirchenführer. In seinen Vorlesungen an der Philosophischen Fakultät betonte er die »verlorene Unmittelbarkeit der Mission« und öffnete die Missionswissenschaft ökumenisch: »Mission ist der Form nach heute ökumenischer Dienst von Kirche zu Kirche, bei dem die Junge Kirche in der Mitte steht«.[21] Aufgrund der Ablösung der Pioniermission durch die Kooperation mit selbstständigen Kirchen müsse sich auch die Rolle der Missionare ändern, die nicht mehr kirchenleitend, sondern lediglich mit speziellen Qualifikationen gebraucht würden, da gelte: »Mission ist nicht mehr Mission!«[22]

Im Gegensatz zum alten Bekehrungsauftrag wurde nun die theologische Wahrnehmung des realen »Lebens der Jungen Kirchen«[23] und die Bereitschaft zu Dialog und Kooperation mit Kirchen wichtig, die zunehmend selbst auf Bildung Wert legten. Auch wenn das Schulsystem in seiner vorbereitenden Rolle für die Kolonialpolitik als auch in seiner Ermöglichung einer antikolonialen Bildungselite ambivalent gewirkt hatte,[24] waren für die Zusammenarbeit mit unabhängig

19 Werner Ustorf, The Documents that Reappeared. The Minute-Books of Council and Federation of German Protestant Missions 1924–1949, in: Lynne Price/Juan Sepúlveda u. a. (Hg.), Mission Matters, Frankfurt 1997, 63–82.

20 Zit. nach Ustorf, The Documents, 81.

21 Walter Freytag, Die neue Stunde der Weltmission, in: Walter Freytag/Karl Hartenstein, Die neue Stunde der Weltmission (Nr. 2 der Schriftenreihe *Weltmission heute*), Stuttgart 1952, 3–21, hier: 14.

22 So der Titel des dritten missionsakademischen Kurses 1954 in Büsum mit 14 Dozenten und 106 Teilnehmern. Vgl. Martin Pörksen, Zehn Jahre Missionsakademie 1959–1969, 2 (Archiv der MA). Freytag versah bis zu seiner Berufung an die theologische Fakultät einen Lehrauftrag an der Kirchlichen Hochschule Hamburg.

23 Johannes Triebel, Bekehrung als Ziel der missionarischen Verkündigung. Die Theologie Walter Freytags und das ökumenische Gespräch, Erlangen 1976, 24. Freytags Entwurf fand weite Beachtung, da er durch seine erfahrungsbezogene Methode die Realität der »Jungen Kirchen« theologisch würdigen konnte.

24 Renate Nestvogel, Mission und Kolonialherrschaft in Kamerun, in: Bade, Kolonialmission, 202.

gewordenen Kirchen die Bildungsansprüche und gefragten Fachkompetenzen gestiegen. Daher warb Freytag bei den im Deutschen Evangelischen Missionsrat (DEMR) zusammengeschlossenen Missionsgesellschaften eindringlich für die Gründung eines akademisch-wissenschaftlichen Ausbildungsinstituts für die bislang lediglich seminaristisch zugerüsteten Missionare oder Missionarinnen.

II. Die Etablierung der Missionsakademie und die Schwerpunktverlagerung auf den Süden

Im Bewusstsein der »neuen Stunde der Weltmission«[25] bot Freytag, der ab 1946 als Nachfolger Schlunks Vorsitzender des DEMR wurde, missionsakademische Kurse für ausreisende Missionare und Missionarinnen, für Ärzte, Lehrerinnen, Krankenschwestern oder Landwirte an, die von den Missionsgesellschaften nach Hamburg entsandt wurden. Im Zuge der 1952 beschlossenen Gründung der Theologischen Fakultät brachte ihr langjähriger Befürworter, Schulsenator Landahl, einen Standort auch für die länger geplante Missionsakademie ins Gespräch.[26] Der mit ihm befreundete Freytag plädierte angesichts der ökumenischen Aufgabe vermehrter zwischenkirchlicher Kooperation dafür, dass die »Fortbildung junger asiatischer und afrikanischer kirchlicher Mitarbeiter«[27] vorzusehen sei und bekam dafür Unterstützung auf der Weltmissionskonferenz in Willingen 1952 und der im selben Jahr in Hannover tagenden Vollversammlung des Lutherischen Weltbundes.[28]

25 Walter Freytag/Karl Hartenstein, Die neue Stunde der Weltmission (Nr. 2 der Schriftenreihe *Weltmission heute*), Stuttgart 1952.

26 Vgl. Rainer Hering, Theologie im Spannungsfeld von Kirche und Staat. Die Entstehung der Evangelisch-Theologischen Fakultät an der Universität Hamburg 1895 bis 1955, Berlin/Hamburg 1992, 257–269. Allerdings konnte die Einrichtung eines missionswissenschaftlichen Lehrstuhls nur mit dem Hinweis auf die Missionsakademie politisch durchgesetzt werden (ebd., 278).

27 Volz, Missionsakademie, 167. In der heutigen Fassung vom 23.07.2018 lautet der Passus: »Fortbildung kirchlicher Mitarbeiterinnen und Mitarbeiter vor allem aus Asien, Afrika, Lateinamerika und Ozeanien«.

28 Bereits 1944 und 1946 hatte der DEMR die Gründung einer Missionsakademie befürwortet (vgl. Volz, Missionsakademie, 158). In Hamburg befand sich auch die Geschäftsstelle des von Freytag geleiteten DEMR sowie die 1953 gegründete Wirtschaftsstelle Evangelischer Missionsgesellschaften. Vgl. zur Frühzeit der Missionsakademie den Bericht von Martin Pörksen, Die Missionsakademie – Ein Erbe Walter Freytags, in: Gerhard Bittner/Friedrich Hammer (Hg.), Hamburger Kirchenkalender 1961, Hamburg 1961, 40–45.

Der Senat erkannte die auf dem Missionstag in Barmen 1954 beschlossene »Missionsakademie an der Universität Hamburg im Aufbau« an, obwohl sie noch über keine eigenen Räume verfügte, sondern ihre missionsakademischen Kurse, die 10 bis 14 Tage dauerten, mit 50 bis über 100 Teilnehmern und Teilnehmerinnen aus 18 Missionsgesellschaften weiterhin an wechselnden Orten im Umkreis von Hamburg veranstalten musste.[29] Sie wurde 1955 in der Rechtsform einer Stiftung bürgerlichen Rechts als gemeinsames akademisches Institut aller deutschen Missionsgesellschaften gegründet, ohne in Konkurrenz zu den regionalen Missionsseminaren treten zu wollen. Eine Abstimmung der Lehrpläne mit der Seminarlehrerkonferenz erwies sich aber als schwierig, zumal sich ein Konflikt zwischen den Glaubensmissionen und einer gesellschaftspolitisch ausgerichteten Ökumene abzeichnete.[30]

Die Raumnot endete mit dem von der Hamburger Bürgerschaft einstimmig beschlossenen Ankauf des früheren Gästehauses der Phrix-AG in der Rupertistrasse 67 in Hamburg-Nienstedten. Die Finanzierung seines Umbaus für insgesamt 30 Wohnplätze wurde auf dem Deutschen Evangelischen Missionstag in Breklum 1956 freigegeben. Bei der Einweihungsfeier 1957 sprach Leslie Newbigin, Generalsekretär des Internationalen Missionsrates: »Im vorigen Jahrhundert waren wir davon überzeugt, das Banner des Kreuzes könne von uns Weißen durch die Welt getragen werden. Doch wir haben dieses Banner mit dem Blut von Menschen befleckt, für die Christus gestorben ist. Das Banner weiterzutragen, ist jetzt die Aufgabe einer Familie von Kirchen, der jungen Kirchen Asiens und Afrikas zusammen mit den alten Kirchen Europas und Amerikas als einer großen Gemeinschaft, in der man voneinander lernt.«[31] Dieses ökumenische Lernen vollzog sich zwischen Gasthörenden verschiedener Fakultäten, die sich auf ihren Auslandsaufenthalt vorbereiteten oder auf Heimaturlaub waren, und Studenten und Studentinnen aus dem Süden. Walter Freytag stellte die Missionsakademie als »eine Stätte der Wissenschaft« und »eine Stätte der Begegnung« vor, die sich darum bemüht, »den Menschen, an den sie sich richtet, wirklich zu verstehen«.[32]

29 Ausführliche Unterlagen finden sich im Archiv des EMW, NL Freytag, Missionsakademische Kurse 1952–1954.

30 Vgl. Zehn-Semester-Bericht der Missionsakademie im DEMT 1959, 6 (Archiv der MA).

31 Leslie Newbigin, Europäische Verantwortung in Asien und Afrika heute, in: Evangelische Missionszeitung (EMZ) 15 (1958), 141.

32 Walter Freytag, Die Missionsakademie an der Universität Hamburg, in: Evangelische Missionszeitung (EMZ) 15 (1958), 139.

Es wurden Themen diskutiert wie: »Was zwingt uns heute, die Mission neu zu sehen?«, »Der Status des Missionars« über »Rassenprobleme und Mission in Südafrika« bis hin zur »Integrationsfrage«.[33]

Schon im Wintersemester 1960/61 reichten die räumlichen Kapazitäten in der Rupertistraße 67 nicht mehr aus.[34] Bis dahin hatten bereits insgesamt 363 Missionare und Missionarinnen, Ärzte, Schwestern, Lehrer, Pastoren und Vikare jeweils für ein Semester an der Missionsakademie studiert, wovon 59 Studierende aus den Kirchen in Übersee stammten.[35] Mit ihrer Gründung ging ein Lebensziel von Walter Freytag in Erfüllung, für das die Eröffnung einer theologischen Fakultät in Hamburg die Voraussetzung war und deren Etablierung zugleich befördert hatte: »Die Missionswissenschaft stellt für die wissenschaftliche protestantische Theologie in Hamburg im 20. Jahrhundert die zentrale Traditionslinie dar und ist von besonderer Bedeutung für die Gründung der Theologischen Fakultät gewesen.«[36]

Während aber die einen im Zusammenschluss von Internationalem Missionsrat (IMR) und Ökumenischem Rat der Kirchen (ÖRK) 1961 einen Verrat am biblischen Missionsauftrag erblickten, rückte für andere das politische Engagement der Befreiung, Armutsüberwindung und Anti-Rassismusarbeit in den Vordergrund. An der Missionsakademie wurden in den 1960er Jahren Seminare angeboten zum Thema »Europa und die Dritte Welt«, »Probleme der Weltchristenheit«, »Entwicklungsorientierter Dialog«, »Mission als Imperialismus«, »Mission – keine Einbahnstraße«. Der Vorstand beklagte, dass es aufgrund der Polarisierung in ein »geistlich-konservatives« und ein »revolutionär-progressives« Lager[37] zu einem Rückgang von Missionsanwärtern gekommen sei. Zentraler Streitpunkt war auch der Umgang mit der historisch-kritischen Bibelexegese. Der Kontaktausschuss der Evangelikalen Missionen forderte daher »eine theo-

33 Vgl. Zehn-Semester-Bericht der Missionsakademie im DEMT 1959, 2 (Archiv der MA).

34 Es wurde 1961 geplant, »auf dem Nachbargrundstück eine Dependance zu errichten« (Volz, Missionsakademie, 169), was 1967 auch gelang. Ab 1960 wurde ein zweisemestriger Diplomkurs eingeführt, um unterhalb der Universitätsvoraussetzungen einen Abschluss anbieten zu können.

35 Herwig Wagner sah sich als erster Studienleiter der Missionsakademie vor die Aufgabe gestellt: »Wie kann die Neubesinnung in der Mission, zumal nach der Weltmissionskonferenz von Willingen (1952), an neu- und wieder ausreisende Missionare vermittelt werden?« Vgl. Herwig Wagner, Die Anfänge der Missionsakademie, in: Hans-Christoph Goßmann u. a. (Hg.), Missionissima. Beiträge zur Zukunft von Mission, Ökumene und Entwicklung (Festschrift Joachim Wietzke), Frankfurt a. M. 2005, 419–422, hier: 419.

36 Hering, Missionswissenschaft, 85.

37 Protokoll des Vorstandes 1971 (Archiv Missionsakademie).

logische Klärung« des Profils der Missionsakademie.[38] 1975 trennten sich die evangelikalen Missionen vom Deutschen Evangelischen Missionstag und somit auch von der gemeinsamen Trägerschaft der Missionsakademie.[39]

Es studierten nun vor allem Promovenden aus Asien und Afrika an der Missionsakademie, die nach ihrem Abschluss zu Leitungspersonen ihrer Kirchen wurden, wie Hirpo Tasgara, Präsident der Mekane Yesus Kirche in Äthiopien, Bischof Johnson, Kirche von Südindien, oder Samuel Amirtham, Prinzipal des Tamilnadu Theological Seminary (TTS) in Madurai und späterer Leiter des Ökumenischen Instituts Bossey sowie O. V. Jathanna, späterer Leiter des United Theological Colleges (UTC) in Bangalore. Im Zuge der hitzig diskutierten Vollversammlung des ÖRK in Uppsala 1968[40] kamen Delegationen von Bischöfen und Kirchenpräsidenten aus aller Welt zu Besuch.

Mission wurde nach der Vollversammlung von Uppsala verstärkt in ihrer sozial-ethischen Dimension verstanden. So erklärten in einem Thesenpapier von 1970 Seminarteilnehmende: »Mission muss von Akten der Barmherzigkeit zu Akten der Gerechtigkeit durchstoßen. [...] Daraus ergibt sich die Notwendigkeit der Aufklärung zum Beispiel über globale Macht- und Wirtschaftsstrukturen. [...] Gegebenenfalls haben Kirchen zu empfehlen, Entwicklungsdienst, statt Wehrdienst zu leisten.« Auch von der EKD-Synode wurde Entwicklungspolitik als eine genuin kirchliche Aufgabe verstanden, als sie 1970 die Arbeitsgemeinschaft Kirchlicher Entwicklungsdienst gründete (AG KED). 1983 formulierte die Studienleitung: »Der entscheidende Kontext von Mission heute ist der Kampf für Gerechtigkeit«.[41]

Mit Hans-Jochen Margulls These, dass sich die »Tertiaterranität des überseeischen Christentums« zum eigentlichen Zentrum der Weltchristenheit ent-

38 Erklärung des Kontaktausschußes der Konferenz Evangelikaler Missionen an den DEMT vom 30.9.1972. Gegenstand der Kritik war, »daß ihre Studenten radikalen Methoden und Ergebnissen der modernen Bibelkritik« in den Veranstaltungen des Theologischen Fachbereichs ausgesetzt seien (Archiv Missionsakademie).

39 Neben dem Evangelischen Missionswerk (EMW) entstand ein Dachverband der evangelikalen Missionsgesellschaften (AEM), mit dem heute Kooperationen bestehen. Eine Akademie existiert in Korntal, https://www.awm-korntal.eu/page/ueber_ uns.html (8.3.2021).

40 Vgl. dazu Ulrich Dehn, Weltweites Christentum und ökumenische Bewegung, Berlin 2013, 86f, und Karl-Heinz Dejung/Gert Rüppell, Ökumenische Gemeinschaft im Wandel der Zeiten. Interkulturelle und interreligiöse Perspektiven der ökumenischen Bewegung, Berlin 2016, 285–289.

41 So Paul Löffler in einem Positionspapier für den Vorstand 1983, Archiv MA. Im Rückblick ist sich Löffler nicht sicher, ob er jetzt noch davon ausgehen würde, »daß wir reale Schritte zur Teilerrichtung des neuen Jerusalem gehen« können (Paul Löffler, Spannungen leben! Gesprächsweise Annäherung an eine ökumenische Biographie, Berlin 2006, 151).

wickele,[42] rückten die Themen der Kirchen des Südens sowie die Anfertigung der Dissertationen ihrer zukünftigen theologischen Lehrer ins Zentrum der Akademiearbeit. Die Anforderungen an die fachliche Begleitung der Promovenden, die bislang durch Tutoren und Vikare erfolgt war, stieg, sodass mit Hilfe der EKD, die sich seit Beginn an deren Finanzierung beteiligt hatte,[43] weitere Studienleiterstellen geschaffen wurden. Die Studienarbeit leistete nun nicht mehr nur Vorarbeit für ausreisendes Personal,[44] sondern erschloss mit den überseeischen Stipendiaten und Stipendiatinnen Themen aus dem globalen Christentum für die Theologie im deutschen Kontext.

Ab 1968 fanden regelmäßig »Ökumenische Praktika« an Hochschulen in Johannesburg oder Nairobi zu den Themen »Work and Mission of the Church in Contemporary Society« statt, die sorgfältig ausgewertet wurden.[45] Die zahlreichen Vikare und Vikarinnen, die jeweils für ein Sondersemester von den Landeskirchen ab 1957 an die Missionsakademie gesandt worden waren, trugen zu einer ökumenischen Sensibilisierung der deutschen Pastorenschaft bei. Die Integration von Mission und Ökumene stellte die Landeskirchen vor die Frage, wie ein Neuanfang der weltweiten Mission unter den veränderten Rahmenbedingungen möglich sein könnte.[46]

III. Aufnahme der entwicklungspolitischen Bildungsarbeit

Neben dem internationalen Stipendienprogramm konnte seit 1975 als zweites Arbeitsfeld der Seminarbetrieb ausgebaut werden, da sich die deutschen Kirchen für Themen aus den jetzt so bezeichneten Entwicklungsländern und der

42 Hans-Jochen Margull, Überseeische Christenheit II. Vermutungen zu einer Tertiaterranität des Christentums (1974), in: Ders., Zeugnis und Dialog. Ausgewählte Schriften mit Einführungen von Theodor Ahrens/Lothar Engel u. a., Hamburg 1992, 208–217.

43 Pörksen, Zehn Jahre Missionsakademie, 17 (Archiv der MA). Bischof Lilje führte auf der Synode in Bethel 1963 die Missionsakademie als erste der Aufgaben der Arbeitsgemeinschaft für Weltmission auf.

44 Etwa in Auslandspfarrerkursen in Kooperation mit der EKD für die Region Südwest-Afrika, vgl. dazu Sebastian Justke, »Brückenbauen« gegen Apartheid? Auslandspfarrer in Südafrika und Namibia, Göttingen 2020.

45 Diesen Hinweis verdanke ich dem ehemaligen »Tutor« Joachim Wietzke. Vgl. MA-Archiv – Dokumentation.

46 Vgl. bereits Walter Freytag, Die Landeskirche als Teil der Weltmission. Tatsachen und Folgerungen (1959), in: Jan Hermelink/Hans Jochen Margull (Hg.), Walter Freytag. Reden und Aufsätze. Zweiter Teil, München 1961, 160–174.

ökumenischen Gemeindeerneuerung öffneten.[47] Die Denkschrift der EKD »Der Entwicklungsdienst der Kirche – ein Beitrag für Frieden und Gerechtigkeit in der Welt« (1973) legte den Akzent auf den sozialpolitischen Aspekt von Mission, was die Gestaltung der zahlreichen Vikarskurse prägte. Der Ausschuss für Bildung und Publizistik (ABP) des Evangelischen Entwicklungsdienstes richtete eine Fachstelle für entwicklungsbezogene Bildungsarbeit in der Missionsakademie ein, die mit einem Vertreter oder einer Vertreterin der überseeischen Kirchen besetzt wurde. Lu Hong Khan aus Vietnam war 1980 der erste Inhaber dieser Stelle, es folgte Sooil Chai aus Korea, Antonio Carlos de Melo Magalhães, Graciela Chamorro, Claudete Beise Ulrich aus Brasilen, Amélé Ekué aus Togo, Daniel Chiquete aus Mexiko und Ruomin Liu aus China.[48]

Die Missionsakademie wurde so zu einer Drehscheibe ökumenischer Bildungsarbeit, die durch ihre Kurse entwicklungspolitische und ökumenische Bewusstseinsbildung in den deutschen Kirchen leisten konnte.[49] Es bildete sich ein thematischer Dreischritt von authentischer Information, Begegnung und Dialog über gemeinsame Fragen heraus,[50] der vielfach übernommen wurde. Angesichts der in Melbourne 1980 befreiungstheologisch zugespitzten Forderung einer Option für die Armen, kam es zu einem Konflikt über eine »Politisierung« des Missionsverständnisses, als der theologische Grundsatzreferent des EMW und ehemalige Studienleiter Wilhelm Wille auf der EKD-Synode in Garmisch-Partenkirchen eine Umverteilung der Macht zur Überwindung der Armut und Gestaltung einer gerechten Welt forderte.[51]

47 Dietrich Werner, Mission in Deutschland, in: Dahling-Sander u. a. (Hg.), Leitfaden, 545–561.

48 Vgl. die Liste der Studienleiter an der Missionsakademie: https://www.missionsakademie.de/files/MA_Studienleitung-seit-Gruendung-2020.pdf (8.3.2021).

49 Impulse kamen auch aus der Ecumenical Association of Third World Theologians (EATWOT). Vgl. Erhard Kamphausen, Die Ökumenische Vereinigung von Theologen und Theologinnen der Dritten Welt (EATWOT). Erfahrungen und Beobachtungen aus dem Blickwinkel der Missionsakademie, in: Theodor Ahrens (Hg.), Zwischen Regionalität und Globalisierung. Studien zu Mission, Ökumene und Religion, Hamburg 1997, 271–301. Vgl. Andreas Heuser/Wolfram Weiße (Hg.), Neuere Religiöse Bewegungen in internationaler Perspektive, Aachen 2005.

50 Vgl. Löffler, Spannungen leben!, 183.

51 Vgl. Klaus Schäfer, Mission im Kontext der Armut. Erinnerungen an eine ökumenische Provokation, in: Ders. (Hg.) Provokation Mission. Lernerfahrungen aus der weltweiten Mission, Hamburg 2000, 104–126, hier: 119. Vgl. dazu Theodor Ahrens, Die Missionsakademie – Rückblick und Ausblick, in: Kahl u. a. (Hg.), Mission Interkulturell, 173–181, hier: 177. Zum Hintergrund: Dejung, Rüppell, Ökumenische Gemeinschaft, 175–195.

Im Zentrum der Debatten stand das Bemühen, die mitunter bedrückenden Realitäten der Partnerkirchen im globalen Süden zu verändern.[52] Schon früh hatte die Missionsakademie Studienprogramme durchgeführt, bei denen jeweils Theologiestudierende und Pfarrerinnen und Pfarrer nach Indien fuhren und dort im Kontakt mit indischen Teilnehmenden und ihren theologischen Institutionen die Bedingungen kennenlernten, unter denen kontextuelle Theologie entstand. Das jeweils zweijährige Programm sah dann auch eine Gegenbegegnung der indischen Partner an der Missionsakademie vor.[53] Mit der 1970 eingerichteten Kommission für Zusammenarbeit in Entwicklungsfragen des ÖRK, dem *United Theological College* in Bangalore und der *United Church of Christ in the Philippines* entstand 1979 ein Drei-Länder-Programm,[54] dessen gemeinsam erarbeitete Lernergebnisse die Teilnehmenden über viele Jahre in Austausch hielt.[55] Spätere Programme fanden in Kooperation mit der methodistischen Kirche von Nigeria statt.[56] In dieser Tradition eines multilateralen akademischen Austausches standen auch die *Joint Consultation of Theologians*, bei denen Vertreter und Vertreterinnen aus Brasilien, Korea, Deutschland und später auch den USA an wechselnden Orten Themen wie »Versöhnung und Heilung« diskutierten und auf eine Anregung der ehemaligen Studienleiter Prof. Chai Soo-il und Prof. Antonio Magalhães zurückgingen. 2014/15 wurde anlässlich der Reformationsdekade gemeinsam mit Brot für die Welt, dem EMW und Partnern eine Twin-Konsultation zum Thema *Reformation – Education – Transformation* in São Leopoldo und in Halle und 2017 federführend von Uta Andrée ein *Global European Ecumenical Institute* (GETI'17) in Berlin durchgeführt.[57] Seit den 1990er Jahren ist

52 Vgl. Dietrich Werner, Armut als Ort der Missio Dei. Ökumenische Missionstheologie im Kontext von Urban Industrial Mission, in: Ders., Mission für das Leben – Mission im Kontext. Ökumenische Perspektiven missionarischer Präsenz in der Diskussion des ÖRK 1961–1991, Rothenburg 1993, 159–264.

53 Vgl. Gert Rüppell (Hg.), Indien. Kontext für Mission und Entwicklung, Frankfurt a. M. 1979.

54 Mission im Kontext des Kampfes für Gerechtigkeit. Ein trilaterales Studienprojekt zu den Bedingungen von Mission und Entwicklung. Missionsakademie Hamburg/ECD Manila 1980.

55 Für diese Hinweise danke ich Gert Rüppell.

56 Werner Simpfendörfer/Gert Rüppell, Our Common Struggle for Justice, Peace and Integrity of Creation. Nigerian-German Learning Experience 1984/1985, Bad Boll 1986. Sowie: Kurt Dockhorn/Gert Rüppell, Justice, Peace and Integrity of Creation – Our Common Struggle. Nigerian German Ecumenical Learning Programme 1985–1986, Bad Boll 1987.

57 Uta Andrée/Anna-Katharina Diehl u. a. (Hg.), Challenged by Ecumenism. Documentation of the Global Ecumenical Theological Institute Berlin 2017, Hamburg 2018. Vgl. Uta Andrée/Benjamin Simon u. a. (Hg.), Reforming Theology. Migrating Church. Transforming Society. A Compendium for Ecumenical Education, Hamburg 2017.

die Missionsakademie zudem Tagungsort der *Arbeitsgemeinschaft Ökumenische Forschung* (AÖF), eines Forums der Nachwuchsförderung im Bereich ökumenischer, ethischer und interreligiöser Forschungsarbeit, und beteiligte sich an Versuchen ökumenisch-liturgischer Erneuerung.[58]

IV. Studien- und Fortbildungsort für Interkulturelle und Interreligiöse Begegnung

Während anfänglich die ökumenischen Beziehungen zu außereuropäischen Kirchen im Mittelpunkt der Studienarbeit standen, rückten im Laufe der Zeit immer stärker interkulturelle und interreligiöse Fragestellungen in Deutschland in den Mittelpunkt des Interesses. Auf einer Tagung der Arbeitsgemeinschaft Christlicher Kirchen (ACK) zum Thema *Die Rolle ausländischer christlicher Gemeinden in der Ökumene vor Ort* wurde 1994 die Notwendigkeit eines Fortbildungsprogramms für Migrationsgemeinden betont.[59] Dieses konnte 2001 durch die Studienleiterin Amélé Adamavi-Aho Ekué in Zusammenarbeit mit Vertretern afrikanischer Gemeinden 2001 als *African Theological Training in Germany* (ATTiG) gegründet werden. Das zunächst von Andreas Heuser durchgeführte Fortbildungsprogramm richtete sich an Leitende afrikanischer, vornehmlich charismatisch geprägter Gemeinden.[60] Bis 2015 wurden über einhundert Gemeindeleiter und Gemeindeleiterinnen mit dem von verschiedenen Dozierenden durchgeführten Programm erreicht und somit in innovativer Weise die Ökumene vor Ort in den Blick genommen. Der von Werner Kahl 2006 gegründete Internationale Gospelgottesdienst zeigte das kirchliche Potential einer interkulturellen Öffnung und regte über Pastoralkonvente neue Gemeindeprojekte an. Auch das sich an ATTiG anschließende Fortbildungsprogramm ÖkuFiT[61] bereitet auf eine

58 Dietrich Werner (Hg.), Sinfonia Oecumenica. Worship with the Churches in the World. Liturgical Workbook in four languages, Gütersloh 1998.

59 Lothar Engel, Zur Entstehung des ATTiG-Programms, in: Evangelisches Missionswerk (Hg.), Gemeinsam lernen in der fremden Heimat. Dokumente des ATTiG-Pilotkurses (Weltmission Heute 56), Hamburg 2004, 20–27, hier: 20.

60 Vgl. Andreas Heuser, Das theologische Ausbildungsprojekt ATTiG (African Theological Training in Germany) an der Missionsakademie – eine Zwischenbilanz, in: Zeitschrift für Missionswissenschaft 1 (2005), 122–130.

61 Vgl. Für das Fortbildungsprogramm ÖkuFIT: https://www.missionsakademie.de/laufende-programme.html (8.3.2021).

interkulturell sensible Gemeindearbeit vor. Durch die Einbeziehung der Stipendiaten und Stipendiatinnen, die sich in ihren Dissertationen oft mit der charismatischen Bewegung in ihren Herkunftsländern Ghana, Tansania, Korea oder Mexiko beschäftigten, trat diese volksreligiöse Befreiungshoffnung eigener Art in den Mittelpunkt der Studienarbeit.[62]

Die Studienleitung stellte eine thematische Verschiebung von Gerechtigkeitsfragen der Befreiungstheologie zu kontroversen Fragen der Lebenspraxis wie dem Streitfall Homosexualität fest, was zu Irritationen im ökumenischen Partnerschaftsverständnis führte: »Wie gelingt Partnerschaft, wenn die Basis der Gemeinsamkeit in Frage gestellt wird? Welche Rolle spielen Religionen und die verschiedenen Spielarten des Christlichen bei der Verhinderung oder Begrenzung von Gewalt?«[63] Die Tagung *Homosexualität als Streitfall zwischen Partnerkirchen* arbeitete 2012 mit Vertretern aus Äthiopien, Tansania und Ghana die Bedeutung kultureller Differenzen, unterschiedlicher Schriftverständnisse, sowie nachwirkender Verletzungen aus der Kolonialgeschichte auf. Das Thema *Religion und Gewaltüberwindung* drängte sich angesichts neuer weltpolitischer Konfliktlagen seit dem 11.9.2001 auf die Agenda.[64] Im ab 2017 veranstalteten »Lateinamerika Forum« ging es um die Verhältnisbestimmung von Befreiungstheologie und Pfingstbewegung, sowie Kirchen und Staat.[65] 2018 fand ein Interreligiöser Dialog mit der *European Pentecostal and Charismatic Research Association* (EPCRA) und dem *Oxford Center for Mission Studies* (OCMS) statt.

Ab 2006 konnte Daniel Chiquete aus Mexiko, der selbst einer pfingstcharismatischen Kirche angehört, als Studienleiter gewonnen werden. In Zusammenarbeit mit dem Evangelischen Entwicklungsdienst fand 2011 eine Konferenz zu den entwicklungspolitischen Kooperationsmöglichkeiten mit Pfingstkirchen Afrikas

62 Vgl. Uta Andrée (Hg.), Einschätzungen zur Pfingstbewegung. Beiträge von Theologinnen und Theologen der Missionsakademie/Hamburg und der Faculdade Unida/Vitória, Hamburg 2016.

63 Bericht des Vorstandes an das Kuratorium 2011/2012, 1 (Archiv MA).

64 Theodor Ahrens/Werner Kahl (Hg.), *Gegen*Gewalt. Ökumenische Bewährungsfelder, Leipzig 2015. Vgl. Erhard Kamphausen/Gerhard Köberlin (Hg.), Gewalt und Gewaltüberwindung: Stationen eines theologischen Dialogs, Frankfurt a. M. 2006.

65 Die Missionsakademie war bereits seit Mitte der 1990er Jahre im Bereich der Migrations- und Pfingstkirchenforschung innovativ, vgl. Dietrich Werner, Charismatisch-pentekostale Gemeindeneugründungen in Deutschland – ihre missionstheologische, pastorale und ökumenische Problematik, in: Ders., Wiederentdeckung, 346–350.

Encounter beyond routine statt.[66] Aufgrund der veränderten Rahmenbedingungen stellte sich 2007 anlässlich des fünfzigsten Jubiläums der Missionsakademie die Frage der inhaltlichen Kontinuität der Missionsakademie. Der Vorstand identifizierte diese trotz des »Wandel(s) der Themenschwerpunkte im Kontext der Zeiten von den 70ern bis ins erste Jahrzehnt des 21. Jahrhunderts«, der sich in der Hinwendung zur »Pfingstbewegung und dem interreligiösen Dialog« zeige, »im Fokus auf ein ökumenisches Lernen«.[67]

Paul Löffler hatte bereits auf dem Kirchentag in Hamburg 1981 einer größeren Öffentlichkeit bei einer Podiumsdiskussion mit Abdoldjavad Falaturi und Hans-Jochen Margull Begegnungen mit dem Islam ermöglicht. Die Veröffentlichungen »Muslime – unsere Nachbarn« (1977)[68], »Zusammenleben mit Muslimen« (1980)[69] oder »Die Begegnung von Christen und Muslimen« (1988)[70] waren aus der Kursarbeit in Kooperation mit Muslimen hervorgegangen. Diese Arbeit war inspiriert von dem interreligiösen Schwerpunkt des Instituts für Mission, Religion und Ökumene und seiner Lehrstuhlinhaber seit Hans-Jochen Margull bis Ulrich Dehn.[71] Margull, der ab 1971 den Vorsitz für die neu geschaffene Abteilung für Dialog beim ÖRK hatte, plädierte dafür, »den anderen so verstehen zu lernen, wie er sich selbst versteht«.[72] So wurde auch das *Europäische Netzwerk für Buddhistisch-Christliche Studien* 1996 an der Missionsakademie gegründet, an der Gerhard Köberlin von 1994 bis 1996 mit Hilfe von *Dienste in Übersee* den Beitrag des christlich-buddhistischen Dialogs für die entwicklungspolitische Bildungsarbeit erkundete.[73] Werner Kahl initiierte gemeinsam getragene Koran-

66 Evangelisches Missionswerk (Hg.), Encounter beyond routine. Cultural roots, cultural transition, understanding of faith and cooperation in development International Consultation, Academy of Mission, Hamburg, 17th-23rd January 2011, Hamburg 2011.

67 Bericht des Vorstandes an das Kuratorium 2007/2008, Punkt 2 (Archiv der Missionsakademie). Vgl. Dejung/Rüppell, Ökumenische Gemeinschaft, 262–277.

68 Gerhard Jasper (Hg.), Muslime – unsere Nachbarn: Beiträge zum Gespräch über den Glauben. Frankfurt am Main 1977.

69 Jürgen Micksch (Hg.), Zusammenleben mit Muslimen: Eine Handreichung, Frankfurt am Main 1980.

70 Vgl. Evangelisches Missionswerk in Deutschland (Hg.), Die Begegnung von Christen und Muslimen: Eine Orientierungshilfe, Hamburg 1988.

71 Vgl. Ulrich Dehn/Ulrike Caspar-Seeger u. a. (Hg.), Handbuch Theologie der Religionen. Texte zur religiösen Vielfalt und zum interreligiösen Dialog, Freiburg 2017.

72 Paul Löffler, Spannungen leben!, 186.

73 Ulrich Dehn, Geschichte des interreligiösen Dialogs, Göttingen 2020, 194. Vgl. auch Evangelisches Missionswerk in Deutschland (Hg.), Wege zu einer gerechten Gesellschaft. Beiträge engagierter Buddhisten zu einer internationalen Debatte, Hamburg 1996, 21.

lektüren von Pastoren und Pastorinnen mit Imamen, aus denen mit *ChrislamFiT* ein neues Fortbildungsformat wurde.[74]

Bedeutsam wurde die Missionsakademie auch im Bereich der interreligiösen Seelsorge durch ihre Vernetzung mit Akteuren und Akteurinnen des interreligiösen Dialogs.[75] Der Arbeitskreis *Mission und Seelsorge* versuchte durch Themen wie »Die Bedeutung der Ahnen und Vorfahren bei der Bewältigung von Krisen und Konflikten« ein kultursensibles Bewusstsein für interkulturelle Seelsorge zu schaffen. Im Rahmen des Themas *Frauen in der Mission* wurde von Sabine Förster 2010 eine Tagung zum Thema *Storytelling – Mission und Seelsorge im Kontext von Gewalt* organisiert. In Zusammenarbeit mit der aus Brasilien stammenden Studienleiterin Claudete Beise Ulrich und dem *Studienzentrum für Genderfragen in Kirchen und Theologie der EKD* beschäftigte sich das Netzwerk ÖKUFEM mit der Fragestellung *Sexualität und Gewalt in Religion und Gesellschaft.* Gemeinsam mit dem Theologischen Ausbildungsprogramm des ÖRK (ETE) und der EKD organisierte Michael Biehl 2012 eine internationale Stipendienkonferenz *Ecumenical Partnership in Theological Education and Theological Scholarship Programs*[76], deren Hauptziel die Entwicklung von Konzepten zur transparenten Abstimmung im Stipendienwesen war. Zentrale Impulse steuerte Biehl zum Studienprozess der 100-Jahrfeier der Weltmissionskonferenz von *Edinburgh 1910–2010* bei,[77] der im gemeinsam mit der DGMW durchgeführten Studienprozess zur 100-Jahrfeier des Internationalen Missionsrats (IMR) in Lake Mohonk 2021 seine Fortsetzung findet.

Zugleich stieg mit dem starken Wachstum des Christentums in China das Interesse an einem theologischen Austausch über die sozial-ethische Bedeutung des Christentums im Zuge von Modernisierung mit dem erst seit den 1980er Jahren wieder zugänglichen, aber weltpolitisch immer wichtiger werdenden Land.

74 Vgl. Uta Andrée/Ruomin Liu u. a. (Hg.), Transkulturelle Begegnungen und interreligiöser Dialog. Erkundungen und Entdeckungen im Anschluss an Werner Kahl, Hamburg 2017 und https://www.missionsakademie.de/files/20210208_Flyer_chrislamFiT_2021_22-2.pdf (8.3.2021).

75 Es sollen gemeinsame Standards für eine interreligiöse Öffnung der Seelsorge entwickelt werden. Vgl. die von dem ehemaligen Studienleiter und jetzigen Islambeauftragten der Nordkirche Sönke Lorberg-Fehring organisierte Tagung, https://www.missionsakademie.de/files/202012023_Flyer_Seelsorgetagung_MA.pdf (8.3.2021).

76 WCC/ETE, Ecumenical Partnership in Theological Education, in: http://www.ftesea.org/Hamburg%20conference%202012.pdf (8.3.2021).

77 Michael Biehl, Das ganze Evangelium der ganzen Welt? Was uns Edinburgh heute noch angehen kann, in: https://www.dimoe.de/fileadmin/mediapool/einrichtungen/E_dimoe/Biehl__Edinburgh_Karlsruhe.pdf (8.3.2021).

So fand dazu 2009 eine deutsch-chinesische Konsultation an der Missionsakademie mit der *Academy of Social Sciences*, der Renmin Universität in Peking und der Universität in Xian statt.[78] Stark nachgefragt werden die von dem aus China stammenden Studienleiter Ruomin Liu angebotenen Kurse für Leitende der chinesischen Gemeinden (China-Kit) sowie von Konferenzen für Dozenten theologischer Hochschulen in China.[79]

Ohne die Programme und Kooperationen der Missionsakademie an dieser Stelle erschöpfend behandeln zu können, dürfte doch die im Laufe der Zeit zunehmende Pluralisierung der Themen und Fragestellungen deutlich geworden sein. Welche postkoloniale Theologie der Mission[80] lässt sich angesichts der unterschiedlichen Wirklichkeitsverständnisse[81] des globalen Christentums formulieren? Welche Möglichkeiten zur Begegnung und Fortbildung sind angesichts der interkulturellen Öffnung der Kirchen erforderlich? Durch die Verbindung des akademischen Stipendiatenprogramms mit der interkulturellen und interreligiösen Studienarbeit verfügt die Missionsakademie über ein bewährtes Bildungsangebot, aus dem viele innovative Beiträge hervorgegangen sind.[82] Sie kann als ein Juwel der interkulturellen Theologie auch zukünftig erforderliche ökumenisch-missionarische Aus- und Fortbildung weiterentwickeln, sofern nicht die dafür nötigen Finanzmitteln gestrichen werden sollten. Dies wäre umso bedauerlicher, als die in den 1960 und 1970er Jahren aufgebrochenen Fronten zwischen Glaubensmission und politischer Ökumene zugunsten eines wirklich ökumenischen Missionsverständnisses wieder zusammenzuführen wären.[83] Mit der Streichung der Zuweisungen entfiele nicht nur für den Universitätsstandort Hamburg und besonders den theologischen Fachbereich ein wichtiges An-Institut, in dem der interreligiöse, interkulturelle und ökumenische Dialog eine auch

78 Michael Biehl/Ulrich Dehn (Hg.), Religion and Culture in Transforming Societies. A Theological Dialogue of Chinese and German Scholars August 25–28, 2009, Frankfurt a. M. 2011.

79 Vgl. Ruomin Liu/Sönke Lorberg-Fehring (Hg.), Theologische Stimmen aus China, Hamburg 2018.

80 Dietrich Werner, Wiederentdeckung einer missionarischen Kirche, Schenefeld 2005.

81 Werner Kahl/Gabriele Lademann-Priemer (Hg.), Hexerei-Anschuldigungen in weltweiter Perspektive. Witchcraft accusations in global perspective, Hamburg 2020. Werner Kahl, Geisterfahrung als Empowerment. Transformationsprozesse innerhalb der weltweiten Pfingstbewegung. Mit einem Fokus auf Westafrika, in: Theologisches Gespräch. Freikirchliche Beiträge zur Theologie 3/42 (2018), 111–128.

82 Vgl. die Studien zu Interkultureller Theologie der Missionsakademie (SITMA)/Theologische Impulse der Missionsakademie (TIMA) in: https://www.missionsakademie.de/sitma.html; https://www.missionsakademie.de/tima.html (8.3.2021).

83 Vgl. Michael Biehl/Traugott Hopp u. a. (Hg.), Witnessing Christ. Contextual and Interconfessional Perspectives on Christology, Stuttgart 2020.

politisch geförderte Rolle spielen.[84] Es wäre auch alarmierend, wenn sich die Evangelische Kirche angesichts der gegenwärtigen Migrationsbewegungen und einer interkulturell und interreligiös pluralisierenden Gesellschaft aus einer ihrer bekanntesten Begegnungs- und Studienzentren zurückzöge.

(Dr. Anton Knuth ist Geschäftsführender Studienleiter an der Missionsakademie an der Universität Hamburg)

ABSTRACT

This article reconstructs the history of the *Missionsakademie an der Universität Hamburg* including its prehistory since the foundation of the Colonial Institute in Hamburg 1909 and the Edinburgh World Missionary Conference in 1910, which emphasized the need for academic training of missionaries. The author assesses the different transformations and paradigm shifts within the program of the internationally well-known Mission Academy which followed from the decolonization of Global Christianity and argues that such ecumenical study-centres are needed for the development of an ecumenical missiology in an intercultural and interreligious context more than ever.

84 Vgl. die brieflichen Einwendungen des theologischen Fachbereichs Hamburgs gegenüber entsprechenden Planungen des Rates der EKD sowie weitere Appelle an den Ratsvorsitzenden der EKD unter https://www.missionsakademie.de/files/FB-Prof.-Brief-an-EKD-Missionsakademie-Hamburg.pdf (8.3.2021).

Forschungsnetzwerk »Begegnung mit dem globalen Christentum vor Ort. Migrationskirchen in Niedersachsen«

Migration verändert Religionsgeographien. Während die Migration von Musliminnen und Muslimen massenmedial und politisch stark wahrgenommen wird, wird oft übersehen, dass in Deutschland über zehn Millionen Christenmenschen mit Migrationshintergrund leben. Viele von ihnen organisieren sich in Migrationskirchen, internationalen und interkulturellen Gemeinden, die das religiöse Leben nachhaltig bereichern.[1] Polyzentrische Strukturen sind nicht länger nur ein Charakteristikum des weltweiten Christentums, sondern prägen die Christenheit vor Ort. Kirchliche Beobachter schätzen, dass sowohl im Ruhrgebiet als auch im Rhein-Main-Gebiet etwa jeweils 600 protestantische bzw. pentekostale Migrationskirchen existieren. Dennoch sind Migrationskirchen ein »Stiefkind« sowohl der Migrations- und Religionswissenschaften[2] als auch der Theologie. Auf einer von uns organisierten Tagung, die im März 2017 unter dem Titel »Begegnung in der Glokalität. Christliche Migrationskirchen in Deutschland im Wandel« an der Ruhr-Universität Bochum stattfand, kam deshalb die Idee auf,

1 Das Netzwerk versteht unter Migrationskirchen solche Kirchen und Gemeinden, in denen die Mehrheit der Mitglieder einen Migrationshintergrund haben, bzw. zugespitzt: Kirchen, die es ohne spätneuzeitliche Migrationsprozesse gar nicht gäbe. Indem wir statt von Migrationsgemeinden von Migrationskirchen reden, wollen wir die theologische Einsicht zum Ausdruck bringen, dass sich in jeder gottesdienstlichen Gemeinschaft von Christenmenschen Kirche realisiert, Migrationskirchen also nichts fehlt, um Kirche zu sein.

2 Alexander-Kenneth Nagel/Nelly Caroline Schubert, Glokale Verflechtungen und zivilgesellschaftliche Potentiale. Migrationskirchen in Niedersachsen in vergleichender Perspektive, in: Claudia Rammelt u. a. (Hg.), Begegnung in der Glokalität. Christliche Migrationskirchen im Wandel, Leipzig 2018, 213–228, 217; in religionswissenschaftlichen und -soziologischen Darstellungen kommen sie oft schlicht nicht vor (vgl. exemplarisch nur Daniel Gerster u. a. [Hg.], Religionspolitik heute. Problemfelder und Perspektiven in Deutschland, Freiburg u. a. 2018.).

ein wissenschaftliches Netzwerk zu gründen, welches diejenigen Forschungen bündelt, die aus theologischer und religionswissenschaftlicher Sicht Migrationskirchen in den Blick nehmen. Da deren bisherige Erforschung vor allem von ehemals missionswissenschaftlichen Lehrstühlen ausging, blendete diese in der Regel die orthodoxen Kirchen aus, da deren Thematisierung, folgt man dem klassischen Fächerkanon der Evangelischen Theologie, in der Kirchengeschichte verortet ist. Dieser Tendenz wollte das Netzwerk von Anfang an durch die Einbeziehung der orientalischen und orthodoxen Kirchen entgegenwirken. Es gilt wahrzunehmen, dass nicht alle (auch nicht alle afrikanischen und asiatischen Migrationskirchen) pentekostal-charismatisch geprägt sind.

Das Netzwerk setzte sich zum Ziel,

a) das glokale Phänomen der Migrationskirchen (in einem historisch weiten und deshalb auch die orientalischen und orthodoxen Kirchen einbeziehenden Sinn) genauer zu erfassen und dicht zu beschreiben, und
b) Möglichkeiten eines lebensförderlichen Zusammenlebens (im Sinne von Konvivenz) und einer fruchtbaren Begegnung zwischen Migrationskirchen und reformatorischen Kirchen samt ihrer akademischen Theologie auszuloten.

Mittlerweile können wir dank der finanziellen Förderung durch die Hanns-Lilje-Stiftung auf eine dreijährige Zusammenarbeit zurückblicken, deren Ergebnisse im Herbst dieses Jahres in einem bei der Evangelischen Verlagsanstalt erscheinenden Band präsentiert werden. Der Band bietet unter dem Titel »Migrationskirchen. Internationalisierung und Pluralisierung des Christentums« grundlegende theologische Zugänge zur Bedeutung von Migrationsprozessen für das Christentum, zahlreiche das Feld der Migrationskirchen erschließende Einzelstudien und lotet die Möglichkeiten aus, welche die Migration von Christenmenschen für Theologie und Kirche eröffnen.

Zum Aufbau des Forschungsnetzwerks haben wir durch persönliche Ansprache und öffentliche Ausschreibungen Forscherinnen und Forscher, vor allem auch aus dem wissenschaftlichen Nachwuchs, gesucht und identifiziert, die sich wissenschaftlich mit Migrationskirchen beschäftigen. Solche finden sich nicht nur an Universitäten und Hochschulen, sondern auch in der kirchlichen Praxis und in intermediären Institutionen. Von der Zusammenführung dieser an unterschiedlichen Orten arbeitenden Wissenschaftlerinnen und Wissenschaftlern hat das Projekt profitiert. Stärkere Theorieorientierung auf der einen Seite, unmittelbare Praxisnähe auf der anderen haben sich beständig und wechselseitig bereichert. In einem respektvoll-kritischen Austausch verschiedener Perspektiven, konkreter

Erfahrungen, aber auch analytischer Zugangsweisen wurde die Vielzahl der Themenfelder offensichtlich, die mit dem Feld der Migrationskirchen verbunden sind.

Dabei war es uns wichtig, nicht ausschließlich als evangelische Theologinnen und Theologen und aus religionswissenschaftlicher Perspektive über Migrationskirchen zu sprechen, sondern auch Wissenschaftler aus Migrationskirchen in das Forschungsnetzwerk zu inkludieren. Zunächst konnten wir zwei zum Promotionsstudium nach Deutschland gekommene rumänisch-orthodoxe Theologen, namentlich PD Dr. Ciprian Burlacioiu (München) und Dr. Vasile-Octavian Mihoc (Genf), für die Mitarbeit gewinnen. Zudem gelang es uns, im Laufe der Arbeit weitere Nachwuchswissenschaftlerinnen und -wissenschaftler aus Migrationskirchen zu identifizieren, die wir entweder für einen einmaligen Beitrag gewinnen oder auch in das Forschungsnetzwerk integrieren konnten: Dr. Egide Muziazia, der an der katholisch-theologischen Fakultät in Münster mit einer Arbeit über afrikanisch-katholische Migrantengemeinden in Nordwesteuropa zwischen Ethnizität und Katholizität promoviert worden ist, Thuy-Evelyn Pham, die am Institut für Evangelische Theologie in Paderborn eine Masterarbeit über vietnamesische Gemeinden in Deutschland geschrieben hat, Nhan Gia Vo, Promovend am Institut für Evangelische Theologie in Osnabrück, Dr. Ruomin Liu, Studienleiter an der Missionsakademie in Hamburg, und Benson Elisamoni Matawana, der in Göttingen eine Dissertation zur Rolle ghanaischer Migrationskirchen in der Arbeit mit Geflüchteten schreibt. Sie alle sind mit Beiträgen in dem genannten Sammelband vertreten. Es gibt also begründete Hoffnung, dass sich an der wissenschaftlichen Erforschung von Migrationskirchen in Zukunft auch Forscherpersönlichkeiten aus diesen Kirchen beteiligen werden.

Neben der Vernetzung einzelner thematisch ausgewiesener Wissenschaftlerinnen und Wissenschaftler dient das Netzwerk der Zusammenführung von Institutionen, an denen Migrationskirchen erforscht werden. Mittlerweile verbindet es die Lehrstühle für Systematische Theologie in Osnabrück, für Interkulturelle Theologie und Körperlichkeit an der Ruhr-Universität Bochum und für Interkulturelle Theologie in Basel, die sozialwissenschaftliche Religionsforschung am Institut für Soziologie der Georg-August-Universität Göttingen, das *CERES* an der Ruhr-Universität Bochum und das Religionswissenschaftliche Institut der Universität Leipzig, das Basler Forschungsprojekt *Conviviality in Motion. Exploring Theologies and Practices of Multiethnic Christian Communities in Europe*, die Fachhochschule für Interkulturelle Theologie (FIT) Hermannsburg sowie die Missionsakademie an der Universität Hamburg.

Um ein bundesweites, bis in die Schweiz ausstrahlendes Netzwerk aufzubauen, konnten wir den einzelnen Forscherinnen und Forschern nicht zumuten, ihre Forschungen auf das Bundesland Niedersachsen zu konzentrieren. Ganz konkret: Wenn eine Pfarrerin aus dem Rheinland sich bereit erklärt, ihre Erfahrungen mit Iranerinnen und Iranern in ihrer Gemeinde wissenschaftlich zu reflektieren, kann man sie nicht nötigen, noch eine Vergleichsgemeinde in Niedersachsen ausfindig zu machen. Wir haben uns deshalb entschlossen, die enge Fokussierung auf Niedersachsen aufzugeben, ohne unsere Forschungen wieder allein auf Metropolregionen zu reduzieren.

Für die jährlichen Treffen des Forschungsnetzwerks wurden Orte ausgewählt, die einen Bezug zum Thema bieten, etwa das koptische Kloster in Brenkhausen, das Missionsseminar an der Universität Hamburg und der Himmelsfels als herausragender Ort interkultureller Ekklesialität. Bei dem ersten Treffen stellten alle Teilnehmerinnen und Teilnehmer in einem drei- bis fünfseitigen Text ihr Forschungsvorhaben dar. Bei den folgenden beiden Treffen hat jeweils die Hälfte der Teilnehmerinnen und Teilnehmer einen vollständig ausgearbeiteten Aufsatz zur Diskussion gestellt. Die Texte wurden jeweils vorweg an alle Teilnehmenden verschickt, so dass die Verfasserinnen und Verfasser nur noch jeweils kurz in ihren Text einführen mussten (zehn Minuten) und nach einer Response durch ein anderes Mitglied des Netzwerks genug Zeit zur Diskussion blieb. Dieses Verfahren bewährte sich: Alle kommen gut vorbereitet zu den einzelnen Treffen und deshalb kann die zur Verfügung stehende Zeit der Interaktion wirklich für das Gespräch genutzt werden. Die tiefe Verbundenheit mit dem Themenfeld und die geteilte Einsicht in die gesellschaftliche und kirchliche Bedeutung desselben führten zu einem intensiven und konstruktiven gemeinschaftlichen Arbeiten. Das Bewusstsein einer Weggemeinschaft ließ das gegenseitige Vertrauen wachsen und ermöglichte, Gedanken, Perspektiven und Forschungsfragen gemeinsam zu entwickeln. Auf einem (digitalen) Treffen im Februar 2021 wurden alle Texte noch einmal im Gesamtkontext des geplanten Sammelbandes diskutiert.

Während die Treffen in der Regel auf ein intensives Arbeiten an zwei halben Tagen mit einer Übernachtung beschränkt waren, diente das dritte Treffen dem Austausch mit Vertreterinnen und Vertretern von Migrationskirchen und umfasste deshalb drei Tage. Die Gruppe erhielt authentische Einblicke in das Leben von Migrationskirchen, die bisher nicht im Zentrum der Forschung standen, und in die Lebenswelt der jeweiligen zweiten und dritten Generation. Dadurch eröffneten sich neue Perspektiven, während manches bereits Diskutierte aber auch bestätigt wurde. Deutlich wurde: Um die Vielfalt nicht zu verspielen, ist jeder Migrationskirche mit vorurteilsfreier und individueller Aufmerksamkeit zu begegnen.

Die Treffen wurden jeweils durch einen Abendvortrag bereichert. Während 2018 Prof. Dr. Sabine Hess (Universität Göttingen) in das Konzept der Grenzregimeforschung einführte, erläuterte 2019 Bischof Damian (Koptisches Kloster Brenkhausen) die Chancen und Herausforderungen koptischen Glaubenslebens in der Diaspora. 2020 berichtete OKR Bendix Balke (EKD) eindrucksvoll von seiner Arbeit als Referent für internationale Gemeinden im Kirchenamt der EKD. Dass diese Projektstelle mittlerweile aufgelöst worden ist, zeigt ebenso wie die angekündigte Schließung der FIT Hermannsburg, dass die evangelischen Kirchen in Deutschland das Potential von Migrationskirchen auch für eigene Erneuerungsprozesse zu verspielen drohen.

Die Arbeit des Netzwerks hat das Phänomen der Migrationskirchen in seiner Pluralität durch zahlreiche Einzelstudien und in unterschiedlichen Forschungsperspektiven umfassend und differenziert erschlossen. Dabei zeigten sich sowohl Spezifika der einzelnen Kirchen als auch interessante Gemeinsamkeiten zwischen ihnen. Dabei hat sich die Entscheidung, orientalische und orthodoxe Gemeinden in die Forschung einzuschließen, bewährt: Zum einen stehen diese Gemeinden oftmals vor ähnlichen Herausforderungen wie andere Migrationskirchen (etwa in der Unterstützung von Geflüchteten, aber auch im Blick auf die zweite und dritte Generation), zum anderen stellen sie ökumenische Konzepte, die zentral auf sichtbare Einheit abstellen, konstruktiv infrage. Was noch aussteht, ist eine ausdifferenzierte Geschichte der verschiedenen Migrationskirchen in Deutschland.

In den Blick geriet die religionsproduktive Kraft von Migration. Durch Migrationsprozesse entstehen Kirchen, die durch die Verschränkung verschiedener Kontexte geprägt sind und diese verschiedenen Kontexte zugleich mitprägen. In der Begegnung vor Ort bilden sich sowohl Formen der gegenseitigen Annäherung bis hin zur Synthese als auch Formen von Differenz-Setzungen und Abgrenzungen. Diese Prozesse werden von Akteurinnen und Akteuren mit ganz verschiedenen Hintergründen, Geschichten und Interessen getragen und gestaltet. Dabei beginnen sich Geschichten zu verknüpfen und es bilden sich Gemeinschaften, die sich nicht in Bindestrich-Identitäten erschöpfen. Zunehmend wurde deutlich, was Migrationskirchen auch als diakonische Akteure leisten.

Für die weitere Forschung zeichnet sich zum einen die Bedeutung von vergleichenden (religions-, konfessions- und Herkunftsländer vergleichenden) Untersuchungen ab. Dem spannenden Vergleich von Migrationskirchen und Moscheegemeinden haben wir nur einen Seitenblick gewidmet, ansonsten der weiteren (dringend benötigten) Forschung überlassen. Ein Vergleich nach Herkunftsländern führt etwa im Blick auf asiatische Migrationskirchen dazu, unterschiedliche Migrationsformen in den Blick zu nehmen, etwa Arbeitsmigration (koreanische, z. T. vietnamesische Gemeinden), Fluchtmigration (vietnamesische Gemeinden) und Bildungsmigration (chinesische Gemeinden).

Zum anderen haben wir zunehmend die Notwendigkeit erkannt, die expliziten und impliziten Theologien von Migrationskirchen (und deren Transformationen im Übergang von der ersten zur zweiten und dritten Generation) zu erforschen. Content matters! Die qualitativen und soziologisch nach den gesellschaftlichen Leistungen von Migrationskirchen fragenden Arbeiten bedürfen der (gerade auch von Religionswissenschaftlern eingeklagten) Ergänzung um theologische Forschungen, welche die lebensweltlich eingebettete Rede von Gott innerhalb von Migrationskirchen methodisch nachvollziehbar erhellt. Wer Migrationskirchen als die gegenwärtige Gestalt des Christentums mitbestimmend ernst nimmt, darf sich nicht nur für deren Glaubens- und Frömmigkeitspraxis interessieren, sondern muss nach der in dieser Praxis verwurzelten Theologie fragen, in der Grundmomente des gelebten Glaubens versprachlicht und damit zugleich reflektiert werden. Der Gefahr, objektivierend über Migrationskirchen zu reden und ihre Gottesrede so nur als eine Variante der eigenen Theologie darzustellen, muss dabei durch die Begegnung (»encountering«) mit Migrationskirchen, den sich in ihnen versammelnden Menschen und deren Theologien entgegengewirkt werden.

Gregor Etzelmüller/Claudia Rammelt

Pentecostal Strategies of Public Engagement

11th GlobPent Conference, 14th–15th February 2020, in Basel

»Pentecostal Strategies of Public Engagement« was the theme of the 11th GlobPent Conference, which took place in Basel/Switzerland from 14th–15th February 2020. GlobPent is an interdisciplinary, international network of scholars committed to the study of Global Pentecostalism and charismatic Christianity. It stimulates the research of Pentecostal and charismatic movements in Asia, Africa, Latin America, and Europe. GlobPent is organized by a steering group »of seven established academics at five major European Universities, all of whom have a dedicated research and teaching focus on« the Pentecostal and Charismatic movement. The following report addresses the proceedings of the 11th GlobPent conference 2020, convened by Andreas Heuser (chair of Extra-European Christianity) at the University of Basel. I bring up observations written from a very personal perspective of a doctoral student engaging in this field of research.

In his opening address, Heuser presented the conference's objective and the central theme, explaining how and why Pentecostal public engagement has become one of the prominent global discourses in academia. Three keynote speakers explored the diversity of public strategies in the Global South: Heinrich Schäfer from the University of Bielefeld discussed »*Pentecostal political agendas in Latin America*«; Ilana van Wyk from the University of Stellenbosch focussed on »*Pentecostal public strategies in Southern Africa*«; and Nanlai Cao from Renmin University, Beijing spoke of »*Pentecostal patterns of public engagement in China and within the Chinese diaspora*«. I experienced an international conference with a surprisingly large contribution of African scholarship. In general, the Basel conference saw the highest numbers of global south participation thus far in the GlobPent history. Many of them had received third-party funding, organised and initiated by Heuser. The GlobPent 11th conference offered professional networking opportunities for most PhD students, and post-doctoral research fellows to interact with expert researchers in the field and a platform to exchange information on different strategies the global Pentecostal movement is using to engage the public sphere. Also, GlobPent Basel presentations provided ample empirical data of effective Pentecostal networking structures. Indeed, the call for papers that asked to study »concepts, strategies, and agendas on how Pentecostals shape the public sphere«, received a massive response from Africa, Europe, Asia, and Latin America. Moreover, contributors were willing to share their knowledge and research findings on how Pentecostals have divergent innovative strategies of engaging the public.

Accordingly, the well-organized conference attracted more than a hundred participants, with some forty-five papers presented in two days. The conference had three plenary sessions. Each session had a keynote speaker and a respondent to the speech, and the moderators led the participants to discuss the presentations. Moreover, there were three parallel sessions in between each plenary session, where different papers were presented. Each panel had sub-themes related to the conference's central theme, organized in twelve-panel sessions, three parallel sessions led by a moderator in each panel. The convention had as contributors both professors, prominent researchers, and authors from different disciplines and expertise. They were well selected to allow a well-coordinated networking interaction between PhD students, PhD holders, and Post-doctoral research fellows from the Global South, North America, and Europe.

On the first day after the opening address and the first plenary session, the first parallel session was held in four-panel sessions, each having a sub-theme related to the conference's central theme. The first panel was »*on re-shaping development- African initiated Christianity's contribution to decolonizing development*«, chaired by Ph. Öhlmann, M.-L. Frost, and J. Stork. Papers within this panel addressed how African independent and African Pentecostal churches re-shaped the concept of development and contributed to the decolonizing agenda. For example, Afe Adogame argued that religion undermined development in many parts of Africa. Religion is often regarded as an impediment to the development and transformation of Africa. Accordingly, for Adogame, religion as a unifying agent is an essential key feature where projects would emerge. In the same vein, Mangaliso Matshobane concurred with Adogame when he emphasized that the concept of development and cooperation with a religious group is not a new phenomenon in Africa. For instance, in Sub-Saharan Africa, Matshobane argues that most of »the developers were engaged with historic mission churches«; however, the »discourse on AICs involvement in development is still an area of research that needs to be explored«.

Chaired by Mika Vähäkangas, the second panel focused on »*Theo-politics*« as Pentecostals' strategy of public engagement in the migration context. Two presenters' focal points were on how the demographic changes in Europe are marked by the increase of immigrants from the Global South with a charismatic Pentecostal background. Leonardo M. Alves focused on Latin American migrant Pentecostalism in Europe, which served as an epitome. One of many impacts caused by the demographic changes is the plantation of Pentecostal charismatic migrant churches in Europe. In his presentation, Tordjörn Arntson gave evidence of how Pentecostal-charismatic migrant churches have become the fastest-growing denomination in Sweden. Moreover, Hadjie Cresencio Sadje explored how Samuel Lee's public theology and advocacy became a new form of Pentecostal strategies of public engagement in the Netherlands. Samuel Lee, a Pentecostal pastor and human rights activist, advocated for social justice for migrants and refugees with no legal documents. Lee's form of ministry portrays a new form of Pentecostalism which is not only about emotionality, fanaticism, and narrow biblical literalism, but involves a holistic mission including social ministry and political action.

The third panel, chaired by Michael Bergunder, discussed how Pentecostals use »›*Prophetism*‹ *and public theology*« to engage the public sphere. E. Okelloh Ogera from Kenya highlighted how the Neo-Pentecostal charismatics in Kenya use spiritual means like prayer, fasting, giving, tithing, divine healing, and miracles in the public sphere. Moreover, in the Kenyan context, the Pentecostal or Charismatics movement seemed to engage the public sphere through its prophetic strategy. The public issues engaged by the Kenyan Charismatic movement discussed by various presenters in this panel were: Charismatic movements and politics, socioeconomics, as well as religious-cultural aspects of private and public life. On the other hand, Ricardo Arakaki reported from a Brazilian perspective on how the Pentecostal church Assembleia de Deus and the Baptist Church used public theology to engage in the public sphere, addressing an economic and political crisis through criticism on theological grounds, even though it was restricted. His focus was on exploring the modalities or strategies of Pentecostals' engagement in the public sphere and their theological bases communicated through sermons.

Chaired by Jörg Haustein, the fourth panel examined how Pentecostals use social media platforms to engage the public. Abimbola A. Adelakun from Texas University argued that social media appropriated by Pentecostal Churches are not only used to broadcast information or to propagate their faith; also through media, Pentecostal and Charismatics' misuse of the tithe collected from members to support church projects and the pastor's glamourous lifestyles was repudiated during online debates. For example, in Cape Town, Pentecostals use live streams to broadcast their activities to all churches in the region, such as the visit to the Holy Land and Jerusalem by Pastor Chris (from Nigeria). Through the program, the viewers are mobilized to use the app to encourage viewership. In the same vein, Nicole Wagner speaks of Kenyan Prophet Dr. David Owuor, known as »the End-Time-Prophet« who emphasizes eschatology. He uses various modern social media technologies to propagate his »godly message« to the Kenyans and to build a personality cult in the public sphere. Accordingly, Peter Oderinde elucidated how Nigerian-led migrant Pentecostal churches in Switzerland use social media to engage in debates on sensitive issues within African communities, such as divorce among members of a born-again movement. Online and WhatsApp groups made it possible for both mega and smaller sized Nigerian-led Pentecostal migrant churches to engage the public on the online platform to interact on diverse issues related to women's rights, shaped by different forms of biblical patriarchy.

The second day of the conference commenced with a plenary session. Later, the second parallel session was held, slotted into three themes, and in three-panel sessions. The fifth panel addressed the theme of »*Global pentecostalism and lived religion*«, chaired by Julia Kuhlin and Yonatan Gez. The first presenter, Stian S. Eriksen from Norway, argued that the proportion of religion in everyday life sheds light on how the practice of faith is a threat to the mainline churches' doctrines and faith life. These »lived religion« settings of the Pentecostal migrant churches in Norway have revealed how the spiritualities of migrant Christians threaten religion's denominational boundaries and affect almost all aspects of daily life. Though migrant congregations in Norway do not get much attention, their proportion of »Lived Religion« defines the current features of Norwegian Pentecostal Christianity. In the same vein, Julia Kuhlin from Sweden explored how »communication technology« has induced people to put religion into practice and how electronic devices like smartphones, tablets, and computers have become part and parcel of people's religious lives. Her presentation focused on women's lived religion from two middle-class Pentecostal churches in India; these women formed a WhatsApp chat group and used it as a platform to express their daily religious life.

Interestingly, the WhatsApp group is used to evangelize their non-Christian relatives; it is used for improvement and motivation and as an online platform for prayer chains. These WhatsApp groups motivate women to integrate and to remain connected. It also helps them to be actively involved in church activities. Hence, because of the people's quest to use electronic devices as a platform to practice their religious lives, it is time for »digital religion« to be given significant consideration. Additionally, the mixture of both online and offline religious platforms should not be underestimated. However, Devaka Premawardhana emphasized in his paper the »relevance of literature for the ethnographic study of Pentecostalism as an everyday religion«. Furthermore, the paper explained the significance of »existential anthropology for the ethnographic study of lived religion«.

The sixth panel, moderated by Sibusiso Masondo, explored the issue of *politics in Southern Africa.* Phillip Musoni investigated whether the Pentecostal churches in Zimbabwe are willing to use their prophetic voice to engage in the political public sphere to restore peace and democracy. For him, the Zimbabwe Pentecostal churches turned a blind eye. They failed to use their prophetic voice to address the political crisis that has been imposed on the country by the corrupt Zimbabwe African National Union-Patriotic Front (ZANU–PF) government – unlike the mainline churches, such as the Catholic Church, who have from time to time condemned the corrupt government. Musoni further argued that the Pentecostal churches in Zimbabwe with their so-called »smart approach to politics« ended up »sanitizing« the corrupt government by adopting what the author called a »spiritualised political theology«, a strategy used by the Pentecostal Church leaders, to avoid any confrontation with the government and thereby sanitize the ZANU–PF political leaders as appointed and ordained by God. According to the presenter, this approach has rendered ZANU–PF untouchable, thereby creating an enabling environment of ongoing political violence in the country. In his presentation, Philipp Öhlmann further argued that, on the one hand, the prominent influencers in politics and society in Africa are the African Pentecostal and Independent Churches.

On the other hand, the African Independent Churches are said to be »apolitical«. However, they are actively engaged in supporting ecological justice and sustainability to advocate for democracy and good governance. In their paper, Nora Milena Vehling and Thabang Rambosha used the case study of Gilgal Bible Church in South Africa's township Tembisa, which is a »Zion Pentecostal Church«, to address two main questions on the double role of AIC as social entity in the society and its structural dominations; AIC socio-economic transformations have also enabled development away from dominating structures. AICs channel actions in societies and then possess the transformative potential to change dominant paradigms and human beings' behavior towards norms and cultures. Hence, AICs might indicate the development of an independent African culture.

The contributions in the eighth panel covered issues on »*Politics of (dis-)continuity*«, moderated by Alan Anderson. The contributions addressed the (dis-) continuity politics from the African traditional beliefs and practices. For example, Judith Bachman explored the idea of African witchcraft beliefs being continued in present Pentecostal churches in Africa, even though African Pentecostalism has discontinuous solutions. Yet, it is holding dear to the traditionally »spirit-filled world« of ancestors, witchcraft, evil spirits, and demons. Based on the works of Alan Anderson and Nigerian debates on witchcraft, Bachmann argued that »… witchcraft must be addressed as global discourse and Pentecostalism as well as its supposed Africanness as a position, which is formed and forming within this discourse«. From a gender perspective, Tumi Mampane illustrates in her paper how the Pentecostal-Charismatic movement has deconstructed the oppressive African perspective on women by giving Pentecostal women a platform to express issues related to the domestic violence they are experiencing. Through prayers they have converted their men to adopt or accept domestic roles, just like »a feminist movement which aims to domesticate men«. She argues that the construction of Christian femininity goes in two opposing directions: a traditional woman waits for the initiative of her man and for God to stand up to the injustice against her.

Moreover, Grace Opare investigated the phenomenon further by addressing the question of (dis-)continuity. She conducted a comparative study between the Ghanaian practice of *duabɔ* and the Pentecostals' imprecation prayers. She argues that there is a similarity between the *duabɔ* practice and the Pentecostal prayers of imprecation offered along with biblical verses to afflict harm or curse others. In the same vein, Juliane Stork addresses the integration of the African Traditional Religions in South Africa and the Zion Christian Churches. She argues that the ZCC protect their members against any threats from traditional spirits by reinterpreting traditional beliefs. Their shared interest during the negotiation is the role played by ecology in both religious streams. The claim is that African Christianity must adopt an African ecology to advocate for ecological justice and environmental protection; for instance, the aspects of the sacredness of land and water and the Ubuntu category reinterpreted in AICs.

The third parallel session had four-panel sessions, whereby the ninth panel was moderated by Miranda Klaver, with the sub-theme »*Pentecostal republics*«. Jörg Haustein and Afework Beyene argued how the public engagement of »Pente« in Ethiopia is evident through the impact of »powerful political figures«. For example, Beyene explores how the Ethiopian Prime Ministership has been led by two »Pentes« in the past nine years. Because of their usage of »mass-media« and private TV stations, they have managed to engage with the public and to show that they are not marginalized in the public and religious sphere. Features of dominion theology shape their ambition to engage in the public sphere. Haustein gave detailed information on Prime Minister Abiy Ahmed, a devoted Pentecostal who acts to renegotiate Pentecostalism and politics. Leonardo Bedin- Fontana pursued a similar concept from a Brazilian perspective on Evangelicals' and Pentecostals' active engagement in the presidential elections; without their intervention, Jair M. Bolsonaro could not have been elected. He further described how these Pentecostal groups were engaged, how they nominated their candidates, and demonized the political opponents. Their prominent Pentecostal pastors offered generous support to the nominated candidates and used religious motives in the political discourse. In the same vein, Denise Austin and Stephen Fogarty gave an example of how Pentecostals engage in Australia's political sphere. The first Pentecostal Prime Minister, Morrison, claimed that his election was nothing but divine intervention in the election's result. Hence, he was nicknamed »the Miracle Man«. Morrison's rise has triggered a new »war of religion« in the country. Politicians were forced to make »public confession of doctrinal allegiance to maintain credibility«. Austin's qualitative data indicate that »Morrison's Pentecostal faith is shaping the public sphere; for example, exuding optimism; supporting the marginalized; and promoting peacemakers«.

The tenth panel, moderated by Jan-Ake Alvarsson, was devoted to the theme »*Transforming values*«. The first presenter, Philomena Mwauara, emphasized the Pentecostals' contribution as agents of transformation through controlling »social and spiritual Capital«. According to her, »social capital« refers to networking and cooperation in private associations. For instance, women's groups, youth groups, men's groups, and widows' groups use networks to empower each other; they link with each other for jobs and social assistance; the networks result in »economic development and effective governance«. On a different note, the spiritual capital refers to religious beliefs, values, norms, and practices used for the economic and political development of the community. For example, Pentecostal beliefs and practices that are the source of social and spiritual capital are the Bible, the doctrine of salvation, Spirit Baptism, and prayers. Her paper's main argument concerned the adoption of social and spiritual capital in Pentecostal churches in Kenya by analyzing the prosperity gospel and some special ministries as transformative tools leading to spiritual, social, and economic transformation and empowerment.

Additionally, Augustine Chikezie Asogwa argued that through the prosperity gospel, Pentecostal Christianity in Nigeria engages in public space as a significant agent of empowerment of the socio-economic and political life of Christians in Nigeria. Asogwa analyzed the teachings of three prominent prosperity preachers in Nigeria to find out how the teachings of prosperity have impacted the lives of the people; those preachers are David Oyedepo, Enoch Adeboye, and Ejike Mbaka. His findings proved that the prosperity gospel, if well-intended and controlled, »can better the lives of people since it entails faith being transformed into praxis as a tool for public empowerment and engagement«. In his paper, Hartness M. Samushonga discussed how Pentecostal public engagement has increased in recent years in the Global South. This offers an opportunity for theological reflections on the development of both theory and practice of the Pentecostal public engagement, most preferably in the field of practical theology. Through the lens of practical theology, the presenter concluded that »Pentecostal Christian movements as contemporary organs have both a missional mandate and a social responsibility for public engagement«.

The eleventh panel was on »*Print and visual media politics*«, chaired by Ilana van Wyk. The first presenter, Mookgo Kgatle examined how the media report on religious practices. Especially news about some Pentecostal pastors seem to dominate the TV, radio and newspaper headlines in recent years. The paper revealed how Pentecostal practices become the top headlines of news reports and commentaries as well as being the main topic of public debates in South Africa, and how Pentecostal pastors have used social media as a strategy to shape public debates on religion. Furthermore, the presenter investigated how the public engagement of Pentecostal churches through broadcasting benefits both the media and the Pentecostal pastors. In her presentation, Anna Droll explored how Pentecostals use the African melodrama as a technique to express spiritual knowledge; it has developed into an alternative perspective for responding to the dehumanizing treatment of accused witches in Ghana. Mainly, the effect in dismantling witchcraft is small, and the sponsorship of this brand's filmmaking is problematic. She attempted to understand the impact of Pentecostal films and the dreams and visions that fund them in the public sphere.

On the other hand, Francis Benyah discussed the overemphasis on African spirituality by the mass media, especially on the spirit world of evil spirits. Witchcraft and demons raise fear in people's lives; thus, they struggle to seek protection by being religiously devoted. Benyah gives an example from an African Pentecostal church in Ghana, the »Pure Fire Miracle Ministry«, and how they used a Ghanaian printed medium, the »Daily Graphic«, to speak of the realities of the African spirit world view and describe different militarizing war strategies used by Christians to attack and destroy the schemes of the enemy in spiritual warfare. Furthermore, the paper focuses on showing the use of media as a platform for Pentecostals to engage the public in spiritual warfare and transformation of the public sphere in Ghana.

The twelfth panel was the last on the list of the second day's activities, the closing day of the 11th GlobPent conference. This panel's contributions generally concerned itself with »*Civil Activism – Social Inequality*«, moderated by Heinrich Schäfer. Among many contributions in this panel, Jens Köhrsen provided a detailed description of how scholars from a perspective of social inequality have often addressed Pentecostalism. He investigated why Pentecostalism has found »a fertile soil« in the Global South, especially in areas affected by poverty. One of the reasons is that Pentecostal churches provide strategies that improve people's lives by improving their socio-economic living standards. Pentecostal churches are regarded as »life-transforming« agents; they offer socio-economic transitions through social services and by transforming their members' perspectives, feelings, and beliefs. His paper offered different approaches to interpreting Pentecostalism by emphasizing the »continuity of everyday lifestyles in the context of conversion and the reproduction of social inequalities within the movement«.

Based on the above highlights on different contributions presented at the conference, this report concludes by acknowledging some important aspects that made it a most successful event. The success of the 11th GlobPent conference was not only due to the differentiated panel sessions and enlightening contributions from more than thirty speakers. Moreover, it presented critical views on the Pentecostal movement as well. Remarkable were the manifold voices of doctoral students, an excellent location at the main campus of the University Basel, but also the conceptual preparation of the conference. Moreover, the 11th GlobPent conference set a thematic cluster on Pentecostal strategies of public engagement that fills a lacuna in current studies on the global Pentecostal movement. Conference proceedings helped to identify emergent and prospective Pentecostal public engagement strategies from different contexts, not exclusively from the Global South. In summary, the conference provided a generalizing picture of how Pentecostal public engagement seems to have similar features and techniques globally, but expressed through different strategies. Pentecostal public engagement takes the form of »glocal«, diverging strategies. They may engage the public as agents of »sustainable development«, as agents of »transformation« in local terms. Pentecostals also use mass media to engage in sensitive debates such as »divorce among born-again members«. Pentecostal migrant churches from the Global South in Europe advocate for the marginalized. Additionally, Pentecostals support the influence of »Pentecostal political leaders« as a strategy to engage in politics, though they sometimes struggle with an »individualistic« theology and they end up »sanitizing« the corrupt political leaders. Unlike the mainline churches, they dare to speak against the evils of society. Such highlights of the conference point to future areas of research in Pentecostal studies.

Leita Ngoy

Report on the International Summer School in China 2019

A Summer School is nothing out of the ordinary. But the fact that a Summer School could take place in Hong Kong, China and Macao in August 2019 was something special. In Hong Kong, the mass protests of the democracy movement had reignited two months earlier, so the security situation was noticeably tense. In mainland China, there were limited opportunities for groups to visit churches; meanwhile, government surveillance had increased significantly. Four months later, the Corona pandemic broke out and made travelling impossible.

Just in time, the Summer School was held from August 16 to 31, 2019, with 22 participants from 7 countries, including professors, pastors, church workers, students and delegates from Mission 21's partner churches. During two weeks, they learned with and from each other in lectures, discussions, excursions and a trip through southern China.

The project was made possible through the cooperation of four institutions: the Divinity School of Chung Chi College, Chinese University in Hong Kong (represented by Tobias Brandner, Professor), the Tsung Tsin Mission in Hong Kong (represented by Oisze Cheung, General Secretary), the Department of Extra-European Christianity at the University of Basel (represented by Andreas Heuser, Professor) and Mission 21 in Basel (represented by Christian Weber, Programme Manager Education).

This short report looks back on the course, problems and outcome of the Summer School and asks for further perspectives.

Political tension in Hong Kong and extraordinary insights into South China

In preparation for the Summer School, the participants worked on thematic statements and partly – but obligatory for Basel students – attended a seminar on »Christianity in China« at the University of Basel in the spring semester of 2019. The two-week study programme in August 2019 was entitled »Currents in Global Christianity« and had two components: In the first week, the focus was on the exchange between the East and the West and the discovery of the cultural melting pot of Hong Kong. In the mornings, lectures and discussion groups dealt with the topics of Christianity and democracy, urbanisation, migration, Pentecostalism and popular culture. The contributions of the speakers from Hong Kong reflected current political events. Lap Yan Kung, professor at the Divinity School of Chung Chi College of the Chinese University of Hong Kong, explained the emergence of the »Anti-Extradition Bill Movement« (see ZMiss 2/2020, 335–348). Yam Chi Keung, publisher of the newspaper »Christian Times«, analysed the surprising significance of the song »Sing Hallelujah to the Lord« as an anthem of the protest movement and a de-escalation strategy. Roy Njuabe, pastor of the Vine Church, spoke on »Migration as a Challenge for the Churches« and told his own story as a refugee from Cameroon and immigrant to Hong Kong.

Depending on the topic of the day, excursions in the afternoon led to churches and temples in Hong Kong, to church educational institutions and social projects. Particularly touching were the encounters with refugees and exploited domestic workers in the counselling centres of the organisation »Christian Ac-tion«, where also young adults work as part of the Professional Exposure Programme (PEP!) of Mission 21.

In the second week, the group members travelled through southern China and to Macao to follow the traces of mission history, encounter other religious communities and discover the Hakka culture. They experienced and reflected on forms of Christian indigenisation and spiritual upheavals, as is only possible through personal contacts and through the network of churches. Outstanding were the visits to two churches and a hospital in Meixian, which go back to the Basel Mission, the visit to the world-famous Hakka round houses and to the historical centre and some temples in Guangzhou/Canton as well as the exchange with students at the Union Theological Seminary there. The diverse shared experiences promoted intensive exchange within the group. The self-confident vision of a student in a discussion on the sinicization of Christianity in China is particularly memorable: »They want to sinicize Christianity (zhongguohua jidujiao) – but we want to christianize China (jiduhua zhongguo)«.

Financial challenges, visa problems and border interrogations

The Summer School had to manage largely without grants. Only delegates from Indonesia, Malaysia and Tanzania were financially supported by their churches or by Mission 21. In order for students to attend at a reasonable price, professionals paid a proportionately higher amount and were accommodated in Hong Kong and Macao at a better standard.

It was a great disappointment that only one delegate from Africa was able to attend the Summer School. The church representatives from South Sudan, D. R. Congo, Nigeria and Cameroon unexpectedly did not receive visas for Hong Kong despite repeated efforts. Only the delegate from Tanzania was able to enter without a visa, but was detained and questioned for several hours on arrival in Hong Kong. He was then also able to accompany the group to South China after the time-consuming visa application was approved.

The border crossing from Hong Kong to mainland China turned into a test of endurance. The group was divided, several of the members were detained for three hours and some were interrogated individually. Only after checking the entire programme of the visit did the authorities allow them to continue their journey. However, the meeting with a Christian woman from a »house church« had to be cancelled. To the regret of the group, it was also not possible to visit the new museum on the history of the Basel mission in Langkou (the first girls' school in China).

International learning community

Despite these limitations, the Summer School 2019 was a formative experience for all participants. The goals were achieved on several levels:

The »international learning community« of Mission 21 became concrete and tangible. Intensive personal relationships between representatives of churches and theological institutions have developed. Disseminators from different churches gained insight into current theological and socio-political topics, especially the development of Christianity in Asia and the international work of Mission 21. Mission 21 was able to get to know and train suitable people from the partner churches for future coordination and leadership tasks. The academic exchange between institutions from different continents was strengthened.

As a follow-up to this Summer School, the idea of a joint research project between the participating professors at the universities in Basel and Hong Kong developed. This project is dedicated to selected African mega-churches in the Basel and Hong Kong region. At a later stage, it is to be expanded to a transnational, comparative perspective to include (West-/East-)African regions as well as those within the People's Republic of China.

One of the students made a film about the Summer School, which exemplifies how different mission concepts came into conversation with each other. In the interview, participants defined mission as »getting in touch with people in other contexts«, »sharing God's love with the world«, »building bridges«, »supporting the people outside of the church« or »working together for a better life for all people«.

Some examples from the personal summaries of participants:

»The Summer School was a completely new experience for me, as I had never travelled to an Asian country before. That alone made the weeks leading up to the trip exciting. In addition, the dynamics of the protest movement brought a lot of uncertainty … We discussed the development possibilities of Christianity today concerning culture, politics, migration, media, prosperity. It was an incredibly memorable trip for me, because we were not tourists, but encountered people.«

»In China we could only visit officially registered churches, which to my astonishment were very lively and large, never had less than 100 church-goers, offered several services on Sundays, as well as house groups, care groups for single mothers, sporting activities for young people, etc. I was immediately struck by the warmth and hospitality and the charitable commitment of the congregations.«

»The second week in China showed how delicate and tense the political situation was just before the 70th anniversary of the People's Republic. Planned meetings with House Churches could unfortunately not take place in order not to put the sisters and brothers in danger. The meeting at the Guangzhou Union Theological Seminary was particularly intensive. We spoke with young students who impressed me with their simple and sincere piety. In the church there, 2–3000 people come to the services every Sunday.«

»The focus of the Summer School was not on tourist attractions, but on meeting, learning, looking, experiencing together – in conversation and devotion. People from three continents met in open, lively exchange and often very personal conversations.«

»The Summer School 2019 has broadened my mind, inspired me in my service, gave me a good chance to learn many things and led me into renewing my focus in mission work. I learned how a church can spread through social service. I observed church centres for refugees and migrant workers, a home for the blind, a big hospital and a theological seminary. I propose to run future summer schools in different countries or continents to discover more of the current issues that churches face.«

»The summer school has enriched me with new insight's that sharpen my calling as a woman theologian from Sumba, eastern Indonesia. This summer school was a space where theologians, social workers and church activists exchanged their ideas, sharing experiences and difficulties that enrich the horizons of thinking and reflection. For me, this program was so excellent because it bridges the theoretical knowledge with the personal and community practices on a grassroot level. I learned many things, especially how Christian communities respond to global issues such as human trafficking, forced migration, violence, poverty, political pressures.«

Perspectives

In addition to international development cooperation, Mission 21 sees the international learning community as a second field of action. The Summer School has proven to be a suitable format to concretise this learning community. Unlike a study trip, it also includes an academic programme with lectures, discussions and related excursions. In this way, it facilitates joint learning, exchange and networking.

The following year (August 21–22, 2020), Mission 21 organised a digital Summer School on the topic of »Protesting for Change – does it matter?«, attended by fifty people from 18 countries. Julian Brown, political scientist at the University of Witwatersrand, Johannesburg, analysed South Africa's anti-apartheid movement. Verena Stern, sociologist from Bielefeld, presented a differentiated picture of protest forms on the topic of migration. Sociologist Nicolás M. Somma from Chile reported on successful protest movements in Latin-America. Finally, reports by activists from Switzerland, Costa Rica, Chile, Tanzania, Nigeria, South Korea and Indonesia showed how people around the world are active against different forms of discrimination.

Another digital Summer School is planned for September 2021, this time on the topic of »Mission, Colonialism and Slavery«.

Christian Weber

550 Jahre globales Christentum

Jens Holger Schjørring, Norman A. Hjelm (Hg.): **Geschichte des globalen Christentums, Teil 1: Frühe Neuzeit**, 709 S., Stuttgart: Kohlhammer 2017, 179 Euro; Jens Holger Schjørring, Norman A. Hjelm (Hg.): **Geschichte des globalen Christentums, Teil 2: 19. Jahrhundert**, 584 S., Stuttgart: Kohlhammer 2018, 179 Euro; Jens Holger Schjørring, Norman A. Hjelm, Kevin Ward (Hg.): **Geschichte des globalen Christentums, Teil 3: 20. Jahrhundert**, 809 S., Stuttgart: Kohlhammer 2018, 179 Euro. Bände 32, 33 und 34 aus der Reihe »Religionen der Menschheit« (Serienpreis bei Abnahme aller Bände der Reihe: je 159 Euro).

In der Reihe »Religionen der Menschheit« sind die drei letzten von sieben Bänden zum Christentum erschienen. Sie umfassen die Zeit von der frühen Neuzeit bis zum Beginn des 21. Jahrhunderts. Zeitgleich mit dem letzten Band ist das vom Kohlhammer Verlag initiierte dreibändige Werk auch auf Englisch erschienen (*History of Global Christianity*, 3 Vol.s, Leiden: Brill [501 Euro]). Mit den drei Herausgebern hat sich der Verlag für eine internationale Besetzung ohne deutsche Beteiligung entschieden: der emeritierte Kirchenhistoriker Holger Schjørring (Dänemark), der theologische Lektor Norman A. Hjelm (USA) und Kevin Ward, Senior Lecturer in African Religious Studies an der Universität Leeds (England). Auf 2100 Seiten sind Beiträge zwischen 12 und über 100 Seiten von 25 Autoren und 5 Autorinnen versammelt. Einige von ihnen sind mit zwei oder mehr Artikeln vertreten. Die einen sind auf Deutsch verfasst und ins Englische übersetzt worden, die anderen vom Englischen ins Deutsche. Was die Autorschaft betrifft, ist das dreibändige Werk überwiegend ein deutsch-britisch-nordeuropäisch-US-amerikanisches Projekt (die im globalen Norden forschenden Autoren mit Wurzeln im globalen Süden miteingerechnet), ergänzt durch wenige Beiträge aus anderen Ländern, z. B. Israel/Palästina, Neuseeland und Brasilien. Das monumentale Werk in seiner Vielschichtigkeit angemessen zu würdigen, sprengt den vorgegebenen Rahmen. Geachtet wird hier vor allem darauf, inwiefern die

Geschichte des Christentums der letzten 500 Jahre nicht eurozentrisch, sondern in *globaler* Perspektive dargestellt wird.

Zunächst jedoch eine Bemerkung zur Frage, was diese Darstellung mit vergleichbaren Beispielen aus dem angelsächsischen Raum verbindet bzw. was sie zum globalhistorischen Diskurs über das Weltchristentum beitragen kann. Seit der Jahrtausendwende sind im englischen Sprachraum mehrere Grossprojekte zur Geschichte des Christentums vorgelegt worden mit dem Ziel, seine Ausrichtung an der Evangeliumsverkündigung »bis an die Enden der Welt« und dementsprechend auch seine Intention, grenzüberschreitend präsent zu sein, darzustellen. Beispiele dafür sind die neunbändige *Cambridge History of Christianity* (Cambridge 2005–2009), die in allen Epochen eine Perspektive zugrunde legt, die auch Christentumsformen ausserhalb der europäischen bzw. westlichen Welt berücksichtigt und würdigt; *A World History of Christianity*, hg. von Adrian Hastings (Cambridge UK 1999); *The Wiley Blackwell Companion to World Christianity*, hg. von Lamin Sanneh und Michael J. McClymont (Oxford 2016). Ausserdem gibt es inzwischen umfangreiche Werke zur Christentumsgeschichte in einzelnen Kontinenten und Weltregionen. Von der auf zehn Bände angelegten Reihe »Edinburgh Companions to Global Christianity« sind bisher vier erschienen: *Christianity in Sub-Sahara Africa* (2017); *Christianity in North Africa and West Asia* (2018); *Christianity in South and Central Asia* (2019); *Christianity in East and Southeast Asia* (2020). Im Vergleich dazu nimmt sich das Angebot auf Deutsch bisher noch bescheiden aus. An erster Stelle zu nennen ist die von Klaus Koschorke und Johannes Meier herausgegebene (deutsch- und englischsprachige) Reihe »Studien zur Außereuropäischen Christentumsgeschichte« (Wiesbaden), in der 34 Bände (2019) erschienen sind und ein weiterer 2020 erscheint. Mit dem dreiteiligen Werk bei Kohlhammer ist nun auch in deutscher Sprache eine konzeptionell und umfangmässig vergleichbare Gesamtdarstellung von 500 Jahren Christentumsgeschichte verfügbar.

Von den englischsprachigen Gesamtdarstellungen unterscheidet sich die deutschsprachige vor allem dadurch, dass die Geschichte des Christentums in Europa – vor allem für die deutschsprachigen Gebiete – umfangmässig bis zur Hälfte der Bände beansprucht. Der verbleibende Raum ist den Entwicklungen des Christentums in Nordamerika, Asien, Nahost, Afrika, Lateinamerika, Australien und in der Pazifikregion gewidmet. Ein Ziel der Bände ist die Überwindung des Eurozentrismus in der Geschichtsschreibung, was z. B. im ersten Band nicht einfach ist, weil »der Schwerpunkt des frühneuzeitlichen Christentums ohne allen Zweifel in Europa« liegt, wie H. Lehmann in der Einleitung zu Band 32, 22, schreibt. Worauf es den Autoren aber ankommt, ist zu zeigen, dass »die christlichen Gemeinschaften in den Ländern außerhalb von Europa relativ früh [...] ein distinktes Eigenleben mit eigenen religiösen Formen und Traditionen» entwickelt haben« (a. a. O., 23).

Die in den USA beheimateten, historiographischen *Studies in World Christianity* zeigen im allgemeinen wenig Interesse an der Geschichte des Christentums in Europa, was am Verständnis von *World Christianity* liegt, das sich an ausser-europäischen bzw. ausserwestlichen Christentumsformen orientiert in bewusster Abgrenzung vom europäischen »*Christendom*«. Das zugleich auf Deutsch und Englisch erschienene Werk bietet nun die Chance eines kritisch-konstruktiven Diskurses über die z. T. vorurteilsbeladenen Wahrnehmungen der europäischen Christentumsgeschichte in Nordamerika und im globalen Süden. Auch in einer anderen Hinsicht ergänzt das dreiteilige Werk die englischsprachigen Beispiele: Es beschränkt »Europa« nicht auf den westlichen Teil des Kontinents, sondern hat ebenfalls Christentumsformen in Osteuropa, besonders in Russland, im Blick. Dasselbe gilt für die östliche Orthodoxie, die in den *World Christianity Studies* oft nur am Rande erwähnt wird.

Die Bände sollen nicht im traditionellen Sinn »*Kirchen*geschichte« sein, sondern umfassender *Christentums*geschichte. »Im Fokus stehen die zahlreichen Wechselwirkungen, die zwischen dem Christentum und den einzelnen Gesellschaften, der Politik, der Ökonomie, der Philosophie, der Kunst sowie den vielfältigen Bemühungen bestehen, welche die Kulturen, Nationen und menschlichen Gemeinschaften ausmachen« (Lehmann, Bd. 32, 16).

Mit den Methoden der allgemeinen Geschichtsschreibung wird das Christentum als *eine* Religion *unter anderen* und z. T. in Wechselwirkung mit anderen Religionen im Gesamtzusammenhang menschlicher Kultur dargestellt. Ausgehend von der Leitfrage, wie das Christentum in die größeren Strukturen des menschlichen Lebens verwoben war, wird die Eingebundenheit des Christentums in weltliche Daseinsformen nachgezeichnet. Wie haben Kirchen, Missionen, christliche Bewegungen auf die »Welt« eingewirkt und sie verändert? Und wie hat sich die umgekehrte Wirkung innerhalb des Christentums manifestiert? Darauf antworten die Beiträge. Das heisst allerdings nicht, dass alle Autoren diesen Vorgaben folgen, wie etwa der Beitrag von Akinade über *Afrikanisches Christentum im 20. Jahrhundert* scheibt: »Nach wie vor richtet Gott seine Selbstoffenbarung an verschiedene Menschen in verschiedenen Kulturen, ohne dabei auf hegemoniale Paradigmen oder westliche Besitzansprüche Rücksicht zu nehmen. […] Das hat Gott mit der afrikanischen Missionsgeschichte und überall auf der Welt bewiesen« (Band 34, 478).

Globalgeschichtlich sind die drei Bände insofern, als es um die Ausbreitung des Christentums in allen Kontinenten und um die dort sich entwickelnden eigenständigen Lebensäusserungen des Christentums geht. Man kann von einer global ausgeweiteten Konfessions- bzw. Christentumskunde sprechen, wenn auch nicht im enzyklopädischen Sinn mit Beiträgen zu sämtlichen Christentumsformen in allen Ländern der Erde. Trotz des 2100-seitigen Umfangs ist es unvermeidlich, Fallbeispiele auszuwählen, thematische Schwerpunkte zu setzen und Schlüsselfragen exemplarisch zu vertiefen. Kurzum: Nur durch eine Kombination von einleitenden Überblicken (z. B. über *Die Revolutionen und die Kirche: Die neue Ära der Moderne* [Hugh McLeod], zeitlichen Längsschnitten über hundert oder zweihundert Jahre (z. B. *Das Christentum in Russland 1700–1917* [Christian Gottlieb], regionalen und kontinentalen Gesamtdarstellungen (z. B. *Christentum in Europa: Das 17. Jahrhundert* [Andreas Holzem] sowie thematischen Vertiefungen (z. B. *Holocaust, Antisemitismus und Neuorientierung* [Siegfried Hermle]) ist es möglich, den globalen Dimensionen des Christentums im vorgegebenen Rahmen Rechnung zu tragen.

»Global« ist die vorgelegte Christentumsgeschichte auch insofern, als in mehreren Beiträgen das Hauptaugenmerk auf den Kommunikationsströmen liegt, die es zu verschiedenen Epochen zwischen Kirchen, christlichen Bewegungen, Organisationen und weiteren Akteuren über konfessionelle, geographische, sprachliche und kulturelle Grenzen hinweg gegeben hat. Das Werk geht davon aus, dass das Christentum wie schon in seinen ersten Jahrhunderten eine Religion mit mehreren Zentren an verschiedenen Orten gewesen ist, zwischen denen es Kontakte, einen lebendigen Austausch und teilweise länger bestehende Verbindungen gegeben hat (vgl. Klaus Koschorke: *Asien im 19. und 20. Jahrhundert*, Band 33), die aber vor allem im 20. Jahrhundert global ausgeweitet worden sind (Dazu Melanie A. Duguid May über die ökumenische Bewegung im 20. Jahrhundert und Gerard Mannion über das Zweite Vatikanische Konzil, Band 34). Wie sich die Kommunikation seit dem 19. Jahrhundert auf andere Religionsgemeinschaften erstreckt hat, zeigen Frieder Ludwig und Ulrike Schröder in zwei Beiträgen: *Das Christentum im Kontext anderer Weltreligionen: Interreligiöse Dynamiken und Entwicklungen im 19. Jahrhundert* (Band 33) bzw. *… im 20. Jahrhundert* (Band 34). Alle Bände zeigen, dass globale Christentumsgeschichte etwas anderes ist als die Summe aller lokalgeschichtlichen Darstellungen.

Zu Teil 1: Frühe Neuzeit (Band 32). Das im europäischen Protestantismus gemeinhin als Reformationsjahrhundert geltende 16. Jahrhundert wird hier hauptsächlich als Epoche der von Europa ausgehenden katholisch-missionarischen Expansion präsentiert: Beginnend mit dem *Katholizismus in Spanien, Portugal und ihren Weltreichen* (Mariano Delgado), folgen *Die Russische Kirche 1448–1701* (Alfons Brüning), ein Kapitel über *Christen unter osmanischer Herrschaft (1453–1800)* (Bruce Masters), *Das Christentum in Afrika zwischen 1500 und 1800* (Kevin Ward), *Das lateineuropäische Christentum im 16. Jahrhundert* (Thomas Kaufmann) und als letzter bis ins 16. Jahrhundert zurückreichender Beitrag *Das Christentum in Asien zwischen ca. 1500 und 1789* (Ronnie Po-chia Hsia). Aus den Überschriften sind die unterschiedlichen Periodisierungen erkennbar, die auf historisch begründete Ungleichzeitigkeiten des Gleichzeitigen hinweisen. Eingebettet in das globale Bild des frühneuzeitlichen Christentums werden Reformation, katholische Erneuerungsbewegung und konfessionelle Spaltungen im europäischen Christentum auch unter der Frage betrachtet, welche Wirkungen sie in der aussereuropäischen Welt gehabt haben. Das Christentum in Afrika, Asien und Lateinamerika wird als Folge europäisch-missionarischer Expansion in den Blick genommen – aber nicht nur: denn gefragt wird zugleich nach indigenen Christentumsvarianten, die sich aus den missionarischen Anfängen heraus eigenständig weiterentwickelt haben oder unabhängig von europäischer Mission entstanden sind (Beispiele dazu bei Delgado zu Lateinamerika; Po-chia Hsia zu Asien; Ward zu Afrika). Bis Ende des 18. Jahrhunderts war das Christentum freilich im aussereuropäischen Raum noch wenig verbreitet. Seinem Profil gemäss war es immer noch überwiegend eine europäisch geprägte Religion. Aber in diesem Zeitraum sind die Grundlagen für die spätere globale Ausweitung des Christentums gelegt worden.

Wie Kaufmann im Beitrag *Das lateineuropäische Christentum im 16. Jahrhundert* zeigt, hat die Verdrängung des teilweise Jahrhunderte alten Christentums aus Westasien, Nordafrika und auf dem Balkan durch den Islam wesentlich dazu beigetragen, dass das Christentum zu Beginn der frühen Neuzeit eine mehrheitlich »europäische« Religion gewesen ist. Kompensiert wurden die »Gebietsverluste« ab Ende des 15. bis ins 17. Jahrhundert durch die Eroberungen der katholischen Weltmächte Spanien und Portugal in der Neuen Welt, in Asien und

Afrika und später aufgrund von Gebietseroberungen der protestantisch geprägten Kolonialmächte Grossbritannien und Niederlande. Im Zuge dieser Ausbreitung stiessen die Europäer in Asien und Afrika mitunter auf sehr viel ältere Kirchen. Aus den Erneuerungsimpulsen und den konfessionellen Abgrenzungen im Europa des 16. Jahrhunderts sind Konfessionskulturen hervorgegangen, die sich in den Gebieten der Weltmission niedergeschlagen und auch dort zu konfessionellen Abgrenzungen gegeneinander geführt haben. Zu den Merkmalen des lateineuropäischen (später: westeuropäischen) Christentums gehörten die territoriale und monokulturelle Einheit von Religion, Nation und Sprache sowie ein enges Bündnis zwischen Staat und Kirche. Genau diese Merkmale werden in den heutigen *Studies in World Christianity* dem *Christendom* zugerechnet und als Vorbild für die ausserwestliche Welt abgelehnt.

Zu Teil 2: Das 19. Jahrhundert (Band 33). Zehn Autoren und zwei Autorinnen befassen sich mit dem globalen Christentum im »langen« 19. Jahrhundert (zwischen 1789 und 1914), das oft auch das »Jahrhundert der Mission« genannt wird. Trotz der grossen missionarischen Anstrengungen vor allem auf protestantischer Seite waren um 1900 erst neun Prozent der Afrikaner*innen Christen, von denen die Mehrheit den historischen Kirchen der Kopten und Äthiopier angehörten. 80 Prozent der Weltchristenheit lebten in Europa, im Russischen Reich und in Nordamerika; lediglich fünf Prozent in Afrika und Asien (Mc Leod, 565). Von daher ist es auch in diesem Band gerechtfertigt, dass Europa gut die Hälfte des Buchumfangs einnimmt. In drei Kapiteln stehen der Katholizismus (Andreas Holzem), das mehrheitlich orthodoxe Christentum in Russland (Christian Gottlieb) und der Protestantismus (Kevin Ward) im Fokus, wobei sich Ward auf die globalgeschichtlich relevante, im 19. Jahrhundert breit entfaltete, protestantische Weltmission beschränkt. Anschliessend werden Christentumsentwicklungen in aussereuropäischen Regionen und Kontinenten in den Blick genommen: Das Christentum im Nahen Osten (Mitri Raheb), in Nordamerika (Margaret Bendroth), Asien (Klaus Koschorke), Afrika (Kevin Ward) sowie Lateinamerika und in der Karibik (Martin N. Dreher). Bis um 1900 gab es in allen Kontinenten Gemeinden, die aus der Westmission hervorgegangen sind. Abgesehen von Nord- und Lateinamerika beschränkten sie sich jedoch meistens auf kleine Stützpunkte in einem mehrheitlich nichtchristlichen Umfeld. Sie standen weitgehend unter dem Einfluss von europäischen oder nordamerikanischen Vorbildern. Es gab aber bereits im 19. Jahrhundert unter den Missionsgemeinden Unabhängigkeits-

und Indigenisierungsbestrebungen, wie Koschorke (*Asien im 19. und frühen 20. Jahrhundert*) an Beispielen aus Indien zeigt. Vor allem aber war die westliche Missionsbewegung »nur ein Faktor unter anderen bei der Entstehung und Entwicklung des asiatischen Christentums. Christliche Kirchen [...] verbreiteten sich vielfach in Gebieten fernab jeglicher westlich-missionarischen Präsenz. [...] In jedem Fall waren es letztlich die einheimischen Akteure, die über Annahme, Ablehnung, selektive Aneignung oder Modifikation der missionarischen Botschaft entschieden« (Koschorke: 427).

Zu Teil 3: Das 20. Jahrhundert (Band 34): Im umfangreichsten der drei Bände (800 S.) befassen sich 20 Beiträge mit dem 20. Jahrhundert. Die Quellenlage dazu ist im Vergleich zu derjenigen von früheren Jahrhunderten viel umfangreicher geworden. Zum grossen Teil sind die neuen Quellen zu den Kirchen des globalen Südens für die Historiographie Neuland und – im Vergleich mit den ausgiebig erforschten Quellen zum Europäischen Christentum – noch kaum erschlossen. In absoluten Zahlen betrachtet ist das Weltchristentum im 20. Jahrhundert enorm gewachsen; vor allem aber ist es durch die Verlagerung des demographischen Schwerpunktes von Nord (20 %) nach Süd und Ost (80 %) bedeutend vielfältiger und disparater geworden.

Angesichts dieser Ausgangslage sind empfindliche Lücken in einer Globalgeschichte des Christentums kaum vermeidbar, und die Entscheidung zwischen Auswahl und Auslassungen ist gut zu überlegen. In Band 34 erweckt die thematische Schwerpunktsetzung den Eindruck, dass sich gegenüber den im globalen Süden entstandenen neuen, weniger erforschten Christentumsformen die europäisch-nordatlantische Perspektive auf die Globalgeschichte zu stark durchgesetzt hat; denn auch in diesem Teil beansprucht die europäische Welt fast die Hälfte des Buches. Diese Priorisierung ist unter anderem aufgrund der »Katastrophen im 20. Jahrhundert« (K. Ward) vorgenommen, die von Deutschland ausgegangen sind und primär in West- und Osteuropa verheerende Auswirkungen gehabt haben. Im Vergleich dazu werden die politischen Katastrophen in Osteuropa zur Zeit von Stalin, in Ostasien durch den Pazifischen Krieg von 1937–1945 und in China unter Mao Tse Tung nur nebenbei erwähnt.

15 Autoren und 4 Autorinnen sind im letzten der drei Bände vertreten. Nach der Einleitung und dem Kapitel über *Das Christentum im ersten Weltkrieg* (beide von Jens Holger Schjørring) schliessen sich weitere an über *Das Christentum in Europa und Nordamerika zwischen den Weltkriegen 1918–1939* (Andrew Chand-

ler), *Die Kirchen im Zweiten Weltkrieg* (Harry Oelke) und *Das Christentum in Europa und Nordamerika zur Zeit des Kalten Krieges* (Andrew Chandler). Den fünf nächsten Beiträgen wird ein thematisches Gliederungsprinzip zugrunde gelegt. Sie befassen sich mit sozialethischen Neuorientierungen (Katharina Kunter), der ökumenischen Bewegung (Melanie A. Duguid-May), dem Zweiten Vatikanischen Konzil (Gerard Mannion), dem Antisemitismus (Siegfried Hermle) und den interreligiösen Dynamiken im 20. Jahrhundert (Frieder Ludwig und Ulrike Schröder). Zum einen zeichnen sie die Entwicklung von regionalen Anfängen zu weltweiten christlichen Bewegungen nach; zum andern fragen sie angesichts von Holocaust, global-wirtschaftlichen und politischen Ereignissen nach sozialethischen Neuorientierungen in der Ökumene.

In den neun nächsten Beiträgen kommt erneut ein geographisches Gliederungsprinzip zum Zug, beginnend mit dem asiatischen Christentum im 20. Jahrhundert (Peter C. Phan), gefolgt von zwei Beiträgen zum Christentum in Afrika (Akintunde E. Akinade und Kevin Ward) sowie zu Lateinamerika (Veit Straßner). Weitere Studien befassen sich mit dem Christentum in Nahost (Mitri Raheb), Nordamerika (Heath W. Carter) und Europa (Grace Davie). Erstmals im dreibändigen Werk folgt ein Beitrag über Australien, Neuseeland und Ozeanien (Geoffrey Troughton). Nach dem letzten regionalen Beitrag zu Russland und dem östlichen Europa (Thomas Bremer) rundet Kevin Wards Zusammenfassung und Ausblick den Band ab.

Der Titel »Geschichte des globalen Christentums« (im Singular) signalisiert, dass der Gegenstand der drei Bände als *eine* Religion in *mannigfaltigen* Ausprägungen perzipiert wird und nicht als eine Mehrzahl von heterogenen, mehr oder weniger unverbunden neben- oder gegeneinander existierenden Religionsformationen. Zwar taucht gelegentlich der Plural »Christentümer« auf (Peter C. Phan, Band 34), aber in diesem Fall sind die Anglikaner, (Afrikanischen) Unabhängigen Kirchen, christlichen Sondergruppen, Orthodoxen, Katholiken und Protestanten damit gemeint, keine Religionen *sui generis*.

Dass das Christentum als *eine* Religion in *mannigfaltigen* Ausprägungen zu denken ist, versteht sich nicht von selbst, ist aber m. E. richtig. Religiöse Phänomene lassen sich nur in Bezug auf den vorausgehenden Gedanken der Einheit als »verschieden« bezeichnen, und das nur unter der Voraussetzung, dass sie durch gewisse Gemeinsamkeiten und Ähnlichkeiten mit anderen religiösen Phänomenen miteinander verbunden sind. Das »globale Christentum« setzt einen gemeinsamen Ursprung in der Jesusbewegung des 1. Jahrhunderts voraus sowie gewisse Merkmale (z. B. den Bibelbezug) und den schon seit dem ersten Jahrhundert erkennbaren Zug zur Einheit in Mannigfaltigkeit. Die schier grenzenlos gewordene Diversität innerhalb des Christentums, die gleichwohl ein Wiedererkennen des Eigenen in anderen Gestalten erlaubt, ist es, was das dreibändige Werk für Fachleute der Theologie, der Missionswissenschaft und der interkulturellen Theologie sehr anregend macht. Das breit angelegte Panorama ist eine Fundgrube von Ausbreitung, Niedergang und Neuaufbrüchen, wechselseitigen Abgrenzungen, Versöhnungen und neuen Kontaktnahmen, Verirrungen und Neuorientierungen christlichen Lebens in unterschiedlichen Kontexten, Epochen, Kontinenten, Kulturen und Gesellschaften. Vor diesem historischen Hintergrund lädt das Werk dazu ein, sich mit vertieften historischen Kenntnissen und neuem Blick mit systematisch-theologischen, missionstheologischen und interkulturellen Grundfragen auseinanderzusetzen.

Christine Lienemann-Perrin

Reik Jagno: **Deutsch-japanischer Wissensaustausch als lokale Praxis in der Meiji- und Taishō-Zeit: Das Beispiel des Kōtō Gakkō-Lehrers Georg Würfel**, Berlin: Wissenschaftlicher Verlag 2020, 327 Seiten, 52,– Euro

Beim vorliegenden Buch handelt es sich um die Dissertation des Göttinger Historikers Reik Jagno. Jagno untersucht den Theologen Georg Würfel (1880–1936), der 1906 als Missionar des Allgemeinen Evangelisch-Protestantischen Missionsvereins (AEPMV) nach Japan kam und von 1908 an in Sendai als Lehrer für deutsche Sprache und Literatur an einer Kōtō Gakkō lehrte. Würfel verstarb 1936 im Dienst. Kōtō Gakkō ist eine Lehranstalt, die in Japan zwischen der Jahrhundertwende und dem Zweiten Weltkrieg existierte und in drei Schuljahren auf die Aufnahmeprüfungen von Universitäten vorbereitete. Diejenige in Sendai war dabei die zweitwichtigste Kōtō Gakkō und bereitete auf die drei großen Kaiserlichen Universitäten in Tokyo, Sendai und Kyoto vor.

Jagno zeichnet in seinem Buch die Biografie von Georg Würfel in die Austauschprozesse seiner Zeit, insbesondere die deutsch-japanischen, ein. Dies unternimmt Jagno mit Hilfe der Netzwerktheorie. Neben der Biografie Jagnos werden folglich immer auch die verschiedenen Netzwerke (japanische Netzwerke in Berlin, der AEMPV, die »Deutsche Gesellschaft für Natur- und Völkerkunde Ostasiens«, und persönliche Netzwerke mit deutschsprachigen Kollegen wie Eugen Herrigel und Wilhelm Gundert und nach Europa) mit untersucht, in denen Würfel sich bewegt hat. Daraus folgt, dass Wissensaustausch als wechselseitige Angelegenheit betont wird.

In der Einleitung (9–46) macht die Literaturdiskussion die Untersuchung des Schultypus und der Biografie Würfels als Forschungslücken plausibel. Es folgen Definitionen einiger grundlegender Begriffe (wie demjenigen des Netzwerkes) und die Darstellung der Quellenlage. Daran schließt ein Abschnitt zur Geschichte Japans an (47–73), der neben viel allgemeinem Wissen über die japanische Geschichte auf die Bildungs- und Austauschprozesse zwischen Japan und »dem Westen« fokussiert.

Der Hauptteil der Arbeit beschäftigt sich mit Georg Würfel. Er beginnt mit Würfels Herkunft und seiner Zeit in Deutschland 1880 bis 1905 (75–106). Inhaltlich werden Würfels Familie, seine (stark liberale) theologische Ausbildung und Verortung, seine Arbeit als Hauslehrer und seine Bewerbung beim AEMPV dargestellt.

In dem Kapitel zu Würfels Station in Tokyo von 1906 bis 1908 (106–130) als Missionar und Lehrer an der Missionsschule wird deutlich, dass Würfel mit seinem äußerst liberalen Verständnis von Religion, Christentum und Mission zwar eigentlich dem Profil der Mission entsprach, aber damit weder den Auslandsdeutschen noch dem Vorgesetzten Hans Haas gefiel. Der Arbeitsvertrag als Missionar wurde schließlich wegen dieser Reibungen und wegen zu geringer Schülerzahlen an der Missionsschule vorzeitig beendet.

Bei der Darstellung von Würfels Leben in Sendai (130–249) werden die Sendaier Schule, Würfels Stellung an der Schule – er galt als strenger Lehrer und er gründete den ersten Eislaufverein Japans als Schulverein seiner Schule – die Hochzeit, sein Engagement für die deutschen Kriegsgefallenen und seine offene Haltung zur japanischen Kultur thematisiert. In den zwanziger Jahren zog sich Würfel vom Stadtgeschehen immer stärker zurück, und die Gesundheit der Familie verschlechterte sich. Schließlich starb die Stieftochter 1935. Georg Würfel starb im Jahr darauf.

Bereits im Kapitel zu Sendai, aber vor allem im abschließenden Kapitel (249–274), geht es um die Einordnung von Würfels Wirken. Aufschlussreich ist hier der durchgeführte Vergleich mit dem Historiker Professor Ludwig Rieß. Hier kommt Jagno zu dem Schluss, dass Rieß zwar deutlicher seine eigene Meinung in seine historischen Vorlesungen einbauen konnte, in alle Richtungen ein weites Netzwerk hatte und somit auch nach Deutschland zurückgewirkt hat, dass jedoch Würfel durch die von ihm ausgewählten Texte und seine längere Arbeit in Japan intensiver gewirkt hat als jener. Auch anhand der Lebenswege seiner Schüler wird deutlich, dass Würfel sie mehr geprägt hat, als sich diese bewusst waren. Die Wirkung nach Deutschland zurück fällt allerdings im Fall Würfels deutlich geringer aus. Sie beschränkt sich lediglich auf seine deutschen Kontakte in Japan und seine Familie in Deutschland. Eine starke Wirkung über die weiteren Netzwerke kann nicht festgestellt werden. An der Biografie Würfels lässt sich mit der Netzwerkanalyse zeigen, von welchen Faktoren es abhängt, dass ein Lehrer stark im Gastland wirkt, aber nur wenig Einfluss auf das Wissen seines Heimatlandes hat. Hier ließe sich sicher noch weiter anknüpfen.

Eine eigenwillige Strukturierung, Redundanzen, wenige Übersetzungs- und einige Flüchtigkeitsfehler erschweren das Lesen der Veröffentlichung. Ungenau wurde der Autor insbesondere im Bereich der Theologie, z. B. bei der Charakterisierung der Theologie Harnacks. Über einige Aussagen und Thesen des Buches ließe sich noch streiten. Ein Beispiel dafür ist das Urteil, »dass die Mission als Träger des Wissensaustausches von geringer Bedeutung« (105) gewesen sei. Hier möchte der Rezensent auf die Zeitschriften der Missionsvereine der Zeit aufmerksam machen, die durchaus hohe Verbreitung hatten, und auf Figuren wie Richard Wilhelm, der als Missionar Wesentliches für den deutsch-chinesischen Kulturtransfer geleistet hat.

Trotzdem bleibt das Buch ein Gewinn für diejenigen, die sich für das deutsch-japanische Verhältnis zwischen 1850 und 1950 interessieren. Die Netzwerkanalyse und der Blick auf den Wissensaustausch als eine wechselseitige Angelegenheit eröffnen fruchtbare Perspektiven und sind insbesondere für die Betrachtung der Kolonial- und Missionsgeschichte hilfreich. Die Quellen, die Jagno zur Beschreibung des Lebens von Georg Würfel auffindet und sichtet, sind beeindruckend und ein Gewinn für das Verständnis des deutsch-japanischen

Kulturaustausches. Der Umgang mit diesen sehr disparaten Quellen ist gekennzeichnet von einer hohen Kreativität und methodischen Flexibilität.

Thomas Linke

Martin Tamcke: **Christliches Leben in islamischer Welt. Exemplarische Erkundungen und west-östliche Interaktionen. Ausgewählte Vorträge und Aufsätze 2003-2018**, durchgesehen und herausgegeben von Egbert Schlarb, Wiesbaden: Harrassowitz Verlag 2020, 288 Seiten, 58,– Euro

Der Sammelband mit Aufsätzen Martin Tamckes aus den Jahren 2003–2018 ist eine Hommage an seine langjährige intensive akademische Arbeit. Jeder oder jede, der/die einen Einblick in Tamckes Tätigkeit erhalten möchte, hat mit diesem Band die Möglichkeit, die weitreichenden Aspekte seiner Forschung gebündelt lesen zu können. Diese Zusammenschau ist vor allem eine Dokumentation eines seiner wichtigsten Forschungsfelder: christliches Leben in islamischer Welt. Im Jahr 2008 erschien auf diesem Gebiet wohl eines seiner grundlegendsten Werke in diesem Bereich mit dem fast gleichlautenden Titel *Christen in der islamischen Welt.* Neben der Beschäftigung mit Fragen des Miteinanders von Christen und Muslimen setzte sich Tamcke auf zahlreichen Reisen von Istanbul bis in den Tur Abdin, von Jerewan über Beirut, Damaskus, Kairo, Addis Abeba bis nach Moskau und auch nach Indien mit den verschiedenen Ausprägungen des Christentums auseinander. Dabei stand immer die Begegnung mit den lokalen Christen und Christinnen und ihren Kirchen im Zentrum. Auch beließ er es nicht bei einem Blick in den Nahen Osten, sondern verband seine Forschungen immer wieder mit einer europäischen Perspektive auf die Situation von Christen und Christinnen in der Region. Vor allem fragte er immer wieder nach der Existenz von christlichem Leben in einer islamisch geprägten Welt.

In seinen Forschungen im Bereich des orientalischen Christentums nahmen die ostsyrischen Christen einen besonderen Stellenwert ein. Aufsätze in diesem Band spiegeln das wider. Der Aufsatz *»Wir sind nicht von Abrahams Samen!« Deutungen Abrahams in der ostsyrischen Literatur* (2003) beschäftigt sich mit herausragenden Persönlichkeiten ostsyrischer Theologie wie Afrahat, dem persischen Weisen aus dem 4. Jahrhundert, oder Elija von Anbar, dem ostsyrischen Bischof über die sassanidische Provinz Peroz Shapur im 10. Jahrhundert. Anhand von Liedzeilen des ostsyrischen Hymnendichters Girwagis Warda des 13. Jahrhunderts schildert der Aufsatz *Heuschrecken, Dürre und Mongolen, Gott und die Katastrophen in der syrischen Literatur* (2008), wie Naturkatastrophen und kriegerische Invasionen literarisch verarbeitet wurden und noch heute für die Gemeinschaft der Gläubigen als Erinnerung an diese Katastrophen dienen. Gezielt mit Girwagis Wardas Verständnis von Lektüre und seiner literarischen Produktion setzt sich der Aufsatz *Leben aus den Ursprüngen. Zur Funktion des Lesens und der schriftlichen Überlieferung bei Girwagis Warda* (2010) auseinander und verbindet diese Gedanken mit der Frage nach der Renaissance der ostsyrischen Literatur. Immer auch fragt Tamcke nach der Verquickung der Christen im Nahen Osten und Europa. Im Aufsatz *Die orientalischen Christen und Europa. »Motor der Modernisierung« oder »Fünfte Kolonne des Westens«?* (2009) greift Tamcke die gängigen Metaphern »Motor der Modernisierung« und »Fünfte Kolonne des Westens« zur Beschreibung des orientalischen Christentums auf und vertieft daraufhin insbesondere die »Mittlerfunktion« orientalischer Christen und Christinnen zwischen dem Nahen Osten und Europa.

Ein weiteres Thema in diesem Band ist das nahöstliche Mönchtum. In dem Aufsatz *Von »Wir begannen, die Anachoreten in einem anderen Licht zu sehen« zu »Jedermann braucht etwas Wüste«. Erhart Kästerns Zeltbuch vom Tumilat und die Kopten* (2017) schildert Tamcke die Erfahrungen Kästerns als Kriegsgefangener in der ägyptischen Wüste und die Veränderung seiner Einstellung zu dem Thema der Abgeschiedenheit der koptischen Mönche. Dieses Erlebnis öffnete Kästern die Augen für das Anachoretentum und für einen ihm vorher fremden Lebenszugang in der Stille und dem Einsiedlerdasein. Am Ende schließt Tamcke mit dem Plädoyer Kästerns aus seinen Aufzeichnungen: »Wir alle brauchen etwas Wüste«. Der Aufsatz *Was macht einen Mönch zum Mönch. Kontroversen um das Mönchsideal in der ostsyrischen Literatur an der Wende des 6. zum 7. Jahrhundert* (2018) geht kirchenhistorisch der Frage nach dem Mönchsein in der ostsyrischen Literatur nach. Innerkirchliche Zerwürfnisse über das richtige Mönchverständnis werden zur Sprache gebracht, genauso eine daraus hervorgegangene Tochtergründung eines neuen Klosters, das besonders wichtig für die Region Asien und China zur Versorgung mit Mönchen wird. Die beiden Beiträge zeigen das breite Spektrum der Themen, mit denen sich Tamcke in diesem Bereich beschäftigt.

Daneben beinhaltet der Band mehrere Beiträge, die das christliche Leben im islamisch geprägten Nahen Osten in den Blick nehmen und das Verhältnis zwischen Christentum und Islam in verschiedenen Kontexten betrachten. *Zwischen Größenwahn und Minderwertigkeitsgefühl. Christsein im Hause des Islams* (2006) behandelt das Aufeinandertreffen beider Religionen ab dem 7. Jahrhundert. Mit der islamischen Eroberung wichtiger christlicher Zentren wechseln sich Nebeneinander, Miteinander und auch Gegeneinander immer wieder ab. Tamcke nimmt dabei die klassischen Topoi dieses Themas in den Blick: Schutzverträge, kultureller Austausch, die Koexistenz und den christlich-islamischen Dialog mit seinen theologischen Kontroversen. Einen weiteren Einblick in das Verhältnis von Islam und Christentum in der Geschichte gibt der Aufsatz *Wie der Islam christliche Bildung beflügelte* (2013). Tamcke führt Beispiele für christliche Bildungsbewegungen auf der arabischen Halbinsel an und nennt mehrere Persönlichkeiten, wie den Gelehrten Isaak von Ninive, die prägend dafür waren. Er sieht Zusammenhänge zwischen der Blüte der ostsyrischen Mystik und Religiosität und der Koexistenz beider Religionen.

Dieser Band sei allen Lesern und Leserinnen ans Herz gelegt, die theologische Einblicke in die Kirche des Ostens mit ihrer reichhaltigen Literatur bekommen möchten. Außerdem bietet sich dieser Band hervorragend an, mehr über das Verhältnis von Christentum und Islam zu verschiedenen Zeiten zu erfahren und es aus verschiedenen Blickwinkeln zu betrachten. Einmal mehr wird durch die Arbeiten von Tamcke deutlich, dass der Nahe Osten ein Schauplatz von komplexen Entwicklungen ist, die meistens außer Acht gelassen werden, wenn es um das globale Christentum geht. Er ist eine besondere Bühne des christlich-islamischen Dialogs, Raum des Wissenstransfers von »Orient« und »Okzident« und der Ort, an dem das Christentum seine orientalischen Ausprägungen entwickelt hat – wie das Beispiel der Apostolischen Kirche des Ostens und ihrer Persönlichkeiten zeigt.

Jan Gehm

Elizabeth A. Foster, **African Catholic. Decolonization and the Transformation of the Church**, Cambridge, MA/ London: Harvard University Press 2019, 369 Seiten

Die Autorin, Professorin für Geschichte an der *Tufts-University* in Medford, Massachusetts und Gastprofessorin am *Center for European Studies* der *Harvard University*, Cambridge (USA), legt mit ihrem zweiten Buch eine ausführliche Geschichte der Entkolonisierung der französischen Gebiete in Afrika mit besonderem Augenmerk auf die katholische Kirche vor. Dabei zeigt sie, dass die Négritude-Bewegung, die Unabhängigkeitsbestrebungen und schließlich die politische Dekolonisierung entscheidende Beiträge auch zur kirchlichen Neuorientierung im Zweiten Vatikanischen Konzil geleistet haben.

In ihrer Einleitung skizziert die Autorin vier Grundmomente, die die Situation Frankreichs und seiner Kolonien und »Besitztümer« zur Mitte des 20. Jahrhunderts prägten: der allmähliche Niedergang des weltweiten französischen Imperiums, das Erstarken der politischen Linken im Nachkriegsfrankreich, eine neue afrikanische Elite mit stark katholischer Prägung sowie Veränderungsprozesse in der katholischen Kirche, die trotz ihrer Nähe zu den Kolonialmächten zu einem wichtigen Faktor in der Entkolonisierung wird und sich zunehmend zu einer von den verschiedenen Kulturen geprägten Weltkirche entwickelt.

Die Schlüsselrolle des Zweiten Weltkriegs sowie der folgenden Transformationsprozesse im Nachkriegsfrankreich und im kolonialen Machtgefüge zeigt die Autorin im ersten Kapitel über das Verhältnis von Kirche und Staat im französischen West- und Zentralafrika. Wichtige Faktoren dabei sind die nunmehr miteinander kooperierenden Missionsgesellschaften und -orden, die zudem auch immer mehr afrikanische Kandidatinnen und Kandidaten aufnehmen, eine verstärkte Betonung seitens des Vatikan, einheimischen Klerus auch für Führungspositionen auszubilden, sowie eine neue französische positive Religionspolitik in den Kolonien, durch die Millionen Francs in die Unterstützung der katholischen französischen Missionen und deren Schulwesen fließen – um den Einfluss Frankreichs in den Kolonien aufrechtzuerhalten. Stärker herausgearbeitet werden könnte m. E. die psychologische Bedeutung des Zweiten Weltkriegs für das Verhältnis von Afrikanern und Europäern.

Die folgenden drei Kapitel behandeln die für die Entkolonisierung entscheidenden Entwicklungen im Nachkriegsfrankreich: die Négritude-Bewegung (Kapitel 2), geprägt u. a. von dem unermüdlichen Netzwerker Alioune Diop, der im Vorfeld des Konzils persönlich bei Papst Johannes XXIII. vorspricht, die theologischen Entwicklungen (Kapitel 3) in der Frage der Kolonien zum Selbstbestimmungsrecht der Völker und zur Identitätsfrage der afrikanischen Christen, und schließlich (Kapitel 4) den Einfluss der afrikanischen Diaspora in Frankreich auf das politische Geschehen und die Bewertung der Unabhängigkeitskämpfe (Indochina, Algerien, Afrika) innerhalb der französischen Gesellschaft.

Die folgenden drei Kapitel beleuchten die Hintergründe aus afrikanischer Sicht und aus der Sicht der in Afrika tätigen Missionare. Im fünften Kapitel geht es um die Afrikanisierung der durch die französischen Missionen geprägten Kirchen in West- und Zentralafrika und die häufig spannungsreiche Besetzung kirchlicher Führungspositionen durch Afrikaner. Kapitel 6 behandelt das vielschichtige Verhältnis zum Islam in Afrika. Als Gefahr wird der Islam von Protagonisten wie Erzbischof Marcel Lefebvre gesehen, während etwa die Weißen Väter und die katholische Hierarchie im Senegal den Schlüssel zur christlichen Gesellschaftsgestaltung im Dialog mit den Muslimen sehen. Das siebte Kapitel widmet sich am Beispiel der Anti-Sklaverei-Gesellschaft den Bemühungen katholischer Amtsträger und Missionare, das Interesse und die Spendenbereitschaft französischer Katholiken nach Ende der Kolonialzeit aufrechtzuerhalten.

In der Schlussfolgerung wird noch einmal die Bedeutung der 1950er und beginnenden 60er Jahre für die weiteren Entwicklungen sowohl in Afrika als auch in der katholischen Kirche deutlich. »Es steht außer Frage, dass die Entkolonisierung die Entwicklungen zum Zweiten Vatikanischen Konzil beschleunigt und seine Ergebnisse geprägt hat« (257). Dies betriff die Fragen, ob die katholische Kirche zuerst eine europäische oder eine universale Kirche ist, ob der Katholizismus ein konservativer Pfeiler kolonialer Ordnung oder eine Kraft für die Befreiung der unterworfenen und ausgebeuteten Völker ist, ob die Kirche an eine unveränderliche Tradition gebunden ist oder sich mit den Zeiten zu ändern hat, und wie Katholiken zu Gläubigen anderer Religion stehen. Eine Schlüsselrolle kommt dabei Papst Johannes XXIII. zu, der zuvor Nuntius im Frankreich der Kolonialzeit und dann vatikanischer Beobachter bei der UNESCO war und somit mit den afrikanischen Gegebenheiten und Hoffnungen bestens vertraut war. Auch vor diesem Hintergrund wollte er mit dem Konzil eine Öffnung im Sinne einer Kirche für die Armen und einer Kirche des Dialogs markieren. Die Konzilsväter, in deren Diskussionen afrikanische Prälaten in der Vernetzung mit anderen Bischöfen südlicher Kontinente eine wichtige Rolle spielten, haben diesen Weg mutig beschritten.

Abkürzungsverzeichnis, Anmerkungen, Literaturverzeichnis und ein ausführlicher Index von Namen und wichtigen Begriffen beschließen das Buch.

Das Buch bearbeitet die Quellenlage, in der insgesamt mehr europäische als afrikanische Stimmen zu Wort kommen, gründlich auf und stellt die verschiedenen Aspekte in spannend zu lesenden Gedankengängen anschaulich dar. Wie sehr haben doch die Entwicklungen in Afrika nicht nur die politische Großwetterlage, sondern auch die Erneuerungsprozesse in der katholischen Kirche geprägt! Eine spannende Forschungsaufgabe wären solche Zeitstudien über Belgien und den Kongo sowie über die britischen Kolonien mit ihren Parallelen und Besonderheiten.

Marco Moerschbacher

Jochen Bauer, **Religionsunterricht für alle: Eine multitheologische Fachdidaktik** (Religionspädagogik innovativ, Band 30), Stuttgart: Kohlhammer 2019, 486 Seiten, 39,– Euro

Jochen Bauer ist einer der Protagonisten des Hamburger »Religionsunterrichts für alle«, in dem Schülerinnen und Schüler aller Religionen und Konfessionen gemeinsam unterrichtet werden – und zwar von Lehrkräften, die ihrerseits unterschiedlichen Religionen angehören. Als Fachreferent für Religion in der Hamburger Schulbehörde und Fachseminarleiter am Landesinstitut für Lehrerbildung und Schulentwicklung hat Bauer die Weiterentwicklung des »Religionsunterrichts für alle in evangelischer Verantwortung« (RUfa 1.0) zum »Religionsunterricht für alle« (RUfa 2.0) maßgeblich mitgestaltet. In seiner Göttinger Dissertation reflektiert er die gemachten Erfahrungen und legt leitende Prinzipien dieses in Deutschland einmaligen Modells dar. Dazu entwirft er eine multitheologische Fachdidaktik, die nicht »selbst *theologisch argumentiert*« und eine »Supra-Theologie« entwirft, sondern »*mit Theologien arbeitet* und ihnen im Hinblick auf den Religionsunterricht für alle eindeutige Rollen und Zuständigkeiten zuweist«. (9)

Säkulare, religionsplurale und multikulturelle Entwicklungen haben schon in den 90er Jahren zum »Hamburger Weg« geführt, einem konfessionsübergreifenden, dem interreligiösen Gespräch geöffneten Religionsunterricht. In der Fortentwicklung zum »Hamburger Modell« übernehmen nun alle Religionsgemeinschaften, die mit der Stadt Hamburg entsprechende Verträge geschlossen haben, gleichberechtigt Verantwortung für den Religionsunterricht. Den Weg dazu hat ein Rechtsgutachten geebnet, dass der »intendierte multireligiös-trägerplurale Religionsunterricht« durch eine bewusste, rechtsgestaltende Neudeutung des Art. 7 Abs. 3 GG begründet werden könnte – »sofern bestimmte Kriterien erfüllt würden« (44). Bauer kommt dieser Forderung nach, indem er das gleichberechtigte Zusammenwirken unterschiedlicher Religionen und Religionsdidaktiken reflektiert und daraus Kriterien ableitet, wie die authentische Vermittlung eigener und die angemessene Vermittlung fremder Glaubenswahrheiten praktisch gestaltet werden kann.

Im ersten Kapitel »*Die didaktische Aufgabe*« zeigt er die speziell hamburgischen Entstehungsfaktoren auf, untersucht die allgemeine religionspädagogische und -didaktische Diskussion auf ihr Potenzial für den Entwurf eines »Religionsunterrichtes *für alle*« hin und nimmt eine wissenschaftstheoretische Verortung seines Ansatzes vor. Zur besseren Veranschaulichung verdeutlicht er seine multitheologische Fachdidaktik mit Hilfe eines dreidimensionalen, würfelförmigen Strukturmodells. Nicht zuletzt hier merkt man deutlich, dass der Autor Lehrer ist und sich – erfolgreich! – darum bemüht, seinen multiperspektivischen Entwurf durch eine verständliche Sprache und einen gut nachvollziehbaren Aufbau lese- und verstehensfreundlich zu gestalten.

Die sechs Außenwände des Würfels sind Thema des zweiten Kapitels »*Der didaktische Raum*«. Sie markieren die religionsrechtlichen, -politischen und -soziologischen sowie die theologischen, schulischen und unterrichtlichen Rahmenbedingungen, Bewegungsmöglichkeiten und Zielbestimmungen des RUfa 2.0. Die Raummetapher verweist auf die Vielfalt der Analyse- und Handlungsmöglichkeiten und gleichzeitig auf die Bestimmungen, die jedes didaktische Handeln ermöglicht und zugleich begrenzt. Innerhalb des so definierten Raumes entwirft Bauer sein Verständnis eines pluralismusfähigen Religionsunterrichtes, dessen zentrale Kennzeichen Dialogizität und die Fähigkeit zum Perspektivwechsel sind.

Im dritten Kapitel »*Die didaktischen Dimensionen*« geht es um Positionen und Bewegungs*möglichkeiten* innerhalb des didaktischen Raumes. Dazu werden Inhalts-, Identitäts- und Wahrheitsdimensionen der neuen Fachdidaktik dargestellt und gezeigt, wie sie die im vorigen Kapitel dargestellten sechs Seiten des didaktischen Raumes miteinander verbinden. Die Inhaltsdimension stellt sicher, dass didaktische Formen und Unterrichtsmöglichkeiten angesichts wandelnder Umfelder und Bewährungssituationen so eingesetzt werden, dass Schülerinnen und Schüler sie autobiographisch wahrnehmen, deuten und kommunizieren können. Die Identitätsdimension erkennt den fragmentarischen Charakter sozialer und kultureller Konstruktionen an und leitet daraus ab, dass Identität nicht in Form binärer Essentialismen erfasst werden kann, sondern als grundsätzlich offener Entwicklungsprozess verstanden werden muss. Die Wahrheitsdimension verhilft dazu, differente Wahrheitsansprüche aufeinander zu beziehen und Geltungsansprüche zu prüfen, damit religiöse Bildung in produktiver Weise zur individuellen Subjektwerdung beitragen kann, ohne dass die beteiligten Religionen gegenseitig relativiert werden müssen.

Das vierte Kapitel untersucht unter der Überschrift »*Die didaktische Orientierung*« die drei didaktischen Dimensionen hinsichtlich ihrer Interdependenzen von Lernen und Lehren. Die beiden Pole der Inhaltsdimension sind dabei die Schülerorientierung auf der einen und die Traditionsorientierung auf der anderen Seite. Die Identitätsdimension steht in Spannung zwischen der Dialog- einerseits und der religionsspezifischen Orientierung anderseits. Die Wahrheitsdimension ist bestimmt durch die beiden Seiten der Authentizitäts- und der Wissenschaftsorientierung. Alle sechs Orientierungen verweisen auf elementare Strukturen, die Realität innerhalb einer religionspluralen Gesellschaft sind und gleichzeitig Unterrichtsprinzipien für einen grundgesetzlich festgeschriebenen Religionsunterricht im Rahmen eines religionsneutralen Staates formulieren.

Das fünfte und abschließende Kapitel »*Die didaktischen Akteure*« konzentriert sich auf die Lehrkräfte, da die Gestaltung religiöser Orientierungsprozesse das »Herzstück der Lehrertätigkeit im Religionsunterricht für alle« ist (423). Ihre religiöse Authentizität ist für den multireligösen Charakter des RUfa ebenso wichtig wie ihre Dialogfähigkeit, da für die intendierte subjektorientierte Identitätsbildung inhaltlich wie personell Positionalität und nicht Relativität nötig ist.

Bauer beansprucht mit seinem Entwurf nicht weniger, als den gordischen Knoten zwischen einer angemessenen Repräsentanz der in Deutschland vertretenen Religionen und der Rettung vor konfessioneller Zersplitterung des Religionsunterrichts zu zerschlagen. Er löst diesen Anspruch ein, indem er konsequent davon ausgeht, dass für eine dialogische und pluralismusfähige religiöse Identität die Begegnung mit fremden Religionen keine sekundäre Aufgabe ist, sondern von Anfang an konstitutiver Bestandteil.

Sönke Lorberg-Fehring

Claudia Hoffmann, **Fremdbegegnung – Das Totenritual Tiwah und die Basler Mission in kontakttheologischer Perspektive** (Studien zur Interkulturellen Geschichte des Christentums Bd. 162), Frankfurt a. M.: Verlag Peter Lang 2018, 378 Seiten, 82,50 Euro

In ihrer an der Universität Basel angenommenen, von Andreas Heuser betreuten Promotionsschrift stellt sich die Autorin der anspruchsvollen Aufgabe, zu einem traditionsreichen, Tiwah genannten Sekundärbestattungsritual auf der indonesischen Insel Kalimantan (Borneo) anhand von Positionierungen Basler Missionare im ersten Drittel des 20. Jahrhunderts eine Diskursanalyse zu erarbeiten. Sie will damit nicht vergleichsbasierte eigene Deutungen fundieren, sondern theologische Verschiebungen in der Basler Mission insgesamt rekonstruieren für die missionsgeschichtlich noch wenig erforschte Zeit der Dreißigerjahre im deutschsprachigen Umfeld. Dies wird mit Hilfe von Beschreibung und Deutung theologisch reflektierter Fremdbegegnung von Missionspersonal mit dem Ritual unternommen, und zwar in »kontakttheologischer Perspektive«. Damit ist gemeint »eine theologische Verarbeitung von verhältnismässig regelmässigen oder auch intensivierten Begegnungen mit indigenen Wissensträgern und Wissensträgerinnen« (263) und den »Veränderungen, die sich durch den Kontakt mit dem Fremden in der theologischen Haltung der Missionare ergeben« – den »kontakttheologische[n] Verschiebungen« (16) und ihren Wirkungen für die Basler Mission also. So sollen lange Zeit selbstverständliche

Auffassungen zu Zentrum und Peripherie von Mission hinterfragbar werden. Für diese Variation des von der Munich School unter dem Terminus »Polyzentrik«, aber auch in neueren Studien zur Transkulturation firmierenden Versuchs einer grundlegenden methodischen Perspektivänderung, nämlich nicht »auf das Missionsfeld hin«, sondern von den forschungsrelevanten Regionen her, wird in der vorliegenden Studie der offenbar vom langjährigen Archivar der Basler Mission Paul Jenkins eingeführte Begriff der »Dort-Zentrik« verwendet. Er bildet die hermeneutische Leitkategorie der Studie, in der nicht nur zahlreiche historische Schrift-, Ton- und Bildzeugnisse aus dem reichen Fundus des Basler Missionsarchivs befragt, sondern auch Reflexionen aus eigener Feldforschung beigesteuert werden. Der Komplexität der Aufgabenstellung und der Diversität der auszuwertenden Befunde entsprechend, wird das Forschungsmaterial mit einem historischen und empirischen »Methodenmix« (62) bearbeitet. Unter ihnen sticht besonders der Einsatz bildanalytischer Verfahren hervor, die im kunst- und kulturwissenschaftlichen Diskurs entwickelt wurden. Sie stellen auf ihre Weise einen kritischen Beitrag zur Frage »sichtbarer Religion« (Daria Pezzoli-Olgiati) dar.

Inhaltlich bietet der Gang der Untersuchung nach einer recht ausführlichen Einleitung zu Zielstellung, Quellen, Methodik und Theorierahmen in zwei Kapiteln zunächst eine Erläuterung zu Ablauf, Bedeutungsfacetten und gesellschaftspolitischen Kontexten des Rituals und seiner bisherigen Beschreibung. Dabei wird auch die heutige, ambivalente Stellung der Evangelischen Kirche Kalimantan zum Tiwah thematisiert. Zwei weitere Kapitel widmen sich Kontexten und Missionsakteuren mit ihren Perspektiven. Dabei werden auch die Text- und Ton-, besonders jedoch Bildmedien vorgestellt und befragt, mit Hilfe derer solche Verstehensbemühungen in Unterstützerkreisen des Missionswerks seinerzeit kommuniziert wurden. Die beiden letzten Kapitel identifizieren zeitgenössische und aktuelle theologische Strömungen, denen die verschiedenen missionsbezogenen Stellungnahmen zugeordnet werden können. Abschließend wird dabei noch einmal der bereits eingangs eingeführte Begriff der »dortzentrischen Kontakttheologie« anhand von religionswissenschaftlichen und theologischen Forschungsreferenzen bilanziert. Durchgängig ist das Bemühen um Berücksichtigung weiblicher theologischer Perspektiven erkennbar. Wohltuend ist auch die geschlechtersensible Sprache ohne Beeinträchtigungen der Lesbarkeit. Das Buch ist ansprechend gestaltet, Bildmaterial wird in guter Druckqualität und erkennbarer Größe wiedergegeben.

An der Studie beeindruckt vor allem die erkennbar sorgfältige und weitgespannte Erhebung des Basler Archivbefunds zum Thema. Aber auch das Wagnis einer »mixed-methods«-Forschung verdient Respekt. Allerdings droht die Mannigfaltigkeit der Zugänge mitunter auch auf Kosten einer tieferen Durchdringung und Verknüpfung der einzelnen Ansätze zu gehen – eine Gefahr, die wohl alle kennen, die sich um Methodenvielfalt innerhalb eines Problemaufrisses bemühen. Das schlägt dann mitunter sogar auf zentrale Anliegen der jeweiligen Forschungsbemühung durch, wie hier zum Beispiel auf die Beantwortung der oben erwähnten Frage nach Zentrum und Peripherie von Mission: Zentren und Ränder von Mission werden ja diskursiv bestimmt. Das dafür in Anschlag gebrachte Verständnis von Diskursanalyse als »Wissen« und »Weg, zu diesem Wissen zu kommen« (47), wird zwar unter Berufung auf die Kulturwissenschaftlerin Gillian Rose als in der Tradition Michel Foucaults stehend erklärt. Der von diesem in seinem Werk »Archäologie des Wissens« entwickelte, komplexe Diskursbegriff, auf den eigens verwiesen wird, bezeichnet jedoch nicht eigentlich selbst Wissen, vielmehr Form und Formation von Wissen, und Diskursanalyse beschreibt nach Foucault kein »Wie« im Gegensatz zum »Warum« (48), sondern in Erklärung der Entstehungszusammenhänge von Wissensformationen durchaus beides. In der Ergebniszusammenfassung zur Diskursanalyse (260f) werden denn auch nur die Vielfalt der Perspektiven als Diskursstränge benannt; deren Zusammenhängen und Abhängigkeiten untereinander, die »den« Tiwah-Diskurs im eigentlichen Sinne ja erst bilden, geht die Studie nicht gesondert nach. Von da ausgehend jedoch wäre missionstheologisch eine »Dort-Zentrik« mit ihren Peripherien nicht nur allgemein einsichtig zu machen, sondern auch argumentativ zu befestigen.

Solche und andere methodische Anfragen an die Studie tun jedoch der immer wieder beeindruckenden Gründlichkeit der archivarischen Recherche keinen Eintrag, die sich in Verwendungsumfang, Sorgfalt der Aufbereitung und Akribie der Nachweise durchgängig zu erkennen gibt. Das Buch erschließt und bearbeitet eine Vielzahl wichtiger Quellen, lenkt den Blick auf eine noch zu gering beforschte Periode in der Geschichte der Basler Mission und regt so zu weiterer Recherche an.

Eckhard Zemmrich

Karl-Josef Kuschel/Shahid Alam, **Goethe und der Koran**. Texte von Johann Wolfgang von Goethe. Kommentar von Karl-Josef Kuschel. Kalligrafien von Shahid Alam, Ostfildern: Verlagsgruppe Patmos 2021, 432 Seiten, 49,– Euro

Der Anlass dieses Buches liegt auf der Hand: Im August 1819 ist Goethes »West-östlicher Divan« bei Cotta in Stuttgart erschienen. Mit einer kleinen Verspätung legen der Tübinger Gelehrte Karl-Josef Kuschel und der bekannte Kalligraph Shahid Alam zum 200. Jahrestag des »Divans« ein Buch vor, das Goethes Begegnung mit Koran und Islam nachzeichnet und für den interreligösen und interkulturellen Dialog heute fruchtbar macht.

Schwerer zu bestimmen ist das Genus des vorliegenden Buches. In seinem ersten Teil werden Texte dokumentiert, in denen sich Goethe mit Koran und Islam auseinandersetzt. Im zweiten Teil kommentiert Karl Josef Kuschel diese Texte aus historischer und religionswissenschaftlicher Sicht. Das Besondere des Bandes liegt in den sechzehn hervorragenden farbigen Bildtafeln aus der Feder des aus Pakistan stammenden und in Deutschland lebenden Kalligraphen

Alam. Auf diese Weise entsteht ein Miteinander von Poesie, Wissenschaft und darstellender Kunst, das dem Geist Goethes sehr angemessen ist.

Alam zitiert in einem kurzen Beitrag ein Wort Goethes: »In keiner Sprache (vielleicht) ist Wort, Geist und Schrift so uranfänglich zusammengekörpert wie in der arabischen Sprache.« (421) Für jede Kalligraphie wurde – soweit es sich nicht um Koranzitate handelt – eine kurzes Gedicht Goethes ins Arabische übersetzt, in einem weiteren Arbeitsgang vokalisiert und dann von Alam mit Öl, Tusche und Tinte auf Birkenholz geschrieben. Hingewiesen sei auch darauf, dass Goethe selbst sich in der arabischen Schrift geübt hat – dies unter Anleitung des Theologen und Orientalisten Heinrich Eberhard Gottlob Paulus, der bis 1811 in Jena lehrte, danach in Heidelberg. Arabische Schreibübungen Goethes sind dem Buch als Faksimile beigefügt (31).

Im Zusammenhang einer »Zeitschrift für interkulturelle Theologie« ist natürlich wichtig, dass Kuschel und Alam eindrücklich auf die Besonderheit darstellender Kunst im Bereich des Islams hinweisen. Wer nach dem Betrachten der Bildtafeln Kalligraphie noch für »ornamentales Beiwerk« halten würde, wäre tatsächlich ein Banause. Zumindest ebenso wichtig aber ist, wie Kuschel Goethes Äußerungen zum Islam in ihrem historischen Zusammenhang nachzeichnet und welche Konsequenzen er in dem Kapitel »Herausforderungen heute« (369ff) zieht.

Für die Darstellung der Entwicklung von Goethes Auffassung des Islams wertet Kuschel gewissenhaft die Erträge der neuen Goethe-Forschung aus, allen voran die Arbeiten von Katharina Mommsen, Anke Bosse und Hendrik Birus.

Dabei gibt es Erstaunliches zu entdecken: So hatte Goethe in der Bibliothek seines Vaters Gottfried Arnolds »Unparteyische Kirchen- und Ketzer-Historie« von 1699 zur Verfügung. In dieser sagt Arnold, Mohammed sei ein Mensch gewesen, der »von natur zu tiefsinnigem nachdenken und einsamem leben geneigt« gewesen sei und »vor aller abgötterey einen abscheu gehabt« habe (173). Noch der alte Goethe äußert sich über Arnold: »Seine Gesinnungen stimmen sehr zu den meinigen« (175).

Ein anderes Beispiel: Voltaire hatte 1739 eine Tragödie unter dem eindeutigen Titel »Le Fanatisme ou Mahomet le Prophète« verfasst. Goethe, der selbst ein Mohammed-Drama mit völlig anderem Charakter begonnen hatte, war auf Wunsch seines Herzogs gezwungen, dieses Stück 1799 im Weimarer Theater aufführen zu lassen, tat aber alles, um die antiislamische Tendenz des Stückes zu mildern.

So könnte man fortfahren. Auch wer glaubt, Goethes Leben und Werk zu kennen, wird noch Neues entdecken. Jedoch muss auch ein Einwand besprochen werden. Hinlänglich bekannt ist Goethes Vierzeiler aus dem Divan:

> »Närrisch, daß jeder in seinem Falle
> Seine besondere Meynung preist!
> Wenn *Islam* Gott ergeben heißt,
> Im Islam leben und sterben wir alle.«

Kuschel zeigt, dass Goethe in der Ergebung in den Willen Gottes ein Verhalten sieht, das ihn mit dem Islam verbindet. Kuschel nennt die »Gottergebenheit« eine »religionsübergreifende Grundhaltung« und urteilt: Das Wort Islam wäre »im Deutschen nicht nur mit ›Gottergebenheit‹ allein, sondern besser noch mit ›Frieden mit Gott im Leben und Sterben‹ zu übersetzen« (354).

Dass »Ergebung in den Willen Gottes … das Wesen des Islam« (353) ausmacht, hatte schon Joseph von Hammer befunden, den Goethe sehr verehrte. Dagegen ist nichts zu sagen. Doch der Ausdruck »Friede mit Gott« ist zumindest für evangelische Theolog*innen mit dem Zusammenhang von Röm 5,1–11 verbunden, also mit der Rechtfertigung der Sünder und Sünderinnen durch Kreuz und Auferweckung Jesu Christi. Hier aber würde Goethe gewiss nicht zustimmen. Wer Ernst Lohmeyers großartige Auslegung des Vaterunsers kennt, wird auch die Vaterunser-Bitte »Dein Wille geschehe« nicht ohne weiteres im Sinne von »Ergebung« deuten. »Widerstand und Ergebung« gehören zusammen.

Bevor wir die »Gottergebenheit« im Islam – die als solche zu tiefem Respekt nötigt – als »religionsübergreifende Grundhaltung« anerkennen, bleibt zwischen Christen und Muslimen noch manches zu besprechen. Nichtsdestotrotz ist Kuschels Hauptanliegen, am Beispiel Goethes zu zeigen, dass Islamfeindlichkeit und Arroganz gegenüber dem Islam Aufmerksamkeit und Wertschätzung weichen müssen, uneingeschränkt begrüßenswert. Mit Goethes eigenen Worten: »Orient und Okzident sind nicht mehr zu trennen.«

Rainer Oechslen

REDAKTION

VERFASSER_INNEN UND REZENSENT_INNEN

Dr. Lahphai Awng Li, Myanmar Institute of Theology, Seminary Hill, 11011, Insein, Yangon, Myanmar, liawng@gmail.com

Dr. Michael Biehl, Evangelische Mission weltweit, Normannenweg 17–21, 20537 Hamburg, Michael.Biehl@emw-d.de

Prof. Dr. theol. Meehyun Chung, United Graduate School of Theology, Yonsei University, Luce Chapel 214, 50 Yonseiro Seodaemungu, Seoul, Korea 03722, gocmh@yonsei.ac.kr

Gregor Etzelmüller, Professur für Systematische Theologie, Neuer Graben 29/Schloss, D-49074 Osnabrück, gregor.etzelmueller@uni-osnabrueck.de

Jan Gehm, Bahrenberstr. 1, D-44801 Bochum, j.gehm@ftr.ru.nl

Daniel Jara J., Schubertgasse 26/19, A-1090 Wien, Daniel.JaraJhayya@ruhr-uni-bochum.de

Dr. Anton Knuth, Missionskademie an der Universität Hamburg, Rupertistr. 67, D-22609 Hamburg, anton.knuth@missionsakademie.de

Prof. em. Dr. Christine Lienemann-Perrin, Manuelstr. 116, CH-3006 Bern, christine.lienemann@theol.unibe.ch

Thomas Linke, Saarbrückenstraße 4, D-04318 Leipzig, thomas.linke@uni-leipzig.de

Ruomin Liu, Missionsakademie an der Universität Hamburg, Rupertistr. 67, D-22609 Hamburg, ruomin.liu@missionsakademie.de

Dr. Sönke Lorberg-Fehring, ZMÖ, Agathe-Lasch-Weg 16, D-22605 Hamburg, s.lorberg-fehring@nordkirche-weltweit.de

Marco Moerschbacher, Missionswissenschaftliches Institut im missio e. V., Goethestr. 43, D-52064 Aachen, m.moerschbacher@mwi-aachen.org

Prof. Dr. Kakule Molo, Université Libre de Pays des Grands Lacs, Avenue du Lac no 2, Quartier Himbi, Goma, République Démocratique du Congo, kamolo53@gmail.com

Leita Ngoy, Ev.-theol. Fakultät der Ruhr-Universität Bochum, Wohlfahrtstr. 215, Z. 15, D-44799 Bochum, lngoy_2002@yahoo.fr

Prof. Dr. Ebenezer Babtunde Obadare, Department of Sociology, The University of Kansas, 1415 Jayhawk Blvd., 716 Fraser Hall, Lawrence, KS 66045-7540, USA, obadare@ku.edu

Dr. Rainer Oechslen, Landeskirchlicher Beauftragter für Islamfragen, Landeskirchenamt, Katharina-von-Bora-Str. 7–13, 80333 München, rainer.oechslen@elkb.de

Claudia Rammelt, Ev.-theol. Fakultät der Ruhr-Universität Bochum, Universitätsstr. 150, D-44780 Bochum, claudia.rammelt@rub.de

PD Dr. Roland Spliesgart, Ludwig-Maximilians-Universität München, Evangelisch-Theologische Fakultät, Lehrstuhl für Kirchengeschichte I, Geschwister-Scholl-Platz 1, D-80539 München, spliesgart@evtheol.uni-muenchen.de

Dr. Christian Weber, mission 21, Missionsstr. 21, CH-4009 Basel, christian.weber@mission-21.org

Rev. Dr. Abraham Silo Wilar, M.Th., M.A., Lecturer in Inter-religious Studies, Jakarta, Theological Seminary/Sekolah Tinggi Filsafat Teologi Jakarta, Jl. Proklamasi 27, Jakarta, Pusat, Indonesia, abraham.wilar@stftjakarta.ac.id

Eckhard Zemmrich, Humboldt-Universität zu Berlin, Hausvogteiplatz 5–7, D-10117 Berlin, zemmrice@hu-berlin.de